Environmental Criminal Liability and Enforcement in European and International Law

Queen Mary Studies in International Law

Edited by

Malgosia Fitzmaurice
Phoebe Okowa
Sarah Singer

VOLUME 21

The titles published in this series are listed at *brill.com/qmil*

Environmental Criminal Liability and Enforcement in European and International Law

By

Ricardo M. Pereira

BRILL
NIJHOFF

LEIDEN | BOSTON

Library of Congress Cataloging-in-Publication Data

Pereira, Ricardo M., author.
Environmental criminal liability and enforcement in European and international law / by Ricardo M. Pereira.
pages cm. -- (Queen Mary studies in international law ; volume 21)
Update and extended version of author's thesis (doctoral - University of Essex Law School, 2009) issued under title: The harmonisation of environmental criminal law in the European Union.
Includes bibliographical references and index.
ISBN 978-90-04-19473-1 (hardback : alk. paper) 1. Offenses against the environment--Law and legislation--European Union countries. 2. Offenses against the environment--Law and legislation. I. Title.

KJE8781.E58P47 2015
345'.0245--dc23

2015029260

This publication has been typeset in the multilingual 'Brill' typeface. With over 5,100 characters covering Latin, IPA, Greek, and Cyrillic, this typeface is especially suitable for use in the humanities.
For more information, please see www.brill.com/brill-typeface.

ISSN 1877-4822
ISBN 978-90-04-19473-1 (hardback)
ISBN 978-90-04-19588-2 (e-book)

This book is printed on acid-free paper.

Contents

Acknowledgements

This monograph is a considerably adapted, updated and extended version of my Ph.D. dissertation submitted for a Ph.D. degree at the University of Essex, Law School, obtained in 2009. Whilst my original Ph.D. thesis focused primarily on developments in Europe, this monograph provides a more expanded coverage of the subject, including from public international law perspectives.

I must thank, specially, Professor Steve Peers, Professor Karen Hulme, Professor Valsamis Mitsilegas and Dr Audrey Guinchard for their advice, constructive comments and intellectual insight into different stages of my research. I must also thank Professor Malgosia Fitzmaurice and Ingeborg van der Laan for their helpful comments to and favourable review of my book proposal and the final manuscript. Any errors are the author's own.

I hope this book will inspire those who also believe in European and international cooperation for a better future.

To my family and friends, with love.

Ricardo M. Pereira
15 April 2015

Abbreviations

AG	Advocate General
BYIL	British Yearbook of International Law
CITES	Convention on International Trade in Endangered Species
CJEL	Columbia Journal of European Law
CJEU	Court of Justice of the European Union
CMLR	Common Market Law Reports
CMLRev.	Common Market Law Review
COREPER	Committee of Permanent Representatives
COM	Communication of the European Commission
EAEC	European Atomic Energy Community
EC	European Community
EC Bull.	Bulletin of the European Communities
ECJ	European Court of Justice
ECOSOC	Economic and Social Committee
ECHR	Reports of Judgements of the European Court of Human Rights
ECR	European Court Reports
ECSC	European Coal and Steel Community
EEA	European Economic Area
EEC	European Economic Community
EEELR	European Energy and Environmental Law Review
EELR	European Environmental Law Review
EESC	European Economic and Social Commitee
EFTA	European Free Trade Association
EL	Environmental Liability
ELJ	European Law Journal
ELM	Environmental Law and Management Journal
ELRev.	European Law Review
Env. LR	Environmental Law Reports
EEELR	European Energy and Environmental Law Review
EJIL	European Journal of International Law
EP	European Parliament
EPL	European Public Law (Journal)
EU	European Union
EU15	European Union of 15 Member States (before 1.5.2004)
EU25	European Union of 25 Member States (as from 1.5.2004)
EU27	European Union of 27 Member States (as from 1.1.2007)
Euratom	European Atomic Energy Community

FIDE	International Federation for European Law
ICJ	International Court of Justice
IMO	International Maritime Organisation
IMPEL	Network for the Implementation and Enforcement of Environmental Law
ITLOS	International Tribunal for the Law of the Sea
JCMS	Journal of Common Market Studies
JEL	Journal of Environmental Law
JECL	Journal of European Criminal Law
JHA	Justice and Home Affairs
LQR	Law Quarterly Review
MARPOL	Convention on Prevention of Marine Pollution from Ships
MEP	Member of the European Parliament
MJ	Maastricht Journal of European and Comparative Law
MLR	Modern Law Review
NGO	Non-governmental organisation
N.y.r.	Not yet reported
OECD	Organisation for Economic Co-operation and Development
OJ	Official Journal (of the European Communities)
OJLS	Oxford Journal of Legal Studies
RECIEL	Review of European Community and International Environmental Law
RMC	Revue du Marche Commun
SEA	Single European Act
SEC	European Commission internal working paper
SSP	Ship-Source Pollution
TEU	Treaty on European Union (Maastricht Agreement)
UNCLOS	United Nations Convention on the Law of the Sea
UNEP	United Nations Environment Programme
YEEL	Yearbook of European Environmental Law
YEL	Yearbook of European Law

CHAPTER 1

Introduction

1.1 Overview of the Book and Subject Matter

The book aims to assess the legal, theoretical and practical implications of interstate cooperation aimed to harmonise environmental criminal law standards. It analyses the rationales for criminalisation of environmental offences and the approaches to harmonisation under specific European and international instruments aimed to prevent and control environmental crime.

The book is centred on the legal questions involving the efforts to harmonise the environmental criminal laws in the Member States of the European Union and the Council of Europe, whilst also considering the scope for legal harmonisation and interstate cooperation under specific international treaties and organisations, in particular the International Criminal Court. In the European Union context, the subject of the book is of the highest political importance since environmental criminal law has lied at the centre of an institutional dispute over the legal basis of the proposed EU/EC[1] measures on environmental crimes, which have delineated features of the adopted Directive on the protection of the environment through criminal law ('environmental crime directive')[2] and the Directive on Ship-Source Pollution and on the Introduction of Penalties for Infringements ('ship source pollution

1 The term EC or 'the Community' is used to refer the three Communities originally established in the 1950s: the European Coal and Steel Community (ECSC, which expired in 2002), the European Economic Community (EEC) and the Atomic Energy Community (Euratom). After the 1992 Maastricht Treaty (Treaty on European Union or TEU), the EEC was renamed European Community (EC); and the European Union (EU) was created. The EU was based on a three-pillar structure formed by the EC (first pillar) and the areas of Common Foreign and Security Policy (second pillar, Title V TEU) and Justice and Home Affairs (third pillar, Title VI TEU – following the Treaty of Amsterdam 1999, Title VI includes only police and judicial cooperation in criminal matters). The term 'EU' was sometimes used to refer to the second and third pillars (as opposed to the EC). Since the abolishment of the pillar structure of the EU by the Lisbon Treaty in 2009, the EU (or EU law) is used to encompass also all the subject areas previously under the competence of the EC.

2 Directive 2008/99/EC of the European Parliament and of the Council of 19 November 2008 on the protection of the environment through criminal law, *Official Journal* L 328, 6 December 2008, pp. 28–37.

 | DOI 10.1163/9789004195882_002

directive').[3] Two ECJ decisions,[4] in particular, have clarified the question of the distribution of competences between the EU/EC Treaties and the EU and its Member States in the area of (environmental) criminal law and policy. The book also considers global developments in the area of environmental criminal law, in particular whether an extension of the International Criminal Court's current jurisdiction over environmental crime is possible or desirable; as well as specific initiatives aimed at criminalisation of environmental offences under multilateral environmental agreements. Moreover, the book aims to assess the approaches and methods adopted for harmonisation of environmental criminal law under the EU Directive on environmental crimes adopted on 24 October 2008[5] and under the EU Directive on ship-source pollution adopted in September 2005 (and amended in October 2009 to require Member States to criminalise shipping pollution offences),[6] as well as under previous EU legislative initiatives aimed to combat environmental crime. Moreover, the book aims to compare the approach to legal harmonisation adopted by the EU directives on environmental crime with that developed under the 1998 Council of Europe convention on the protection of the environment through criminal law.[7]

Finally, focusing on developments in Europe, the book aims to assess whether the harmonisation of environmental criminal law could lead to the improvement of the enforcement of environmental law. In particular, it discusses whether harmonisation could improve the levels of implementation of EU environmental law; contribute to the completion of the EU internal market; and to the improvement of interstate criminal-law cooperation against environmental crime.

3 Directive 2005/35/EC of the European Parliament and of the Council on Ship-Source Pollution and on the Introduction of Penalties for Infringements, 7 September 2005, *Official Journal* L 255/11; 30.9.2005 and Directive 2009/123/EC of the European Parliament and of the Council of 21 October 2009 amending Directive 2005/35/EC on ship-source pollution and on the introduction of penalties for infringements; *Official Journal*, L 280/52. 27.10.2009.

4 *Commission v Council* C-176/03 [2005] E.C.R. I-7879; [2005] 3 C.M.L.R. 20; Case C-440/05, *Commission of the European Communities v Council of the European Union* [2008] 1 C.M.L.R. 22.

5 Directive 2008/99/EC of the European Parliament and of the Council of 19 November 2008 on the protection of the environment through criminal law, Official Journal L 328, 6 December 2008, pp. 28–37.

6 Directive 2005/35/EC of the European Parliament and of the Council on Ship-Source Pollution and on the Introduction of Penalties for Infringements, 7 September 2005, *Official Journal* L 255/11; 30.9.2005 and Directive 2009/123/EC of the European Parliament and of the Council of 21 October 2009 amending Directive 2005/35/EC on ship-source pollution and on the introduction of penalties for infringements; *Official Journal*, L 280/52. 27.10.2009.

7 Council of Europe Convention on the Protection of the Environment through Criminal Law (1998), Strasbourg, 4.XI.1998, ETS no. 172 (not yet in force).

1.2 Overview of International and European Developments

This section starts by considering the figures and estimates relating to the scale of environmental crime globally. This is followed by an overview of the international and European initiatives aimed at the harmonisation of environmental criminal law.

1.2.1 *The Scale of Environmental Criminality Worldwide and in Europe*

Environmental crime is one of the most profitable and fastest growing areas of international criminal activity. The three main drivers to environmental crime are the growing global demand for environmental goods; the economic benefits arising from environmental crime (which includes both the potential of high profits for those engaged in the trade and the desire for access to illegal goods); as well as specific regulatory gaps, which includes deficiencies in international and national laws and their enforcement.[8]

Organised criminal groups, corporations and individual actors make significant profits from environmental criminality, as estimated by international organisations and national governments. The government of the United States estimated in 2000 that local and international criminal groups earn $22–31 billion annually from a range of environmental criminal activities, including hazardous waste dumping, smuggling proscribed hazardous waste materials, and exploiting and trafficking protected natural resources.[9]

Developed countries are major consumer markets for the products originating from environmental crime. The illegal wildlife and timber trade are classic examples of trade that flows predominantly from less developed countries to

8 See generally, Charles Schmidt, 'Environmental Crimes: Profiting at the Earth's Expense' in Rob White (ed.) Environmental Crime: A Reader' (Willan Publishing, 2009); Hayman, Gavin and Brack, Dunkan, *Workshop Report: International Environmental Crime: The Nature and Control of Environmental Black Markets* (the Royal Institute of International Affairs, London 1998); and '*The Growth and Control of International Environmental Crime*', (Chatham House, 2007) available at http://www.illegal-logging.info/uploads/Intenvcrime2007background papers.pdf.

9 The *International Crime Threat Assessment*, December 2000, USA, available at http://www.fas.org/irp/threat/pub45270index.html (accessed on 20 February 2015). This international crime threat assessment was prepared by a US Government interagency working group in support of and pursuant to the President's International Crime Control Strategy. For a discussion, see also F. Comte 'Environmental Crime and the Police in Europe: A Panorama and Possible Paths for Future Action' (2006) *European Environmental Law Review* 190.

more developed countries, i.e. South–North trade.[10] For example, one study suggested that between 60% and 70% of tropical timber imported into the European Union come from illegal sources.[11] Moreover, it has been estimated that the EU is one of the world's largest import markets of live birds, live reptiles, reptile's skin and sturgeon caviar.[12] Yet increasingly China and other Asian emerging economies are becoming major consumer markets in the trade for illegal environmental goods, including part components of wildlife such as rhino horns and elephant tusks due to the belief on their medicinal benefits held by some consumers in those countries, as well as for ornamental reasons.[13]

In addition, industrialised countries 'export' the product of environmental crime to third countries, in particular developing countries. The increased cost of safe waste disposal has driven an export trade to many of the world's least developed countries, where there are often gaps and weaknesses in the regulatory framework applicable to the waste disposal sector.[14] Illegal waste imports are widely thought to cross national borders easily, particularly in developing countries which have few inspection systems and technologies available.[15] The illegal trade and dumping of hazardous waste materials is estimated to have an

10 Hayman, Gavin and Brack, Dunkan, *Workshop Report: International Environmental Crime: The Nature and Control of Environmental Black Markets* (the Royal Institute of International Affairs, London 1998) at 10.

11 The Royal Institute of International Affairs: Controlling the international trade in illegally logged timber and wood products, London 2002, at 9. See also, Albrecht, Hans-Jorg 'The Extent of Organised Environmental Crime: A European Perspective' in Comte, Françoise and Kramer, Ludwig (eds.) *Environmental Crime in Europe: Rules of Sanctions* (Europa Law Publishing, Groningen 2004) at 89.

12 From 1996 through 2002, the EU15 imported approximately 6 million live birds, 1.6 million live reptiles, 10 million reptile skins, and almost 600 tonnes of sturgeon caviar listed under CITES. For live birds, the EU was the predominant market, accounting for over 80% of global net imports; for caviar, the EU imported about 45% of global trade. See Milieu Consortium, *Study on the Enforcement of the EU Wildlife Trade Regulations in the EU-25: Final Report*, November 2006.

13 Rhino horns are composed largely of the protein keratin, also the chief component in hair, fingernails, and animal hooves. See 'Rhinoceros. Rhino Horn Use: Fact vs. Fiction', *Nature*, August 20, 2010.

14 Frohlich et al, *Organised Environmental Crime in the EU Member States: Final Report*, Betreuungsgesellschaft fur Umweltfragen (BfU) and Partners, May 2003. at 3.

15 Charles W Schmidt, *Environmental crimes: profiting at earth's expense*, Environ Health Perspect. 2004 February; 112(2): A96–103, available at http://www.ncbi.nlm.nih.gov/pmc/articles/PMC1241843/pdf/ehp0112-a00096.pdf (accessed on 10 February 2015).

overall value of between U$10 and 12 billion.[16] Moreover, it has been estimated that organised crime generates revenues of between US$1 billion and 2 billion annually through dumping of toxic waste.[17] This practice of 'waste dumping' has been condemned by some NGOs as amounting to 'garbage imperialism'.[18] This problem is exacerbated in light of the increased costs of waste disposal in developed countries.[19]

According to a 2014 UNEP-Interpol study, the overall illegal wildlife and natural resources trade is worth between US$70 billion and $213 billion a year.[20] This includes the illegal trade in fauna and flora which could be worth US$ 7–23 billion annually, according to the same study.[21] This would place illegal trade in fauna and flora as the second largest market for global illegal trade, behind only illegal drugs trafficking.[22] A less wide range is present in the figures released by the 2000 *International Crime Threat Assessment* report, which estimates that the illegal trade in animal parts and endangered species generates revenues of between U$6 and 10 billion annually.[23] Overall, a number of studies have sug-

---

16 Ibid. See also Nellemann, C., Henriksen, R., Raxter, P., Ash, N., Mrema, E. (eds). 2014. *The Environmental Crime Crisis: Threats to Sustainable Development from Illegal Exploitation and Trade in Wildlife and Forest Resources, infra* at 19.

17 *Ibid.*

18 See e.g. Kenyon Rainier Stebbins, *Garbage imperialism: Health implications of dumping hazardous wastes in third world countries*, Medical Anthropology: Cross-Cultural Studies in Health and Illness Volume 15, Issue 1, 1993.

19 There are estimates suggesting that while in the late 1980s the average cost of safe waste disposal in an OECD country was between US$100 and US$2,000, in Africa it was between U$2.50 and $50. See Hayman, Gavin and Brack, Dunkan, *Workshop Report: International Environmental Crime: The Nature and Control of Environmental Black Markets* (the Royal Institute of International Affairs, London 1998) at 13.

20 Nellemann, C., Henriksen, R., Raxter, P., Ash, N.,Mrema, E. (Eds). 2014. *The Environmental Crime Crisis: Threats to Sustainable Development from Illegal Exploitation and Trade in Wildlife and Forest Resources. A Rapid Response Assessment.* A UNEP Rapid Response Assessment. United Nations Environment Programme and GRID-Arendal, Nairobi and Arendal, at 4. available at http://www.unep.org/unea/docs/rracrimecrisis.pdf (accessed on 15 February 2015).

21 *Ibid.*

22 *Ibid.*

23 The *International Crime Threat Assessment*, December 2000, USA. Moreover, statistics from the British Central Office of Information show that every year as many as five million wild birds, 30,000 primates, 15 million furs, 12 million orchids, 8 million cacti and countless other species are sold on the international market. BBC News, *Environmental Crime: A Global Problem, available at* April 5, 1998, at http://news.bbc.co.uk/1/hi/74317.stm (accessed on 15 February 2015); and Comte (2006), 15 *EELR* 190; p. 199.

gested that the illegal trade in endangered species may account to approximately 25% of the level of legal trade.[24]

As regards illegal, unreported and unregulated (IUU) fishing, it has been estimated to be of an annual value globally of between $US 4.2 billion to 9.5 billion, according to a MRAG 2005 report.[25] Yet citing a 2012 OECD study[26] and other sources,[27] the 2014 UNEP-Interpol study suggests that there may be an even larger scale of criminality in the fisheries sector, which could be worth 11–30 billion annually (accounting for 12–32% of the global trade).[28] Furthermore, it has been estimated that about two-thirds of the world's fishing stocks are at, or beyond, their sustainable capacity.[29]

According to the 2000 *International Crime Threat Assessment* report, the illegal trade in ozone depleting substances (ODS) generates between U$1 and

---

24 Fröhlich et al , Organised environmental crime in the EU Member States: Final Report, Betreuungsgesellschaft für Umweltfragen (BfU) and partners, May 2003; and Milieu Consortium, *Study on the Enforcement of the EU Wildlife Trade Regulations in the EU-25: Final Report*, November 2006 at 13.

25 MRAG (2005) *IUU Fishing on the High Seas: Impacts on Ecosystems and Future Science Need;* and Chatham House (Royal Institute of International Affairs) 2008. See also, *The Growth and Control of International Environmental Crime,* available at http://www.illegal-logging.info/uploads/Intenvcrime2007backgroundpapers.pdf (accessed on 15 February 2015) at 5.

26 OECD (2012) *Illegal Trade in Environmentally Sensitive Goods*. Executive Summary.

27 UNODC (2011). *Transnational organized crime in the fishing industry*. Nellemann, C., INTERPOL Environmental Crime Programme (eds). *Green carbon, black trade: Illegal Logging, Tax Fraud and Laundering in the World's Tropical Forests,* A Rapid Response Assessment. United Nations Environment Programme, GRIDArendal (2012); available at http://www.unep.org/pdf/RRAlogging_english_scr.pdf (accessed on 15 February 2015).

28 OECD (2012) *Illegal Trade in Environmentally Sensitive Goods*. Executive Summary. This figure came from extrapolating the findings of a study of 10 developing countries in Africa and Oceania. See also, Doulmann, D.J. 'A General Overview of some Aspects of Illegal, Unreported and Unregulated Fishing. Report at the FAO Expert Consultation on Illegal Unreported and Unregulated Fishing, 2000 at 2. Illegal, unreported and undocumented fishing accounts according to some estimates to some 30% of all catches. See Albrecht, Hans-Jorg 'The Extent of Organised Environmental Crime: A European Perspective' in Comte, Françoise and Kramer, Ludwig (eds.) *Environmental Crime in Europe: Rules of Sanctions* (Europa Law Publishing, Groningen 2004) at 91. Doulmann, D.J. 'A General Overview of some Aspects of Illegal, Unreported and Unregulated Fishing. Report at the FAO Expert Consultation on Illegal Unreported and Unregulated Fishing, 2000 at 2.

29 Rayman and Brack (1998) above note 10 at 14; FAO, World Review of Fisheries and Aquaculture. Fisheries Resources: Trends in Production, Utilization and Trade (Rome: FAO, 1999).; and Doulmann, D.J. (2000) *supra* at 2.

2 billion annually.[30] Those are considerably higher figures than those presented by a EIA-Chatham House 2006 study,[31] which suggested that in the early 2000s smuggling of ODS was in a range of 7,000 – 14,000 tonnes annually and had a value of US$25–60 million (representing 10–20% of the legitimate trade in ODS).[32] This same study suggested that the illegal trade in ODS was decreasing in absolute numbers since the mid-1990s, when the illegal trade in chlorofluorocarbons (CFCs) was worth US$150–300 million – or 20,000 tonnes per year (equivalent to over 12% of global ODS production).[33]

According to the 2014 UNEP-Interpol report, illegal logging and illegal timber trade leads to annual loss of resources of between US$30–100 billion, corresponding to 10–30% of the global timber trade.[34] Thus the illegal logging trade represents a considerably higher value than is the illegal trade in fauna and flora, which as discussed above is estimated by the UNEP-Interpol 2014 report to be in the range of US$7–23 billion annually. Yet the 2000 *International Crime Threat Assessment* report presents considerably more modest figures, suggesting that illegal logging may generate revenues of between U$0.5 and 1 billion annually (these figures, however, do not relate to costs connected to loss of resources, but to the profits made from illegal trade).[35] It is worth noting that the market for illegally extracted natural resources also includes mineral resources, which was estimated by the UNEP-Interpol study to be in the order of U$ 12–48 billion (or 1–4% by industry of the global trade in minerals).[36]

It is in the context of organised crime that the figures of environmental crime have been more widely estimated.[37] It has been suggested that even

---

30 The *International Crime Threat Assessment*, December 2000, USA. See also, Comte, F. (2006) above n. 9, at 198.

31 Chatham House and Environmental Investigation Agency (2006), ODS TRACKING *Feasibility study on developing a system for monitoring the transboundary movement of controlled ozone-depleting substances between the Parties.* Report produced according to the terms of reference of Decision XVII/16 September 2006.

32 *Ibid.*

33 *Ibid.*

34 Nellemann, C., et al (Eds).(2014) above note 20; Nellemann, C., INTERPOL Environmental Crime Programme (eds). 2012, above note 27; and OECD (2012) above note 28.

35 The 2000 *International Crime Threat Assessment* report, above note 10.

36 Nellemann, C., et al. (Eds). 2014, *supra*. OECD (2012) above note 28.

37 See Albrecht, H-J (2004) above note 12; Final Report: *Organised environmental crime in the EU Member States*, Max-Planck-Institute for Foreign and International Criminal Law, Kassel, 15 May 2003, available at http://ec.europa.eu/environment/legal/crime/pdf/organised_member_states.pdf (accessed on 15 February 2015). See also, Watson, Michael 'Organised Crime and the Environment: The British Experience' (2005) *EELR* 207, who

though it is often overlooked, the extent of organised crime involving environmental impairment is very high, especially in the contexts of wildlife crime[38] and illegal trade in and disposal of waste.[39] The so-called 'eco-mafia' in Italy in many ways personifies the worse forms of environmental criminality in Europe carried out by criminal organisations. Italy's waste disposal contracts are notoriously controlled by criminal groups. According to the Italian authorities 11 million metric tones of toxic and industrial waste are deposited annually in some 2,000 illegal domestic dump sites in local waterways or in the Mediterranean. It was estimated that 11.2 million tons of special waste were illegally dumped in 1999; and that at least 15–20% of waste in Italy disappears annually between production and final storage and disposal.[40] Research by the Italian environmental NGO Legambiente on Italy's 'Ecomafia' shows a far higher than average incidence of recorded environmental crime in the traditional Mafia strongholds of Campania, Puglia, Calabria and Sicily.[41] Among the 1,734 waste-related infractions recorded in Italy in 2002, 39% were committed in those four regions.[42] Not only in Italy but in the EU Member Sates generally several studies have shown the infiltration of criminal organisations into the waste disposal sector.[43]

Those developments reflect the fact that criminal organisations are increasingly moving away from traditional areas of transnational crime – such as drug trafficking – to focus on environmental crime, due to the perceived low risk and high profits associated with environmental crime. But unlike narcotics and other illegally traded commodities, there is a finite stock of endangered species and forestry resources, which leads to their progressively increased

---

suggests that in the UK there is a high infiltration of criminal organisations in the fields of waste disposal, fly-tipping and wildlife crime.

38 It has been suggested that 'drawing on the comments received and on the basis of more in-depth research, it appears that organized crime, while not involved in all forms of trafficking in protected species of fauna and flora, is strongly present in various sectors. Even when organized crime, as such, is not fully involved, much of the trafficking is highly organized'. See *International Crime Assessment* (2000) above note 9.

39 See Albrecht, H-J above note 11.

40 Legambiente, *The Illegal Trafficking in Hazardous Waste in Italy and Spain: Final Report*, GEPEC-EC, October 2003 at 21.

41 *Ibid.*

42 *Ibid.*

43 Final Report: *Organised environmental crime in the EU Member States* (2003) above note 37. See also Final Report Organised environmental crime in a few Candidate Countries, Kassel, 10 September 2003, available at http://ec.europa.eu/environment/legal/crime/pdf/organised_candidate_countries.pdf (accessed on 15 February 2015).

price in international markets and thus higher profits to traders, who are also attracted to the low risks connected to environmental offences in comparison with traditional crimes.[44]

What is clear from the above discussion is that there are considerable variations and discrepancies in the figures estimating the scale of environmental criminality in specific markets, which depend on the measurements applied in different studies. For example, the *International Crime Assessment* Report estimates annual illegal wildlife trade to be between 6 and 10 billion, exposing a considerable gap between the lowest to the highest estimates of revenues for that particular market. Moreover, those estimations are considerably lower than those presented by the more comprehensive UNEP-Interpol 2014 study, which has provided estimates of the annual illegal wildlife trade in the range of US$ 7–23 billion annually.[45] The variations and incongruences in the findings of those studies may be explained by the fact that there are considerable complexities and uncertainties in assessing the levels and costs of illicit wildlife trade. This includes challenges in estimating the number of animals or plants in the wild; the numbers that are illegally but successfully trafficked to customers; and the percentage of those trafficked that are intercepted and the prices that are paid.[46] Data is recognizably difficult to obtain, particularly in developing countries where data on illegal trade tends to be unreliable or patchy.[47] Moreover, global estimates are particularly tenuous as typically they are made by extrapolating from national data and sometimes from anecdotal evidence.[48]

The disparities in the findings of those studies can also be attributed to other difficulties in measuring the scale of environmental illicit activity. For example, in order to estimate the scale of illegal production or trade in stolen timber, wildlife, ozone depleting substances or illegal fishing, commonly figures

44 Hayman and Brack (1998), above note 10, at 10.

45 Nellemann, C., et al (eds.) 2014, above note 20.

46 Sam Lawson, 'International Environmental Crime: Data Collection, Transparency and Auditing' in *The Growth and Control of International Environmental Crime* (2007), available at http://www.illegal-logging.info/uploads/Intenvcrime2007backgroundpapers.pdf (accessed on 15 February 2015).

47 *ibid.*

48 Nellemann, C., et al (eds.) 2014, *supra*. One study by the British Central Office of Information suggested that 'data [is] not available to allow estimation of scale [of organized environmental crime]'. See, Hannah Mills, Sara Skodbo and Peter Blyth, *Understanding organised crime: estimating the scale and the social and economic costs*, Research Report 73 October 2013 available at https://www.gov.uk/government/uploads/system/uploads/attachment_data/file/246390/horr73.pdf (accessed on 15 February 2015).

of prevalence of illegal activity (in percentage terms) are assessed against overall figures for legal production and trade (typically estimated to account for 10–20% of the legal trade in many cases, and even more for certain products).[49] Another method used to estimate levels of environmental criminality is to compare the legal production against actual consumption. If, in a particular country, overall consumption of a controlled good (domestic use plus legal exports) significantly exceeds legal production (domestic legal production and legal imports), then this can be a strong indicator of illegality.[50]

One of the main difficulties in finding comprehensive and reliable figures on the scale of environmental crime is that only crimes which are reported are taken into consideration in crime statistics.[51] The difference between the crimes which are reported and those which are not is commonly referred to as the 'dark figure'.[52] In the case of environmental crime, it has been suggested that the extent of the 'dark figure' may be very high: estimates range from 20 per cent to 40 per cent and in certain cases as much as 90 per cent falls in this category.[53] Possible explanations for the high number of unreported environmental crime is that those crimes are in many instances 'victimless' in the sense that they do not directly affect any person or property, and therefore authorities tend to regard such crimes as of lower importance in comparison with traditional crimes.

The difficulties in identifying and reporting environmental crime are particularly evident in the context of environmental criminality occurring in the 'global commons' (i.e. in areas beyond national jurisdiction), such as illegal fishing or the dumping of hazardous wastes in the high seas, in violation of the provisions of international agreements and national laws. In this context, waste dumping and illegal fishing in the high seas can be regarded as lucrative

49 Customs data was used by TRAFFIC in the early 1990s estimate the overall international trade in wildlife (excluding timber and commercial fish). See also, Sam Lawson, (2007), above note 46. In this vein, an estimate of the scale of international illegal trade in ODS by the Environmental Investigation Agency (EIA) and Chatham House in 2007 ($25-$60 million) was produced by multiplying the known legal trade volume by an estimate of the relative percentage of illegal trade of between ten and twenty percent, itself based on anecdotal information such as seizure data, market surveys, and admissions by illegal traders. See Chatham House (2007) above note 8.

50 *Ibid.*

51 Comte, F. (2006) above note 9, at 190.

52 Moreover, there is also a 'grey figure', which consists of those crimes regarded to be of minor importance which, despite being reported to the authorities, nonetheless do not appear in the official statistics. *Ibid* at 197.

53 *Ibid.*

and carrying few risks, given the sheer size of the world's oceans and weak interstate cooperation and enforcement, which means that infringement of fisheries or waste disposal laws are particularly difficult to detect.

1.2.2 *Overview of International Declarations and Initiatives on Environmental Criminal Law*

The need for protection of the environment through criminal law is recognised in a number of international instruments which call on states to enact criminal provisions for the enforcement of environmental law. One of the earliest initiatives was the Eighth United Nations Congress on the Prevention of Crime and the Treatment of Offenders (Havana, Cuba, 1990) which issued a resolution on 'the role of criminal law in the protection of nature and the environment' endorsed by the General Assembly Resolution 45/121. This General Assembly Resolution called upon states to 'to modify or enact, where necessary, and to enforce national criminal laws designed to protect the environment'[54] and 'to encourage the harmonisation of national and regional legislation',[55] as well as to 'cooperate in the prevention, investigation and prosecution of criminal acts against the environment'.[56] Moreover, the Resolution requested the UN Secretary General 'to encourage the incorporation, where appropriate, in future international conventions for the protection of the environment, of provisions under which States would be expected to enact sanctions under national criminal law'[57] as well as to 'examine the possibilities of further harmonisation of the provisions of existing international instruments entailing penal sanctions under national criminal law'.[58] Subsequently, the General Assembly resolution 67/189 of 20 December 2012 expressed deep concern about environmental crimes, including trafficking in endangered and protected species of wild fauna and flora. It emphasized the need to combat such crimes by strengthening international cooperation, capacity-building, criminal justice responses and law enforcement efforts.[59]

In a similar vein, the Economic and Social Council (ECOSOC) Resolution 1993 on the role of criminal law in the protection of the environment '[c]alls upon Member States and the bodies concerned to continue their efforts to protect nature and the environment using, in addition to measures provided by

54 General Assembly Resolution 45/121, 2.1 (a).

55 ibid, 2.2 (d).

56 ibid, 2.2. (e).

57 ibid, 2.3 (a).

58 ibid 2.3(b).

59 General Assembly resolution 67/189 of 20 December 2012.

administrative law and liability under civil law, measures in the field of national criminal law, and to provide requesting Member States with technical cooperation in the field of environmental crime'.[60] The resolution further suggested that '(…) Member States should consider acknowledging the most serious forms of environmental crimes in an international convention'.[61] Furthermore, ECOSOC Resolution 2013/40 adopted in July 2013[62] strongly encouraged states to 'strengthen, where necessary, their national legal and criminal regimes and law enforcement and judicial capacity, consistent with international legal obligations, to ensure that relevant criminal laws, including appropriate penalties and sanctions, are available to address illicit trafficking in protected species of wild fauna and flora;'[63] and 'to make illicit trafficking in protected species of wild fauna and flora involving organized criminal groups a serious crime'.[64]

The Vienna Declaration and Programme of Action, adopted by the World Conference on Human Rights[65] recognized, *inter alia*, that illicit dumping of toxic and dangerous substances and wastes potentially constituted a serious threat to the human rights to life and health of everyone, and called on all states 'to adopt and vigorously implement existing conventions relating to the dumping of toxic and dangerous products and waste and to cooperate in the prevention of illicit dumping'.[66] This statement is in line with a number of UN General Assembly Resolutions recognising that environmental protection is inseparable from human rights.[67]

Moreover, the International Law Commission (ILC) has adopted or proposed a number of initiatives calling for the establishment of offences against the environment as international crimes, in particular the ILC Draft Code of Crimes Against the Peace and Security of Mankind (1954) (adopted in second

60 ECOSOC 43rd plenary meeting, 27 July 1993, para. 4.

61 'On the basis of proposals put forward by the International Law Commission and the discussions at the United Nations Conference on Environment and Development'. See 43rd Plenary Meeting 25 July 1994, Annex: Recommendations Concerning The Role Of Criminal Law In Protecting The Environment, Paragraph (K).

62 Resolution 2013/40 on '*Crime Prevention and Criminal Justice Responses to Illicit Trafficking in Protected Species of Wild Fauna and Flora*' adopted by the United States Economic and Social Council on 25 July 2013, Distr.: General 17 October 2013.

63 *Ibid*, para. 5.

64 As defined in article 2, paragraph (b), of the United Nations Convention against Transnational Organized Crime. Ibid, para. 4.

65 Vienna Declaration and Programme of Action Adopted by the World Conference on Human Rights in Vienna on 25 June 1993.

66 *Ibid.*

67 See e.g. UN GA Resolution A/RES/45/94, 68th plenary meeting, 14 December 1990.

reading in 1996);[68] and the original proposal by the ILC to include international environmental crime in its Draft Articles on State Responsibility.[69]

The view that criminal sanctions are necessary for the enforcement of environmental field was also expressed in international conferences with leading experts in the field. This includes the 'Conclusions of the Seminar on the Policy of Criminal Law in the Protection of Nature and the Environment in a European Perspective', held at Lauchhammer, Germany (25–29 April 1992) in which it was stated that: '[t]he environment must be protected not only at the national but also at the international level. In this respect criminal law for the protection of the environment should also be developed at the international level'.[70] Moreover, it was stated that further 'European standards of environmental substantive criminal law should be developed (...) [and] efforts of the Council of Europe in elaborating a convention and a recommendation on environmental offences should be supported'.[71] The importance of criminal law enforcement in the environmental field was echoed in the Twelfth Congress on Crime Prevention and Criminal Justice in April 2010 held in the city of Salvador, Brazil. The 2010 '*Salvador Declaration*' acknowledged the 'challenge posed by emerging forms of crime that have a significant impact on the environment'.[72]

In addition, there have been initiatives focusing on specific areas of environmental criminality. For example, growing international concern over pollution of the marine environment has led the General Assembly of the International Union for the Conservation of Nature and Natural Resources (IUCN) in 1978 to approve a resolution inviting governments and the International Maritime Consultative Organisation to adopt the principle that 'those responsible for damage to marine species and ecosystems due to negligent operation of large oil tankers *should be heavily penalised*' (emphasis added).[73]

Another notable development was the G8's statement on environmental protection and transnational crimes issued in 1997 in the Denver summit.[74]

---

68 Draft Code of Crimes Against the Peace and Security of Mankind, adopted by the International Law Commission at its forty-eighth session, Yearbook of the International Law Commission, 1996, vol. II, Part Two.

69 ILC Draft Articles on State Responsibility (1996), Official Records of the General Assembly, Fifty-first session, A/51/10, Article 19 (2) and Article 19 (3) (d). See further, Chapter 3.

70 See Hans-Jorg Albrecht and Seppo Leppa, (ed.) *Criminal Law and the Environment*, Proceedings of the European Seminar held in Lauchhammer, Land Brandenburg, Germany, April 1992, para. 13.

71 *Ibid*, para 15.

72 The *Salvador Declaration*, adopted at the Twelfth Congress on Crime Prevention and Criminal Justice in April 2010, Salvador, Brazil.

73 IUCN, 14th session of the G.A. of the IUCN, Ashkhasbad, USSR, 1978, 8(b).

74 G8 summit Communiqué. Denver, June 22, 1997, in particular points 12–30.

Significantly, in a high-level meeting held by the UN Security Council in 2007 a link was made between climate change and peace and security of mankind.[75] Furthermore, transnational environmental crime was included as a serious form of crime in the sixth session of the COP of the UN Convention against Transnational Organised Crime in 2012, in which it was held that '[c]riminal activities affecting the environment, once an emerging threat, have evolved to become a serious form of transnational organized crime with links to other crimes associated with high levels of violence and corruption'.[76]

In the 2014 *London Declaration* adopted by the conference on the illegal wildlife trade that took place in London on 12–13 February 2014, the representatives of governments and regional economic integration organisations held their commitment 'to curb the illegal wildlife trade' and to ensure that criminals 'are prosecuted and penalised to provide an effective deterrent'.[77] Moreover, the declaration called on states to 'address the problem of the illegal wildlife trade by adopting or amending legislation, as necessary, to criminalise poaching and wildlife trafficking and related crimes including by ensuring such criminal offences are "serious crimes" within the UN Convention on Transnational Organised Crime'.[78] Importantly, the governments represented in the conference have agreed to establish a global £10million fund to address conservation projects aimed to prevent and combat wildlife crime.[79] The March 2015 Progress Report on the implementation of the London Declaration has suggested that a number of countries have taken action to strengthen penalties and enforcement against wildlife crime.[80] For example, Vietnam has reported

---

75 Following the Security Council on 'Energy, security and climate' held on 17 April 2007. See *Security Council Holds First-Ever Debate On Impact Of Climate Change On Peace, Security, Hearing Over 50 Speakers,* 5663rd Meeting, SC/9000, 17 April 2007. Resolution adopted by the General Assembly [without reference to a Main Committee (A/63/L.8/Rev.1 and Add.1)] 63/281. Climate change and its possible security implications, Sixty-third session, Agenda item 107.

76 Conference of the Parties to the United Nations Convention against Transnational Crime, Sixth Session, CTOC/COP/2012/7, 5 July 2012 point 30.

77 Declaration of the London conference on Illegal Wildlife Trade (2014), b), point 16, available at https://www.gov.uk/government/uploads/system/uploads/attachment_data/file/281289/london-wildlife-conference-declaration-140213.pdf (accessed on 15 February 2015).

78 *Ibid*, VIII.

79 UK Commitment to Action on the Illegal Wildlife Trade (IWT) February 2014, available at https://www.gov.uk/government/uploads/system/uploads/attachment_data/file/277772/pb14129-commitment-action-illegal-wildlife-trade.pdf (accessed on 10 February 2015).

80 *Kasane Conference On The Illegal Wildlife Trade – London Declaration on the Illegal Wildlife Trade: Review of Progress*, 25th March 2015, Points 52–58, available at https://www.gov.uk/

that it is reforming its Penal Code to incorporate stronger and more deterrent sanctions over environmental crimes, including illegal trade in endangered species; China has amended its Wildlife Conservation Law in 2014 in order to criminalise illegal purchases of rare or endangered species of wildlife as food or for other purposes; and Mozambique passed the Conservation Law in April 2014 to include prison sentences for offenders and stiffer fines.[81]

The above developments suggest that there is growing international recognition that states must cooperate towards combatting and punishing environmental crime (in particular transnational environmental crime) through criminal liability standards and enforcement. Although resolutions adopted by international organisations such as the UN General Assembly or ECOSOC are not legally binding, the fact that these resolutions have called for a degree of harmonisation and coordination of criminal sanctions demonstrates an intention and commitment by states to pursue integration and cooperation in the criminal-law field to protect the environment. This is an evidence of state practice (and indeed *opiniu iuris*) which could eventually lead to the development of a rule under customary international law that would require that states establish that serious infringements of international environmental law must be subject to effective sanctions, including the possibility of criminal law enforcement by the national authorities.

1.2.3 *Overview of European Legislative Initiatives to Combat Environmental Crime*

1.2.3.1 The Council of Europe Convention on the Protection of the Environment through Criminal Law

The Council of Europe ('CoE') was established in May 1949 in order to promote European cooperation in the aftermath of the Second Wold War with ten founding countries. Currently it covers virtually the entire European continent with forty-seven member states.[82] The Council of Europe seeks to develop throughout Europe common and democratic principles based on the European Convention on Human Rights and other instruments on the protection of human rights.[83]

---

government/uploads/system/uploads/attachment_data/file/415690/review-progress-kasane-conf-150317.pdf (accessed 10 April 2015).

81 Points 52–56 ibid.

82 *The Council of Europe in Brief*, http://www.coe.int/en/web/about-us/who-we-are (accessed on 15 February 2015).

83 See European Convention for the Protection of Human Rights and Fundamental Freedoms, adopted on 4 November 1950, in force on 3 September 1953, ETS 5; 213 UNTS 221.

One of the primary functions of the Council of Europe is to develop the law of the participating states, by harmonising and improving legislation with the view to protect human rights. Unlike the European Union, the Council of Europe has no supranational powers, yet it may influence the development of the criminal law in Member States through international conventions – including conventions on extradition and mutual assistance and transfer of criminals[84] – or recommendations and through the case-law of the European Court of Human Rights.[85] In the field of criminal procedure the European Convention on Human Rights (ECHR) has contributed significantly to the harmonisation of standards in Europe, in particular through the interpretation of the right to a fair trial recognized under Article 6 ECHR by the European Court of Human Rights.[86] Unlike is the case of the EU judicial protection framework in which citizens do not have standing to bring judicial proceedings directly before the Court of Justice of the EU,[87] every citizen of a Council of Europe Member State can make an individual application to the European Court of Human Rights (ECtHR) after the domestic remedies have been exhausted.[88]

As was mentioned above, Council of Europe has adopted a number of treaties in the criminal-law field.[89] Yet the role of the ECtHR lies primarily in overseeing the compatibility of signatory states' (criminal) law and procedure with the European Convention on the Human Rights. Hence it has been suggested that 'the European Convention on Human Rights is not an adequate instrument for real harmonisation of the criminal law and procedure in Europe'.[90]

---

84 The European Convention on Extradition, Paris, ETS no. 24, 13 December 1957; the European Convention on Mutual Assistance in Criminal Matters, Strasbourg, ETS n.30 20 April 1959 and European Convention on the Transfer of Proceedings in Criminal Matters, Strasbourg, ETS no. 73, 15 May 1972.

85 Perron, Walter, 'Perspectives of the Harmonization of Criminal Law and Criminal Procedure in the European Union' in Husabø, E.J. and Strandbakken, Asbjørn (ed.) *Harmonization of Criminal Law in Europe* (Intersentia, 2005) at 11.

86 The ECtHR case-law on the right to a fair trial is discussed in Chapters 2 and 7.

87 If a question of EU law arises in a criminal prosecution in a member state, the CJEU may decide on that aspect of the dispute if a question for a preliminary ruling is submitted by the national court to the CJEU. Yet the existing rules establishing the jurisdiction of the court (although a subsequent Treaty amendment could change this) do not allow for direct prosecutions to be brought before the CJEU.

88 Article 34 ECHR.

89 See e.g. the European Convention on Extradition, Paris, ETS no. 24, 13 December 1957; the European Convention on Mutual Assistance in Criminal Matters, Strasbourg, ETS n.30 20 April 1959 and European Convention on the Transfer of Proceedings in Criminal Matters, Strasbourg, ETS no. 73, 15 May 1972.

90 Perron (2005) above note 85, at 12.

Specific efforts towards the harmonisation of environmental criminal law by the Council of Europe started in the late 1970s. In 1978 the Committee of Ministers of the Council of Europe adopted Resolution (77) 28 on the Contribution of Criminal Law to the Protection of the Environment.[91] This resolution concluded that it was necessary to resort to criminal law as an 'ultima ratio' when other measures proved ineffective or inappropriate; and recommended that Member States introduced a number of measures relating to criminal law for the protection of the environment, including specific criminal penalties.[92] Moreover, the Resolution draws attention to the advantages which certain member states may derive from gradually compiling in a single collection their criminal provisions relating to environmental protection with a view to: (a) subsequent consolidation at a national level, e.g. by codification, of the entire legislation on the environment 'in so far as this appeared desirable or feasible'; and (b) an eventual future *harmonisation of all legislations* of the member states of the Council of Europe in this field (emphasis added).[93] Although the Council of Europe Committee of Ministers resolutions lack legally binding force, they represented an important first step towards acceptance of the general and underlying principles and standards before the drafting of a regional treaty on environmental crime.[94]

91 Adopted by the Committee of Ministers on 28 September 1977 at the 275th meeting of the Ministers' Deputies. For a discussion see Vercher, A. 'The Use of Criminal Law for the Protection of the Environment in Europe: Council of Europe Resolution (77) 28' Northwestern Journal of International Law & Business 10:442 (1990) p. 445.

92 This included (1) examination of criminal penalties for damage to the environment and whilst maintaining the traditional penalties of fine and imprisonment (possibly conditional) in the most serious cases: *a.* introduction in this field of particular forms of pecuniary penalty, such as daily fines ('astreintes'), day fines, suspended fines and conditional fines; *b.* allocation of proceeds from pecuniary penalties for pollution to environmental uses, *c.* introduction in this field of measures such as restoration of the former state possibly; ordered in connection with a suspended custodial penalty, work for the benefit of the community, disqualifications (as principal penalties) and publication of convictions; (2). re-examination of the principles of criminal liability, with a view, in particular, to the possible introduction in certain cases of the liability of corporate bodies, public or private; (3) examination of the advisability of criminalising acts and omissions which culpably (intentionally or negligently) expose the life or health of human beings or property of substantial value.

93 Resolution (77) 28, paragraph 4, penultimate recital.

94 Moreover, the resolution invites the governments of Member States to report to the Secretary General every five years on the action they have taken on the recommendations contained therein.

Subsequently, in the early 1990s there were calls for a comprehensive treaty addressing the growing evidence of the costs and risks associated with environmental criminality. In the seventeenth Conference of European Ministers of Justice (Istanbul, 1990) adopted Resolution No. 1, leading the Committee of Ministers of the Council of Europe to set up in 1991 a new select committee of experts on the protection of the environment through criminal law. In its first meeting, the Committee decided to draft a binding international Treaty.[95] The Council of Europe Convention on the Protection of the Environment through Criminal Law adopted on 4 November 1998 in Strasbourg (herein after, 'Council of Europe/CoE environmental crime convention')[96] was the first international treaty to require more broadly the criminalisation of a number of offences causing or likely to cause environmental damage.[97] Although it is a convention adopted by the Council of Europe, it is also open for accession by 'non-member States which have participated in its elaboration'.[98] Moreover, '[a]fter the entry into force of this Convention, the Committee of Ministers of the Council of Europe, after consulting the Contracting States to the Convention, may invite any State not a member of the Council of Europe to accede to this Convention (...)'.[99]

The CoE convention aims at criminalising environmental harm and harmonising environmental criminal offences and administrative infringements and penalties. The Council of Europe treaty aimed at harmonising environmental criminal law is based on the idea that criminal law is essential in order to strengthen the protection of the environment, whilst also recognising the effectiveness of other penalties, in particular administrative penalties. In this vein, the Convention aims to establish a minimum standard for a common

95 The draft Convention and explanatory memorandum were approved by the European Committee on Crime Problems (CDPC) and adopted by the Committee of Ministers in June/September 1996.

96 Council of Europe Convention on the Protection of the Environment through Criminal Law, ETS no. 172, adopted on 4 November 1998 (not in force at the time of writing).

97 See also, Comte, Françoise, 'Protection of the Environment through Criminal Law: Destiny of the Various European Union's Initiatives' in Odina, Marco (ed.) *Europe and the Environment* (Groningen, 2004) at 46.

98 Art. 13 (1) Council of Europe environmental crime convention. This provision only applies to Canada, which has participated in the drafting of the convention. However, at the time of writing Canada has not yet signed or ratified the convention.

99 Art. 14, ibid. This article subjects the accession by a non-Council of Europe member state to the condition that there is 'a decision taken by the majority provided for in Article 20.d of the Statute of the Council of Europe and by the unanimous vote of the representatives of the Contracting States entitled to sit on the Committee'.

criminal policy on the protection of the environment. The Explanatory Report to the Convention states that 'the Convention seeks to harmonise national legislation in the particular field of environmental offences' and creates an obligation for contracting States to introduce criminal offences and penalties or modify their existing criminal law provisions in relation to the protection of the environment 'on the understanding that harmonisation of legislation in this area also enhances international co-operation'.[100] Even though the preamble to the Convention recognises that 'the prevention of the impairment of the environment must be achieved primarily through other measures',[101] the Convention recognises the need for criminalisation of the most serious environmental offences when committed intentionally or with negligence.[102]

At the time of writing, the Council of Europe Convention has not reached the minimum number of ratifications required for it to enter into force. It has only attracted one ratification by Estonia on 26 April 2002 and a total of fourteen signatures.[103] Since the convention requires three ratifications for it to enter into force,[104] it remains inoperative. Initially, it should be noted that, in comparison with other international or even regional agreements, the requirement for a minimum of three ratifications is a particularly low threshold. It is also important to note that the majority of the current fourteen states that *have signed* the convention are in fact also EU member states,[105] who are already bound in any event by the EU instruments on environmental criminal law, i.e. the EU directives on environmental crime and ship-source pollution (further discussed in Section 1.2.3.2 below). Since the EU member states are

100 Explanatory Report, point 1) of the Council of Europe environmental crime convention. Recital 9 to the preamble to the convention links effective intestate cooperation with the harmonisation of legislation. It states that states should 'take effective measures to ensure that the perpetrators of such acts do not escape prosecution and punishment and desirous of fostering international co-operation to this end'.

101 Recital 7 of the Preamble, Council of Europe environmental crime convention.

102 See Art. 2 and 3 (1) ibid.

103 See http://conventions.coe.int/Treaty/Commun/ChercheSig.asp?NT=172&CM=8&DF=3/8/2007&CL=ENG (accessed on 10 February 2015). The states that have signed the convention at the time of writing are: Austria, Belgium, Denmark, Estonia, Finland, France, Germany, Greece, Iceland, Italy, Luxembourg, Romania, Sweden and Ukraine.

104 Article 13 (3) states that the Convention shall enter into force following the period of three months after the date on which three States have expressed their consent to be bound by the convention.

105 Ukraine and Iceland are the only non-EU member states to have signed the convention (in 2006 and 1998 respectively). It should be noted that some signatory parties (such as Estonia and Romania) have joined the EU after they had signed the Council of Europe environmental crime convention.

already bound by those EU directives establishing environmental criminal liability standards, an eventual ratification of the convention by those member states would have limited legal or practical significance.[106] Yet one of the advantages of a Council of Europe instrument on environmental crimes over a European Union instrument is that the former could potentially bind a higher number of states.[107]

Although the Council of Europe member states have not expressed official reasons for not having (yet) ratified the convention, it is possible to assess some of the reasons which may explain why the Convention has not been particularly well received by the member states of the Council of Europe. One reason for this is that they may regard the Convention as a threat to their sovereignty over national criminal laws – a position which however is difficult to reconcile with the fact that many of those states have ratified other (Council of Europe) conventions harmonising substantive and procedural criminal law.[108] More convincingly, it could be argued that improving the levels of environmental enforcement is not seen as a priority by those states; or even that there remains a certain degree of scepticism over the effectiveness of the use of criminal law for protection of the environment. The lack of interest in the environmental crime convention could also be attributed to a level of criticism on the part of certain states as regards some of the provisions of the convention – for example, it has been suggested that Germany was discontent with the provisions of the CoE environmental crime convention on corporate criminal liability.[109]

Yet the lack of interest in the Council of Europe convention could be a reflection of a more generalised aversion by states to ratify international conventions

---

106 Even though the text of the EU environmental crime directive was influenced by the Council of Europe convention, as will be discussed in Chapter 6, there are considerable differences between the two instruments.

107 Presently, the Council of Europe has 47 Member States, while the EU has, following the two most recent EU enlargements in 2007 and 2013, 28 Member States. However, it is not necessarily true that the CoE convention would ensure a wider participation than the EU environmental crime directive, as the convention only requires three ratifications for it to enter into force.

108 See for example, the Council of Europe Criminal Law Convention on Corruption CETS No.: 173, which currently has 45 ratifications. Montenegro and Serbia are the only Council of Europe member states which have not yet ratified that convention. See also the Council of Europe Convention on Cybercrime CETS no. 185, with 45 ratifications. Andorra, Greece, Ireland, Lichtenstein, Russia and San Marino are the only Council of Europe member states which have not yet ratified that convention.

109 Kramer, Ludwig. 'Case Law Analysis: Environment, Crime and EC Law', (2006) 18 (2) *Journal of Environmental Law*, at 285.

or protocols focusing on the harmonisation of liability standards. This can be illustrated with reference to the ratification process of environmental civil liability conventions or protocols.[110] In general, there is a noticeable lack of political will by states to implement the provisions under multilateral environmental agreements calling for the establishment of civil liability regimes, which commonly become 'dead letter'.[111]

Another reason which may explain the lack of interest in the Council of Europe environmental crime convention is that the EU member states were in the process of negotiating since 2000 the first proposed EU instruments of harmonisation of environmental criminal law[112] (therefore only two years after the adoption of the Council of Europe convention). In fact, as will be seen in Chapter 6 in particular, there are some similarities between the adopted (or proposed) EU legal instruments on environmental crime and the CoE environmental crime convention.

It is apparent that there will be insufficient interest by the European governments to boost the ratification process of the Council of Europe environmental crime convention, given that the EU member states are themselves already bound by the EU standards under the environmental criminal law directive. So unless the political will across Europe increases for adoption of more effective measures to improve interstate cooperation against environmental crime, it is likely that the CoE environmental crime convention will face a similar fate of the Lugano Convention on civil liability for environmental damage,[113] which has not at the time of writing yet attracted one single

110 See e.g. Liability Protocol to the Basel Convention on the Control of Transboundary Movements of Hazardous Wastes and their Disposal (1999) (not yet in force). The Nagoya-Kuala Lumpur Protocol on Liability and Reddress (2010) (at the time of writing, not yet in force). See also, the Council of Europe *Lugano Convention on Civil Liabiliy for Environmental Damage* (1993) (not yet in force).

111 See e.g. UN Convention on Biological Diversity (1992), Article 14 (1); Basel Convention on the Control of Transboundary Movements of Hazardous Wastes and their Disposal, adopted on 22 March 1989; entered into force on 5 May 1992, Article 12; Convention for the Protection of the Marine Environment and the Coastal Region of the Mediterranean (Barcelona Convention, 1976) Article 16.

112 In 2000 Denmark launched a proposal for a Framework Decision on the Protection of the Environment through criminal law. See Initiative of the Kingdom of Denmark with the view of Adopting a Framework Decision on Combating Serious Environmental Crime (2000/C 39/05) of 11 February 2000. See 1.2.3.2 below.

113 The Council of Europe Convention on Civil Liability for Damage resulting from Activities Dangerous to the Environment, adopted in Lugano on 21 June 1993, CETS No.: 150 ('the Lugano Convention').

ratification by the Council of Europe member states, even after more than ten years since its adoption (a minimum of three ratifications is required for the convention to enter into force).[114]

On the other hand, the adoption of a Council of Europe and EU instruments on environmental criminal law could be regarded as complementary. Indeed, there are adopted Council of Europe conventions in the area of criminal law and procedure (including, for example, on cybercrime, corruption and human trafficking) which overlap with the content of EU criminal-law cooperation instruments on those subjects. Those conventions are widely ratified and could be regarded as complementary to existing EU criminal-law initiatives.[115]

This suggests that the regionalisation of environmental criminal liability standards in Europe may be confined to the EU Member States for some time. On the other hand, it might be necessary to control and prevent cross-boundary environmental crime affecting the Council of Europe member states, including cross-border environmental damage involving non-EU states. This includes cooperation with third-country (non-EU) Council of Europe member states (for example Russia, Ukraine or Turkey) which have considerable real and

114 Similarly, in this case the EU member states are already bound by the EU civil liability directive adopted in 2004, which entered into force in 2007. See Directive 2004/35 on Environmental Liability with Regard to the Prevention and Remedying of Environmental Damage [2004] OJ L143/56. The provisions on strict liability under the Lugano Convention proved particularly contentious. See Article 6 of the Lugano Convention as regards '[l] iability in respect of substances, organisms, and certain waste installations or site'. According to the Explanatory Report to the Lugano Covention (51): '[Article 6] lays down the general principle of strict liability which applies only to the operator who was in control of the dangerous activity which caused the damage at the time when the incident took place (Article 6, paragraph 1). This general principle is therefore a strict liability principle, which does not require proof of any fault of the operator who was in control of the activity which caused the damage. The purpose of this rule is to encourage the operator to adopt all useful preventive measures to avoid the damage. The operator may avoid all or part of his liability by claiming an exemption (Article 8) or the fault of the person who suffered damage (Article 9)'.

115 Compare, for example, the Council of Europe Criminal Law Convention on Corruption CETS No.: 173 and the EU Council Framework Decision 2003/568/JHA of 22 July 2003 on Combating Corruption in the Private Sector, OJ L328 (2003), at 54; OJC195/2 (1997); OJ L279/1 (1997); OJ L358/2 (1998); the Council of Europe Convention on Cybercrime CETS no. 185 and the EU Council Framework Decision 2005/667/JHA of 24 February 2005 on Attacks Against Information Systems, OJ L69 (2005), at 67; and Council of Europe Convention on Action against Trafficking in Human Beings, Warsaw, 3 May 2005 (CETS No. 197) and Council Framework Decision 2002/629/JHA of 19 July 2002 on Combating Trafficking in Human Beings, OJ L2003 (2002), at (2).

potential cross-border environmental impacts in neighbouring EU member states. In fact, the most serious nuclear power plant accident in Europe to date (Chernobyl in 1986) happened in Ukraine (not a EU member state, but currently a Council of Europe member state). This accident had considerable cross-border health and environmental impacts not only on neighbouring states in the former Soviet Union, but also on countries in Eastern and Northern Europe.[116] Other examples of possible transboundary environmental impacts arising from a Council of Europe (non-EU) member state to EU member states include transboundary pollution from oil and gas activities carried out by Russia in the Arctic sea; or a cross-boundary gas pipeline running from Russia to Turkey via the Black Sea, such as the proposed Turkey Stream project (Turkey is currently a candidate country, but not a EU member state). Another example is in the context of illegal fishing and wildlife crime. The 2000 *International Crime Assessment* report suggested that Russian crime syndicates are believed to earn as much as $4 billion annually from the illegal export of some 2 million metric tons of seafood, including to the European market.[117]

It should also be noted that as part of the enlargement process, candidate countries to EU membership – which includes for example Serbia and Turkey – are required to implement the directive on environmental crime so as to comply with the EU's *acquis communaitaire*.[118] Therefore, the process of

116 Marc Lallanilla, *Chernobyl: Facts About the Nuclear Disaster*, September 25, 2013, http://www.livescience.com/39961-chernobyl.html (accessed on 15 February 2015).

117 'According to press reports citing Russian law enforcement estimates.' See the 2000 *International Crime Assessment* report. Russia ratified the Convention on Trade in Endangered Species (CITES) on 13 January 1992. It has been suggested that although the Russian federation has adopted specific legislation relating to environmental crime, there are considerable gaps and shortcomings in its legislation and enforcement. See Sally Stoecker and Ramziya Shakirova, *'Environmental crime and corruption in Russia: federal and regional perspectives'*, (Routledge, 2014), who noted that 'in 1910, the criminal code, as it was then called, addressed the protection of trees and for the first time named forest fires a crime. (...)' Furthermore, they suggest that the 1960 Criminal Code expanded the code of 1926 and contained 12 norms that could be applied for environmental protection. Environmental crime were contained in the criminal code's chapter on economic crimes thereby illustrating their subordination to the latter. In the 1960s few convictions for environmental crime: for example, in 1963 there were only 5, and in 1967 only 12. Yet they note that under the Criminal Code and Criminal Procedural Code adopted in late 1996, environmental protection crimes assumed a higher status in a new separate chapter of the code, and were not subsumed under economic crimes. *Ibid* at 10.

118 See *European Neighbourhood Policy and Enlargement Negotiations: Conditions for Membership*, http://ec.europa.eu/enlargement/policy/conditions-membership/index_en.htm (accessed on 15 February 2015).

enlargement could lead to broader regionalisation of environmental criminal law standards in Europe beyond the EU Member States (and help to address some of the cross-boundary environmental impacts between Council of Europe and EU member states), even if the situation remains that there is lack of interest by the Council of Europe member states to ratify the environmental crime convention.

Obviously the entering into force of the Council of Europe Convention is not dependant on the ratifications of the EU member states, as it could still enter into force with a minimum of three ratifications including non-EU, Council of Europe Member States. Yet this scenario would not be without legal implications for the EU as at least one EU Member State – Estonia! – would be bound by both the EU and Council of Europe environmental crime instruments. In this connection, as will be discussed in section 1.2.3.3. below, the adoption of the environmental crime directive could have implications to the external competence of the EU member states to negotiate and adopt the CoE environmental crime convention.

1.2.3.2 Overview of Developments in European Union Environmental Criminal Law

Since the entry into force of the Maastricht Treaty in 1993, the regionalisation of penal law in the EU appeared to be limited to a process of co-operation in criminal matters between the Member States.[119] The European Union was based on a three-pillar structure formed by the European Community ('first pillar') as well as the areas of Common Foreign and Security Policy ('second pillar', Title V TEU) and Justice and Home Affairs/police and judicial cooperation in criminal matters ('third pillar', Title VI TEU).[120] By creating the third pillar, the Maastricht Treaty established a formal framework to allow Member States to improve mutual assistance, cooperation and legislative harmonisation in criminal matters. The main rationale for the creation of the pillar-structure is that certain areas were considered to be important and sensitive areas of policy at the core of national sovereignty and therefore should not be subject to the supranational controls of the European Community (EC).

119 Under the 1992 Maastricht Treaty (Treaty on European Union or TEU), the EEC was renamed European Community (EC); and the European Union (EU) was created.

120 Following the Treaty of Amsterdam (1999), Title VI includes only police and judicial cooperation in criminal matters. The Treaty of Amsterdam incorporated other areas relating to Justice and Home Affairs which previously belonged to the Third Pillar – including asylum, border controls and visas – into Title IV of the EC Treaty (First Pillar), since they raise issues connected with fundamental human rights that were considered to deserve greater scrutiny by the European Parliament and review jurisdiction by the ECJ. See also, Craig, P. and de Burca, G., EU Law: Text, Cases and Materials (Oxford 2007, Fourth ed.) at 230.

The lack of competence of the European Communities under the first pillar in criminal matters appeared to be confirmed by the fact that there was no express competence to legislate in criminal matters under the former EC Treaty. In this vein, Professor Valsamis Mitsilegas has suggested that:

'The central factor leading to uncertainty and conflicting views on the existence of competence of the European Community in criminal matters has been the silence of the EC Treaty [...] on the matter, and the introduction of explicit EU powers to act in criminal matters in the third pillar by the Maastricht Treaty'.[121]

So if the Member States considered that criminal measures were necessary to enforce EC law, a parallel third pillar measure had to be adopted alongside the first pillar measure. This was the so-called double-text mechanism.[122] Even though criminal law remained outside the competence of the Communities, national criminal law was influenced by the developments at the Community level, either by requiring them to strike down penal measures which were incompatible with Community law[123] or by requiring member states to introduce 'effective, proportionate and dissuasive' measures for implementation of EC law.[124]

In the context of environmental crime, the European Union institutions and Member States have attempted to find an instrument of harmonisation of environmental criminal law which would respect the distribution of competences between the EC and EU Treaties but which would also offer an effective response to environmental criminality within the EU. Following the Kingdom of Denmark's initiative for a Framework Decision on environmental crimes in February 2000 founded on the EU's third pillar,[125] the Commission subsequently launched a rival parallel proposal in March 2001 for a directive on environmental

---

121 Mitsilegas, Valsamis 'The Transformation of Criminal Law in the "Area of Freedom, Security and Justice"' (2007) 26 *YEEL* 1, at 2.

122 The shipping pollution Directive and Framework Decision (discussed below) were adopted in 2005 following this double-text mechanism. Another example is the Directive 2002/90/EC of 28 November 2002 defining the facilitation of unauthorised entry, transit and residence (OJ L 328, 5.12.2002, p. 17), which was accompanied by Framework Decision 2002/946/JHA of 28 November 2002 aimed to strengthen the penal framework on the same subject.

123 Case C-106/89, *Marleasing SA v. La Commercial International de Alimentacion SA* [1990] E.C.R. 1–4135; Case 34/79 *R v Henn and Darby*, [1979] E.C.R. 3795.

124 Case 68/88 *Commission v. Hellenic Republic* [1989] ECR 2965; Case 265/95 *Commission v. France* [1997] ECR. See further discussion in chapters 4 and 5.

125 Initiative of the Kingdom of Denmark with the view of Adopting a Framework Decision on Combating Serious Environmental Crime (2000/C 39/05) of 11 February 2000. This proposal was on based on Articles 31 and 34 (2) (b) of the TEU (pre-Lisbon).

crimes[126] based on former Article 175 EC (now Article 192 TFEU).[127] The Commission reinforced its position that the third pillar instrument proposed by Denmark encroached upon the Community's competence under the former first pillar. The presentation of the 2001 directive proposal has successfully delayed the adoption of the Framework Decision by the Council, but it was not sufficient to convince the Member States that the Community had competence in the area of environmental criminal law, culminating in the adoption by the Council of Ministers of a Framework Decision on environmental crimes in January 2003.[128]

The final text of the Framework Decision agreed by the Council substantially improves the text of the original Danish proposal, and mirrors more closely the text of the Council of Europe 1998 environmental crime convention.[129] The Framework Decision needed to be implemented by the Member States within two years after it came into force on 27 January 2003, i.e. by no later than 27 January 2005. Given the legally binding nature of third pillar measures, Member States were expected to have introduced the necessary changes to their national environmental laws in order to fulfil their obligations under the Framework Decision by the implementation deadline. Yet it was well known that the Commission, supported by the European Parliament, had brought an annulment action against the Council Framework Decision on environmental crimes in April 2003 before the European Court of Justice, challenging the legal basis of the adopted third pillar instrument. In their view, the third pillar instrument encroached upon the Community's competence under the first pillar. The objective of the Commission's action was to annul the Framework Decision adopted under the third pillar; and to obtain a declaration of the Court on the criminal-law powers of the European Communities under the former first pillar. In particular, an environmental criminal law measure adopted under the 'environmental title' of the EC Treaty would have allowed

126 Proposal for a Directive of the European Parliament and of the Council on the Protection of the Environment through Criminal Law, COM (2001) 139 final, 13 March 2001, *Official Journal* C 180 E/20, 26 June 2001.

127 The Commission's 2001 directive proposal takes account of the amendments proposed by the European Parliament in 2002. See Amended Proposal for a Directive of the European Parliament and of the Council on the Protection of the Environment through Criminal Law, COM (2002) 544 final, 30 September 2002, *Official Journal* C20E/284, 28 January 2003, adopted in accordance with former Art. 250 (2) EC.

128 Council Framework Decision 2003/80/JHA on the Protection of the Environment through Criminal Law, 27 January 2003, *Official Journal* L 29, 5 February 2003.

129 It also borrows to a more limited extent some elements of the 2001 environmental crime directive proposal.

the Commission and ECJ to exercise stronger enforcement powers and the European Parliament to have greater participation in decision-making.

In its landmark ruling in the summer of 2005, the ECJ provided some clarification to the question of distribution of competences between the former EC and EU Treaties in the area of criminal law and policy. The European Court of Justice decision of 13 September 2005 in *Commission v. Council*[130] (*'Environmental Crimes'*) has established that while the Community did not have competence in criminal matters *per se*, the Community institutions might require Member States to introduce criminal sanctions in the case of serious violations of EC environmental law in order to ensure the effective implementation of EC environmental law.[131] Thus the Court in *Environmental Crimes* embraced the overall arguments raised by the Commission and the European Parliament and ruled that despite the fact that 'as general rule, neither criminal law nor the rules of criminal procedure fall within the Community's competence',[132] 'the last-mentioned finding does not prevent the Community legislature, when the application of effective, proportionate and dissuasive criminal penalties by the competent national authorities is *an essential measure for combating serious environmental offences, from taking measures which relate to the criminal law of the Member States which it considers necessary in order to ensure that the rules which it lays down on environmental protection are fully effective*'. (emphasis added).[133] Further, the Court ruled that 'the entire framework decision, *being indivisible*, infringes Article 47 EU as it encroaches on the powers which Article 175 EC confers on the Community',[134] and ultimately annulled the 2003 Framework Decision on environmental crimes.

The three central premises lending support to the Court's findings in the *Environmental Crimes* case are: (1) in line with ex Article 47 TEU, the Community competence is not affected by the Treaty on the European Union;[135] (2) the main objective of the Framework Decision was the protection of the environment and hence could been properly adopted under former Article 175 EC (post-Lisbon, Article 192 TFEU); (3) the principle of loyal co-operation, enshrined

130 Case 176/03 *Commission v Council* [2005] ECR I-7879; [2005] 3 CMLR 20 (*'Environmental Crimes'*).

131 See, in particular, paras 48, 49 and 53 of the judgment.

132 *Environmental Crimes*, par. 47.

133 *Environmental Crimes* par. 48.

134 *Environmental Crimes* par. 53.

135 Post-Lisbon, repealed and replaced by Article 40 TEU. Article 47 TEU literally stated that '[...] nothing in [the TEU Treaty] shall affect the Treaties establishing the European Communities or the subsequent Treaties and Acts modifying or supplementing them'.

in former Article 10 EC,[136] calls on Member States to introduce 'effective, proportionate and dissuasive' criminal penalties in order to enforce Community law.

It should be noted that although the national Parliaments of the then EU 15/25 Member States[137] were required to implement the Framework Decision on environmental crimes by January 2005, the EU Member States were technically discharged from this obligation when the Framework Decision was finally annulled in September 2005 in the *Environmental Crimes* case.[138] The *temporal effect* of this judgment had the effect of discharging Member States from their legal obligations under the Framework Decision, despite the fact that the legal action itself had no suspensive effect as regards the period for implementation.[139]

Following the ECJ decision in *Environmental Crimes*, the Commission published a Communication in November 2005 outlining its interpretation of the judgment.[140] The Commission found that the *Environmental Crimes* ruling provided the Community with the power to define criminal offences and penalties, and perhaps also the rules on police and judicial cooperation in criminal matters which had traditionally been regarded by the Commission as belonging to the third pillar.[141] Thus the Commission interpreted the judgment broadly, suggesting that 'from the point of view of subject matter, in addition to environmental protection, the Court's reasoning can therefore be applied to all Community policies and freedoms which involve binding legislation with which criminal penalties should be associated in order to ensure their effectiveness'.[142] The Commission proposed an alternative for fast review and restoration of legality of a number of third pillar instruments – which had, according

136 Replaced, in substance, by Article 4, paragraph 3, TEU.

137 The EU enlargement in 2004 brought 10 new member states from central, Eastern and Southern Europe to the EU-15.

138 *Commission v Council* C-176/03 [2005] E.C.R. I-7879; [2005] 3 C.M.L.R. 20. Annulment actions brought under former Article 230 EC and 231 EC had retroactive and *erga omnes* effects, whereas under the TEU they did not have those same effects.

139 Indeed, the Commission fully supported the aims and content – a high level of environmental protection in the European Union – enshrined in the Framework Decision on environmental crimes.

140 Communication from the European Commission to the European Parliament and the Council on the Implications of the Court's Judgement of 13 September 2005 (Case C-176/03 Commission *v* Council) COM (2005) 583 final/2, 24 November 2005.

141 See paragraph 12 of the Communication, in which the Commission claims that the Community has the power not only to define criminal offences and penalties, but also 'other criminal-law measures appropriate to the area concerned'.

142 *Ibid*, para. 8.

to the Commission's interpretation of the ECJ decision, been adopted under the wrong legal basis. This would involve the achievement of political agreement between the Commission, the Council and the Parliament on the transfer of certain third pillar measures, listed in an Annex to the Communication, to the first pillar.[143] The case for adoption of the environmental crimes directive proposal was particularly strong[144] as no framework for harmonisation of environmental criminal law at the EU level existed following the successful annulment action in the *Environmental Crimes* case (this, of course, outside the context of ship-source pollution offences, which was subject to specific legislative measures, as will be discussed below). However, not only the Member States[145] but also the Parliament ultimately rejected the Commission's proposal for fast adoption of those measures with the aim of bringing them into the first pillar, in line with the Commission's expansive interpretation of the *Environmental Crimes* judgment.[146]

Despite the Commission's failure to engage the other institutions in its endeavour to restore the legality of the third pillar measures outlined in an

---

143 The list include the EU Framework Decisions which could be regarded as providing criminal enforcement to recognised EC policies, i.e. the framework decisions on counterfeiting, fraud and forgery in respect of non-cash payment, money laundering, illegal migration, corruption in the private sector, hacking, and ship-source pollution. See also, Fletcher, Loof and Gilmore 'EU Criminal Law and Justice' Edward Elgar (2008) at 178.

144 In principle, the Commission could have sought to reach political agreement on the adoption of the 2001 proposal for a directive on environmental crimes, even though this proposal is not listed in the Annex to the 2005 Communication, and it would have been difficult in any event for the Commission to bypass the co-decision procedure for the adoption of the directive, as it appears that the Commission's intention was to restore the legality of pre-existing third pillar instruments.

145 The February 2006 Justice and Home Affairs Council only adopted a procedure for the examination of future Commission legislative proposals containing criminal law provisions (Doc. 6077/06) (Presse 18), 10. There is a summary of the reactions in the Council in Council doc. 13103/06, Brussels, 22 September 2006. See Mitsilegas, V. 'The Competence Question: The European Community and Criminal Law' in Guild, Elspeth and Geyer, *Florian (e.d.) Security versus Justice? Police and Judicial Cooperation in the European Union* (Ashgate, 2008) at 158.

146 European Parliament Resolution on the consequences of the judgement of the Court of 13 September 2005 (C-176/03 *Commission v Council*) (2006/2007 (INI)) Committee on Legal Affairs (Rapporteur Giuseppe Gargani). In paras. 8–11 the Parliament urged a case-by-case approach as any review should not deprive the Parliament 'of its inalienable role as co-legislator and thus sacrificing the democratic input provided by the Parliament (…)'. Yet the Parliament supported the Commission's broad interpretation of the ruling regarding the Community competence in criminal matters.

Annex to its 2005 Communication, the Commission reignited the institutional conflict with the Council by bringing an annulment action against a Council Framework Decision to strengthen the criminal law-framework relating to Ship-Source Pollution on 23 November 2005.[147] This Framework Decision was adopted on 30 September 2005[148] to complement Directive 2005/35 on Ship-Source pollution.[149] The Directive and Framework Decision on ship-source pollution are based on two original proposals adopted in 2003 in the aftermath of the *Prestige* oil-spill disaster, which caused severe loss of wildlife in the coasts of Portugal, Spain and France.[150] They aimed to strengthen the implementation and enforcement of maritime anti-pollution rules by means of criminal sanctions and to ensure adequate implementation by the Member States of the IMO International Convention for Prevention of Pollution from Ships ('MARPOL') rules on shipping pollution.[151] The Commission defended its

147 See Council Framework Decision 2005/667/JHA to Strengthen the Criminal-Law Framework for the Enforcement of the Law against Ship-Source Pollution, 12 July 2005.

148 Adopted under Article 35 (6) TEU (pre-Lisbon). Hence it was not possible for the Commission to bring annulment actions against the legal basis of other criminal-law measures adopted under the third pillar due to the time limit enshrined in former Article 35 TEU for the Commission to bring annulment actions against Framework Decisions adopted by the Council.

149 Directive 2005/35/EC of the European Parliament and of the Council on Ship-Source Pollution and on the Introduction of Penalties for Infringements, 7 September 2005, *Official Journal* L 255/11; 30.9.2005, based on former Article 80 (2) EC (post-Lisbon, Art. 100 (2) TFEU) (which deals with the Community common transport policy),

150 See Proposal for a Directive on Ship-Source Pollution and on the Introduction of Sanctions, including Criminal Sanctions, for Pollution Offences COM (2003) 92 final 2003/0037 (COD); and Proposal for a Council Framework Decision to Strengthen the Criminal-Law Framework for the Law Against Ship-Source Pollution COM (2003) 227 final 2003/0088.

151 COM (2003) 92, para. 2.1. The view that urgent measures in this field were needed was also echoed by the EU Member States who, represented in the Transport and Telecommunications Council on 6 December 2002 and the Justice and Home Affairs Council on 19 December 2002, embraced the need for measures to ensure that ship-source pollution was subject to appropriate sanctions and to 'strengthen the protection of the environment, in particular the seas, through criminal law'. See, paragraph 14 of the Transport and Telecommunication Council's conclusions on Ship Safety and Pollution of 6 December 2002 and the Statement of the Justice Home Affairs Council of 19 December 2002. For a discussion of the maritime safety measures taken by the EU following the *Erika* and *Prestige* disasters see e.g. Veronica Frank 'Consequences of the Prestige Sinking for European and International Law' [2005] 20 *The Int J Mar Coast Law* 44; Wang Hui 'The EU Marine Oil Pollution Prevention Regime – Recent Developments' [2004] *EELR* 292; and Farkhanda Zia-Mansoor, 'International Regime and the EU Developments for Preventing and Controlling Vessel-Source Oil Pollution', (2005) *EELR* 165.

legislative initiative by arguing that the international and Community legal instruments to eliminate illegal discharges from ships failed to establish specific offences and penalties for the violation of the applicable pollution standards and hence that action to strengthen enforcement by Member States at the Community level was necessary.[152]

The Ship-Source Pollution 2005/35/EC Directive (hereafter 'shipping pollution directive')[153] sets out 'infringements' but not criminal sanctions and the parallel Framework Decision 2005/667/JHA[154] (hereafter 'shipping pollution framework decision') contained the underlining criminal sanctions. They were adopted on 7 September 2005 and 12 July 2005 respectively.[155] So the Community institutions applied the 'double-text' mechanism in which a Framework Decision under the third pillar is used to complement a Directive under the first pillar. Therefore, the Directive on shipping pollution adopted in 2005 itself did not prescribe criminal obligations on Member States, which could have been in principle implemented by means of administrative penalties. This thus reflects the necessary compromise struck by the EU institutions: the Directive defines specific 'infringements' under Article 4 which, if committed with intent, recklessness or by serious negligence, needed to be criminalised by Member States under the conditions established under the Framework Decision.[156]

There are a number of reasons for the Commission and the Council to pursue a separate directive and Framework Decision on ship-source pollution crimes. Firstly, unlike in case of the offences contained in the environmental crime directive, there was no specific EU secondary legislation in force implementing MARPOL,[157] thus calling for the adoption of specific implementation

---

152 Explanatory Memorandum to the Proposal for a Directive on Ship-Source Pollution and on the Introduction of Sanctions, above note 150, page 4.

153 Directive 2005/35/EC of the European Parliament and of the Council on Ship-Source Pollution and on the Introduction of Penalties for Infringements, 7 September 2005.

154 Council Framework Decision 2005/667/JHA to Strengthen the Criminal-Law Framework for the Enforcement of the Law against Ship-Source Pollution, 12 July 2005.

155 The difference of the dates of adoption of those measures reflects *inter alia* the differences of the procedures for their adoption. The adoption of the Directive based on Article 80(2) EC (now Art. 100 (2)) required qualified majority voting and co-decision between the Council and the European Parliament, whereas measures adopted under Title VI TEU required unanimity in the Council and the Parliament was merely consulted.

156 Council's Common Position on the Draft Directive on Ship-Source Pollution (1964/04) 29/09, para. 8. References to criminal sanctions and offences have also been dropped from the Title and Art. 1 of the shipping pollution directive.

157 See Recital 3 to the shipping pollution directive. Although all Member States were parties to MARPOL, the EC was not a party to that convention, which does not permit regional organisations such as the EU to become parties.

measures, for example, in relation to the 'defences' available and 'jurisdiction'. Moreover, the Prestige oil tanker disaster occurred in 2002 – so after the environmental crime directive and framework decision proposals were already being negotiated – making it clear that urgent EU cooperative measures were needed in the context of ship-source pollution also. Finally, unlike in the case of the environmental crime directive which was based on former Article 175EC (post-Lisbon, Article 192TFEU), the Commission sought to use Article 100 TFEU (ex Article 80EC) – which relates to the EU common transport policy – as the legal basis for the ship-source pollution directive.[158]

Fuelled by the Court's findings in the *Environmental Crimes* case, in case C-440/05 ('*Ship-Source Pollution*') the Commission attempted to annul the ship-source pollution framework decision adopted under the third pillar.[159] One of the important consequences of this annulment action brought against the legal basis of the Framework Decision on shipping pollution is that the Member States represented in the Council declared that no progress towards the adoption of the environmental crimes directive proposal (tabled in March 2001) would be made until the outcome of the *Ship-Source Pollution* case, which was expected to be handed down in late 2007. Moreover, this legal action had no suspensive effects[160] and thus it was expected that the shipping pollution crime Framework Decision would be implemented by the Member States by 12 January 2007.

In its decision in *Ship-Source Pollution* on 23 October 2007 the ECJ confirmed its position regarding the EC criminal-law powers in the *Environmental Crimes* case. The court ruled that the shipping Framework Decision encroached upon the Community competence under the first pillar and has decided thus to annul it.[161] Yet the Court stated in clear terms that the 'definition of the types and levels of criminal penalties are outside the Community's sphere of competence'.[162] Hence the provisions on the type (e.g. imprisonment, fines) and levels ('minimum maximum' custodial sentences and fines, in line with the Justice and Home Affairs Council conclusions on penalties in April 2002[163]) had been properly adopted under the third pillar.

---

158 As will be discussed in Chapter 5, Article 80EC was also used as the legal basis for other EU marine environment protection legislation.

159 Case C-440/05, *Commission of the European Communities v Council of the European Union* [2008] 1 C.M.L.R. 22 ('*Ship-Source Pollution*').

160 Though the temporal effect of the ruling would discharge Member States from the obligations under the Framework Decision when it was finally annulled on 23 October 2007.

161 *Ship-Source Pollution*, para. 66.

162 *Ship-Source Pollution*, para. 70.

163 Justice and Home Affairs Council 2423rd meeting, Luxembourg, April 2002, 25/26.IV.2002.

Just under eight months before the *Ship-Source Pollution* ruling, the Commission had presented a new proposal for a Directive in February 2007 on environmental crimes[164] based on former Article 175 EC, superseding the 2001 proposal.[165] Unlike the 2001 Directive proposal which contained a general provision on the types of criminal sanctions to be introduced by Member States,[166] the 2007 proposal specified not only the types but also minimum levels of criminal penalties to be introduced by Member States.[167] The Commission thereby hoped that harmonisation of environmental criminal law would help improve the implementation deficit of EC environmental legislation and provide a strong deterrent against transboundary environmental crimes within the EU.[168] In the aftermath of the *Ship-Source Pollution* case, the 2007 Directive proposal on environmental crimes was discussed by the Council of Ministers[169] and European Parliament[170] following the co-decision procedure.[171] Subsequently, the Draft Report of Hartmut Nassauer[172] was approved by the members of the European Parliament Legal Affairs Committee in a close vote[173] on 8 April 2008.

---

164 Proposal for a Directive of the European Parliament and of the Council on the Protection of the Environment through Criminal Law, COM (2007) 51 final, 9 February 2007.

165 Formally withdrawn in the *Official Journal* 2008/C 68/02 on 13 March 2008.

166 Article 4 (a) of the 2001 Directive Proposal states that '[a]s concerns natural persons, Member States shall provide for criminal penalties, involving in serious cases deprivation of liberty'.

167 See Articles 5 and 7 of the 2007 Directive proposal on environmental crimes. See also the September 2007 Opinion of the European Economic and Social Committee (EESC) on the 2007 draft directive (para. 1.4 of the EESC Opinion COM (2007) 51 final – 2007/0022 (COD) 2008/C 10/12).

168 See forth Recital to the Explanatory Memorandum of the 2007 environmental crime directive proposal.

169 See for example Working Party on Substantive Criminal Law, Proposal for a Directive of the European Parliament and of the Council on the Protection of the Environment through Criminal Law 5152/08 DROIPEN 1ENV 12 CODEC 17 11 January 2008, available at http://register.consilium.eu.int/ (accessed on 10 February 2015).

170 Draft Report on the Directive on the Protection of the Environment through Criminal Law. European Parliament, Committee on Legal Affairs, Rapporteur: Hartmut Nassauer, 26 February 2008.

171 The co-decision procedure is set out under Article 294 TFEU (former Article 251 EC).

172 See Report on proposal for a directive of the European Parliament and of the Council on the protection of the environment through criminal law, A6-0154/2008 of 15 April 2008 [COM(2007)0051 – C6-0063/2007 – 2007/0022(COD)] European Parliament, Committee on Legal Affairs, Rapporteur: Hartmut Nassauer.

173 15 Committee members voted in favour while 11 voted against the proposal. There were two abstentions. See http://www.euractiv.com/en/environment/meps-vote-outlaw-green-crimes/article-171498 (accessed on 10 February 2015).

The Council and the European Parliament (following the first-reading Plenary session) reached an agreement on the final compromise text of the Directive on 21 May 2008[174] and the Directive was finally adopted with minor amendments by the unanimous vote of the Member States represented in the Council on 24 October 2008.[175]

However, the provisions on the minimum levels of penalties which were present in the original directive proposal, in line with the ECJ ruling in the *Ship-Source Pollution* case, have been dropped in the text agreed by the three institutions involved in the first-reading legislative process (the Parliament, the Council and the Commission) as well as in the documents that preceded the adoption of the final compromise text.[176] Another difference between the original proposal and the final compromise text of the directive is that only violations of EC environmental law, not national environmental law, were required to be criminalised at the EC level, in line with the findings of the *Ship-Source Pollution* ruling.[177] Hence the directive refers in Annexes A and B to over 70 pieces of EC environmental legislation[178] which relate to the environmental offences defined in the directive, instead of criminalising violations of purely national environmental law.

The shipping industry was particularly against the adoption of the ship-source pollution directive, which it argued established higher standards than those established under international agreements binding the Community. As individuals or corporations do not have direct access to bring proceedings before the ECJ to challenge Community legislation, the shipping industry

174 See Position of the European Parliament Adopted at First Reading on 21 May 2008 with a View to the Adoption of the Directive 2008/…/EC of the European Parliament and of the Council on the Protection of the Environment through Criminal Law, available at www.europarl.europa.eu (accessed on 10 February 2015).

175 Directive 2008/99/EC of the European Parliament and of the Council of 19 November 2008 on the protection of the environment through criminal law, *Official Journal* L 328, 6 December 2008, pp. 28–37.

176 Compare Nassaeur's Report (European Parliament) *supra* and the several Reports of the Council Working Party on Substantive Criminal Law, for example Council of the European Union, Proposal for a Directive on the Protection of the Environment through Criminal Law, DROIPEN 19 ENV 122 CODEC 260 10 March 2008. See also the Draft Opinion of the EP Committee on Civil Liberties, Justice and Home Affairs for the Committee on Legal Affairs, Rapporteur Luis Herrero-Tejedor of 15.12.2007 (2007/0022 (COD)). These documents are available at the Council's register: http://register.consilium.eu.int/.

177 *Ship-Source Pollution*, para. 66: '[…] the Community legislature may require the Member States to introduce such penalties in order to ensure that *the rules which it lays down in that field* are fully effective' (emphasis added).

178 Annex B concern legislative measures adopted by EURATOM.

brought a legal action before the English High Court, which in turn referred questions on 4 July 2006 to the ECJ for a preliminary ruling, leading to the initiation of the proceedings of Case C-308/06 (Intertanko and others) (hereinafter '*Intertanko*').[179] Therefore this case offered an opportunity for the European Court of Justice to rule on the question of the compatibility of the 2005 Directive on ship-source pollution with international law. In its ruling handed down on 3 June 2008, the ECJ held, as it had done in *Peralta*,[180] that the Community itself was not bound directly by the IMO International Convention for Prevention of Pollution from Ships ('MARPOL'),[181] as the Community is not a signatory party to that Convention, despite the fact that all Member States are signatories to it. Consequently, the ECJ could not review the legality of the shipping Directive in light of MARPOL.[182] As regards the legality of the Directive in light of the 1982 UN Convention on the Law of the Sea ('UNCLOS')[183] – to which the Community is a party – the ECJ held that the Community was bound by that Convention and that it formed an integral part of the Community legal order.[184] Yet it established that the nature and broad logic of UNCLOS precluded the examination of the validity of the shipping directive in light of its provisions, as UNCLOS was not directly applicable in the Community legal order.[185] This reasoning allowed the ECJ to ultimately declare that it was not possible for it to examine the compatibility of directive on shipping pollution with either MARPOL or UNCLOS.

It could be argued that the shipping pollution directive is a reflection of coastal states (or regional groupings of such states) either resorting to unilateral

---

179 Case C-308/06 *The Queen on the Application of: International Association of Independent Tanker Owners (Intertanko), International Association of Dry Cargo Shipowners (Intercargo), Greek Shipping Co-operation Committee, Lloyd's Register, International Salvage Union v Secretary of State for Transport*, 3 June 2008. See also, R. Pereira, 'On the Legality of the Ship-Source Pollution Directive – The *Intertanko* Case and Selected Others' (2008) 17 European Energy & Environmental Law Review, 6, 372.

180 Case C-379/92 *Peralta* [1994] ECR I-3453, para. 16.

181 *IMO International Convention for the Prevention of Pollution from Ships 1973/1978 ('MARPOL')*, adopted on 2 November 1973, in force on 2 October 1983, 12 ILM 1319.

182 *Intertanko*, para. 50: 'Since the Community is not bound by Marpol 73/78, the mere fact that Directive 2005/35 has the objective of incorporating certain rules set out in that Convention into Community law is likewise not sufficient for it to be incumbent upon the Court to review the directive's legality in the light of the Convention'.

183 UN Convention on the Law of the Sea 1833 UNTS 3/[1994] ATS 31/21 ILM 1261 (1982) ('UNCLOS').

184 *Intertanko*, para. 53.

185 Ibid.

measures going beyond those standards permitted by international law or dictating the development of new international regulations which accord them greater powers to deal with pollution and safety safeguards. The unilateralism pursued by the EU in the aftermath of the sinking of the *Erika* and *Prestige* tankers is explained partially by its failure to achieve progress within the International Maritime Organisation ('IMO') – to which the EU is still not a party; and the fact that some Conventions (e.g. MARPOL) only allow the participation of *States*.[186] Therefore, the EU has found it difficult to negotiate collectively with other nations on common maritime environmental standards. Moreover, there is an argument that stringent regulatory measures in the US must be accompanied by equally strong regulatory measures in Europe, in particular as substandardised ships could move their operations from the US to European waters.[187] It is suggested that the European states are developing a 'pro-coastal' Community posture, while states with large shipping interests (such as Greece, Cyprus and Malta) are being compelled to go along with the stricter regulation over ships.[188]

Only a few months prior to the *Intertanko* ruling, the European Commission proposed a directive on 11 March 2008 to amend the directive on ship-source pollution,[189] introducing *inter alia* the requirement that sanctions for certain forms of ship-source pollution committed intentionally, recklessly or with serious negligence are of a criminal nature. In line with the *Ship-Source Pollution* ruling, this proposal does not contain provisions on specific types and levels of criminal penalties. On 17 February 2009 the European Parliament's Transport Committee voted in favour of the shipping amending directive proposal's report drafted by Luis de Grandes Pascual[190] and the amending Directive was finally adopted by the unanimous vote of the Member States represented in the Council of Ministers on 14 September 2009 (see Table 1.1.).[191]

186 See also, Pereira, R. (2008), above note 179.

187 See Khee-Jin Tan, Alan. *Vessel-Source Marine Pollution: The Law and Politics of International Regulation'*, Cambridge 2006.

188 *Ibid* at 157. See generally, R. Churchill and A. Lowe, *The Law of the Sea*, (third ed., 1999) at 89.

189 Proposal for a Directive of the European Parliament and of the Council amending Directive 2005/35/EC on ship source pollution and on the introduction of penalties for infringements, COM/2008/0134 final – COD 2008/0055.

190 There were 37 votes in favour of the proposal and 1 against. See 'Pollution at Sea: MEPS Vote for Compulsory Criminal Law Penalties' http://www.europarl.europa.eu/news (accessed on 10 February 2015).

191 2960th meeting of the Council of the European Union (General Affairs and External Relations) Brussels, Monday 14 September 2009. See Directive 2009/123/EC of the European

Another significant development in the area of criminal-law cooperation in the EU was the adoption on 13 December 2007 of the Lisbon Treaty. The Treaty was signed by the heads of government and state of the Member States and was ratified in November 2009, following the Irish second referendum and the Czech and Polish ratifications, and came into force in December 2009.[192] The Lisbon Treaty has abolished the pillar structure of the EU whilst simultaneously defining more clearly the power of the European Union to adopt, at the supranational level, criminal law legislative measures (including criminal penalties and other measures on police and judicial cooperation in criminal matters).[193] Under Lisbon, the intergovernmental third pillar is abolished and two separate bodies of law are generated: an amended version of the Treaty on the European Union (TEU) and the Treaty on the Functioning of the Union (TFEU), which replaces the Treaty establishing the European Community (TEC).[194] Moreover, with the introduction of Articles 82 and 83 TFEU, the Treaty of Lisbon provided a clearer legal basis for the harmonisation of (environmental) criminal law and criminal procedure.[195] Hence the dispute over the legal basis for the harmonization of environmental criminal law, highlighted in the ECJ *Environmental Crimes* and *Ship-Source Pollution* cases, will no longer be as relevant following the ratification of the Treaty of Lisbon.

1.2.3.3 The Relationship between the Environmental Crime Directive and Council of Europe Environmental Crime Convention

From the perspective of the EU's external relations, the adoption of the EU directive on environmental crimes would have important implications as regards Member States' external competence to negotiate and eventually adopt the Council of Europe environmental crime convention. This might require the involvement of both the Union and the Member States in the negotiations of a (criminal-law) Convention under the auspices of the Council of

Parliament and of the Council of 21 October 2009 amending Directive 2005/35/EC on ship-source pollution and on the introduction of penalties for infringements; *Official Journal*, L 280/52. 27.10.2009.

192 The Irish 'no vote' in a national referendum on the Treaty on 12 June 2008 had shed doubt on whether the Treaty of Lisbon would indeed be ratified by all Member States.

193 See Art. 83 of the Treaty on the Functioning of the European Union. This Article is the successor to Art. III-271 of the 2005 Draft Constitutional Treaty.

194 S. Carrera, and F. Geyer, 'The Reform Treaty and Justice and Home Affairs: Implication for the Common Area of Freedom, Security and Justice', in E. Guild and F. Geyer (eds.) *Security versus Justice: Police and Judicial Cooperation in the European Union* (2008), at 291.

195 See Chapter 5.

TABLE 1.1 *European environmental crime initiatives*

Legislative proposal	Adopted text	Entry into force and current status	Implementation deadline
–	**Text adopted on 4 November 1998** Council of Europe Convention on the Protection of the Environment through Criminal Law (1998), Strasbourg, 4.XI.1998, ETS no. 172	**Not yet in force**	–
11 February 2000 Initiative of the Kingdom of Denmark with the view of Adopting a Framework Decision on Combating Serious Environmental Crime (2000/C 39/05)	**Adopted on 27 January 2003** Council Framework Decision 2003/80/JHA on the Protection of the Environment through Criminal Law, 27 January 2003, *Official Journal* L 29.	**Annulled on 13 September 2005 by the ECJ**	**27 January 2005**
26 June 2001 Proposal for a Directive of the European Parliament and of the Council on the Protection of the Environment through Criminal Law, COM (2001) 139 final, 13 March 2001, *Official Journal* C 180 E/20	–	**Formally withdrawn on 13 March 2008**	–
02 May 2003 Proposal for a Council Framework Decision to Strengthen the Criminal-Law Framework for the Law Against Ship-Source Pollution COM (2003) 227 final 2003/0088.	**Adopted on 12 July 2005** Council Framework Decision 2005/667/JHA to Strengthen the Criminal-Law Framework for the Enforcement of the Law against Ship-Source Pollution	**Annulled on 23 October 2007 by the ECJ**	**12 January 2007**

05 March 2003 **Proposal for a Directive on Ship-Source Pollution and on the Introduction of Sanctions, including Criminal Sanctions, for Pollution Offences COM (2003) 92 final 2003/0037 (COD)**	**Adopted on 07 September 2005** Directive 2005/35/EC of the European Parliament and of the Council on Ship-Source Pollution and on the Introduction of Penalties for Infringements	**In force**	**1 March 2007**
9 February 2007 **Proposal for a Directive of the European Parliament and of the Council on the Protection of the Environment through Criminal Law, COM (2007) 51 final**	**19 November 2008,** Directive 2008/99/EC of the European Parliament and of the Council of 19 November 2008 on the protection of the environment through criminal law, *Official Journal* L 328	**In force**	**26 December 2010**
11 March 2008 **Proposal for a Directive of the European Parliament and of the Council amending** Directive 2005/35/EC on ship source pollution and on the introduction of penalties for infringements, COM/2008/0134 final - COD 2008/0055	**Adopted on 21 October 2009** Directive 2009/123/EC of the European Parliament and of the Council of 21 October 2009 **amending Directive 2005/35/EC on ship-source pollution and on the introduction of penalties for infringements; *Official Journal,*** L 280/52. **27.10.2009.**	**In force**	**16 November 2010**

Europe.[196] Yet the EC has not participated in the negotiations of the environmental crime convention, which only foresees the accession by states, but not regional organisations such as the EC/EU.[197]

Article 3 (2) TFEU provides that the Union will have exclusive competence for the conclusion of an international agreement 'insofar as its conclusion may affect common rules and their scope'. So if the EU exercises its internal competence (as in the case of the EU environmental crime directive), this could lead to the exclusivity of the EU external competence.[198] Yet for the EU competence to be exclusive following the adoption of EU legislation, the conclusion of an international agreement would need to 'affect common rules or alter their scope'. This, in turn, might require the EU institutions to 'specify in detail the aspects of Community legislation which could be prejudiced by the agreement'.[199]

The EU exclusive competence would generally arise when the EU internal legislation involves total harmonization of standards. Minimum standards such as those pursuant to Articles 192 and 193 TFEU applied for adoption of the EU environmental crime directive normally give rise to non-exclusive EU

196 See House of Lords, European Union Committee, 42nd Report of Session 2005–2006 'The Criminal Law Competence of the European Community. Report with Evidence' 28 July 2006 *infra* at 45: 'Another consequence of moving policing and criminal law into the First Pillar is that if the Community were to act internally (for example, by adopting a Directive on a particular subject) then the Member States would lose competence, in favour of the Community, to conclude treaties or other agreements with third States on that subject. Even if the Community rules are only a partial harmonisation, Member States' freedom would be restricted. They would share competence with the Community.' Consequently, as Professor Peers pointed out, 'almost any future negotiations, certainly at a multilateral level within the Council of Europe, for instance, on international criminal treaties, would involve both the Community and the Member States'. He further argued that there might be some areas where the Community would have exclusive competence, for example, arising from the European Arrest Warrant in relation to competing extradition requests. But he concluded that there would only be a handful of areas where exclusive competence of the Community would apply therefore leaving Member States the capacity to exercise their competence in international negotiations (Q 110)' (para. 158).

197 See Article 13 (1) and Article 14 of the Council of Europe environmental crime convention.

198 This manner of acquiring exclusive external competences was recognized for the first time by the ECJ in the *ERTA* case and was further refined, inter alia, in the *Open Skies* cases. See Geert de Baere, *EU External Action*, in Catherine Barnard and Steve Peers (eds.) *European Union Law* (OUP, 2014) at 715.

199 Opinion of Advocate General Tizzano in Open Skyies case, (Case C-466-98 Commission v. UK (2002) ECR I-9427; See also, e.g. Case C-467/98 Commission v Denmark ECR I-9519).

competences.[200] In this vein, as the Court held in *Opinion 1/03*, the fact that both the Union rules and international agreement in question lay down minimum standards: 'may justify the conclusion that the [Union] rules are not affected, even if the [Union] rules and the provisions of the agreement cover the same area'.[201] Although this suggests that the EU Member States would then remain free to negotiate the Council of Europe environmental crime convention, the principle of sincere cooperation enshrined in Article 4 (3) TEU could still restrict Member States' external actions, even if they were to be acting within their own sphere of competence.[202]

Another problem is that the CoE environmental crime convention does not contain a 'disconnection clause' to protect the future status of Community/ Union law, which have become common in the Council of Europe Conventions adopted since 1989.[203] For example, the Council of Europe convention on civil liability for environmental damage states that 'in their mutual relations, Parties which are members of the European Economic Community shall apply Community rules and shall therefore not apply the rules arising from this Convention except in so far as there is no Community rule governing the particular subject concerned'.[204] According to the Explanatory report to that convention, the purpose of this clause is twofold:[205] firstly, it aims at permitting the EC Member States, when a Convention contains subjects for which the Community has exercised its competence, to sign and ratify the Convention together with the Community without the need to make declarations about the division of their competence. The second purpose of the 'disconnection clause' is to ensure that the 'EEC Member States and the Community would not have to abstain from becoming a Party to the Convention in the case of possible minor discrepancies between the provisions of the Convention and Community rules during the period needed to bring these rules in conformity with the provisions of the Convention'.[206] Despite this, it has been suggested that 'a disconnection clause' to protect the status and future development of

---

200 Geert de Baere (2014) above note 198.

201 Opinion 1/03, Opinion pursuant to Article 300(6) EC (*'Competence of the Community to conclude the new Lugano Convention on jurisdiction and the recognition and enforcement of judgments in civil and commercial matters'*).

202 Geert de Baere (2014) supra at pp. 721–722.

203 Frank Hoffmeister, 'The Contribution of EU Practice to International Law' in Marisa Cremona (ed.), *'Developments in EU External Relations Law'* (OUP, 2008).

204 The Council of Europe Convention on Civil Liability for Damage resulting from Activities Dangerous to the Environment CETS No.: 150 ('the Lugano Convention'), Article 25.

205 Explanatory report, Article 25, 88, ibid.

206 *Ibid.*

Community/Union law in the text of the [Council of Europe] Convention does not seem to be strictly necessary. The same legal result can be deduced from the mixed ratification of the Convention and may be confirmed through a declaratory statement to that effect'.[207]

The above analysis suggests that the EU member states remain competent to negotiate the Council of Europe environmental crime convention so long as it does not 'affect common rules or alter their scope'. Chapter 6 of this book discusses the similarities and possible incompatibilities between the two instruments, which could thus hinder the ability of the member states to negotiate independently and ratify the CoE environmental crime convention.

1.3 The Structure of the Book

In Chapter 2 the book considers the role of the criminal law for the protection of the environment. It analyses whether reaching a common definition of environmental crime is possible; and assesses the rationales for the criminalisation of environmental offences in light of the theories of punishment, whilst considering alternatives to the protection of the environment through criminal law. Chapter 3 discusses the rationales and basis for the internationalisation of environmental criminal law, analysing in particular the potential scope for an extension of the jurisdiction of the International Criminal Court (ICC) over environmental crime, as well as the role of multilateral environmental agreements (MEAs) in driving states to introduce criminal measures to protect the environment.

Chapter 4 aims to assess the degrees to which states may pursue the harmonisation of environmental criminal law, considering the merits and demerits of unification, approximation, cooperation and coordination as models for the harmonisation of environmental criminal law. Chapter 5 discusses the question of the competence and mandate of the European Union to harmonise the environmental criminal laws of the EU Member States, in light of the limits of this competence as defined by the jurisprudence of the European Court of Justice. In particular, it analyses the impacts of two ECJ decisions which have for the first time explicitly recognised the power of the European Communities in criminal matters: the '*Environmental Crimes*' ruling on 13 September 2005[208] and the '*Ship-Source Pollution*' ruling on 23 October 2007.[209] In addition, this chapter investigates the legal implications of the ratification of the Lisbon Treaty

207 Frank Hoffmeister (2008) above note 203, at 69.

208 Case C-176/03 [2005], *Commission v Council* [2005] E.C.R. I-78793 C.M.L.R. 20.

209 Case C-440/05, *Commission v Council* [2007] 1 C.M.L.R. 22.

in 2009 to future attempts of harmonisation of environmental criminal law in the EU. It also discusses the extent to which the application and evolution of the general principles of law and EU law (including legality, effectiveness, subsidiarity and proportionality) limit the power of the EU to adopt future environmental crime legislation.

Chapter 6 discusses the specific features of the legislative instruments that have been adopted or proposed to harmonise environmental criminal law, including the legal implications arising from the harmonisation of criminal offences, complicity, corporate liability and penalties. In particular, it analyses the specific features of the EU Environmental Crime Directive adopted on 24 October 2008[210] and under the 2005 Directive on Ship-Source Pollution (as amended in October 2009);[211] as well as under the Council of Europe Convention on the protection of the environment through criminal law adopted in 1998.[212] Moreover, this chapter discusses the enforcement and implementation provisions under specific multinational environmental agreements relevant to the field of environmental criminal law, including under the Basel Convention on the Control of Transboundary Movement of Hazardous Waste and their Disposal[213] and the Convention on the International Trade of Endangered Species.[214]

Chapter 7 of the book examines the extent to which the harmonisation of environmental criminal law could lead to the improvement of the enforcement of environmental law, focusing on developments in the EU. This chapter will initially compare the effectiveness of environmental criminal law enforcement on the one hand with other enforcement mechanisms (particularly administrative law) on the other, which is fundamental for answering the question of

210 Directive 2008/99/EC of the European Parliament and of the Council of 19 November 2008 on the protection of the environment through criminal law, Official Journal L 328, 6 December 2008, pp. 28–37.

211 Directive 2005/35/EC of the European Parliament and of the Council on Ship-Source Pollution and on the Introduction of Penalties for Infringements, 7 September 2005, *Official Journal* L 255/11; 30.9.2005 and Directive 2009/123/EC of the European Parliament and of the Council of 21 October 2009 amending Directive 2005/35/EC on ship-source pollution and on the introduction of penalties for infringements; *Official Journal*, L 280/52. 27.10.2009.

212 Council of Europe Convention on the Protection of the Environment through Criminal Law (1998), Strasbourg, 4.XI.1998, ETS no. 172 (not yet in force).

213 Basel Convention on the Control of Transboundary Movements of Hazardous Wastes and their Disposal, adopted on 22 March 1989; entered into force on 5 May 1992, 1673 UNTS 126; 28 ILM 657 (1989).

214 Convention on International Trade in Endangered Species of Wild Fauna and Flora. Signed at Washington, D.C., adopted on 3 March 1973, entered into force on 1 January 1975, 27 UST 1087.

the necessity and effectiveness of environmental criminal law. This is followed by an analysis of the extent to which the *harmonisation* of environmental criminal law could lead to the achievement of specific goals, in particular to the improvement to the implementation of EU environmental law; to the development of the EU internal market; and to the enhancement of interstate cooperation in criminal matters in the EU.

Chapter 8 provides the concluding remarks regarding the necessity of criminal-law standards in the environmental field and regarding the necessity of harmonisation of those standards in the international and European settings. It will be argued that the seriousness of certain environmental offences requires an effective response from states and that the criminal law is a crucial tool for the effective enforcement of environmental law. Moreover, it will be suggested that advancing the role of the International Criminal Court for protection of the environment (beyond its current mandate primarily limited to the context of armed conflicts) would offer only limited deterrent effects against transnational environmental crime. It will also be argued that there is considerable fragmentation of the enforcement and penalties provisions under multilateral environmental agreements (MEAS), which calls for a more cohesive and coherent approach to implementation and enforcement under MEAS or, perhaps more ambitiously, for the adoption of global environmental crime convention. In general, it will be argued that states should seek to harmonise specific penalties, including criminal penalties, for the implementation of international environmental obligations, yet MEAS should simultaneously allow flexibility in the choice of national enforcement action to be taken in individual cases. Moreover, based on developments in the EU, it will be suggested that harmonisation of substantive environmental criminal rules could improve the implementation deficit of environmental law only to a limited extent, i.e. in so far as criminal sanctions have stronger deterrent effects than those of an administrative or civil nature. It is further suggested that the creation of a level playing field in a common market is an important aspect of harmonisation of environmental criminal law, although market integration should not be considered a determinant element for establishing the necessity of a measure harmonising environmental criminal law. Finally, it will be argued that measures aimed at fostering police and judicial cooperation in the EU are unlikely to be effective without a regime harmonising penalties and jurisdictional and prosecutorial rules.

CHAPTER 2

The Role of the Criminal Law for the Protection of the Environment

2.1 Introduction

Even prior to the adoption of the EU environmental crime directive in 2008, the majority of countries in the European Union used the criminal justice system as a means to enforce environmental law.[1] However, there has been significant variation as regards the choice of penalties and enforcement practices for different violations of environmental law within different jurisdictions. While some EU Member States have traditionally relied heavily on criminal sanctions (for example, the UK), other Member States generally applied a more flexible approach including administrative sanctions for the enforcement of environmental law (for example, the Netherlands).

This chapter aims to identify the rationales for the use criminal law in the environmental field. It starts by exploring the definition of environmental crime so that boundaries are set to the range of offences which may be categorised as falling under the auspices of the criminal law. It then discusses the rationales for the criminalisation of environmental offences in light of the theories of punishment; as well as the philosophical foundations for criminalisation of acts or omissions that cause or may cause damage to the environment. It finally discusses other forms of environmental liability, in particular civil and administrative liability, as well as non-command-and-control measures, as possible alternatives (or perhaps as complementary measures) to criminal liability.

2.2 Defining 'Environmental Crime'

It is important to define environmental crime, in particular, because it helps to frame many of the key aspects of criminal liability for environmental harm, for example whether an activity is viewed as a technical regulatory

1 See Faure, Michael and Heine, Gunter 'Criminal Enforcement of Environmental Law in the European Union' Kluwer Law International (2005); Huglo Lepage & Partners, *Study on Environmental Crime in the 27 Member States*, JLS/D3/2006/05 Final Report April 2007; and Faure, Michael and Heine, Günter, Final Report: Criminal Penalties in EU Member States Environmental Law, Maastricht 4 October 2002.

 | DOI 10.1163/9789004195882_003

breach or a 'crime against the environment'.[2] Moreover, defining environmental crime allows for the drawing of limits to the offences which may be subject to a degree of legislative harmonisation at the international or European levels.

Legal history reveals a traditional resort to criminal law by the sovereign state as a primary and effective way to solve numerous social, political and economic problems.[3] Criminal law is the strongest formal condemnation that society can inflict and the principal state tool impacting upon individual (and arguably also 'corporate'[4]) civil liberties.[5] Hence state promulgation and exercise of criminal law could be regarded as intrinsic to state sovereignty.

Smith and Hogan identify two characteristics which are generally found in a conduct classified as 'criminal': a 'public' wrong and a 'moral' wrong.[6] A crime generally has particularly harmful effects on the public and goes beyond a mere interference with private rights.[7] It affects the security and well-being of society and hence it is not safe to leave a crime addressable only by means of compensation of the party injured.[8] As put by Hart, 'a crime is a conduct which, if duly shown to have taken place, will incur a formal and solemn pronouncement of the moral condemnation of the community'.[9]

The above definitions reinforce the traditional position that crimes are 'moral wrongs' impacting upon public interests. However, many acts are now prohibited by means of criminal sanctions on the grounds of social expediency and not because of their immoral nature – in fact, this is the case of many regulatory environmental offences. Moreover, some acts which are often regarded as immoral, for example adultery, have been de-criminalised in virtually all

---

2 Bell, Stuart & McGillivray, Donald 'Environmental Law' (sixth ed., OUP 2006) at 278.

3 Noguera Vercher, A. 'The Use of Criminal Law for the Protection of the Environment in Europe: Council of Europe Resolution (77) 28' (1990) 10 *Northwestern Journal of International Law & Business* 442, 442.

4 Although it has been suggested that the very idea of companies having human rights is in itself a 'conceptual oxymoron'. See Emberland, Marius, *The Human Rights of Companies: Exploring the Structure of ECHR Protection* (OUP, Oxford 2006) at 27.

5 Asworth, Andrew. *Principles of Criminal Law* (Fifth ed. OUP, Oxford 2006) at 1.

6 Ormerod, David *Smith and Hogan Criminal Law* (11th ed. OUP, Oxford 2005), at 11.

7 *Ibid.*

8 Allen, 'Legal Duties and Other Essays in Jurisprudence' (1931) 233–234, cited in Simester, A.P. and Sullivan, G.R. *Criminal Law: Theory and Doctrine* (3rd ed. Hart Publishing, Oxford 2007) at 2.

9 H. Hart, 'The Aims of the Criminal Law' (1958) 23 *Law and Contemporary Problems*, 401, at 404.

Western countries.[10] Another problem is that it would be difficult in any event to establish a benchmark of morality which could be enforced by criminal law.[11] There is a tendency for the term 'crime' to be used to stigmatise almost any intentional behaviour of which the speaker disapproves. Indeed, calling a rubbish-dump a crime is a conservationist's way of stimulating public protest against something which is deplorable.[12] Even though it is unlikely that it would be considered an immoral act for an industrial plant to surpass by a small margin the limits of pollutant's emissions threshold, the killing and trade of endangered species or waste dumping in protected sites are more likely to be subject to moral condemnation by the wider society. Yet the criminalisation of the former, despite lacking the element of moral disapproval of the latter, may be justified for reasons of expediency and as a means to ensure the effectiveness of the regulatory system.

The academic literature has attempted to define the boundaries of the notion of environmental crime. A relatively broad definition of environmental crime is given by Mary Clifford who defines it as '[a]n act committed with the intent to harm or with a potential to cause harm to ecological and/or biological systems and for the purpose of securing business or personal advantage'.[13] A narrower definition, which emphasises the illegality of the activity and the degree of harm, is given by Situ and Emmons who define environmental crime as: '[a]n unauthorized act or omission that violates the law and is therefore subject to criminal prosecution and criminal sanctions. This offence causes harm or endangers people's physical safety or health as well as the environment and serves the interests of either organisations – typically corporations – or individuals.'[14] The 'green criminology' literature also tends to focus on the degree of harm when conceptualising environmental crime.[15]

10 On decriminalisation in the Council of Europe Member States, see e.g. European Committee on Crime Problems, *Report on Decriminalisation,* Strasbourg: Council of Europe (1980) 275.

11 The standard of morality is arguably that of 'the man in the jury box' based on the 'mass of continuous experience half-consciously or unconsciously accumulated and embodied in the morality common sense'. *See* Ormerod, above note 6, citing Lord Devlin.

12 Antonio Vercher Noguera, 'Some Reflections on the Use of Criminal Law for the Protection of the Environment' (2002) 10 *Env. liability* 3 107.

13 M. Clifford, *Environmental Crime: Enforcement, Policy and Social Responsibility* (Gaitherburg: Aspen, 1998) at 26.

14 Yingyi Situ and David Emmons. *Environmental Crime: The Criminal Justice System's Role in Protecting the Environment.*, Sage Publications, 2000 at 4.

15 See e.g. White, Rob 'Environmental Issues and Criminological Imagination' (2003) 7 *Theoretical Criminology* 483 at 485–486 and M. Lynch and P. Stretsky, 'The Meaning of Green: Contrasting Criminological Perspectives' (2003) 7 *Theoretical Criminology* 217.

Interestingly, Andrew Ashworth affirms that the contours of criminal law are 'historically contingent' – not the product of any principled inquiry or consistent application of certain criteria, but largely dependent on the fortunes of successive governments, on campaigns in the mass media, on the activities of various pressure groups, and so forth.[16] In particular, criminalisation of environmental offences in many countries (and indeed within the European Union setting) appears to be 'historically contingent' and coincides with the growing awareness about the importance of preserving environmental values and resources. From a historical perspective, the advent of the industrial revolution in the eighteenth century, despite bringing prosperity to some parts of the globe – in particular to the European powers – has led to increasing levels of industrial pollution which had detrimental effect to the environment and human health. This, in turn, led to the response of several European countries to introduce legislation in the nineteenth and twentieth centuries to regulate and prevent harmful levels of industrial pollution.[17] Moreover, the resort to criminalisation is often a reaction of legislators and governments in light of certain catastrophic environmental disasters or as a result of a penal code reform.[18] It is this 'unprincipled' and 'chaotic' construction of criminal law

16 Ashworth, Andrew. 'Is the Criminal Law a Lost Cause?' *Law Quarterly Review* (2000) at 226.

17 Including for example the German General Industrial Code (1845), the British Waterworks Clauses Act (1845), the French Dangerous Industrial and Commercial Activities Act (1917) and the Spanish Water Act (1878). For a discussion, see Noguera (1990) above note 3, at 444. Moreover, in France a crime of poaching was introduced to the Law of 15 April 1829 on 'River Fishing'. It has been applied by the courts since 1859 to manufactures that discharged pollutants into water. See also, Tiedemann, 'Theorie et Reforme du Droit Penal de L'Environment: Etude de Droit Penal Compare' *Revue de Science Criminelle et Droit Penal Compare* 264 (1986).

18 Indeed, many European states have introduced into their penal codes specific provisions on the protection of the environment: following the example of the German *Strafgezetzbuch* of 1980, an amendment to which introduced a chapter entitled 'Crimes against the Environment', a number of European countries reformed their penal codes: for example, Austria in 1974/1987 (Bundesgesetz of 23 January 1974; Strafrechtsanderungsgesetz of 1987); Spain in 1996 (Nuevo Codigo Penal, Articles 325–331, which was promulgated on November 23 1995 and entered into force on 24 July 1996); and Portugal in 1995 (Codigo Penal of October 1995, Articles 278–281 dealing with environmental crimes). Also, Finland, Denmark, the Netherlands and Sweden have incorporated environmental offences into their penal codes. (see further, Chapter 6) In France, the Environment Code (2008) lays down criminal sanctions for violations of environmental law. See generally, Ringelmann, C. 'Recent Trends in Environmental Criminal Legislation' (1997) 5 *Eur. J. Crime L. & Crim. Just.* 393, pp. 394–395.

which prompted Ashworth to question whether it may be a lost cause.[19] The adoption of the Ship-Source Pollution Directive and Framework Decision on shipping pollution in 2005 in response to the *Erika* oil tanker disaster in 1999 off the coast of France, and particularly the *Prestige* oil tanker disaster in 2002 off the coasts of Spain and Portugal, are examples of reactive legislation.[20] On the other hand, the adoption of the EU framework decision and directive on environmental crime in 2003 and 2008 respectively could not be said to have been influenced by specific environmental disasters. Indeed, those legislative developments could be said to be the product of the growing consensus over the need for criminal sanctions for environmental law enforcement; as well as the need to ensure the effective enforcement of EU environmental law. Moreover, the adoption of the Council of Europe environmental crime convention in 1998 could be said to have influenced the decision of the EU to adopt a legislative instrument on environmental crime.

There is no definition of environmental crime in the Council of Europe Convention nor in the European Union instruments on environmental crimes. Although the EU 2008 environmental crime directive does not define environmental crime, it states that 'effective protection' requires 'more dissuasive penalties for environmental protection, which typically cause or are likely to cause substantial damage to the air, including the stratosphere, to soil, water, animals or plants, including to the conservation of species'.[21] The Impact Assessment accompanying the 2007 environmental crime directive proposal broadly defines environmental crime 'as comprising acts or omissions which directly

---

19 Ashworth (2000), above note 16, at 225.

20 Other legislative measures in response to those accidents include Regulation (EC) No 1726/2003 of the European Parliament and of the Council of 22 July 2003 amending Regulation EC No 417/2002 on the accelerating of phasing in of double hull or equivalent requirements for single hull oil tankers OJ 01.10.2003 L249/1. Directive 2001/105/EC of the European Parliament and of the Council of 19 December 2001 of 19 December 2001 amending Council Directive 94/57/EC on common rules and standards for ship inspection and survey organisations and for the relevant activities of maritime administrations, OJ 22.01.2002 L19/16. Directive 2001/106/EC (as part of the Erika I package) of the European Parliament and of the Council of 19 December 2001 amending Council Directive 95/21/EC concerning the enforcement, in respect of shipping using Community ports and sailing in the waters under the jurisdiction of the Member States, of international standards for ship safety, pollution prevention and shipboard living and working conditions (port state control) OJ 22.01.2002 L19/17.

21 Recital 5 of Directive 2008/99/EC of the European Parliament and of the Council of 19 November 2008 on the protection of the environment through criminal law, *Official Journal* L 328, 6 December 2008.

or indirectly damage the environment and which constitute *a breach of legislation*' (emphasis added).[22] This is reflected in the actual offences under the directive, which require that the activity harmful or potentially harmful to the environment is 'unlawful' under national laws.[23] While on the one hand this legalistic definition emphasising the illegality of the activity has the advantage of being value free and objective, on the other hand it has the disadvantage of providing a narrow definition of environmental crime which is contingent on the legality of the activity, which may vary from one country to another.[24] Yet one of the advantages of the approach to criminalisation adopted under the EU environmental crime directive is that it separates the more serious environmental crimes – which deserve stronger degree of moral condemnation and hence higher punishment – from those which could be regarded as regulatory breaches and therefore generally subject to a lower degree of moral condemnation.

Even though there is no clear definition of 'environmental crime' within the European Union setting, the term appears in a number of EU criminal law instruments, in particular in instruments on interstate cooperation in criminal matters.[25] It is thus particularly important to define the limits of the definition of environmental crime for establishing the scope of a number of EU instruments on interstate cooperation in criminal matters – for example the 2002 European Arrest Warrant Framework Decision;[26] the 2005 European Evidence Warrant Framework Decision[27] and the Framework Decision on Mutual Recognition of Financial Penalties.[28] Indeed, one of the 32 offences for

22 Commission Staff Working Document, *Accompanying document to the proposal for a Directive on the Protection of the Environment through Criminal Law: Impact Assessment*, COM (2007) 51 SEC (2007) ('2007 Directive proposal Impact Assessment') at 4.

23 See Article 3 of the environmental crime directive.

24 See also Bell & McGillivray (2006), above note 2, at 278.

25 See e.g. Article 14 (2) of the Council Framework Decision on the European Evidence Warrant for the purpose of obtaining objects, documents and data for use in proceedings in criminal matters, 2008/978/JHA, 18 December 2008, *Official Journal* L 350/72, 30 December 2008.

26 Article 2 (2) of Council Framework Decision of 13 June 2002 on the European Arrest Warrant and the Surrender of Procedures between Member States, *Official Journal* L 190 18 July 2002. ('EAW Framework Decision').

27 Article 14 (2) of Council Framework Decision on the European Evidence Warrant for the purpose of obtaining objects, documents and data for use in proceedings in criminal matters, 2008/978/JHA, 18 December 2008, *Official Journal* L 350/72, 30 December 2008.

28 See Article 5(1) of Council Framework Decision 2005/214/JHA on the application of the principle of mutual recognition to financial penalties of 24 February 2005, *Official Journal* L76/16 22 March 2005.

which the dual-criminality principle is abolished in EU mutual recognition instruments (provided that certain conditions are met) is 'environmental crime, including illicit trafficking in endangered animal species and in endangered plant species and varieties'.[29] So other than the illegal trade in endangered species, the range of offences falling into the scope of the definition of 'environmental crime' is not clearly defined in those Framework Decisions and could potentially be far-reaching.[30] According to Article 2 (2) of the EAW Framework Decision, the possibility of surrender applies to certain listed offences if they attract certain punishments in the issuing Member State '*and as they are defined by the law of the issuing State*' (emphasis added).[31] Therefore, it is ultimately for the law of the issuing state to establish the scope and possible limits to the definition of environmental crime and thus which offences could lead to the surrender of a criminal from one member state to another.

2.2.1 *Anthropocentric v Ecocentric Approaches to Defining Environmental Crime*

A related debate to the one above, which influences the contours of a legislative or academic definition of environmental criminal offences, lies in deciding whether environmental law should follow an anthropocentric or eco-centric approach to environmental protection. The anthropocentric view suggests that the environment should be protected chiefly as a necessary means to protect human quality of life, while the 'eco-centric' approach requires that the natural environment *per se* is protected.[32] If the latter approach were adopted,

29 See e.g. Article 2 (2) of the Council Framework Decision of 13 June 2002 on the European arrest warrant and the surrender procedures between Member States, Official Journal, L 190 Volume 45, 18 July 2002.

30 On whether this and other undefined offences in the 2002 EAW Framework Decision violate the principle of legal certainty, see C-303/05, *Advocaten voor de Wereld*, judgement of 3 May 2007, discussed in Chapter 5.

31 See Council Framework Decision of 13 June 2002 on the European Arrest Warrant and the Surrender of Procedures between Member States, *Official Journal* L 190 18 July 2002.

32 As will be further discussed below, the English civil liability regime, under which traditionally direct victims of environmental pollution needed to be identified, is predictably anthropocentric. However, this has changed since the adoption of the EU Civil Liability Directive (2004), which requires the EU member states to establish administrative environmental enforcement mechanisms. See Directive 2004/35 on Environmental Liability with Regard to the Prevention and Remedying of Environmental Damage (2004) OJ L 143/56.

then it could be said that the natural environment has inherent rights.[33] Despite its obvious limitations, the 'anthropocentric' model can be open to flexible and wider interpretation. Indeed, even if no direct human victim exists, there could still be a case to answer under the criminal law if the amenity or economic value pertaining to natural resources or the environment were affected, for example by the pollution of a watercourse or oceans.

Some international environmental conventions and soft-law declarations follow an anthropocentric approach by establishing the principle that the 'human environment' should be protected, while others aim at protecting the environment as such. Moreover, some treaties provide for *comprehensive environmental protection,* including humans and the environment as such.[34] The landmark UN 1972 Stockholm Declaration on the *Human Environment*[35] could be said to generally follow an anthropocentric approach. The same could be said of Principle 1 of the Rio Declaration on Environment and Development[36] which reflects an anthropocentric approach to environmental protection.[37] On the other hand, a number of international environmental agreements define 'environmental damage' in a way that suggests a move away from a predominantly anthropocentric approach towards an eco-centric approach.[38]

33 See Christopher D. Stone, *Should trees have standing? Toward legal rights for natural objects', in Should Trees Have Standing?* (Oceana Publications, 1996). The recognition of the welfare principle (discussed below) as a basis for the criminalisation of violations of environmental law enables one to avoid the question of whether animals and plants have inherent rights. Even if environmental rights are accorded to humans and to human interests, the protection of the environment and natural resources, if not regarded as the *subjects* of legal rights, could be regarded as the *objects* of legal protection.

34 For example Article 2 of the Protocol on Environmental Protection to the Antarctic Treaty (Madrid) (1991) 30 ILM 1461 1991.

35 The 1972 United Nations Stockholm Declaration on the Human Environment (1972) YUN 319. *Declaration of the United Nations Conference on the Human Environment. Report of the United Nations Conference on the Human Environment,* UN Doc A/CONF.48/14/Rev.1 (1 January 1973).

36 *Report of the United Nations Conference on Environment and Development,* UN Doc A/CONF.151/26/Rev.1 (Vol.1) (12 August 1992) annex 1, principle 1 (*'Rio Declaration on Environment and Development'*) (*'Rio Declaration'*).

37 Principle 1 of the Rio Declaration states that humans are at the centre of concerns for sustainable development' and that they are 'entitled to a healthy and productive life in harmony with nature', thus falling short of aiming to establish a right to clean and healthy environment as such. See *ibid.*

38 In respect of state liability for environmental damage, the only definition in a treaty is provided by the 1988 Convention on Regulation of Antarctic Mineral Resources Activities (CRAMRA) (not in force), which defines environmental damage as: 'any impact on the

Indeed, when defining 'environmental damage' these environmental agreements adopt a narrow definition of natural resources in their interaction with air, soil, fauna and flaura and therefore recognise the protection of the environment as such, regardless of any harm to property or human health. In fact, the definition of environmental damage adopted under those international environmental agreements generally do not include damage to persons or damage to property, although such damage can be consequential to environmental damage.[39] One exception is the 2010 Nagoya-Kuala Lumpur Supplementary Liability Protocol to the Biosafety Protocol which defines damage to mean 'an adverse effect on the conservation and sustainable use of biological diversity, *taking also into account risks to human health*' (emphasis added).[40] Another exception is environmental damage caused in the context of extraction of mineral resources of the deep seabed, which are regarded as 'common heritage of mankind'.[41] Moreover, oil pollution civil liability international agreements define 'pollution damage' to include both compensation for impairment of the environment and reinstatement thereof 'other than loss of profit', as well as for the costs of preventive measures,[42] which hence could include economic losses connected to property damage or personal injury.[43]

---

living or non-living components of the environment or those ecosystems, including environmental harm to atmosphere, marine or terrestrial life, beyond that which is negligible or which has been assessed and judged to be acceptable pursuant to [the] Convention'. (Article 1(15)) See further, Sands, P. and Peel, J. (2012) *Principles of International Environmental Law*, (CUP, 2012) at 706–707.

39 *Ibid* at 706. Loss of environmental amenity, which may be included under the provisions of the 1993 Council of Europe Convention on Liability for Environmental Damage (not in force) relating to the 'characteristic aspects of the landscape', could be treated as environmental damage or damage to property, depending on the definition of the latter (*ibid*).

40 Article 2 (b) Nagoya-Kuala Lumpur Supplementary Liability Protocol to the Cartagena Protocol on Biosafety (2010), (not yet in force).

41 See *Responsibilities and obligations of States sponsoring persons and entities with respect to activities in the Area* (Feb 2011) (Request for Advisory Opinion submitted to the Seabed Disputes Chamber), para. 179, the Tribunal held that 'the damage in question would include damage to the Deep Seabed Area and its resources constituting the common heritage of mankind, and damage to the marine environment'.

42 See Article I (6) of the International Convention on Civil Liability for Oil Pollution Damage (CLC) (adopted in 27 November 1992; entry into force 30 May 1996) ('Oil Pollution CLC 1992'). See also, the International Convention on the Establishment of an international Fund for Compensation for Oil Pollution Damage (1992).

43 Oil spills from tankers give rise to compensation claims for damage to property; costs of clean-up and measures to prevent or minimize pollution damage; loss of income in the fisheries, mariculture and tourism sectors; as well as environmental damage. See also,

The anthropocentric approach to environmental protection is supported by the development of a human right to health and to property under international human rights law. The right to health was first articulated at the international level under the 1946 Constitution of the World Health Organisation (WHO) and subsequently established in a number of international human rights treaties[44] and national constitutions,[45] and is recognized by decisions of international tribunals and human rights treaty monitoring bodies.[46] The right to property is also recognized as a human right in international human rights instruments.[47] Yet not all environmental crimes impact directly on human health or property rights – for example, the trafficking in endangered species is one example in which biodiversity is affected but where there is no identifiable human victim, thus calling for a liability regime that protects the environment as such. Therefore, the criminal legislation of

---

Kyriaki Noussia, BP Oil Spill – Environmental Pollution Liability and Other Legal Ramifications, 20 *European Energy and Environmental Law Review*, 3, 98 (2011).

44 See *e.g.* Article 12 of the International Covenant on Economic, Social and Cultural Rights; Article 25.1 of the Universal Declaration on Human Rights; Article 5 (e) (iv) of the International Convention on the Elimination of All Forms of Racial Discrimination of 1965; Articles 11.1 (f) and 12 of the Convention on the Elimination of All Forms of Discrimination against Women of 1979 and Article 24 of the Convention on the Rights of the Child of 1989. The right to health is also recognised in a number of regional human rights instruments, for example in Article 11 of the European Social Charter of 1961 (as revised), Article 16 of the African Charter on Human and Peoples' Rights of 1981 and Article 10 of the Additional Protocol to the American Convention on Human Rights in the Area of Economic, Social and Cultural Rights of 1988. *See* also, Paul Hunt, *The Right to the Highest Attainable Standard of Health*. 370 The Lancet, 369 (2007).

45 See e.g. the 1988 Constitution of Brazil, Articles 6 and Article 196; and the 1996 South African constitution, Chapter 2, 2.19, which recognise the right to 'health care'.

46 See e.g. Inter-American Court of Human Rights, Case of Xakmok Kasek Indigenous Community v. Paraguay, Judgment of August 24, 2010, Case 12, 420. African Commission on Human and Peoples' Rights, Communication No 155/96: The Social and Economic Rights Action Center and the Center for Economic and Social Rights v Nigeria, 30th sess (27 October 2001) [56] ('Ogoni'). [68]–[69]; Case 12.191. Report no. 66/00 *Maria Mamerita Mestanza Chavez*. See further, Pereira, R. 'The Right to Reproductive Self-Determination of Indigenous Peoples under Human Rights Law' in S. Berking and M. Zolkos (eds.), *Between Life and Death: Governing Populations in an Era of Human Rights*, Peter Lang, 2009.

47 See e.g. Convention for the Protection of Human Rights and Fundamental Freedoms, Art 1 of Optional Protocol 1 [1952], which recognises the right to property as a fundamental human right: 'Every natural or legal person is entitled to the peaceful enjoyment of his possessions. No one shall be deprived of his possessions except in the public interest and subject to the conditions provided for by law and by the general principles of international law'.

several countries have introduced criminal offences relating to the illegal interference with certain elements of the natural environment (such as water, air or soil) without the requirement that there is harm or a risk of harm to humans or property. For example, there are a number of offences in the German Criminal Code (*Strafgesetzbuch*) of 1980 that do not require harm to humans,[48] although harm to humans may be an aggravating circumstance.[49] Similarly, in a study of five countries which at the time were candidate countries to join the EU, it was suggested that the criminal codes of those countries have abandoned the anthropocentric conception of environmental crime and moved to a more ecocentric approach.[50] In general, many national legal systems have created criminal offences to protect the environment as such without the need to evoke the harm or potential harm to human health or property as a prerequisite.[51]

The Council of Europe Convention on environmental criminal law aims at the criminalisation of offences which were regarded by the drafters of the convention as the most serious environmental offences, including pollution offences impacting on human health.[52] Indeed, the 'autonomous' offence under Article 2 (1) of the Council of Europe Convention regards damage to human health as an element that aggravates liability.[53] In the case of the EU directive on environmental crime, despite the fact that there is no reference to the protection of human health as a general objective in the Recitals to the directive, the actual offences in the directive go beyond protecting the environment as such, and aim to prohibit activities which cause or are likely to cause

48 For example StGB 324 (water pollution) and StGB 325 (air pollution).

49 StGB 330 (2) 1–2.

50 The countries analysed in that study are Poland, Hungary, the Czech Republic, Lithuania and Slovakia. See *Study on Criminal Penalties in a Few Candidate Countries' Environmental Law*, Final Report, October 2003.

51 This includes the civil liability regimes in Europe which, in particular since the adoption of the EU civil liability directive (2004), requires Member States to make damage to the environment as such as compensable.

52 Indeed, while the unlawful transport and disposal of hazardous waste endangering human and animal life falls under Section 2 ('intentional offences' for which signatory parties *must* introduce criminal sanctions), the unlawful disposal and transport of non-hazardous waste (or other wastes that are not likely to endanger human and animal life) fall under Section 4, leaving it to the discretion of national Parliaments the choice between enacting criminal or non-criminal sanctions.

53 The autonomous offence under the CoE environmental crime convention relates to the intentional 'discharge, emission or introduction of a quantity of substances or ionising radiation into air, soil or water [which either] causes death or serious injury to any person, or creates a significant risk of causing death or risk of serious injury to any person'. See further, Chapter 6.

death or serious injury to 'any person'.[54] In this regard, one important difference between those two instruments is that the EU environmental crime directive does not distinguish damage to the environment from damage to property or human health when defining the standards of liability.

2.3 Rationales for the Criminalisation of Environmental Offences

Some commentators suggest that criminal law is not always the most effective mechanism to prevent or control violations of environmental law[55] and it has been suggested even that criminal law enforcement is inherently antithetical to environmental law.[56] Yet this does not mean that there is a lack of theoretical foundation for the use of criminal law for the protection of the environment.

Any political decision to criminalize offences against the environment will invariably be based either on (1) utilitarian or (2) retributivist grounds. These are the two main pillars designing the contours of any move towards the criminalization of offences. The retributivist theory of crime and punishment holds that there is a need to introduce criminal sanctions whenever an element of moral culpability in the wrongful act can be identified (or 'just deserts'). On the other hand, utilitarians advocate that the only rationale for introducing criminal penalties is the maximisation of society's welfare under a cost-benefit analysis in order to improve deterrence and not simply to punish offenders for their past conduct. While the retributivist goal is to punish an offender for his or her intrinsically morally wrong behaviour (past-orientated), the utilitarian objective is to create a mechanism of punishment that enjoys efficiency in deterring the commission of future crimes (future-orientated). While retributive and utilitarian goals may be obtained simultaneously,[57] the emphasis put

54 Article 3, paragraphs (a) – (b); (d) –(e).

55 For example Pagh, Peter, 'Administrative Criminal Law Systems in Europe: an Asset for the Environment?' in Comte, Françoise and Kramer, Ludwig (eds.) *Environmental Crime in Europe: Rules of Sanctions* (Europa Law Publishing, Groningen 2004); Faure, Michael. 'European Environmental Criminal Law: Do we really need?' (2004) 13 *EELR* 18; Macrory, Richard. 'Regulatory Justice: Making Sanctions Effective: Final Report' Cabinet Office, November 2006.

56 Lazarus, Richard, 'Meeting the Demands of Integration in the Evolution of Environmental Law: Reforming Environmental Criminal Law', (1993) 83 *Georgetown Law Journal.* On Lazarus' arguments, see Chapter 6.

57 See Wood, David, 'Retribution, Crime Reduction and the Justification of Punishment' *Oxford JLS*, vol.22, no.2 (2002) pp. 301–321, who calls for the integration of the utilitarian and retributivist theories.

on either of those goals may have a significant impact on criminal policies and sentencing practices.

In the context of corporate crimes, the theories of punishment could also be applied to justify the punishment of corporations. As argued by Celia Wells, a theory of corporate criminal liability satisfies both the retributive and deterrence theories of punishment, and therefore there is no fundamental challenge to their application to corporate offenders.[58]

2.3.1 *Retributive Notions*

Many environmentalists defending the use of criminal sanctions for the protection of the environment base their position on retributivist grounds and not necessarily on cost-benefit analysis. After all, cargo-operators such as that of the *Prestige,* responsible for an oil-spill that caused severe damage to wildlife on the coasts of Spain and Portugal, or the smuggler of endangered species who destroys their natural habitat or traffics them would surely deserve penal punishment regardless of whether or not others would be deterred from committing similar offences in future. Indeed, as the awareness of the public in environmental issues increase, it is likely that (serious) environmental offences will not be regarded as mere regulatory offences (or *'mala prohibita'*) but real crimes (*'mala in se'*).[59] It has been suggested that the population at large may regard some major forms of pollution as serious crimes – even as serious as some of the most severe street crimes.[60]

The core of the retributive view is that punishment should aim to address the wrong represented by the criminal act.[61] Hegel argued that punishment cancels the wrong and restores 'the Right'.[62] Some absolutist states and some dictatorial governments have followed an extreme side of the retributivist theory, i.e. the old 'lex-talionis' that regards punishment as 'an eye for an eye,

58 Wells, C. *Corporations and Criminal Responsibility* (OUP, Oxford 2001).

59 Bell & McGillivray (2006), above note 2, at 281.

60 Gerhard Mueller cites a national survey carried out in the US (Wolfgang et al. 1985) and a multi-country study conducted by the United Nations Interregional Crime and Justice Research (UNICRI). See Mueller, Gerhard, 'An Essay on Environmental Criminality' in Sally M. Edwards, Terry D. Edwards, Charles B. Fields (eds.) *Environmental Crime and Criminality: Theoretical and Practical Issues* (Garland Pub, New York 1996) at 8. Moreover, a Eurobarometer 2008 survey suggests that environmental issues rank very high among the concerns of Europeans. European Commission: Eurobarometer, 'Attitudes of European Citizens Towards the Environment', March 2008 available at http://ec.europa.eu/public_opinion/archives/ebs/ebs_295_en.pdf.

61 Fletcher, George, *Basic Principles of Criminal Law* (OUP USA, 1998) at 32.

62 Georg W.F. Hegel, *The Philosophy of Right* 69 (TM Knox trans., 1991).

a tooth for a tooth'. Yet beginning in the Seventeenth Century early legal philosophers such as Beccaria expressed the view that penalties must be fair and proportionate to the offence.[63] Indeed, it would be wrong to imply that the retributivist theory is necessarily incompatible with the principle of proportionality of penalties. Despite being fair and proportionate, the criminal sanction could be regarded as a retribution for the wrongdoing. So regardless of whether criminal sanctions are efficient or not, criminal sanctions might be necessary as an expression of society's moral condemnation of some serious forms of impairment to the environment.[64]

Retributive considerations may also be reflected in sentencing practices: although in general it could be said that low penalties are applied in most countries in respect of environmental offences, one of the most severe penalties imposed for wildlife offences in the UK was handed down in a case in early 2002 involving three men who captured threatened birds of prey in Thailand and smuggled them to the United Kingdom, leading to the death of seven animals and the placement of others in cruel conditions.[65] A search on one of the men's home led to the discovery of a further 54 birds of prey, seven slow Ioris, five tortoises and a golden checked gibbon, as well as several dead birds and a slow Ioris in a freezer.[66] This man was sentenced to six and half years in prison with a recommendation of at least two thirds before release.[67] Another example is British Petroleum (BP) which was fined US$4.5 Billion (the highest in U.S. history) in November 2012 as part of a settlement related to the *Deepwater Horizon* oil rig spill disaster for the crimes of involuntary manslaughter and for

63 See Cesare Beccaria, *Beccaria On Crimes and Punishments and Other Writings*. Cambridge Texts in the History of Political Thought (1764).

64 It has been suggested that 'it may appear as a necessity, even a duty of government to provide the criminal law with adequate instruments for the protection of the environment' given the general acceptance of the theory of climate change and its potentially dramatic effect on the course of human development'. Heine, Günter 'Environmental Protection and Criminal Law' in Owe Lomas ed. *Frontiers of Environmental Law* (Chancery Law Publishing, 1991) at 76–77.

65 Willem Wijnstekers, 'Protection of Endangered Species of Fauna and Flora' Comte, Françoise and Kramer, Ludwig (eds.) *Environmental Crime in Europe: Rules of Sanctions* (Europa Law Publishing, Groningen 2004) at 22.

66 *Ibid.*

67 Under UK customs legislation in force at the time of the incident, the maximum penalty for illegal wildlife imports was seven years imprisonment and an unlimited fine. Moreover, the Thai man pleaded guilty, and was sentenced to 22 months, half of which was suspended; while the third person was acquitted. *Ibid.*

violations of the Clean Water Act.[68] It should be noted that although the judicial authorities in those two cases surely must have given weight to the retributivist goal of the criminal law when sentencing, those severe penalties also serve a deterrence purpose.

On the other hand, there is generally no moral stigma attached to certain regulatory offences (and a considerable number of environmental offences fall into this category). Indeed, there is little intrinsic moral difference, for example, between driving at 70 miles per hour on a highway (not an offence) and driving at 75 (a criminal offence);[69] or, equally, in the case of a violation of emissions control standards by a negligible percentage margin.

Moreover, when environmental offences are labelled as 'regulatory' – which is the case of many of environmental offences in the UK – this generally implies that strict liability standards are applied.[70] This certainly diminishes the stigma connected to the application of criminal sanctions and it could ultimately trivialise the use of criminal sanctions.[71] Therefore the 'just deserts' or retributivist approach described above would be difficult to reconcile with the absence of culpability in the case of strict liability offences.[72]

The retributivist theory has also been conceptualised in the context of white-collar crimes. Edwin Sutherland, a leading theorist of modern criminology, launched the social legalistic perspective of crime which argues that some acts, especially by corporations, are so violent in their expression as to merit being defined as criminal.[73] He observed in a classic study of white-collar crime that harmful acts of large U.S. corporations were often treated as mere regulatory violations or civil infringements, and hence carried neither criminal

68 *See BBC News, BP Gets Record Criminal Fine over Deepwater Disaster,* 15 November 2012, http://www.bbc.co.uk/news/business-20336898 (accessed on 15 February 2015).

69 A.P. Simester and G.R. Sullivan, *Criminal Law: Theory and Doctrine* (3rd edn. Hart Publishing, Oxford 2007) at 3.

70 See e.g. *Alphacell v. Woodward* [1972] A.C. 824.

71 See also, Macrory, Richard. 'Regulatory Justice: Making Sanctions Effective: Final Report' Cabinet Office, November 2006.

72 The reason for use of strict liability offences is primarily pragmatic: in a typical pollution case the contravention itself may not be intentional, but resulting from a normal and continuous activity deliberately undertaken. Thus, requiring proof of knowledge of the quantity or quality of discharge which rendered the conduct unlawful would impose a heavy burden on the enforcement agency. See also, Burrows, Paul; Ogus, Anthony I.; Richardson, Generva *Policing Pollution: A Study of Regulation and Enforcement* (Oxford, 1982) at 57.

73 Sutherland, H. Edwin, 'White Collar Criminality' (1949) 5 *American Sociological Review* 1.

stigma nor the typical sanction of imprisonment.[74] He advocated a much stronger role for criminal justice in the context of corporate crimes. In this regard, it is not uncommon for environmentalists to label the actions of certain corporate groups as 'criminal', apparently taking the view that the corporation is itself responsible for environmental crimes.[75]

2.3.2 *Utilitarian Notions*

Utilitarianism holds that, in deciding what one should do, one should consider only the consequences of one's actions: an action cannot be justified purely by its relationship to past facts.[76] Since the ultimate aim of environmental law is the protection of ecological resources, its role must not only be punishment for the offender's past-misconduct, but primarily that of harm prevention (deterrence).[77]

The main utilitarian notions applied to justify punishment are the welfare principle, the harm principle and deterrence. The principles of effectiveness and minimalism are also relevant in the decision of whether or not to criminalise. The relevance of those utilitarian notions to environmental criminal law will be examined next.[78]

2.3.2.1 The Welfare Principle

According to the welfare principle, the main basis for criminalisation would be to protect collective interests belonging to the whole community (*res communis*).[79] In this context, there seems to be a strong basis for the support of criminalisation of environmental offences, as it is in the public interest that the environment is protected. Significantly, environmental protection tends to be identified as a third generation right, reflecting communal values and

---

74 *Ibid* at 3.

75 This can be epitomised by the statements posted in the Greenpeace website in relation to some corporations such as Exxon Mobil. See e.g. http://www.greenpeace.org/usa/en/campaigns/global-warming-and-energy/exxon-secrets/ (accessed on 15 February 2015).

76 N.E. Simmonds, *Central Issues in Jurisprudence. Justice, Law and Rights* (Sweet and Maxwell, London 1987) at 15/17, cited in Noguera (2002), above note 12, at 10.

77 In a seminal paper developing an economic analysis of the criminal law, Gary Baker argues that firms and individuals are rational economic actors who are motivated by wealth or utility-maximising intentions. Becker, G. 'Crime and Punishment: An Economic Approach' 76 *Journal of Political Economy* (1968) 161.

78 Other prominent utilitarian theories of criminalisation applicable to the environmental context – the rehabilitation of offenders and restoration of the natural environment – will be discussed in Chapter 6 (in the context of criminal penalties and corporate crimes).

79 Ashworth (2006) above note 5, at 28.

interests that cannot be divided or singularised. Hence the welfare principle is an important philosophical foundation for the criminalization of environmental offences.

Yet while it appears legitimate to raise the notion of 'community welfare' in support of policies emphasising public safety and the need for greater measures to ensure security (for example laws relating to industrial safety, food safety and environmental protection), the legitimacy of criminalisation on the basis of welfare may be at odds with the principle of individual autonomy. Whereas the principle of autonomy suggests that individual rights should be given priority in the legal structure, the principle of welfare recognises the social context in which the law operates and gives stronger weight to collective goals.[80] This suggests that the decision to criminalise requires a balancing test between the individual and collective goals – a test which is particularly challenging in the environmental field, since polluting (economic) activities can be detrimental to the environment and the public but are also generally socially useful and vital for prosperity. Furthermore, elements and resources pertaining to the natural environment are considered in some legal systems to be *res communis* (meaning that they belong to an indeterminate number of persons within a state) thus calling for state intervention for protection of those environmental interests.[81]

The welfare principle cannot be considered a determinant factor in the decision by lawmakers as to whether or not to criminalise violations of environmental law. Following the recognition that environmental protection is a 'community' or 'public' goal, it is still necessary to establish whether violations

---

80 *Ibid.*

81 In fact, some States have established in their Constitutions the division of property of certain elements of the natural environment (flora, fauna, rivers etc.) to the different spheres of governance (federal, state and municipal levels). This may also have implications in the determination of which legal action may be brought to protect the environment, since in some countries an *actio popularis* can only be brought in the defence of the *res communis*. This is the case of the Brazilian Constitution, see Art. 20 and 26 which divide different natural resources between the Federal and State governments. *Constituicao da Republica Federativa do Brasil*, 1988. The regime has, on occasion, been reinforced by decisions of national courts (for example, in Nigeria), which have established ownership of oil and gas to the federal or state governments: see, eg, *Attorney-General of the Federation v Attorney-General of Abia State* (2002) 6 NWLR Part 764, 542–905 (Supreme Court of Nigeria). See also Yinka Omorogbe and Peter Oniemola, 'Property Rights in Oil and Gas under Domanial Regimes' in Aileen McHarg et al. (eds), *Property and the Law in Energy and Natural Resources* (Oxford University Press, 2010), at 120–1.

of environmental norms could not be dealt with in other more effective or less costly ways, for example under civil or administrative law.[82] So public interest arguments in favour of criminalisation must meet certain criteria such as urgency, unavoidability, effectiveness and so forth.[83]

2.3.2.2 The Harm Principle

Notwithstanding the importance of the welfare principle, it is the harm principle that has been more widely debated as a possible philosophical basis for the criminalisation of environmental offences. John Stuart Mill, one of the fathers of utilitarianism, has famously written that 'the only purpose for which power can be rightly exercised over any member of a civilized community, against his will, is to prevent harm to others'.[84] This statement is one of the earliest formulations of the harm principle, under which criminal legislation could only be introduced in order to protect others from harm. Therefore, those human acts that do not have the potential of causing harm to others (for example, adultery or homosexual acts in private)[85] could not be criminalized since any objection to them would be merely based on moral grounds. The objective of the application of the harm principle is thus to secure moral neutrality. Yet as Andrew Ashworth notes, 'harm' itself is a 'morally loaded' concept.[86]

Controversially, Joel Feinberg argues that the harm principle does not apply in the case of pollution offences since, as a cumulative harm, it is impossible to determine the degree of contribution of each polluter to the harm.[87] To illustrate his proposition, he argues that it would be impossible to individualise the degree of contribution of each motor vehicle for the air pollution caused by the discharge of carbon dioxide from its engine. It then becomes impossible to assign responsibility to each offender.

Another approach, which was embraced by the Law Reform Commission of Canada in 1986, would be to regard the responsibility in such cases as shared

---

82 Ashworth (2006) above note 5, at 29. On this question, see further below and Chapter 7.

83 *Ibid.*

84 J.S. Mill, *On Liberty*, Ch. 5, quoted in Ashworth, *supra* at 30.

85 However, an arguably more conservative approach was adopted by the UK House of Lords decision in *Brown* in the context of consensual sado-masochist sexual acts in private. See *R v Brown* [1994] 1 AC 212.

86 He suggests that since harm is defined in terms of violations of peoples' legitimate interests, then account must be taken of the moral, cultural and political nature of the interests affected in a particular system. See Ashworth (2006) above note 5, at 28, citing D. MacCormick, Legal Right and Social Democracy (1982), 29.

87 Feinberg, Joel. *The Moral Limits of the Criminal Law: Harm to Others* (OUP USA 1984) p. 227.

and independent of the identification of specific offenders.[88] Similarly, many jurisdictions appear to have circumvented any limitations to the harm principle by recognising types of endangerment offences which are independent of actual harm as long as there is potential for harm. In contrast to 'real crimes' which relate to the commission of, or attempt to commit, a real harm, many regulatory crimes are abstract endangerment offences that require the mere potential of causing harm.[89] In such cases, the breach of pollution emission standards by industrial enterprises could be a regulatory crime regardless of whether or not any real harm to the environment occurs.[90]

Moreover, it is commonplace for the responsibility to be regarded as 'shared' in several areas of environmental regulation – one could mention the case of environmental taxes or the internalisation of the clean-up costs of pollution in the price of vehicles, meaning that ultimately it will be for consumers and tax payers to pay collectively for the costs of cleaning up the pollution.[91] However, it becomes less evident how the *criminal* responsibility could be shared in such cases.[92]

Another criticism that could be made to Feinberg's conceptualization of the harm principle as a limitative theory to criminalisation of pollution offences is that it may disregard the wide range of offences that could be regarded as 'environmental crimes'. Indeed, despite the fact that some forms of environmental impairment are cumulative, for example the pollution-control offences discussed in Feinberg's work, there are other examples of environmental crimes

88 See the Law Reform Commission of Canada, *Sentencing in Environmental Cases* (1986). In the Canadian *Panarctic* case it was held that: 'The destruction of the ecosystem is a gradual process, effected by cumulative acts – a death by a thousand cuts, as it were. Each offender is as responsible is as responsible for the total harm as the last one, who triggers the end. The first offender can't be allowed to escape with only nominal consequences because his input is not as readily apparent'.

89 Rowan-Robinson J., Watchman P., and Barker C., *Crime and Regulation: A Study of the Enforcement of Regulatory Codes* (T&T Clark 1990) p. 205.

90 Celia Wells, notes that 'health and safety offences (...) do not refer to the result which the unguarded machine might endanger, they prohibit the failure to guard'. See Wells, Celia. *Corporations and Criminal Responsibility*, (Oxford 2001) at 5. On the definition of abstract endangerment offences, see further Chapter 6.

91 For a definition of the polluter-pays principle, see Principle 16 of the United Nations Rio Declaration on the Environment and Development (1992).

92 It could be argued not to be fair to single out one individual company and declare it guilty of a criminal offence of causing the damage to the environment that had already been initiated by the action of others. Yet it should be noted that selective prosecutions are commonplace in a number of jurisdictions. See Hubbard, R., Peter M. Brauti, and C. Welsh. 'Selective Prosecutions and the Stinchcombe Model for Disclosure' (1999). *CLQ* 42: 338.

(for example, the killing and trading of endangered species or illegal logging) in which the harm happens instantly or imminently. Moreover, in such instances the source of harm, and the environmental harm itself, are identifiable and could thus be directly attributable to a company, individuals or criminal organisations.

Yet it does not appear likely that the degree of harm will be the only determinant element when it comes to graduating environmental offences. Not only the degree of harm but also the interests affected are to be taken into account when offences are graduated. Since environmental concerns are intertwined with economic interests, policy-makers may decide not to criminalize violations of environmental law – despite their harmful or potentially harmful consequences – in view of the perceived priority of the economic interests affected. This helps to explain why some potentially very harmful environmental offences are treated leniently by legislators who are also lobbied and pressured to act in accordance with economic imperatives. Moreover, the harm alone cannot justify criminalisation, but the *wrongful* causing of harm in the sense of one's culpability in setting back another's interest.[93]

2.3.2.3 Deterrence

For utilitarianism, the main goal of the criminal law is deterrence.[94] There are two forms of deterrence: specific deterrence, which applies to individual offenders; and general deterrence, which applies to the general public. Hence the objectives of deterrence policies are twofold: to stop the individual offender from committing further crimes (either by fear of punishment or by incapacitation in the case of incarceration), or to prevent the general public from committing crimes after the exemplary punishment system is introduced and applied. The existence of deterrence arising from the introduction of criminal punishment has been tested and confirmed in criminological studies, particularly in those carried out in the context of drink driving or the use of seatbelt in private cars.[95] But no conclusive studies have been able to prove marginal deterrence, that is, how much *extra* deterrence is achieved by increasing the

93 Feinberg defines harm as 'those states of set-back interest that are the consequence of *wrongful* acts or omissions of others' (emphasis added). Feinberg (1984) above note 87, at 215.

94 The deterrence approach not only predicts behavioural outcomes, but also provides the theoretical basis for determining the quantum of penalties for regulatory offences. See also, Abott, C., '*Enforcing Pollution Control Regulation: Strengthening Sanctions and Improving Deterrence*' (Hart Publishing 2009) at. 17.

95 See e.g. Von Hirsch, Andrew. *Criminal Deterrence and Sentence Severity: an Analysis of Recent Research*. Oxford: Hard (2000) at 47.

certainty (e.g. improving policing) or severity (penalty levels) of punishment, though current research does indicate that there are consistent and significant negative correlations between likelihood of conviction and crime rates.[96]

Those studies on deterrence suggest that while the presence of a criminal justice system imposing penalties (or the allocation of police resources or application of enhanced enforcement methods increasing detection rates) *do have* recognisable positive deterrent effects, the same cannot be said about manipulating criminal law rules within that system to achieve heightened deterrence effects (e.g. increasing penalty levels).[97] Despite this, law and policy makers often act in the belief that compliance can be enhanced by either enhancing the detection rate or increasing the expected penalty.[98] Since enhancing the detection rate is more costly, they tend to choose to increase the level of penalty, which must be high enough to account for the low detection rate.[99] This is significant since when legal rules are formulated to enhance deterrence, overriding other goals, such as doing justice, such emphasis on deterrence may frustrate those other goals for no overriding benefit.[100] On the other hand, other studies have suggested that the manipulation of legal norms to enhance prison terms has proved in fact to have deterrent effects, even though the effect of incarceration has been played down for failing to take into account the effect of 'incapacitation'.[101] So the deterrent effect of criminal law may not necessarily be linked primarily to the level of penalties applicable, but to the presence of criminal offences and the actual levels of law enforcement.[102]

---

96 *Ibid.*

97 Paul Robinson and John Darley, 'Does Criminal Law Deter? A Behavioural Science Investigation' *Oxford Journal of Legal Studies*, Vol. 24, No. 2 (2004) at 173.

98 Faure, Michael and Heine, Günter '*Criminal Enforcement of Environmental Law in the European Union*' IMPEL Network, July 2000, at 57.

99 Robinson and Darley (2004), *supra.*

100 *Ibid* at 174.

101 Indeed, when criminals are imprisoned they are not in general able to commit further crimes against the public. This might explain the fall in crime rates when prison terms are extended. *Ibid.*

102 This view was echoed by a UK Audit Committee on 'Corporate Environmental Crime' report which emphasised the need for further measures to increase detection with the ultimate aim of enhancing deterrence: 'time and again over the course of our inquiries into environmental crime, it has been brought home to us that unless there is a real threat of being detected, the offender will continue to offend. We cannot stress strongly enough the importance of the threat of detection as a deterrent.' See Environmental Audit Committee 2nd Report, *Corporate Environmental Crime* HC (8 February 2005) 136 [38].

The degree of compliance that can be achieved within the group susceptible to deterrence policies has been the subject of debate in the law and economics literature.[103] The starting point for this literature is that perfect compliance is not possible nor desirable since regulation is not self-enforcing and requires compliance through enforcement agencies which involves substantial resources. Thus it is argued that the goal of the enforcement system must be optimal compliance, i.e. the point at which marginal social benefits accruing from compliance are equivalent to the marginal social costs incurred in securing that level of compliance.[104] Optimal deterrence aims to strike the right balance between the utility/benefit of the unlawful activity, and the cost of preventing it. If expected sanctions rise with the harm caused by the offence, then it will in principle encourage individuals to commit less harmful rather than more harmful acts.[105] Therefore, the main economic goal of enforcement policy is to minimise the total cost to society when the costs from non-compliance are added to the costs of enforcement, which is in line with Gary Becker's view that individuals and firms comply with regulatory obligations if the benefits arising from contravention are exceeded by the costs.[106] Becker then developed a model suggesting that the potential offender will only be deterred from committing the offence if the anticipated profit to be derived from the illegal activity is lower than the costs consequent on being caught as discounted by the perceived risk of apprehension.[107] So the most important element in this model is the expected punishment costs, which is calculated by multiplying the amount of the penalty imposed on a successful conviction and the probability of detection and conviction.[108] Therefore, the aim of any enforcement agency should be optimal deterrence, i.e. to ensure that the social costs of enforcement (taking account of the avoided harm) equal the costs of enforcement.[109]

---

103 See e.g. G. Stigler, 'The Optimum Enforcement of Laws' 78 *Journal of Political Economy* 78 (1978) 526; and G. Becker, 'Crime and Punishment: An Economic Approach' 76 *Journal of Political Economy* (1968) 161.

104 Anthony Ogus and Carolyn Abbot 'Sanctions for Pollution: Do we have the Right Regime?' *Journal of Environmental Law* vol. 14 no. 3 (2002) at 289.

105 Abott, C., '*Enforcing Pollution Control Regulation: Strengthening Sanctions and Improving Deterrence*' (Hart Publishing 2009) at 17.

106 Becker (1968) above note 104, at 161.

107 Ogus and Abbot (2002), *supra* at 290.

108 Burrows et al. (1982), above note 73, at 60.

109 According to Polinsky and Shavell's analysis of public law enforcement the optimal penalty (D) under this normative model can be determined by assessing the harm caused by the unlawful act (including enforcement costs as part of the wider social costs of an

Criminologists have a word of caution in this regard and suggest that it could be substantially flawed to make certain generalised conclusions about deterrence studies. They argue that deterrence is *subjective* in character – i.e. different social groups and people respond differently to deterrence policies. It seems that strong evidence that such group exists comes from the numerous studies demonstrating the increase in crime rates during police strikes.[110] Moreover, deterrence policies must target in particular the so-called 'career criminals' who have been reported to commit the majority of crimes, which may explain the high rate of recidivism for some types of crime.[111] This calls on the application of the criminal justice system for protection of environmental values in order to deter criminal organisations and companies from engaging in criminal activity in the environmental field – in light of the high profitability and low detection rate of environmental crime – as an alternative to, for example, drug trafficking, money laundering and other forms of highly profitable crimes.[112] So the model suggested by Gary Becker may not always be an accurate guidance to deterrence strategies, in that the potential offender's *subjective* perception of the probability of detection, associated costs, defence expenditures and any stigma or loss of reputation are not taken into account in Becker's model.[113]

It must be emphasised though that the social group of interest for this study of deterrence are not necessarily career-criminals, for example criminal organisations, but in many instances industrialists and companies that are regulated by environmental law. If it were not for the effects of stigmatisation on businesses – and the possibility of incarceration of corporate managers and officials – criminal sanctions such as fines could be seen as a cost of doing business and passed on to consumers. However, imposing very severe penalties on companies and corporate officials in order to achieve deterrence may also be problematic: firstly, criminal laws could result in over-deterrence and consequently

---

unlawful activity) and the probability of detection. Polinsky and Shavell 'Public Enforcement of Law', in Bouckaert and Geest (eds.) *Encyclopedia of Law and Economics* (Cheltenham, Edward Elgar, 2000) vol. 307, 320.

110 Commonly cited in this connection are the police strikes in Liverpool in 1919 and Melbourne in 1918. Broadly speaking, property offences (looting) tend to increase during police strikes, whereas sexual and violent crimes do not. See Ashworth (2006) above note 5, at 16.

111 It has been suggested that 'career criminals' tend to commit a disproportionate number of crimes and that 7% of criminals commit 2/3 of all violent crimes. See discussion in Robinson and Carley, above note 97 at 184.

112 Wijnstekers, (2004) above note 65, at 20.

113 Ogus and Abbot (2002), *supra* at 290.

disrupt some socially useful activities. This would be the case if the (socially desirable) activity of developing and managing waste disposal sites were subject to such strict and burdensome regulations on businesses that actually no (or perhaps only very few) companies would be willing to take the risk of carrying out that business. Secondly, over-deterrence also raises questions of fairness – despite probably providing 100% deterrence, it would certainly be unfair (and disproportionate to the offence) if for a relatively minor pollution discharge offence the penalty of capital punishment were to be imposed, for example. Since this penalty would appear to be disproportionate to the offence committed, the effect would be to bring the whole criminal law system into disrepute in a democratic society. It follows from the foregoing analysis that deterrence cannot in itself be the sole goal of applying the criminal law, and other goals of the criminal justice system such as its correctional and educational functions need to be given at least the same weight.

There are also limits to the application of the general deterrence theory specifically in the context of corporate crime. Slapper and Tombs suggest that there are no studies providing evidence that the general deterrence theory applies in the context of corporate crimes – perhaps because it is difficult many times for the prosecution to lift the corporate veil, corporations may feel relatively 'safe' from effective prosecutions.[114] Yet this position may underestimate the difficulties in enforcing individual accountability. Slapper and Tombs themselves recognise that there appears to be evidence that punishing a corporation with an appropriately serious sanction for an offence has a chastening effect on others.[115]

In this vein, 'individualists' base their proposition against corporate criminal punishment primarily on the ground that it does not provide sufficient deterrence. They argue that punishment should target the individual agents or representatives of the company (who are in fact deterred by the threat of punishment), and not the company itself (which is not capable of moral blameworthiness and could not be deterred by the threat of punishment). Hence there is an assumption by individualists that sufficient deterrence of corporations can be achieved through punishment of the individual persons responsible for offences.[116] This view suggests that criminal law presupposes

114 Slapper, Gary and Tombs, Steve. *Corporate Crime* (Longman, 1999) at 205.

115 *Ibid.*

116 *Ibid* at 36. This view is supported by the following assertions (1) only human agents are capable of responding to the deterrent threat of punishment; (2) corporations are not wrongdoers to be punished but entities to be reformed (3) and that deterrence of corporate crime can be achieved by punishing the individual persons responsible. Fisse, B. And

human choice and therefore criminal liability should be based exclusively on individual guilt and hence that the general deterrence theory – which is based on an element of human choice – does not apply in the context of corporate crime.

In contrast to the view of 'individualist' scholars, it could be argued that in some circumstances the prosecution of the corporation has a *higher* deterrent effect than the prosecution of individual offenders, for example when there is bad publicity associated with the prosecution of environmental crime and the development of 'naming and shaming' enforcement policies targeting such corporate offenders.[117] Hence it is suggested that the punishment directed at the corporate entity will typically seek to deter a wide array of individual associates from engaging in conduct directly or indirectly connected with the criminal offence. It does appear that if sufficiently serious penalties are applied to corporations, individual associates will be deterred in engaging in action which could lead to substantial losses to the company – and perhaps even the end of the legal entity, for example if a sanction of plant shut down for poor health and safety standards were to be applied.[118]

2.3.2.4 The Principle of Effectiveness

The principle of effectiveness is in line with the '*de minimis*' principle – i.e. that the law should not criminalise trifling wrongs. This is in line with the definition of the harm principle and the other theories of criminalisation discussed above – the criminal law is to be used as a last resort and only when other sanctions

---

Braithwaite, J. *Corporations, Crime and Accountability* (Cambridge University Press, Cambridge 1993)at 32.

117 Bell and McGillivray (2006) above note 2, at 288. Another mistaken assumption made by individualists is that corporations can be punished simply by means of fines or other monetary penalties, and therefore managers will not be deterred by criminal punishment unless the spill-over effects of fines were high enough to affect severely shareholders, workers, consumers and perhaps the whole economy. Indeed, a sufficiently serious sanction may in certain circumstances not be passed on to consumers in a competitive market, as it would otherwise put a company in competitive disadvantage vis-à-vis its competitors. Moreover, there are other forms of sanctions applicable to corporate entities that go beyond financial penalties (for example corporate probation and prohibition orders), including sanctions as severe as equivalent to individual capital punishment (for example the revocation of a licence to operate).

118 This implies that in order to have sufficient deterrent effects, criminal enforcement should target not only the corporations *but also* the individuals responsible for the environmental crime within the corporation. On the question of harmonisation of rules on corporate criminal liability, see further Chapter 6.

could not achieve the same result at lesser costs to society. Hence the principle of effectiveness is closely connected to the minimalist theory and requires the use of criminal law only if it is the most efficient and cost-effective means of enforcing the law.[119] This approach is generally recognized under the preamble to the Council of Europe environmental crime convention, which states that 'the prevention of the impairment of the environment must be achieved primarily through other measures',[120] leaving the use of criminal law for the most serious environmental offences when committed intentionally or with negligence.[121]

Although, as discussed above, the harm principle is primarily a negative principle in its impact on criminalisation (i.e. it mainly suggests which conducts *should not be* criminalised), it also contains some positive principles of criminalisation, including the key fundamental utilitarian principle of effectiveness. In this regard, Feinberg proposes the following application of the harm principle as a positive principle for criminalisation based on the principle of effectiveness: '[i]t is always a good reason in support of penal legislation that it would probably be effective in preventing (eliminating, reducing) harm to persons other than the actor and there is probably no other means that is equally effective at no greater cost to other values'.[122]

Although as was argued above there are strong arguments for the more serious violations of environmental law to be criminalised, it could be argued that for the sake of efficiency (and effectiveness) civil and administrative sanctions should play a stronger role in the environmental field. This is in line with the definition of the harm principle and other theories of criminalisation discussed above – the criminal law is to be used as a last resort and only when other sanctions could not achieve the same result at lesser costs to society. Thus minimalism demands stronger justifications for criminalisation than when civil or administrative strategies are used (see Chapter 7).[123]

However, this purely utilitarian view may be challenged since if the wrongdoing is serious or harmful enough, then there is at least an important symbolic reason for declaring it to be criminal, bearing in mind that the 'declaratory' function of criminal law plays a significant role in reassuring some members of

119 J. Bentham 'Introduction to the Principles of Morals and Legislation' (1789) ch 13. See also, Ashworth (2006) above note 5, at 34. The question of effectiveness of criminal law enforcement is further analysed in Chapter 7.

120 Recital 7 of the Preamble, Council of Europe environmental crime convention.

121 See Art. 2 and 3 (1) *ibid.*

122 J. Feinberg, (1984) above note 87, at 26.

123 Ashworth (2006) *supra* at 31.

society and deterring others, thereby further contributing to the deterrent effect of the criminal law.[124] Moreover the view that the criminal law should only be used as 'a last resort' has been criticised by some authors in particular because they envision a broader role for the criminal law in ensuring compliance *ex-ante* with environmental law.[125] On the other hand, the minimalist theory is not only limited to utilitarian arguments, and the detrimental side effects of criminalisation and over-criminalisation are well documented in the literature.[126] In particular, it has been argued that the right not to be criminalised is a basic human right that aims to protect individuals from unwarranted state intervention of a penal nature.[127]

In the corporate crime context, one pragmatic rationale for corporate liability is the efficiency of the prosecution. It is argued that it is particularly challenging for prosecutors to pierce the corporate veil, i.e. to identify an individual or group of individuals inside the corporation who is responsible for the crime.[128] So the main problem with the individualist theory (which negates the effectiveness of corporate criminal punishment) is that it may underestimate the difficulties in enforcing individual liability: including enforcement overload; the lack of clarity of internal lines of accountability; expendability of individuals within organisations and corporate self-harbouring of individual suspects.[129] On this last point, it has been suggested that organisations have a well-developed capacity for obscuring internal accountability if confronted by outsiders and that '[r]egulatory agencies, prosecutors and courts find it difficult

124 *Ibid* at 34.

125 See Husak, Douglas. 'The criminal law as last resort'. *Oxford Journal of Legal Studies* 24.2 (2004): 207–235.

126 Dennis Baker notes that the bulk of the literature addressing the over-criminalisation problem tends to focus on the case for decriminalising crimes that are usually victimless. See Dennis Baker, *The Right not to be Crimininalised: Demarcating Criminal Law's Authority* (Ashgate, 2011) at 3. He further notes that the arguments for decriminalisation have tended to focus on instrumental issues (such as law enforcement costs), rather than alluding to the constitutional requirements of fairness and justice (*ibid* at 9). See also, Sanford Hadish, 'The Crisis of Overcriminalisation' (1967) 374 *The Annals of American Academy of Political and Social Science*, 157; Hebert Packerm *The Limits of the Criminal Sanction* (Stanford: Stanford University Press, 2008); and Douglas Husak, Overcriminalisation: *The Limits of the Criminal Law* (New York: Oxford University Press, 2008).

127 It is enshrined in Fifth and Eighth amendments of the US Constitution, and Arts. 3, 5 and 8 of the European Convention. See Dennis Baker (2011) ibid.

128 In fact those who influence the commission of offences indirectly may fall outside the scope of liability for complicity or other ancillary heads of criminal liability. Fisse and Braithwaite (1993) above note 116, at 32.

129 *Ibid* at 37.

or even impossible to unravel lines of accountability after the event because of the incentives personnel have to protect each other with a cover-up'.[130] Hence 'given the difficulties and expense of convicting individuals for crimes within complex organisations, a policy of individualism almost certainly would reduce the number of convictions for corporate crime and thereby worsen the inequality between "crime in the streets" and "crime in the suites"'.[131]

Moreover, the rationale for criminalisation based on the effectiveness of prosecutions has been criticised because in practice corporate criminal liability could be used as an *alternative to* individual liability. It has been suggested that '[p]rosecutors are able to take the short-cut of proceedings against corporations rather than their more elusive personnel and so individual accountability is frequently displaced by corporate liability, which now serves a rough-and-ready catch-all device'.[132] In this respect, in the UK context it is recognised that while corporate criminal liability plays a significant role in ensuring compliance with the law by measures of fines and costs of restoration, it has been noted that a disproportionate number of cases are prosecuted against the company because of the strict liability standard.[133]

It does appear problematic if corporations are prosecuted and not the individuals responsible for environmental crime on the basis that it is more economical for prosecutors to do so. Yet in this regard it must be noted that most international instruments establishing some form of corporate liability, including the EU environmental crime directive, establish that corporate responsibility is not to be regarded as an alternative to individual liability.[134] In fact, many EU Member States allow for the possibility of imposing criminal liability on directors and managers[135] and recognise that criminal sanctions may apply to those corporate officials *as well as* the corporation.

2.4 Alternatives to Criminal Liability

This section discusses the systems of environmental liability which could be regarded as alternatives to (or, more likely, complementary to) criminal liability.

130 *Ibid.*

131 *Ibid* at 510.

132 Ibid at 1.

133 IMPEL Network Report (2005) above note 1, at 44.

134 Article 6 (3) of the environmental crime directive states that '[l]iability of legal persons (…) *shall not exclude* criminal proceedings against natural persons who are perpetrators, inciters or accessories in the offences referred to in Articles 3 and 4'. (emphasis added). See further, Chapter 6.

135 IMPEL Network Report 2005, above note 1 at 44.

It must be noted at the outset that there is no general prohibition of accumulation of administrative, civil and criminal sanctions for the same incident in international human rights law.[136] According to Article 4 (1) of Protocol, no. 7 of the European Convention on Human Rights:

'No one shall be liable to be tried or punished again in *criminal proceedings* under the jurisdiction of the same State for an offence for which he has already been finally acquitted or convicted in accordance with the law and penal procedure of the State'. (emphasis added).

In some countries the accumulation of administrative and criminal sanctions may be forbidden depending on the nature of the administrative measure. Some administrative measures have both a repressive and deterrent character and could be considered to have the same nature and aim as criminal ones.[137] Examples of administrative penalties of a punitive and deterrent character are fines, closure of establishment or the withdrawal of a permit, though imprisonment is generally not possible in administrative infringement proceedings. However, even in such cases, in some legal systems administrative sanctions aim to protect the interest of the administration and not superior values of the society. Hence in those countries there is no social blame attached to the administrative sanction which has a regulatory function to restore public order, and there is no violation of the *ne bis in idem* principle if both administrative and criminal sanctions are applied cumulatively for the same violation of the law.[138]

On the other hand, it must be noted that some legal systems which allow for the imposition of administrative sanctions have a form of *electa una via* rule, which means that the authorities must choose (unless the goals are totally different) between an administrative sanction or a criminal penalty.[139]

2.4.1 *Differentiating the Criminal Law from other Liability Regimes*

With the first codifications in the 19th Century, sanctions were differentiated, isolated from each other in their specific legal regimes: a simple juxtaposition of independent sanctions with nothing to prevent their being imposed with

136 See generally Peers, Steve 'Double Jeopardy and EU Law: Time for a Change?' *European Journal of Law Reform* Vol. VIII no. 2/3.

137 Milieu & Huglo Lepage '*Summary Report: Study on Measures other than Criminal Ones in Cases where Environmental Community Law has not been Respected in the EU Member States*', 20 September 2004, at 52. (B4-3040A/2003/369724/MAR/A.3) ('Studies on Non-Criminal Measures') at 13.

138 *Ibid.*

139 E.g. Austria, Germany, Spain and Italy. See IMPEL Network Report (2005) above note 1, at 49.

regard to the same acts.[140] For example, the victim of an offence may be awarded civil damages, which could be compounded with the criminal sanction *per se* of fine or imprisonment of the offender. This poses no difficulties as long as the implicit foundation of each category of sanction is different: punishment (criminal sanctions), disciplinary (disciplinary sanctions), regulation (administrative sanctions), reparation (civil sanctions) or even reconciliation (in the case of mandatory mediation), which arguably could be regarded as a sanction in the broad sense.[141]

In light of a number of common features between the enforcement systems for environmental protection, it is not surprising that the same act of environmental damage can lead to both criminal and civil liabilities. That is so because most crimes are torts as well, though some torts are not crimes and some crimes are not torts. Indeed, even though sometimes it is suggested that a choice needs to be made between recognising a conduct as a crime or a civil wrong, in fact some conducts are both a civil wrong and a crime. However, in each case the objective of the liability regime is substantially different: whilst the emphasis of criminal law is on *punishment*, civil law generally seeks the *reparation* of injured parties; while administrative law generally seeks the *regulation* of an activity.[142]

Once most constitutions of continental Europe incorporated the principle of separation of powers, it became possible to draw a distinctive line between criminal law and other areas of the legal system.[143] Yet the increasing cross-fertilisation between the different regulatory and enforcement systems has led to the blurring of the distinction between civil and criminal law.[144] The blurring line between civil and criminal law is visible, for example, when 'punitive' or 'exemplary' damages are awarded in civil proceedings, or when private parties are granted the right to start a criminal prosecution under the criminal procedural laws of certain countries. Moreover, a general trend in recent years can be identified in the criminal justice processes of some countries that have

140 Delmas-Marty, Mireille, *Towards a Truly Common Law*, (Cambridge University Press, Cambridge 2002) at 137.

141 *Ibid.*

142 Ibid. See further, Chapter 7.

143 Noguera (2002) above note 12. However, long before then the criminal and civil law systems were regarded as separate – for example under the Roman legal system. See Robinson, *infra*.

144 See Robinson, Paul 'The Criminal-Civil Distinction and the Utility of Desert' (1996) 76 *Boston University Law Review* 201.

turned increasingly to require offenders to provide monetary restitution to the victims of crime.[145]

Despite these similarities and converging features, there are some unique features accruing to criminal law which distinguish it from other enforcement systems. The criminal justice system provides the most coercive method of regulating an individual or legal entity's behaviour and infringes upon one's personal autonomy through the investigation, surveillance, arrest, search, seizure (which may include pre-trial detention), to punishment which may include imprisonment.[146] The degree of stigma and coercion of criminal law is qualitatively different from that in civil law,[147] and is characterised by its dissuasive and deterrent nature.[148]

Durkheim proposed the classification of legal rules according to the sanctions attached to them. He draws a distinction between 'repressive sanctions' which 'consist essentially of pain, or at least a diminution, inflicted on the agent' and compensatory sanctions, which 'consist solely of restoring the *status quo*, or re-establishing normal relations', for example an injunction to perform, damages or cancellation. This would imply placing criminal sanctions in the repressive category, and all others in the compensatory category.[149] Yet the difference between repressive and punitive sanctions on the one hand, and restitution on the other, does not necessarily correspond to the categorisation of penalties in some countries. In the European setting, the case-law of the European Court of Human Rights (ECtHR) suggests that the definition of whether sanctions are 'criminal' or 'civil' is determined by reference to an entire set of criteria that go beyond domestic legal categories. Article 6 (1) of the European Convention of Human Rights guarantees the right of a fair trial in the Council of Europe member states 'in the determination of a person's civil rights and obligations or of any criminal charge against him'. The European

145 Either directly through the imposition of court-based orders; or through the establishment of victim's funds maintained by offender surcharges and fine payments. This is the case of the U.S. Mandatory Restitution Act (1996) aimed 'to help victims recover from any financial hardship caused due to a criminal activity'. See Matthew Hall, *Victims of Environmental Harm: Rights Recognition and Redress under National and International Law* (Routledge, 2013) at 100.

146 Even though 'detention' may be possible under some disciplinary proceedings, 'imprisonment' is only available as a punishment in criminal proceedings. See the discussion of the case-law of the ECtHRs below interpreting the right to a fair trial under Article 6 ECHR.

147 Ormerod (2005) above note 6, at 13.

148 In a similar vein, see Advocate General Mazak's opinion in the *Ship-Source Pollution* case. ECJ *Mazak AG*, Point 71.

149 Durkheim, E., The Evolution of Punishment, in Lukes and Scull (eds.) Durkheim and the Law (Oxford: Martin Robertson 1983). See further, Delmas-Marty, above note 140, at 137.

Court of Human Rights has given an autonomous meaning to the concept of 'criminal charge' which is independent of the categorisations given in the domestic legal systems of the Member States. So it is not possible for ECHR signatory States to circumvent Convention controls by indiscriminately classifying offences as either criminal, administrative or civil wrongs.[150] If the member states were free to determine what matters were to be regarded as criminal, the scope of protection offered by Article 6 would differ substantially from one country to another.[151] So the European Court of Human Rights (ECtHR) has held in a number of cases that a sanction, regardless of its classification under national law, could be considered *criminal in nature* for the purposes of the Convention, hence requiring the procedural guarantees of Article 6 ECHR.[152] This suggests that if certain petty offences are decriminalised by the contracting party, they would continue to belong to criminal law for the purposes of the fair trial guarantees of Article 6 ECHR.[153]

Specifically, the European Court of Human Rights applies the following criteria when deciding whether a sanction is 'criminal in nature': (1) 'Does the text defining the offence belong to criminal law?' In case the offence is not classified as criminal, the Court may investigate and interpret the national law, its legal history or the case law relating to the relevant norm.[154] (2) The court then asks what the nature of the offence is. To answer this question, the ECtHRs must define the scope of the norm. In particular, the Court is concerned about its addressees, hence whether the norm is only addressed to a specific group or

150 *Ezeh and Conners v. United Kingdom* (Apps. 39665/98 and 400086/98) Judgement of the Grand Chamber of 9 October 2003 (2004) 39 EHRR 1. See also, Ovey, Clare and White, Robin, *Jacobs & White: The European Convention on Human Rights* (OUP, Oxford 2006) at 160.

151 Trechsel, Stefan. *Human Rights in Criminal Proceedings* (OUP, Oxford 2006) at 16.

152 *Özturk v. Germany* (Application no. 8544/79), ECHR, 1984, available at echr.coe.int. The Court stated that 'if the Contracting States were able at their discretion, by classifying an offence as "regulatory" instead of criminal, to exclude the operation of the fundamental clauses of Articles 6 and 7, the application of these provisions would be subordinated to their sovereign will. A latitude extending thus far might lead to results incompatible with the object and purpose of the Convention' (Par. 49).

153 *Lutz v. Germany*, 25 August 1897, Series A no. 123 (1988) 10 EHRR 182; and *Schmautzer v. Austria*, 23 October 1995, Series A no. 328-A (1996) 21 EHRR 511.

154 As regards the first criterion applied by the Court relating to the classification of the norm under domestic law, the first step for the Court is to consider whether the classification of the allegedly violated norm belongs to criminal or to disciplinary or administrative law. In case the violation is classified as *criminal* under the domestic law of the Contracting Party, then Article 6 is applicable and this question is settled. See van Dijk et al., *Theory and Practice of the European Convention on Human Rights*, Intersentia, Oxford 2006 at 544.

whether it is of a generally binding character.[155] In order for an offence to be considered criminal, the scope of the violated norm must be of a *general character*. In the *Özturk* case the Court held that the decriminalisation of certain offences under the domestic law of the Contracting Parties does not mean that Article 6 is no longer applicable, so long as the penalty maintains its 'deterrent' and 'punitive' character.[156] (3) Finally, the court assesses 'the nature and severity of the penalty that the person concerned risked incurring',[157] having regard to the object and nature of Article 6.[158] For example, if the disciplinary or administrative procedure imposes the penalty of imprisonment – which is the classic criminal penalty – of *considerable duration*, then the conditions of Article 6 (1) need to be observed in the procedure in question. This same principle was applied in *Engel*, in which a maximum of two-day arrest was not considered sufficiently severe to amount to a criminal penalty.[159]

It is clear from the case-law of the ECtHRs that it adopts an autonomous meaning of the concept of 'criminal charge' and that the deterrent and punitive character of the penalty is decisive for the determination of whether an environmental offence is 'criminal in nature' regardless of its classification under national law.

155 As for the second criterion (the scope of the norm and the purpose of the penalty) the court must define the nature of the offence. Another aspect of the second criterion is the *purpose* of the penalty, which aims at distinguishing criminal sanctions from simply reparatory or compensatory ones. Hence fines which are merely intended as pecuniary compensation for the damage caused are to be distinguished from those which have a deterrent or punitive character. *Ibid.*

156 *Özturk* [*1984*] paras. 49 and 53.

157 See *Ozturk* [1984] para. 54. Moreover, it is the maximum penalty that the accused *risked incurring* which will determine whether Article 6 is applicable or not, not the penalty actually applied. Article 6 does not distinguish between criminal *charges* of a serious nature and those of a less serious nature. Indeed, the determination of a criminal charge concerning a petty offence may be of great importance for the person – hence all procedural guarantees of Article 6 must be present in the case of a criminal charge, regardless of the seriousness of the penalty that may be imposed. See *Adolf v Austria* Series A No 49, (1982) 4 EHRR 313 para. 33 (even in proceedings that may not amount to any penalty at all); and *Ozturk* 1984 para. 53, which confirm that the severity of the penalty cannot be a decisive element for the determination of its 'punitive' character.

158 *Engel and others v the Netherlands* [1976] ECHR, Judgement of 8 June 1976, para. 82. This test was replicated in the *Özturk* case, *supra*. So if Article 6 is found to be applicable, it does not follow from the Court's case-law that the administrative procedure will need to be converted into one of a criminal nature, but that the relevant administrative procedure will need to observe the minimum procedural rights of Article 6. See van Dijk et al. (2006) above note 154.

159 *Ibid.*

2.4.1.1 Civil Liability

Civil law (or the law of torts) provides a mechanism for injured parties to claim compensation for the damage caused by others. It allows the victim(s) who suffered individual harm to claim compensation in the courts. Thus it is a system used for the protection of private interests, though the environment as a public good may be protected as an indirect consequence of civil claims.

In order to claim compensation the victim must prove the damage and the causal link between the act or omission and the damage caused. One area in which the standard of proof is more flexible in civil cases is for the establishment of causation. In the environmental law context, it is a perennial and thorny problem to establish the casual link between the environmental damage and the wrongdoing of the individual.[160]

The civil claim is generally brought directly against the polluter though in some countries it is possible for individuals to sue the administration for its failure to control the pollution.[161] In some countries it is possible for the victim to claim 'punitive' awards in civil claims which might raise damage awards to a level that could have significant deterrent effects and even drive corporations out of business.[162] In particular because most companies regard profit-maximization as their main business objective, damage awards must exceed the gain from illegal conduct so that they take account of the economic benefits of the illegal activity.[163] If a company causes the death of several people through the discharge of harmful pollutants, the risk of paying a criminal fine of €100,000 has less dissuasive effects than the payment of millions of Euros in compensation to the families of the victims.[164] For example, the asbestos litigation in the U.S. is the longest running mass tort litigation in U.S. history. The total corporate liability costs for asbestos-related diseases in the U.S. has

160 Spindler, Gerald, 'Alternatives to Criminal Responsibility of Corporations – Considerations by a Corporate Lawyer' in *Criminal Responsibility of Legal and Collective Entities*, Albin Eser/Günter Heine/Barbara Huber (eds.), International Colloquium Berlin 1998, at 344. Given the difficulties in establishing the casual link between the act or omission and the damage caused, Finland adopted a concept of 'probable casual link' (based on a 50% probability that they were the cause of damage). ibid.

161 E.g. Austria, Belgium, Germany, Spain, UK, Portugal, France and Luxembourg. 'Studies on non-criminal measures' above note 137, at 15.

162 See Cohen, A. Mark, 'Criminal Law: Environmental Crime and Punishment: Legal/Economic Theory and Empirical Evidence on Enforcement of Federal Environmental Statutes' [1992] 82 *Journal of Criminal Law & Criminology*, 1054.

163 This is also true in the case of criminal or administrative fines.

164 See also, Simester and Sullivan (2007) above note 8.

been estimated at US$30 billion, which is far more than the product ever earned its manufacturers.[165]

The main shortcoming of the traditional civil law enforcement is that it only allows compensation for damage caused to a victim's property or health and not for the restoration of the environment as such. Moreover, the public apparatus will not generally be available for the investigation of those civil claims of a private law nature.[166] Hence since private enforcement is dependent on individual victims bringing civil claims it leaves the environment as a 'public good' unprotected, though the civil action may indirectly offer a degree of protection to the environment. By contrast, criminal and administrative law protects the public interest and have a public apparatus available to investigate and apply sanctions,[167] although in some countries this negative feature of private enforcement to protect the environment is addressed to some extent by the use of collective civil actions which may be brought by a number of individuals who wish to collectively claim compensation.[168]

Before the coming into force of Civil Liability Directive in 2004,[169] only some EU Member States had a specific liability regime for environmental damage.[170] Compensation was still determined by damage to individual property in some Member States. They also retained the traditional system of civil liability based on fault,[171] though the standard of proof of the fault element (*on a balance of probabilities*) was generally substantially relaxed in comparison with the standard generally applied *beyond reasonable doubt* requirement in criminal cases.[172] Therefore, from the perspective of efficiency, civil law has a clear

---

165 See Dunphy, A. Griffiths and S Benn, '*Organizational Change for Corporate Sustainability*' (Routledge, 2003).

166 See Cohen (1992) above note 162.

167 'Study on non-criminal measures' above note 137, at 9.

168 Such as, for example, for the protection of collective rights, such as employees' rights, or in defence of 'public goods' such as environmental and aesthetic values for which an unidentifiable number of individuals can claim to have suffered damage, also known as *erga omnes* rights. This is the case with class actions which are commonly used in the United States, for example. For a discussion of class actions see e.g. Gidi, Antonio 'Class Actions in Brazil – A Model for Civil Law Countries' (2003) *American Journal of Comparative Law* 311.

169 Directive 2004/35 on Environmental Liability with Regard to the Prevention and Remedying of Environmental Damage (2004) OJ L 143/56.

170 This included Finland, Greece, Denmark, Germany and Sweden and Ireland. 'Study on non-criminal measures' *supra* at 9.

171 *Ibid.*

172 See generally, e.g. Allen, Michael. *Textbook on Criminal Law* (8th ed. OUP, Oxford 2005).

advantage since the standard of proof is lower to establish the fault element than in criminal law. Moreover, in England and Wales and the Republic of Ireland the courts developed the concept of strict liability based on a House of Lords decision in *Rylands v Fletcher*.[173] Similarly, Spain applied strict liability in certain civil actions, which means that it was not necessary to prove fault on the part of defendant.[174]

After the deadline for transposition of the Environmental Civil Liability Directive[175] on 30 April 2007, all EU Member States are expected to have a specific liability regime for environmental damage aside from the traditional civil liability regime based on fault. The Environmental Civil Liability Directive[176] addresses many of the criticisms raised above to civil law enforcement as a means to protect the environment. Indeed, one of the main advantages of a specific regime of civil liability for environmental damage is that restoration of damage caused to the environment can be enforced against the polluter despite the absence of individual victims if the public authorities decide to bring the action.[177] Thus the Directive represents a move away from an emphasis on monetary compensation, to preventive or remedial action aimed at rectifying actual or threatened environmental damage, and from private enforcement to enforcement by competent authorities.[178] In this vein, Lin argues that a key advantage of administrative compensation schemes in cases of environmental harm is that they have the potential to compensate those who are not yet affected by environmental damage but are at a significant risk of becoming so.[179] Moreover, the regime established by the Directive is based on strict or objective liability for activities which are dangerous to the environment.[180] This means that evidence of fault or negligence on the part of the polluter is not be necessary for certain activities under the Directive.

173 *Rylands v Fletcher* (1868) LR3 HL 330, House of Lords.

174 Spanish Civil Code, Article 1902. See 'Study on Non-Criminal Measures' above note 137 at 9.

175 Directive 2004/35 on environmental liability with regard to the prevention and remedying of environmental damage, OJ 2004 L143/56, 21 April 2004, as amended by Directive 2006/21, OJ 2006 L102/15. For an analysis of the Directive see e.g. Winter et al. 'Weighing up the EC Civil Liability Directive' (2008) *Journal of Environmental Law* 20(2):163.

176 Dir 2004/35 on Environmental Liability with Regard to the Prevention and Remedying of Environmental Damage [2004] OJ L 143/56.

177 'Study on non-criminal law measures' above note 137, at 9.

178 Hedemann-Robinson, M. *Enforcement of European Union Environmental Law: Legal Issues and Challenges*, (Routledge-Cavendish, 2007) at 514.

179 See Lin, A.C. (2005) Beyond Tort: Compensating Victims of Environmental Toxic Injury, *Southern California Law Review* 78, 1 439; and Hall M (2013) above note 145 at 100.

180 As regards the so-called 'Annex III activities'. Liability may also be based on fault under the Directive (for the non-Annex III activities).

2.4.1.2 Administrative Liability

Most EU Member States provide for different kinds of administrative sanctions which can be applied by administrative bodies in their legal systems.[181] The United Kingdom (not until recently), Denmark, Ireland and Finland, on the other hand, do not have a very well developed system of administrative sanctions.[182] Those countries have a tradition of applying administrative enforcement *measures* (warnings, orders, notices, injunctions and other soft measures) which can be followed by a criminal prosecution, but the administrative authorities may not directly apply sanctions as such.[183] So whereas in the UK, Ireland and Denmark the administrative agency would generally bring a criminal prosecution for the failure of an operator to comply with the administrative measure, in other Member States such as France, Belgium, Luxembourg and the Netherlands the sanction for non-compliance would be applied by the agency itself.[184]

Even in countries with a more developed system of administrative sanctions (which may include administrative fines, revocation of licences and the shutdown of an installation), those sanctions may only be applied as a last resort – for example in France or Belgium. In this respect, the administrative systems of the Member States can be classified as having a preventive character[185] or a more repressive character.[186] In those systems with a preventive character, enforcement authorities tend to choose either fine-accessory sanctions or warning notices (in most cases in very moderate levels of severity).[187]

As regards the culpability requirement to establish an administrative infringement, the traditional difference of criminal and administrative law in this respect is somewhat blurred by the increasing application of strict liability in criminal proceedings and the requirement of negligence/endangerment for

181 IMPEL Network Report (2005) above note 1, at 17.

182 *Ibid* at 70.

183 'Studies on non-criminal measures' above note 137, at 15.

184 *Ibid.*

185 Belgium, France, Luxembourg, Denmark, Finland, the Netherlands, UK and Ireland. *Ibid* at 61.

186 Greece, Italy, Spain, Portugal and the quasi-criminal administrative systems of Austria and Germany. *Ibid.*

187 It is interesting to note that France, the archetype of the administrative law system based on powerful administration, may find itself more in line with the UK and Ireland – which have a much less developed system of administrative law – than with countries that have a more coercive or repressive system of administrative law. One explanation for this is that in some countries (in particular those with an authoritarian past) the administration was stripped of any punitive power and which is only later partly recovered. *Ibid* at 18.

the commission of an administrative infringement.[188] This means that the mere breach of an administrative provision without some element of fault may not be sufficient to establish an administrative infringement. Yet it should be noted that in some countries – such as the UK – strict liability standards are generally applicable to regulatory offences.[189]

There is a strong accessoriarity between the criminal law and administrative law in some countries, and an environmental regulatory infringement is often required for the establishment of a criminal offence. For example, Anglo-Saxon countries have a well developed system of regulatory offences.[190] Moreover, a hybrid system of enforcement which lies in between administrative and criminal law is the quasi-criminal system. The quasi-criminal system allows the administrative agencies in some countries to apply *repressive* sanctions against breaches of environmental regulations. Germany and Austria for example have a well established system of administrative criminal sanctions (*Ordnungwidrigkeiten*).[191] One of the advantages of this quasi-criminal system is that it allows the administration in countries that do not accept the concept of criminal liability of corporations, such as Austria, Germany, Spain and Portugal, to apply non-criminal fines of a deterrent character as enforcement tools to corporate entities.[192]

Even though there may be some ideological basis for the creation of the administrative criminal system,[193] the main reason for its creation was pragmatic, i.e.: (a) to avoid the congestion of already busy criminal courts; (b) to avoid the trivialisation and deterioration of criminal law overrun by petty offences and (c) to prevent citizens from going through the lengthy procedures and defamatory nature of the criminal penalty.[194]

---

188 *Ibid.*

189 The emergence of strict liability is linked to the establishment of the public nuisance offences in the 19th Century. See Leigh, L.H., *Strict and Vicarious Liability: a Study in Administrative Criminal Law* (Sweet & Maxwell, London 1986) at 11.

190 IMPEL Network Report (2005) above note 1, at 42.

191 'Study on non-criminal measures' above note 137, at 17. This quasi-criminal system was also found to play an important role in environmental enforcement in at least three of the Member States that joined the EU in 2004: Hungary, Czech Republic and Slovakia. See 'Study on Criminal Penalties in a Few Candidate Countries' Environmental Law: Final Report' 6 October 2003 at 10, hereinafter 'Study on criminal penalties in candidate countries'.

192 'Study on non-criminal measures' *supra* at 61.

193 For example, that the values protected by those repressive sanctions could not be regarded as fundamental values of society.

194 'Study on non criminal measures' *supra* at 19. Yet the study notes that 'nowadays administrative courts are also overwhelmed by a heavy caseload'. *ibid.*

There is an ongoing debate regarding the *nature* of administrative-penal fines. While there is a tendency for them to be considered as having a 'mixed' nature, some countries regard them as being closer to either criminal law or administrative law and provide for different guarantees in the infringement procedure accordingly.[195] This is the case of Austria which has a quasi-criminal system more in line with criminal law and which thus provides similar procedural guarantees to that of criminal proceedings.[196]

Those *repressive penalties* (administrative penal law) are alien to Denmark and the Netherlands that apply instead *coercive fines* as a means of achieving compliance with environmental law.[197] The United Kingdom has traditionally not recognised the power of regulators to apply sanctions directly, and criminal sanctions have only been applied in their unique form. However, the environment agency and other regulators in England and Wales were granted considerable additional powers to apply civil penalties under the Regulatory Enforcement and Sanctions Act 2008.[198] 'Civil penalties' lie in between criminal and civil law and can be used in order to provide for retribution, social condemnation, specific deterrence, general deterrence, the protection of third parties and the payment of compensation or reparation.[199] Civil penalties are thus more similar to criminal fines than private law civil damages, 'in particular because they retain a punitive element, even if their purpose is more focussed on deterrence'.[200] Moreover, civil penalties are to be distinguished

195 IMPEL Network Report (2005) above note 1, at 27.

196 Also Germany, Italy and Portugal apply stronger procedural guarantees than in the ordinary administrative procedure and thus have their system of administrative penal law more aligned with criminal law than administrative law. *Ibid.*

197 *Ibid* at 17.

198 In his advice to the British government in relation to corporate regulatory non-compliance, Richard Macrory called for sanctioning powers to be given to regulators in the case of non serious violations, instead of the heavy reliance on criminal prosecutions which was the practice then. Macrory, R. 'Regulatory Justice: Making Sanctions Effective' Final Report, November 2006. hereinafter 'Macrory Report'. The advice triggered the Draft Regulatory Enforcement and Sanctions Bill, Cabitet Office (May 2007) which went into review in the House of Lords and was finally given royal assent in 21 July 2008. For a discussion of the original Bill, see Macrory, Richard 'New Approaches to Regulatory Sanctions' (2008) 20 *Environmental Law & Management* 5, 210 and Kellett, P. 'Is the Better Regulation Agenda Producing Better Regulation?' (2008) 20 *Environmental Law & Management* 5, 210.

199 Macrory, Richard and Woods, Michael. 'Environmental Civil Penalties: A More Proportionate Response to Regulatory Breach', available at www.ucl.ac.uk/laws/environment/civil-penalty (accessed on 10 February 2015).

200 Holder, Jane and Lee, Maria. *Environmental Protection, Law and Policy* (Cambridge University Press, Cambridge 2007) at 401.

from 'administrative' and 'fixed' penalties which are enforced by a regulator, without the discretion in assessing the amount of the civil penalty. Civil penalties could hence be defined as 'a discretionary monetary sum which is imposed flexibly under the civil law rather than the criminal law, in order to achieve deterrence and reparation'.[201]

It has been suggested that in the case of civil penalties, the regulated community would be less likely to risk non-compliance in the knowledge that regulators would be better equipped to take enforcement action without having to resort to criminal proceedings. It is then argued that 'civil penalties' would fit well with the 'compliance' approach to regulation used in the UK, by avoiding the need for more severe enforcement action which might endanger ongoing relationships between the regulator and regulated.[202] Yet it is acknowledged that for any civil penalty regime to function it is vital that there is a suitable means of appeal in order to allow the independent review of the regulator's discretion. Moreover, if 'civil rights or obligations' are at issue, the guarantees of Article 6 (1) ECHR must be available in the administrative proceedings applying civil penalties.

Yet it should be noted that administrative measures of a punitive character, such as licence revocation or the shut down of an installation, were available to regulators in the UK even before the 2008 Regulatory Enforcement and Sanctions Act 2008, and they are at least as serious as – but often even more serious than – other formal sanctions.[203] These penalties could arguably be as powerful a deterrent as criminal sanctions.[204] The revocation of a licence to operate or the shut down of an installation, in particular, are extremely serious and are equivalent to the corporate 'death sentence'. Since the agencies may apply those sanctions themselves without the need of recourse to a court and the rules of administrative procedure are generally simplified, it could be argued that a system of administrative sanctions would be an effective alternative to the criminal justice system.

201 *Ibid.*

202 *Ibid* at 402.

203 However, Ogus and Abbot noted that these administrative penalties have not been used with frequency in practice. See Ogus and Abbot (2002) above note 104. See also, Bell & McGillivray (2006) note 2, chapter 9.

204 Other administrative sanctions which have been recognised to provide the desired deterrent/remedial effect are the restoration of damage, publicity of the enforcement measure or registration of the administrative penalty in commercial records of the company. See 'Study on non-criminal measures' above note 137, at 61.

2.4.1.3 Market-based Incentives and Voluntary Action

The command-and-control enforcement mechanisms discussed above specify the required or prohibited conduct, and includes prohibitions or limitations on discharge of certain pollutants or wastes, adoption of certain technologies or the setting of specific standards, attaching liability for non-compliance.[205] Market-based legal instruments, in contrast, aim to establish a price to environmental goods that reflects the true costs of pollution and natural resources use. Market-based incentives require an established market or commodity that can be traded, so the first step is that property rights are accorded under a permit system which can be traded at a later stage.

Some economists tend to take a strong view that environmental protection is better achieved in many cases through market-incentive legal mechanisms than through command-and-control measures.[206] Although the trend towards market-based instruments, deregulation and liberalisation in the 1980s and 1990s could be regarded as necessary in a globalised capitalist economy, the electricity crisis in California, the collapse of Enron in 2001 and the global financial crisis in 2007–2009 have triggered calls for stronger government control and intervention in business activities, in particular in the natural resources and financial services sectors. So unlike the general tendency towards deregulation and market-based incentives in other sectors, command-and-control is still the preferred method of regulation in natural resources management.[207]

It is expected that the law should provide adequate safeguards against companies that recklessly harm citizens, which requires regulatory measures and compensation schemes to be available to prevent and punish reckless behaviour.[208] This might be the case, for example, of a company that uses illegal sites to dispose of hazardous waste or knowingly dumps dangerous chemicals in a water basin causing environmental damage and health risks. Given the serious potential

---

205 E. Blanco and J. Razzaque, *Globalisation and Natural Resources Law*, Edward Elgar, 2011; Pereira, R. 'Environmental Regulation, Business Competitiveness and Corporate Responsibility', in K. Makuch and R. Pereira (eds.) *Environmental and Energy Law* (Wiley-Blackwell, 2012).

206 See Elkins, P. and S Speck, The impacts of environmental policy on competitiveness: the theory and evidence, in Baker, T. and Kohler (eds.) *International Competitiveness and Environmental Policies*, (Edward Elgar, 1998); Palmer, K., Oates, W., and Portney, P., (1995) Tightening Environmental Standards: The Benefit-Cost or the No-Cost Paradigm, *Journal of Economic Perspectives*, vol. 9, no.4: 119–132; Hanley, N., Jason Shogren and Ben White, *Introduction to Environmental Economics*, (OUP 2001).

207 Blanco and Razzaque (2011) *supra*.

208 Porter, M. and C. Van der Linde, 'Toward a New Conception of the Environment-Competitiveness Relationship', *Journal of Economic Perspective*, 9 (4): 97–118.

impacts of those actions, and the fact that they may cause significant identifiable harm to humans and the environment, more severe forms of command-and-control tools should be available to the public authorities.[209] On the other hand, the use of market incentives, which includes pollution taxes, deposit-refund schemes and tradable permits often allows greater flexibility and reinforces resource productivity.[210] Market incentives are also perhaps better understood by and more palatable to business leaders than are traditional elements command-and-control regulations. Moreover, market-based mechanisms are held by business and certain regulators to be the best way of establishing the best value and price attached to these compliance mechanisms in order for them to be effective.[211] Indeed, it could be argued that the mandating of specific outcomes by setting emission level targets – which is typical of command-and-control regulation – provides less incentive for innovation as it will tend to freeze the *status quo* before new regulations appear. In contrast, market incentives allow for greater flexibility, which in turn could be an incentive for innovation.[212]

In one example, there has been a shift in Brazilian environmental policy from sole reliance on command-and control regulation to embrace a wider range of market-based tools in forest protection efforts.[213] Federal Decree 6.321/2007 on 'prevention, monitoring and control of deforestation' is the

---

209 To provide an illustration of the legal response to environmental offences: in the U.S. public authorities were held responsible for allowing development, including the building of houses and schools, upon an abandoned storage dump containing 21.800 tons of toxic chemical waste (Dunphy, A. Griffiths and S Benn, 'Organizational Change for Corporate Sustainability,' Routledge 2003). In response to that infringement of EPA regulations, the US government introduced a comprehensive legislation on environmental compensation and liability (the so-called Superfund) under which both the government and corporations are deemed responsible for toxic site clean-up.

210 Pereira (2012) above note 205, at 67.

211 *Ibid.*

212 For example, in Germany an eco-labelling programme introduced in 1977 – which only allowed their display in products meeting very strict environmental criteria-led to greater energy efficiency in the case of oil and gas heating appliances and ultimately to the reduction by 30 per cent of emissions of sulphur dioxide, carbon monoxide and nitrogen oxide. Policies such as this have led Germany to maximize its export potential in the pollution control sector. See, Porter, M. *The Competitive Advantage of Nations*, New York: The Free Press, 1990.

213 See generally, Brito, B. & Barreto, P. (2011) Enforcement against Illegal Logging in the Brazilian Amazon. In: Kotze, L., Paddock, L., Qun, D., Markell, D.L., Markowitz, K.J., Zaelke, D. & Kotze, L.J. (eds.) *Compliance and Enforcement in Environmental Law: Toward More Effective Implementation* Edward Elgar Pub, pp. 449–470.

clearest example of this shift in strategy in Brazil, as it aims to implement a number of financial and market-based tools and self-regulatory measures in the forestry sector. The decree emphasizes supply-chain accountability, uses suspension of tax benefits and access to public credit as sanctions, and it requires that landowners demonstrate compliance with environmental conditions in order to access credit, thus encouraging self-regulation by producers and landowners in the Amazon region. These market-based incentives have the potential to be more efficient than classic command-and-control style regulations as they reduce the incentives for illegal activities by reducing the financial reward rather than requiring the environment agency to undertake enforcement action.

The use of these market incentives will not always be satisfactory since polluters may pass on those added costs to consumers (although this may not always be possible in the case of industries in a competitive market), who would then be effectively paying for the costs of cleaning up. This implies that the potential deterrent effect against companies going over emission targets is limited since the price of goods may be raised in order to internalise the costs of compliance with environmental regulations.[214]

Alternative approaches to laws and regulations include, for example, voluntary codes of conduct, stakeholder's guidelines and corporate social responsibility programmes. Voluntary instruments have the advantage of greater adaptability to the market and changing conditions, and could have a global reach as their application is not confined to the borders of a particular state.[215] In the 1990s the idea of corporate self-regulation grew in popularity, and corporate social responsibility and Voluntary Codes of Conduct (VCC) emerged as an alternative to the failure of states' to reach agreement on international rules to regulate multinational corporations. U.S. companies began introducing codes of conduct in the early 1990s, and the practice spread to Europe in the mid-1990s. Voluntary codes of conduct range from vague declarations of business principles applicable to international operations, to more substantive efforts at self-regulation.[216] Yet only a small proportion of codes make provision for

214 On the impact of environmental regulation on business competitiveness, see Chapter 7.

215 E. Blanco and J. Razzaque (2011) above note 205.

216 The OECD inventory of 246 codes found that 60 per cent of them referred to labour standards and 59 per cent to environmental stewardship. See OECD Codes of Conduct: An Expanded Review of their Contents: OECD Working Party of the Trade Committee, Paris, 2000; and Jenkins, R. *Corporate Codes of Conduct Self-Regulation in a Global Economy*. Technology, Business and Society Programme Paper number 2 April 2001, United Nations Research Institute for Social Development.

independent monitoring, and the underlying principles are at times drafted in vague language, making it difficult for one to assess the effectiveness of such codes.

A number of arguments have been raised for deregulation and for companies to voluntarily act to protect the environment. Businesses tend to argue that *de*regulation enhances business competitiveness: for example the requirement of environmental impact assessment leads to costs for firms. Moreover, the possibility of infringement and liability arising from non-compliance with regulations means that firms need to introduce expensive and burdensome monitoring mechanisms to guarantee the best practices from employees. This argument for deregulation is often made along political lines, in which conservative parties push the agenda for the *laissez-faire* state, while liberal parties call for stronger government intervention on business activities.[217] The 'business case' for corporate social responsibility is also made based on the argument that companies can gain competitive advantage in relation to competitors by acting voluntarily to protect the environment, regardless of the presence of environmental regulations.[218]

On the other hand, environmental regulation is also seen as a necessary instrument for creation of a level playing field in which firms operate, and thus avoiding a race to the bottom. It also ensures that at least a certain minimum threshold of environmental protection will be observed, but leaving unimpaired the ability of firms and countries to adopt higher standards. What is more, environmental regulation is accompanied by legal mechanisms of enforcement that aim to ensure that they are complied with and to punish non-compliance. So one of the main weaknesses of voluntary mechanisms is that they lack the enforcement mechanisms of prescriptive legal instruments.[219] Corporate social responsibility is also often criticised for amounting

217 This can illustrated by the calls by the conservative parties in the US at state level for the cut of the budget in Environment Departments and for reduction of environmental regulation that they regard as too burdensome to business interests. See The New York Times, 16 April 2011). See Pereira, (2012) above note 205, 67–68.

218 See e.g. Orlitzky, Marc, Frank L. Schmidt, and Sara L. Rynes, 'Corporate social and financial performance: A meta-analysis' *Organization studies* 24.3 (2003): 403–441; and Margolis, Joshua D., and James P. Walsh, 'Misery loves companies: Rethinking social initiatives by business' *Administrative science quarterly* 48.2 (2003): 268–305.

219 Although some voluntary certified schemes such as environmental management systems (such as ISO 14001) allows for third party certification, which reduces the need for all the customers to audit suppliers, and for the establishment of a *monitoring system* to ensure compliance.

to nothing more than 'green washing', i.e. it is a public relations instrument to improve a company's image.

2.5 Conclusions

This chapter has suggested that there are important rationales for criminalisation of environmental offences. In particular, this chapter has suggested that there are important utilitarian (as well as retributivist) grounds for the more serious environmental offences to be criminalised. Moreover, in line with the fair labelling principle,[220] as the awareness of environmental issues increase around the globe, there is a pressing need to provide a stamp of moral disapproval from society against those serious violations of environmental law by categorising them as criminal. In this vein, the European Court of Human Rights is prepared to consider certain regulatory or disciplinary infringements as 'criminal in nature' depending on the seriousness of the offence and the nature or severity of the sanction applicable. Therefore the decriminalisation of certain types of serious environmental offences together with the application of particularly serious penalties under the administrative procedural law of the member states of the Council of Europe could be found to contravene Article 6 of the ECHR.[221] It is clear that the court aims to strike a balance between the effective application of administrative sanctions on the one hand, and the need for observing the rules of fair trial, the rule of law and other procedural guarantees of the accused, on the other.

Yet it must be reminded that the trend towards decriminalisation of minor offences in several European countries may be in the interest of the accused who may wish to remove some types of conduct from the stigma of criminality.[222] But from the perspective of environmental protection, the decriminalisation or deregulation trend in some countries may be problematic. For example, it has been suggested that this may explain the increasing infiltration of criminal

220 This principle is directed at the legislature and suggests that offences are subdivided and labelled so as to represent fairly the nature and magnitude of the law-breaking. Ashworth (2006) above note 5, at 88.

221 In paragraph 49 of *Özturk* the Court stated that 'The Convention is not opposed to States, in the performance of their task as guardians of the public interest, both creating or maintaining a distinction between different categories of offences for the purposes of their domestic law and drawing the dividing line, *but it does not follow that the classification thus made by the States is decisive for the purposes of the Convention*' (emphasis added).

222 Ovey, Clare And White, Robin, *Jacobs & White: The European Convention on Human Rights* (OUP, Oxford 2006) at 161.

organisations in the waste disposal sector in Italy.[223] Moreover, even if regarded in countries as 'economic' or 'regulatory' crimes, non-compliance with environmental regulations can lead to substantial cost savings for businesses which may place them in a competitive advantage vis-à-vis their competitors and thus, as in the field of competition law, an appropriately stringent and effective penalty for violations of environmental law may be needed.[224]

Furthermore, from the discussion above it would seem reasonable to conclude that voluntary codes and guidelines are complementary, rather than alternatives, to compliance with environmental regulations. So both instruments must co-exist in order to optimize the level of environmental protection. Policy-makers must establish a regulatory framework that creates a level playing field and the necessary threshold of environmental protection, depending on the seriousness and urgency of action needed to address the environmental problem. This provides a guarantee that companies do not lose out by acting unilaterally to guarantee a minimum level of environmental protection. The main benefactor of voluntary codes or CSR strategies – even if ultimately motivated by the wish to improve a company's image – is the environment itself.

Although there are strong arguments for the more serious violations of environmental law to be criminalised, it could be argued that for the sake of efficiency (and effectiveness) civil and administrative sanctions should play a stronger role in the environmental field. This is in line with the definition of the harm principle and other theories of criminalisation discussed above – the criminal law is to be used as a last resort and only when other sanctions could not achieve the same result at lesser costs to society. Thus minimalism demands stronger justifications for criminalisation than when civil or administrative strategies are used.[225] This analysis will be further developed in Chapter 7 of this book, in which the effectiveness of criminal law enforcement is compared with that of other enforcement options, in particular administrative law enforcement.

---

223 See Amendola, Gianfranco 'Need for a Strengthening of Criminal Environmental Law? The Italian Case' in Comte, Françoise and Kramer, Ludwig (eds.) *Environmental Crime in Europe: Rules of Sanctions* (Europa Law Publishing, Groningen 2004).

224 The different liability regimes can also be regarded as complementary, as there is no general prohibition in international law for accumulation of penalties of a different nature for the same offence.

225 Ashworth (2006) above note 5, at 31.

CHAPTER 3

The Internationalisation of Environmental Criminal Law: Rationales, Basis and Prospects

3.1 Introduction

This chapter assesses the rationales, basis and prospects for the internationalisation of environmental criminal law, discussing the extent to which existing international legal frameworks could be used to prevent and punish environmental crime. It analyses in particular the potential scope for an extension of the current jurisdiction of the International Criminal Court (ICC) over environmental crime; the role of multilateral environmental agreements (MEA s) in leading countries to implement criminal measures for the protection of the environment; as well as the existing international legal frameworks aimed at facilitating interstate cooperation to combat environmental crime.

3.2 Rationales for the Internationalisation of Environmental Criminal Law

It is generally recognized that transnational crime does not recognize national borders and states may pursue, bilaterally or on a regional/multilateral basis, measures to combat crimes as a counterweight to reduced border controls. Hence concerted international action is generally more effective to deal with common security threats, in particular in the case of crimes which are necessarily 'international' in nature (such as cybercrimes). Globalization and the consequent loosening of border controls diminishes the ability of nation states to be the sole guardians of values protected by criminal law as the principal means to control criminal activities. These transnational criminal activities weaken the ability of states to maintain security within their own boundaries. The individual failure of nation states to combat crime (in particular transnational crime) calls for forms of police and judicial cooperation in criminal matters between states, as recognized in several international and regional agreements (for example, on extraction and mutual assistance on criminal matters[1]).

1 See e.g. the 1957 The European Convention on Extradition, ETS 24, 359 UNTS 273; 1959 European Convention on Mutual Assistance in Criminal Matters, ETS 30; 1972 European

 | DOI 10.1163/9789004195882_004

The fact that criminals are able to exploit the differences in legislation and legal enforcement techniques in different states to their benefit is a main driver for the harmonisation of both substantive and procedural criminal law. In general, the diversity of national penal systems allows criminals to select the legal system that is regarded as less effective and use them as sanctuaries or safe havens.[2]

Furthermore, harmonisation of criminal legislation could be regarded as a means to facilitate police and judicial cooperation in criminal matters. Classic extradition agreements require double-criminality in both executing and issuing states, so harmonisation of criminal law would facilitate the operation of those agreements because both states would have criminalised similar offences.[3] So one of the main justifications for legal harmonisation is that the comparability of legal norms is fundamental for an effective transnational crime control.[4]

Yet the harmonisation of criminal legislation could also be regarded as an objective in itself. Indeed, some environmental offences have global or transboundary effects (for example, the illegal trade in endangered species or the illegal trade in ozone-depleting substances). Because of their global or transboundary implications, it is suggested that eco-criminals should be punished with a similar degree of severity wherever these offences are committed or their effects are felt. Moreover, it could be argued that certain animal and plant species and habitats, especially endangered species or ecosystems,

Convention on the Transfer of Proceedings in Criminal Matters, ETS 73, 72 UNTS 185. See generally, S. Peers, *EU Justice and Home Affairs Law*, (OUP, 2011), Ch. 9.

2 See Weyembergh, A. 'Approximation of Criminal Laws, the Constitutional Treaty and the Hague Programme' (2005) 42 *Common Market Law Review* at 1579.

3 However, as will be further discussed in Chapter 4, the European Arrest Warrant and other EU instruments based on the principle of mutual recognition do not require double-criminality for certain crimes, including environmental crimes, when punishable by a maximum custodial sentence or detention order of at least 3 years.

4 For example, the lack of a common definition of crime may have an impact on crime statistics, as the collection of data and statistics depends on the legal categorisation given by each legal system and the comparability of the figures may be compromised by variations. See Harding, C. 'European Regimes of Crime Control: Objectives, Legal Bases and Accountability' 7 *MJ* 3 (2000) p. 227. The Commission set up an expert group to remedy the lack of EU statistics on crime and criminal justice (Press Release, IP/06/1089) (8 August 2006). See Herlin-Karnell, E. (2007) 'Recent Developments in the Area of European Criminal Law' 14 *Maastricht Journal of European and Comparative Law* 1, at 20.

should be regarded as a 'common concern'[5] or 'common heritage' of mankind,[6] therefore calling for strengthened international and national regulatory measures.

Another rationale for the criminalisation of environmental harm at the global level is connected to the fact that the conservation of natural resources found in the so-called 'global commons' i.e. areas that are beyond national jurisdiction such as the high seas, transcends individual harm and concerns the protection of collective interests. As international environmental law incorporates *erga omnes* obligations, it includes obligations imposed on states towards the international community as a whole.[7] In the *Seabed Chamber Advisory Opinion*, the International Tribunal on the Law of the Sea (ITLOS)

---

5 The Preamble to the 1992 UN Framework Convention on Climate Change states that change of earth's climate is a 'common concern of mankind' and reaffirms 'the principle of sovereignty of States in international cooperation in addressing climate change'. United Nations Framework Convention on Climate Change, 1771 UNTS 107 ('UNFCCC') opened for signature on 9 June 1992 in Rio de Janeiro during the Conference on Environment and Development (UNCED) entered into force on 21 March 1994. Moreover, the UN General Assembly has declared that the global climate is 'the common concern of mankind'. See G.A. Res. 43/53 1 UN Doc. A/RES/43/53 (Dec 6, 1988). See also, Frederic Megret, The Problem of an International Criminal Law of the Environment, (2011) *Columbia Journal of Environmental Law* (vol. 36:2) at 245.

6 See e.g. Recital 2 to the Agreement on the Implementation of Part XI of the UN Convention on the Law of the Sea (adopted in 10 December 1982; in force on 16 November 1994). The principle of common heritage of mankind is expressly or implicitly recognized in a number of international environmental agreements. For example, Recital 3 of the Preamble to the UN *Convention on Biological Diversity*, 1760 UNTS 79 (1992) affirms that 'the conservation of biological diversity is a common concern of mankind'. Moreover, Article 2 of the *Ramsar Convention on Wetlands of International Importance Especially at Waterfowl Habitat*, 996 UNTS 245 (1971) requires state parties to designate within their territory a 'List of Wetlands of International Importance'. There are a number of international agreements aimed at establishing rules on conservation of cultural and natural heritage and landscape. See, in particular, the *Convention for the Protection of World Cultural and Natural Heritage* 1037 UNTS 151, Art. 2. See further, Francesco Francioni (ed.), '*The 1972 World Heritage Convention, Oxford Commentaries on International Law*' (OUP, 2008).

7 For example, two dissenting opinions in the ICJ *East Timor* case took the view that the principle of permanent sovereignty over natural resources has legally binding consequences and embraced the view that permanent sovereignty is one of the essential principles of contemporary international law with *erga omnes* character. See *East Timor (Portugal v Australia) (Judgment)* [1995] ICJ Rep 90, 142, 197–9, 204 (Judge Weeramantry), 264, 270, 276 (Judge Skubiszewski) [1980]. See further, Per Magnus Wijman, *Managing the Global Commons*, 36 Int' Org. 511; and Maurizio Ragazzi, *The Concept of International Obligations Erga Omnes* 1 (Oxford, 2000).

upheld its recognition of the '*erga omnes* character of the obligations relating to the preservation of the environment of the high seas and the Area'.[8]

Moreover, natural resources in the global commons are *res nullius*[9] and hence are not private property or under the jurisdictional control of any state, which also means that these resources are not subject to private vigilance from either States or individuals. Therefore, unless cooperative frameworks are in place to govern the extraction of the natural resources in these common spaces, open competition between states or between private operators could ultimately have the effect of depleting these resources against the interests of present as well as future generations.[10] In 1968 Hardin famously called this phenomenon the 'tragedy of the commons'.[11] The 'global commons' are thus especially vulnerable to environmental damage and therefore require international cooperation for the effective enforcement of environmental law, arguably also through criminal-law cooperation frameworks and sanctions.[12]

---

8 *Responsibilities and obligations of States sponsoring persons and entities with respect to activities in the Area* (Feb 2011) (Request for Advisory Opinion submitted to the Seabed Disputes Chamber, case no. 17, International Tribunal on the Law of the Sea), para. 180. See also, P. Sands and J. Peel, *Principles of International Environmental Law* (CUP, 2012).

9 '*Res nullius*' are resources which belong to no one, and therefore exploitable by anyone, for example fisheries in high seas. This is to be contrasted with *res communis or 'common heritage'* – the resources could be exploitable by anyone, but only with the permission of the world community and upon such conditions as the institutions representing that community (i.e. the International Sea Bed Authority, in the context of deep seabed mining) lays down. See also, Pereira, R., 'The Exploration and Exploitation of Energy Resources in International Law', in K. Makuch and R. Pereira (eds.) *Environmental and Energy Law* (Wiley-Blackwell, 2012).

10 On the elaboration of the rights of future generations, *see* e.g. UN GA Resolution 35/36 on International Development Strategy for Third UN Development Decade 1980 (para. 41) which states that 'Natural resources are to be used to maintain optimum sustainable productivity and living resources must not be utilised in excess of their natural capacity for regeneration'. See also, the 1997 UNESCO *Declaration on Responsibilities of Present Generations toward Future Generations*. In the 1996 ICJ *Nuclear Weapons Test* case, the dissenting opinion of judge Weeramantry argued that 'it is imperative that the court takes account of the unique characteristics of nuclear weapons, in particular *their ability to cause damage to generations to come*'(emphasis added).

11 See G. Hardin (1968), 'The Tragedy of the Commons', *Science*, 162(1968):1243–1248. It must be noted that the ocean space which is currently considered high seas has reduced significantly since states were given the power to claim exclusive economic zones (EEZ s) under 1982 UN *Convention on the Law of the Sea* (UNCLOS). It is estimated that the high seas currently represents about 60% of the ocean space. *See* Rothwell and Stephens, *International Law of the Sea*, Hart Publishing, 2010.

12 *See* Stephen C. McCaffrey, 'Crimes against the environment', in Bassiouri, C. '*International Criminal Law: Sources, Subjects and Contents* (Vol.1)', (BRILL, 2008) at 985.

For law enforcement authorities, one of the main challenges remains how to monitor and enforce international and national laws and regulations in the high seas. This includes the fact that the enforcement of environmental law in the high seas is limited by the principle the exclusive jurisdiction of flag states; and the unwillingness of flags-of-convenience states to enforce environmental standards on their own vessels in the high seas.[13] In this regard, some international agreements contain 'policing provisions' allowing signatory parties to take action on the spot to enforce the rules of the agreement, but they are often constrained to a limited geographical area, or to a specific environmental resource or medium.[14] This is the case of a number of regional fisheries agreements which tend to contain enforcement provisions requiring parties to oversee the management of shared fish stocks; whilst recognising that interstate concerted action and common management are necessary to give effect to the conservation of those high seas resources.[15] Yet there are a number of weaknesses in the enforcement provisions present in specific regional fisheries agreements, including the fact that they do not generally apply to third-country vessels.[16]

13 *See* further, Tanaka, Y., *'The International Law of the Sea'* (CUP, 2012); and Rothwell and Stephens, *International Law of the Sea*, (Hart Publishing, 2010).

14 *See* e.g. the 1911 *Convention for the Preservation of Fur Seals in the North Pacific*, articles 1 and 7; and the 1937 *International Agreement for the Regulation of Whaling*, article 1.

15 There are are presently sixteen Regional Fisheries Management Organisations, which are the main governance structures for interstate cooperation for conservation of fisheries (they protect the Bluefin tuna, the Patagonian toothfish, among other migratory, straddling and endangered fish stocks in the high seas). In one example of enforcement action under a RFMO, the International Commission for Conservation of the Atlantic Tunas (ICCAT) has attempted to actively manage and conserve fish stocks through compliance measures including implementing an on-board observer program and maintaining a list of IUU vessels. The 1995 UN *Fish Stocks Agreement* is particularly noteworthy (it presently has 78 parties, including the EU) as it requires states to cooperate in the high seas via RFMO s (regional fisheries management organisations). See *Agreement for the Implementation of the Provisions of The United Nations Convention On The Law Of The Sea of 10 December 1982 Relating to the Conservation and Management of Straddling Fish Stocks and Highly Migratory Fish Stocks* (1995).

16 For example, the International Commission for Conservation of the Atlantic Tunas (ICCAT) relies on member countries to implement and enforce management policies. Although they can board and inspect foreign vessels fishing in the RFMO s regulated areas, they cannot detain and prosecute vessels in the high seas without the consent of the flag state. One often overlooked but related problem is that some RFMO s member states are not always willing to enforce obligations against their own vessels. Another limitation is that RFMO s can only attract a limited number of members (states must have a 'special

Despite the rationales discussed above which suggest that there are a number of reasons for states to pursue the internationalisation of environmental criminal law, there is a belief shared by some states that criminal law reflects part of their legal culture and is a symbol of state sovereignty. This leads to the fear of loss of sovereignty in this sensitive area to supranational or intergovernmental institutions.[17] Sovereignty over criminal laws then is raised as a fundamental argument for states to resist the harmonisation of (environmental) criminal law. Although it is true that many states have agreed to forfeit a degree of their sovereignty to the international or European legal orders in the interest of international cooperation, they certainly did not intend that those supranational or intergovernmental mechanisms of criminal-law cooperation would compromise their ability to determine their own future and develop their criminal laws according to their national aspirations. National sovereignty over criminal law is arguably an essential element of the state entity and identity, since to secure its stability and cohesion every nation is dependent on the criminal law's ability to balance society's conflicting interests (through its unique implications for liability and coercive mechanisms of enforcement).

Then, one could wonder, what about the recent developments in international criminal law? Are they not a sign that states are willing to give away their sovereignty over criminal matters? Firstly, it should be noted that the coming into force of the Rome Statute on 1 July 2002 and the consequent creation of the International Criminal Court[18] affects states' sovereignty over criminal matters only in a very limited context, namely that of those crimes listed in the Court's Statute. Moreover, those crimes are, purposively, restricted to serious crimes impacting on the peace and security of mankind (although a connection with an armed conflict, as seen in the cases of the crimes of genocide or crimes against humanity, is not necessary).[19] Since the Rome Statute does not cover many other international crimes, such as drug trafficking, money laundering, or illegal logging[20] – nor, obviously, any other strictly 'national' crimes –

---

interest' in the relevant fish stocks to become a member of the RFMO). See generally, M. Fitzmaurice, 'Natural Resources Management: Protecting Fisheries in the 21st Century', in E. Blanco and J. Razzaque (eds.), *Natural Resources and the Green Economy: Redefining the Challenges for People, States and Corporations*, Martinus Nijhoff/BRILL, 2012. On law enforcement against illegal, unreported and unregulated (IUU) fisheries, see Chapter 6.

17 *See* G.J.M. Corstens, 'Criminal Law in the First Pillar?' (2003) 11 *European Journal of Crime, Criminal Law and Criminal Justice* 131.

18 1998 Rome Statute of the International Criminal Court, 37 ILM 1002 (1998).

19 *See* A. Cassese, *International Criminal Law* (OUP, 2003) at 24.

20 In the context of an armed conflict, 'pillage' could be considered a war crime. See e.g. Article 4 (f) of the ICTR Statute.

it suggests that consensus would not be easily reached on the harmonisation of international criminal law in those areas or that they are not perceived as posing a threat to the peace and security of mankind. Moreover, the ICC applies the complementary principle, that is, it should only exercise its jurisdiction when states are unable or unwilling to prosecute.[21] This suggests that states are not willing to compromise significantly their sovereignty over criminal matters even in the limited context of the international crimes which currently fall under the jurisdiction of the ICC.

Other rationales for criminalization of environmental law at the international level are similar to those raised for criminalization at the national level, as was discussed in Chapter 2. They revolve around retributive grounds (linked to the seriousness of the offence) and utilitarian grounds (i.e. deterrence and criminalization as means to ensure the effectiveness of the enforcement system).[22] The utilitarian rationales for criminalisation include the fact that the criminal law offers potentially the strongest deterrent effect against eco-criminals; and the fact that some criminal non-monetary penalties (such as imprisonment) cannot be seen as a cost of doing business or passed on to consumers; and therefore they have a stronger deterrent effect than penalties of a civil or administrative nature.

Yet it could be argued that the main role of international criminal law is to act as a punitive system and therefore to fulfil a retributive role.[23] In contrast, it is generally accepted that international environmental law is most effective when it succeeds in preventing harm from occurring in the first place, rather than repairing the damage or punishing the wrongful act after it occurs.[24] This

21 *See* Rome Statute, *supra*, Preamble, para. 10, and art. 1. This is unlike the approach taken by the *ad hoc* International Criminal Tribunal for the former Yugoslavia (ICTY) and the International Criminal Tribunal for Rwanda (ICTR). See also Cassese, above note 19, at 351.

22 Moreover, there are secondary functions of international criminal law, which include: (a) the creation of historical records of international crimes (b) the education of present and future generations. *See* Rene Provost, 'International Criminal Environmental Law', in Good-Gill, G. and Talmon, S (eds.) *The Reality of International Law: Essays in Honour of Ian Brownlie*, (Oxford 1999).

23 See, for example, *Aleksovski*, ICTY A Ch. 24.3.2000, para 185 '(…) a sentence of the International Tribunal should make plain the condemnation of the international community of the behaviour in question and show "that the international community was not ready to tolerate serious violations of international humanitarian law and human rights"'.

24 *See* also, McLaughlin, Robert 'Improving Compliance: Making Non-State International Actors Responsible for Environmental Crimes', 11 *Colorado Journal of International Law and Policy*, 2000; Regina Rauxloh, 'The Role of International Criminal Law in Environmental

can be seen in many pollution-control regimes in national legal systems which implement integrated pollution prevention and control (IPCC) strategies with the view of implementing preventative measures, rather than end-of-pipe solutions or measures aimed to rectify environmental damage after pollution discharges occur.[25] So there is an apparent paradox in that the mainly preventive nature of international environmental law should be complemented by the essentially punitive nature of international criminal law.[26] The extension of the ICC jurisdiction over international environmental crimes could hence be criticised since it would necessarily be 'punitive, ex post facto, and to some degree restitutional, rather than preventive in nature'.[27]

Notwithstanding those constraints, increasing deterrence and therefore compliance *ex ante* could be regarded also as one of the rationales for extending the jurisdiction of the International Criminal Court to include international environmental crimes beyond the context of war crimes. In fact, the ICC Statute itself recognises a role for deterrence in international criminal law.[28] In a similar vein, the International Criminal Tribunal for the former Yugoslavia (ICTY) came to the conclusion that deterrence plays an important part in international penal responsibility, i.e. the prevention of future violations of the same norm; in addition to reprobation and retribution, i.e. the expression of societal condemnation of the offence and to satisfy the victim's need for justice.[29] Moreover, the UN Security Council declared, in connection with the ICTY, that the prosecution and punishment of the guilty would contribute to the prevention of future human rights violations.[30] Likewise, arguments surrounding deterrence have been raised as one of the justifications for the adoption of civil liability regimes under a number of international environmental agreements aimed at the reparation and compensation of environmental damage, as they increase the likelihood that the operator will be held accountable

---

Protection' in F. Botchway (ed.) *Natural Resource Investment and Africa's Development*, Edward Elgar, 2011.

25 See e.g. the EU Directive on Industrial Emissions (COM [2007] 844 Final). See further, Chapter 6.

26 Rauxloh (2011) above note 24.

27 McLaughlin (2000) *supra* at 389.

28 See Preambluar para. 5 of the Statute which states that parties are '[d]etermined to put an end impunity for the perpetrators of these crimes and thus contribute to prevention of such crimes'.

29 See Case No. IT-96-22-A, 7 October 1997, Prosecutor v. *Erdemovic*.

30 *See* Security Council Resolution 827 of 25 May 1993 UN Doc. S/Res/827 (1993). See further, Werle and Jessberger, *Principles of International Criminal Law*, Third ed. (OUP, 2014) at 37.

for environmental damage.[31] It is expected that the jurisdiction of the ICC over international environmental crimes would send a strong message through the exemplary publicity that follows from punishment and, additionally, it could lead to the adoption of higher and tougher penalties than those commonly applied at the national level, and thus to increased deterrence. On the other hand, it is not clear whether the jurisdiction of an international criminal tribunal such as the ICC would indeed have stronger deterrent effects on international environmental crime than the jurisdiction of national courts (armed with powers established under multilateral criminal-law cooperation agreements) already does, in particular in light of the complementary nature of the ICC jurisdiction in relation to national courts.[32] However, the harmonization of international environmental crimes under the ICC Statute in itself could be a welcome development, in particular if 'a culture of accountability is created, and domestic courts play their part in prosecution of international crimes as the drafters of the ICC Statute intended (...)'.[33]

3.3 The Rationales for Regionalisation of Environmental Criminal Law

The willingness of a group of states to pursue integration in criminal matters on a regional basis may arise for a number of reasons. In particular, the 'regionalization' of national criminal justice systems could arise from the willingness

31 See e.g. International Convention on Civil Liability for Oil Pollution Damage (CLC) (adopted in 27 November 1992; entry into force 30 May 1996) ('Oil Pollution CLC 1992') and the International Convention on the Establishment of an international Fund for Compensation for Oil Pollution Damage (1992); the Vienna Convention Civil Liability for Nuclear Damage (adopted on 21 May1963, entry into force on 17 November 1977); the Paris Convention on Nuclear Third Party Liability (1960); and the Nagoya – Kuala Lumpur Supplementary Protocol on Liability and Redress to the Cartagena Protocol (2010) (not yet in force). See also, Council of Europe Lugano Convention Civil Liability for Environmental Damage (1993), not yet in force.

32 *See* Rome Statute, above note 18, Preamble, para. 10, and article 1. In addition to treaties which provide for mutual legal assistance and extradition between States in respect of crimes with a foreign element' other treaties require States to criminalise certain types of conduct by creating offences in their domestic law, and to bring criminals to justice when they are found in their territory or to extradite them to States that will prosecute. *See* Neil Bolster, 'Transnational Criminal Law?' (2003) 14 *European Journal of International Law* 953 at 967–77.

33 R. Cryer. H. Friman, D. Robinson and E. Wilmshurst, 'An Introduction to International Criminal Law and Procedure'(second ed., CUP, 2011) at 28.

of a regional group of states to form a concerted response to a common security threat (for example terrorism, child pornography or human trafficking). Another reason for states to pursue regionalisation in criminal matters is with the view of adoption of effective and coherent regional measures for implementation of international agreements that establish common definition of offences or penalties.[34] For example, the European Commission justified the adoption of the EU directive and framework decision on criminal sanctions for shipping pollution on need to implement effectively the MARPOL standards[35] on enforcement against shipping pollution discharges.[36] It has been suggested then that 'the global and regional approaches can supplement each other, while (...) the regional approaches take into account specific circumstances of a particular region'.[37] Depending on the type of pollution and area of pollution, a regional approach would be regarded as appropriate. Hence in some circumstances, a regional or national legal framework would be preferable to a global regulatory framework since the interests and impacts pertaining to certain environmental problems will tend to be regional or national. In particular, the existence of regional machineries established under some regional organisations or programmes, such as those governed by UNEP for marine environment protection, arguably weaken the case for a global treaty regime.[38] These regional machineries are already in place and could better address the intricacies and the relevant interests pertaining to these regional seas. This suggests that concerted action at the regional or national levels would better respond to certain environmental challenges.

---

34 See, for example, the 2000 Palermo Convention Against Transnational Organized Crime, 40 ILM 335 (adopted 15 November 2001; in force 29 September 2003); which has influenced the adoption of the EU Framework Decision on organised crime. See Council Framework Decision on the Fight Against Organised Crime of 24 October 2008 (O.J. L300/42, 11.11.2008).

35 Convention on the Prevention of Pollution from Ships, 12 ILM 1319 (MARPOL 1973/1978).

36 Recital (3) of the Preamble to the ship-source pollution directive (2005).

37 M. Fitzmaurice, *International Legal Problems of the Environmental Protection of the Baltic Sea*, (Springer, 1992) at 17.

38 For example, as regards pollution arising from offshore seabed activities, the UN Commission on Sustainable Development, which acts within the UN Economic and Social Council (ECOSOC), after noting the outcome of an international expert meeting on environmental practices in offshore oil and gas activities held in 1997, recommended that the primary focus of action on the environmental aspects of offshore oil and gas operations should continue to be at the national, subregional and regional levels. See Decision 7/1, Report of the IMO to the Conference on Sustainable Development at its seventh session, A/53/456, para. 258. See also, *Report of the Secretary General on the Oceans and the Law of the Sea*, UN Doc. A/57/57 (2002) para. 406.

Moreover, the very nature of the regional institutional arrangement – in the case of the EU, a common market with limited border controls – may facilitate cross-border crimes and hence a regional solution would be called for. Indeed, when the European Union decided to abolish border controls under the 1986 Single European Act (SEA) in an ambitious programme to complete the single market by 1992 (where goods, persons, services and capital would move freely), it recognized that flanking policies would need to be introduced in order to combat cross-border crime.[39]

There is also an indication that regional cooperation could facilitate the development of common rules and principles in criminal matters because of the relative homogeneity of the interests or outlooks of actors, which could ensure a more efficient or equitable implementation of the relevant norms. This view assumes that cultural and/or economic similarities are more likely to exist within a region and hence that it could better ensure the legitimacy of the regulations and that they are understood and applied in a coherent way.[40] It is thus suggested that as a matter of law and policy, it may often be more efficient to proceed by way of taking a regional approach.

The main advantages of 'regionalization' of environmental criminal law (in contrast to 'internationalization' of criminal law) could be summarised as follows:[41]

(a) the likelihood of being able to reach agreement on common definitions of the elements of the offences;
(b) the greater deterrent effect in relation to transboundary conduct;
(c) the contribution towards achieving greater consistency in legal provisions;
(d) the existence of regional extradition and mutual assistance in criminal matters arrangements which could contribute to effective investigation and prosecution.

---

39 Even though the abolition of border controls was initially developed outside the context of European Union law (the so-called 'Schengen Acquis'), it was later incorporated into EU law by the Treaty of Amsterdam. See the 1985 Schengen Agreement and the 1990 Convention on the Application of the Schengen Agreement of 14th June 1985.

40 See M. Kostenniemi, Martti and P. Leino, 'Fragmentation of International Law? Postmodern Anxieties', (2002) 15 *LJIL* 553.

41 See International Centre for Criminal Law Reform and Criminal Justice Policy, '*International Meeting of Experts on the Use of Criminal Sanctions for the Protection of the Environment: Internationally, Domestically, Regionally*', (1994), available at www.icclr.law.ubc.ca/Publications/Reports/Portland2.PDF (accessed on 10 February 2015).

Hence a number of 'pragmatic' reasons could be given for regional integration in criminal matters. Point (a) above implies that it is easier to achieve harmonization at the regional level than at the international level, where agreement on the common definitions of the elements of the offences is less likely to be found. Points (a), (b) and (c) are closely related: if there is greater consistency among the legal provisions of the member states, it will be more difficult for criminals to cross borders and remain unaffected. This is so, as suggested by point (d), in particular because instruments for the cooperation in the investigation and prosecution of crimes are more likely to be found at the regional setting.

In the European Union context, the reasons for harmonization of criminal law can be traced back to the Treaty on European Union (TEU, 1993) as amended by the Lisbon Treaty in 2009. There are both ideological reasons – the TEU mentions the Union's aim to 'promote peace, its value and the well-being of its peoples'[42] and its contribution towards 'solidarity and mutual respect among people'[43] and pragmatic reasons for this – the need to facilitate the free movement of persons within Europe by establishing an area of freedom, security and justice.[44] The European Commission itself has justified its proposal for a directive on environmental crimes mainly on pragmatic grounds, rather than alluding to broader ideological arguments.[45] There is no doubt though that there are ideological reasons underlying the Commission's programme of harmonisation of criminal law, as seen in a Commission Green Paper on Approximation of Penal Law which emphasises ideological reasons for harmonisation, such as 'giving the general public a shared sense of justice'.[46] So one cannot understate the importance of ideological and symbolic arguments for harmonization of penal law, including the desire to have a new and unified law as a symbol of a new and unified statehood, which were used similarly as grounds for national codifications of penal law in the Nineteenth century.[47]

---

42 Art. 3 (1) TFEU. See also Point 15 of the Vienna Action Plan which highlights a 'shared sense of justice'. *See* Action Plan of the Council and the Commission on How Best to Implement the Provisions of the Treaty of Amsterdam on an Area of Freedom, Security, 31999Y0123(01), (1998), para. 15.

43 Art. 3 (5) TEU.

44 See Art. 3 (2) TEU.

45 See further, Chapter 7.

46 European Commission Green Paper on the Approximation, Mutual Recognition and Enforcement of Criminal Sanctions in the European Union, Brussels 30.04.2004 COM (2004) 334 final pp. 10–11.

47 J. Spencer, 'Why is the Harmonisation of Penal Law necessary?', in A. Klip and H. van der Wilt (eds.) *Harmonisation and Harmonising Measures in Criminal Law* (2002), 43.

This range of pragmatic and ideological rationales surrounding the need for harmonisation of criminal laws can illustrated by the Dutch reluctance to accept any outside interference in its liberal laws on the use of cannabis. One argument which is typically made in this context is that countries should retain their sovereignty over their criminal laws, the most severe mechanism of interference by the State in the matter of individual liberties.[48] Hence it might be difficult to argue that the EU should be given powers to constrain Dutch liberal attitudes by requiring the Netherlands to criminalize the use of cannabis. However, it is possible to argue that any EU attempt to restrict the Dutch legislation on cannabis would be justified on the grounds that there are possible cross-border effects of the Dutch liberal policies. For instance, German or Belgian nationals could buy and smuggle drugs from the Netherlands into their home countries which could pose an extra burden on their healthcare systems in connection with the treatment of drug addiction or other drug-related health problems. Hence the *transnational* nature of some crimes is a particularly strong justification for legislative harmonization.[49]

Crucially, cooperation in criminal matters at the EU level is regarded as necessary in order to ensure that individuals do not escape prosecution simply by exercising their free movement rights. This has been termed an *auxiliary function* of the approximation of European criminal law – that is, approximation as a tool to support judicial co-operation in the field of criminal law – which is regarded as perhaps one the most important goals of the harmonization programme.[50] The differences in criminal (substantive and procedural) laws in the EU member states undermines the principle of free movement of persons since 'people travelling abroad should be confident that existing standards [in criminal proceedings] offer equivalent protection whatever the Member State so as not to impede their free movement for fear of encountering a system operating lower standards'.[51] However, it should be noted that since the Treaty of Amsterdam – and in particular following the entry into force of the Lisbon Treaty in 2009 – a number of EU instruments are devoted to approximation as

48 For a discussion see E. Berkman, 'Sacrificed Sovereignty? Dutch Soft Drug Policy in the Spectre of Europe Without Borders', (1996) 19 *Boston College International and Comparative Law Review* 173–185, at 180.

49 However, as will be discussed in Chapter 5, 'transnationality' is not a requirement for the EU to harmonize all types of criminal offences in the member states (see Art. 83 (2) TFEU).

50 Weyembergh, A. 'Approximation of Criminal Laws, the Constitutional Treaty and the Hague Programme' (2005) 42 *Common Market Law Review*, at 1583.

51 Commission of the European Communities, Consultation Document, European Commission's Green Paper on Procedural Safeguards for Suspects and defendants in criminal proceedings throughout the European Union, (2003).

an autonomous goal, showing that 'approximation is slowly gaining some independence from judicial cooperation mechanisms'.[52]

More generally, the regionalisation of criminal law arguably could be regarded as a product of the fragmentation of international criminal law. Indeed, the development of EU criminal law could be regarded as an example of (institutional) fragmentation of international criminal law. In its Fifty-Eighth Session, the International Law Commission analyses the notion of legal 'regionalism' and the extent to which legal regional integration is a reflection of the fragmentation of international law, stressing the role played by regional systems such as the Council of Europe and European Union institutions in the development of international law.[53] To the extent that those regional systems have developed general principles and rules which may at times develop, complement or diverge from those upheld by other international institutions, it is suggested that international law becomes fragmented. The rise in the number of regional *fora* engaged in the formulation of international regulation is also recognized in the literature as one of the causes of fragmentation of international law.[54] By implication, a similar relationship could be found between international criminal law (as a branch of international law) and European Union criminal law (as a branch of European Union law): EU criminal law could be regarded as an example of fragmentation of international criminal law to the extent that distinctive rules and principles have been developed for the EU member states, as a regional block, to cooperate in criminal matters. It is important to emphasize however that the idea that EU criminal law could be considered a fragmented part of international criminal law is more telling in the case of horizontal international criminal law or 'transnational' criminal law (i.e. the law on extradition and mutual assistance), than in the case of 'vertical' international criminal – i.e. the codification by the ICC of the core international crimes. Indeed, it would be more difficult to perceive EU criminal law as a fragmented part international criminal law in the 'vertical' sense. In that sense it is rather a different body of law, with different rules regulating different interests, as the international crimes codified by the ICC do not correspond in substance to the crimes harmonised at the European level.[55]

---

52 Weyembergh, above note 50, at 1583. See Article 83 (2) TFEU.

53 See M. Koskenniemi, The Fragmentation of International Law: Difficulties arising from the Diversification and Expansion of International Law, UN Doc. A/CN.4/L.682 (2006).

54 See e.g. G. Hafner, 'Pros and Cons Ensuing from Fragmentation of International Law', (2004) 25 *Michigan Journal of International Law* 849.

55 *See* Pereira, R. 'The Regionalisation of Criminal Law – The Example of European Criminal Law' in L. van den Herik and C. Stahn (eds.), *The Diversification and Fragmentation of International Criminal Law*, Martinus Nijhoff Publishers/Brill, 2012.

But beyond the mechanisms for interstate criminal law cooperation in criminal matters (in the horizontal sense), could international criminal law in the vertical sense establish the jurisdiction of an international court or tribunal over environmental crimes? If so, what would be the basis for international criminal liability for environmental damage? Should the International Criminal Court have jurisdiction over environmental crimes in the peacetime context? These are the questions to be addressed in the next sections of this chapter.

3.4 The Basis for Environmental Criminal Liability under International Law

International enforcement is understood as the right to take measures to ensure the fulfilment of international legal obligations or to obtain a ruling from an appropriate international court, tribunal, or an organ within an international organisation.[56] As proposals for creation of an International Environmental Court have not yet been successful,[57] the main forum for adjudication of interstate disputes in the environmental field remains the International Court of Justice (ICJ),[58] and as well as international arbitration.[59] The responsibility of

56 P. Sands and J. Peel, *Principles of International Environmental Law* (CUP, 2012).

57 A number of arguments have been advanced to justify the establishment of an international environmental court. This includes, for example, arguments relating to the very many pressing environmental problems that exist today and the need for a bench consisting of experts in international environmental law to consider these problems; the need for individuals and groups to have access to environmental justice at the international level; the need to enable international organizations to be parties to disputes related to the protection of the environment; and the need for dispute settlement procedures that enable the common interest in the environment to be addressed. Arguments against the establishment of an international environmental court include the following: the proliferation of international courts and tribunals would result in the fragmentation of international law; existing courts and tribunals are, or can be, well equipped to consider cases involving environmental issues; and disputes involving international environmental law also involve other aspects of international law. See Hey, E. *Reflections on an International Environmental Court*, Martinus Nijhoff Publishers, 2000; and Murphy, Sean D. *Does the World Need a New International Environmental Court?* 32 *Geo. Wash. J. Int'l L. & Econ.* 333 (1999–2000).

58 See e.g. the *Gabčíkovo-Nagymaros Project* case (Hungary/Slovakia) (ICJ Reports, 1997); and the *Pulp Mills on the River Uruguay* case (Argentina *v.* Uruguay) (ICJ Reports, 2010).

59 See e.g. *Pacific Fur Seal Arbitration United States v. Great Britain* (1893) and *Lac Lanoux Arbitration* (Spain v. France) [1957]. In addition, the Appellate Body of the World Trade

states for transboundary environmental damage has been consistently recognized in the international jurisprudence.[60]

There is considerable state practice consolidating the principle of state liability for environmental damage, including in soft-law instruments adopted in major intergovernmental environmental conferences, such as the Stockholm Declaration on *Human Environment* (1972)[61] and the Rio Declaration on *Environment and Development* (1992).[62] State liability for transboundary environmental damage is based on the no-harm customary rule, under which no state can allow its territory to be used for causing environmental harm to other states or areas beyond national jurisdiction.[63] Yet only a few treaties recognize state liability for environmental damage.[64]

Organization (WTO) has handed down decisions in cases dealing with environmental issues. See e.g. US-*Gasoline Case* (1996) (United States – Standards for Reformulated and Conventional Gasoline WT/DS2/9 20 May 1996); *Brazil-Retreaded Tyres Case* (2007) Appellate Body Report, Brazil – Measures Affecting Imports of Retreaded Tyres, WT/DS332/AB/R, adopted 17 Dec 2007, DSR 2007:IV, 1527; *Tuna-Dolphin case* (1992) (United States – Restrictions on Imports of Tuna; not adopted, circulated on 3 September 1991); *Tuna Dolphin case* (1994) II (United States – Restrictions on Imports of Tuna; not adopted, circulated on 16 June 1994). *Shrimps-Turtles* case (1998) (WTO, United States: Import Prohibition of Certain Shrimps and Shrimp Products – Report of the Appellate Body (1998) WT/DS58/AB/R). As regards investment disputes addressing environmental issues, see e.g. Compania de Desarrollo de Santa Elena v Costa Rica ICSID Case ARB/96/1 Award of 17 February 2000.

60 See e.g. *Gabcikovo-Nagymoros (Hungary v Slovakia)* ICJ *Reports (1997); Pulp Mills in River Uruguay case,* ICJ *Reports (2010);* and *Responsibilities and obligations of States sponsoring persons and entities with respect to activities in the Area* (Feb 2011) (Request for Advisory Opinion submitted to the Seabed Disputes Chamber, case no. 17, International Tribunal on the Law of the Sea). As regards the development of the notion of state responsibility for transboundary damage more generally, see e.g. *Corfu Channel* case (Merits) United Kingdom of Great Britain and Northern Ireland, Judgment of 9 April 1949 (ICJ *Reports,* 1949); and *Lake Lanoux* Arbitration, (Spain v France) (1957).

61 See Principle 22 of the *Stockholm Declaration on Human Environment* (1972). *Report of the United Nations Conference on the Human Environment,* UN Doc A/CONF.48/14/Rev.1 (1 January 1973) ch 1.

62 See Principle 13 of the *Rio Declaration on Environment and Development* (1992). *Report of the United Nations Conference on Environment and Development,* UN Doc A/CONF.151/26/Rev.1 (Vol.1) (12 August 1992) annex 1.

63 See e.g. the *Trail Smelter United States v Canada Arbitration* (1941); Principle 21 of the Stockholm Declaration on the Human Environment (1972) *supra*; and Principle 2 of the Rio Declaration on the Environment and Development (1992), *supra.*

64 See e.g. the *Convention on International Liability for Damage Caused by Space Objects,* 961 UNTS 187 ('Space Liability Convention', 1972). Under Article II, a state which launches a space object could be held 'absolutely liable to pay compensation for damage caused by

The rules of international law on state responsibility are further elaborated under the 2001 International Law Commission (ILC) Articles on the Responsibility for Internationally Wrongful Acts ('The ILC Articles').[65] The ILC Articles state that 'every internationally wrongful act of a State entails the international responsibility of that State',[66] and this responsibility arises irrespective of the 'origin and character' of the international obligation.[67] It also recognizes that state responsibility can arise for the breach an international obligation from the state,[68] which could arise from a breach of a treaty norm or customary international law. Indeed, the 'injured state' may invoke the responsibility of another state if the obligation breached is owned to other states, or when the obligation affects the collective interest of a group of states or is owned to the international community as a whole.[69] Moreover, a breach of such an obligation is serious if it involves a gross or systematic failure by the responsible State to fulfil its obligation.[70]

The first initiative by the International Law Commission calling for the criminalisation of offences against the environment was the Draft Code of Crimes Against the Peace and Security of Mankind (1954), adopted in second reading in 1996.[71] The original draft code recognised under article 22 'widespread

its space object on the surface of the earth or to aircraft in flight'. See further, Pierre-Marie Dupuy, *The International Law Of State Responsibility: Revolution Or Evolution?* 11 *Mich. J. Int'l L.* 105 1989–1990 p. 106.

65 2001 ILC Articles on State Responsibility, 48, Report of the ILC to the United Nations General Assembly, UN Doc. A/56/10 (2001).

66 Ibid, article 1.

67 Ibid, article 12.

68 Ibid, article 2 (b).

69 *See* also, A.E. Boyle, '*Globalising Globalising Environmental Liability: The Interplay of National and International Law*', Journal of Environmental Law (2005) Vol 17 No 1, 3–26; and Pereira, R. 'Compliance and Enforcement in International, European and National Environmental Law' in *Environmental and Energy Law* (Wiley Blackwell, 2012).

70 Article 40 (2), 2001 ILC 'Articles on State Responsibility'. This provision also calls on states to cooperate to bring an end to serious breaches. Further standards on state responsibility for transboundary damage are found in the draft Articles on the Prevention of Transboundary Harm adopted in 2001 by the International Law Commission, *Draft Articles on the Prevention of Transboundary Harm from Hazardous Actbivies* (2001). Although the Draft 'Transboudary Harm' Articles attempts to codify the international legal framework for regulation of activities which pose a risk of transboundary harm, one of its main weaknesses is that it does not address liability issues, including the issue of compensation for transboundary harm.

71 *ILC Draft Code of Crimes Against the Peace and Security of Mankind* (1996), adopted by the International Law Commission at its Forty-Eighth Session. The ILC provisionally adopted a set of articles in 1991 which revised and updated the 1954 Draft Code.

environmental damage' as a 'crime against the peace and security of mankind' and envisaged penal protection under article 26 against 'wilful and severe damage to the environment'.[72] It thus identifies widespread environmental damage as a crime against the peace and security of mankind, which is a prerequisite for establishment of an international crime. Even though it has been suggested that the draft code appeared to aim at 'codifying the most serious crimes of individuals under international law in *Nuremberg-like* processes',[73] it does not appear that article 26 ('on environmental protection') of the Draft Code was confined to the context of an armed conflict. In contrast to article 22 (on 'war crimes') of the same draft code, article 26 was not limited to the context of an armed conflict.[74] As argued by Mark Gray, 'though only certain instances of ecocide would therefore fall within article 26 [of the Draft Code], it lays the foundation for wider recognition, particularly should the link to war crimes disappear'.[75]

However, during the second reading of the draft code the special rapporteur recommended significant changes to article 22, and the deletion of article 26.[76] This is because article 22 received little support in government comments on the draft adopted on first reading, and article 26 faced strong opposition from member governments.[77] In particular, there was opposition from the United States, United Kingdom and the Netherlands to the inclusion of environmental crimes in the ILC Draft Code.[78] Those governments have expressed doubt over

72 *See ibid*, articles 22 and 26.

73 McCaffrey, Stephen C., 'Crimes Against the Environment', in Bassiouni, Cherif M., *International Criminal Law*, 2008, at 1021.

74 *Compare* it with Article 55 of the Additional Protocol I to the 1949 Geneva Conventions. Protocol additional to the Geneva Conventions of 12 August 1949, and relating to the Protection of Victims of International Armed Conflicts of 1977 (Protocol I), Article 55 (1.): 'Care shall be taken in warfare to protect the natural environment against widespread, long-term and severe damage (…)'.

75 Gray, Mark A. 'The International Crime of Ecocide', *California Western International Law Journal*, (1996) at 331.

76 See McCaffrey, Stephen C., 'Crimes Against the Environment', in Bassiouni, Cherif M., *International Criminal Law*, 1996, at 1104.

77 *Ibid.*

78 A/CN.4/448 and Yearbook of the ILC 1993, Vol. II, Pt. 1. Documents of the 45th session. A/CN.4/SER.A/1993/Add.1 (Part 1) (includes A/CN.4/448 and Add.1); and the discussions in the Sixth Committee (Legal) of the General Assembly addressing the draft Code: 12th – 25th meeting; summary records: A/C.6/50/SR.12 to A/C.6/50/SR.25. See further, Anja Gauger, Mai Pouye Rabatel-Fernel, Louise Kulbicki, Damien Short and Polly Higgins, *'Ecocide is the Missing 5th Crime Against Peace'* July 2012, Human Rights Consortium, School of Advanced Study, University of London.

whether environmental issues can affect the peace and security of humankind, which stands at odds with the expanding interpretation of given to that concept by the UN Security Council,[79] and with the development of the notion of ecological security.[80] So the final version of the Draft Code adopted in 1996 recognises a limited scope to the criminalization of environmental offences, specifically in the context of war crimes. It states that 'war crimes' constitute crimes against peace and security of mankind when committed in a systemic manner or on large scale with intent to cause 'widespread, long-term and severe damage to the environment'.[81]

Another significant development was the proposal by the ILC to include in its Draft Articles on State Responsibility a provision stating that 'the breach of rules concerning the environment may constitute (…) in some cases, an international crime'.[82] Furthermore, Article 19(2) of the ILC's Draft Articles on State Responsibility provided some guidance for a definition of international crimes: 'an internationally wrongful act… [is one] which results from the breach…of an international obligation so essential for the protection of fundamental interests of the international community that its breach is recognised as a crime by that international community as a whole'.[83] Specifically, Article 19 (3) (d) of the Draft Articles added that 'a serious breach of an international obligation of essential importance for the safeguarding and preservation of the human environment' could constitute an international crime, such as *'massive pollution of the atmosphere and the high seas'*.[84] Hence, according to the original version of the ILC Articles on State Responsibility, an international crime could include the serious breach by a state of an obligation essential for the protection of fundamental world interests. This included peace and security of

79 Provost, R. (1999) above note 22, at 444.

80 See Barnett, Jon. *The meaning of environmental security: Ecological politics and policy in the new security era*. Zed Books, 2001.

81 *See* art. 20 (g) ILC Draft Code of Crimes Against the Peace and Security of Mankind 'in the case of armed conflict, using methods or means of warfare not justified by military necessity with the intent to cause widespread, long-term and severe damage to the natural environment and thereby gravely prejudice the health or survival of the population and such damage occurs'.

82 See ILC's *Draft Articles on State Responsibility for Internationally Wrongful Acts* (1954) (A/CN.4/88) Report of the International Law Commission Covering the Work of its Sixth Session, 3 28 July 1954, Official Records of the General Assembly, Ninth Session, Supplement No. 9 (A/2693).

83 Article 19(2) of the ILC's Draft Articles on State Responsibility, *ibid.*

84 Article 19 (3) (d) *ibid* (emphasis added).

mankind, human rights, and safeguarding and preservation of the human environment.[85]

In light of those developments, Mark A. Gray argued in 1996 that at least in the instances of massive pollution of the atmosphere or high seas, customary international law has developed to accept the concept of international environmental crimes.[86] Indeed, it could be argued that as States have the primary role in enforcing the rules of international environmental law, international law should evolve to recognise the criminal liability of States for environmental damage. In particular, state criminal liability would establish a higher degree of responsibility and culpability than that established under the present rules on state responsibility.

Yet some members of the ILC took the view that paragraph 3 (d) of Article 19 was premature in terms of community recognition.[87] The ILC thus decided against including the concept of state crimes in its final draft on state responsibility by taking the view that 'there has been (...) no development of penal consequences for states of breaches of (...) fundamental norms'.[88] So the ILC focused instead on serious breaches of obligations under peremptory norms of general international law. Therefore, the Articles on State Responsibility finally adopted in November 2001 by the ILC its fifty-third session omit the reference to international crimes as triggering the criminal responsibility of states.[89] Moreover, the examples given in the Commission's commentary – although they 'may not be exhaustive' – do not include harm to the environment of the kind listed in the former Article 19 of the Draft Articles on State Responsibility.[90] Instead of recognizing environmental crime as international crimes, the final version of the 2001 ILC Articles on State Responsibility identifies the legal consequences of the breach of peremptory norms of international law, but does not state exhaustively what those norms are.[91] So the original proposal for codification

---

85 See also, Gray, Mark A (1996) above note 75, at 266–267.

86 *Ibid.*

87 See Report on the forty-fifth session, at 49–53 (discussing Article 19).

88 *See* James Crawford, '*The International Law Commission's Articles on State Responsibility: Introduction, Texts and Commentaries*' (CUP, 2002) at 243; and A. Pronto and M Woods, '*The International Law Commission 1999–2009, vol. IV: Treaties, Final Draft Articles and Other Matters*' at 296.

89 See 2001 International Law Commission (ILC) Draft Articles on the Responsibility for Internationally Wrongful Acts 48, Report of the ILC to the United Nations General Assembly adopted in the fifty-third sesssion, UN Doc. A/56/10 (2001).

90 See Draft articles on Responsibility of States for Internationally Wrongful Acts, with commentaries 2001, Artilcle 40, commentary 6, at 286.

91 *See* ibid, Articles 40 and 41.

of the international crime of 'ecocide' was ultimately never incorporated in the final draft adopted by the Commission, and 'massive pollution' or 'other environmental catastrophes' are not listed as examples of serious breaches in the 2001 Draft Articles or in the accompanying ILC commentaries. On the other hand, it is possible to interpret the adopted provisions (i.e. Articles 40 and 41) recognizing the existence of 'serious breaches' as also leading to state responsibility for environmental damage. This is because the ILC Articles on State Responsibility are open-ended and non-exhaustive; and therefore they were not supposed to exclude the development of rules under international law detailing the consequences of serious breaches which 'fulfill the criteria for peremptory norms under article 53'.[92]

It should be emphasised that the original ILC draft articles were concerned with *state* responsibility (as opposed to *individual* responsibility), which explains the resistance by the members of the ILC to recognise the criminal liability of states for environmental offences. Whereas international criminal law has traditionally recognised the principle of individual criminal responsibility, the principle of criminal liability of states is not yet developed in state or jurisprudential practice.[93] In this regard, Robert McLaughlin argues that that it is paradoxical that whereas international environmental law is based on the predominant role of States and their responsibility for environmental harm, the subjects of ICC jurisdiction would be necessarily non-state international actors.[94] To quote that author, 'an environmental Pinochet would be subject to

92 *Ibid*, Article 40, commentary 6. See also Article 41, commentary 14: 'By setting out certain basic legal consequences of serious breaches in the sense of article 40, article 41 does not intend to preclude the future development of a more elaborate regime of consequences entailed by such breaches'.

93 See C. Tomuschat, 'International crimes by States: an endangered species?', International Law: Theory and Practice – Essays in Honour of Eric Suy, K. Wellens, ed. (The Hague, Martinus Nijhoff, 1998) at 259; G. Gilbert, 'The Criminal Responsibility of States' (1990) 39 I.C.L.Q 345. Meron, Theodor, Is International Law Moving Towards Criminalization? *European Journal of International Law* 9 (1998) at 21. However, since the definition of the crime of aggression was given by the by the ICC review conference in 2010, at least this form of state responsibility for international crimes is now recognized in the ICC Statute. See Resolution RC/Res.6; adopted at the 13th plenary meeting, on 11 June 2010, by consensus. Annex I Amendments to the Rome Statute of the International Criminal Court on the crime of aggression, 2 Article 8 bis Crime of aggression (2). For the purpose of paragraph 1, 'act of aggression' means the use of armed force *by a State* against the sovereignty, territorial integrity or political independence of another State' (emphasis added).

94 Mclaughlin (2000) above note 24, at 389.

ICC jurisdiction, while an environmental Chile would remain apparently insulated'.[95] On the other hand, McCaffrey questioned whether 'an entire population of a nation should be treated as international criminals because of the actions of their leaders'.[96] So while States remain responsible under international law for the environmental harm caused by individual actors who operate in their territory under the general international rules on state responsibility for environmental damage, no *criminal* liability would be attached to states under international law. This is reflected in the ICC Statute itself, which expressly states that 'no provision in this Statute relating to individual responsibility shall affect the responsibility of states under international law'.[97] Moreover, the ILC Articles on State Responsibility adopts a restrictive approach as regards the public organs of a state whose actions or omissions could trigger state responsibility under international law.[98]

The advantage of also recognising the international criminal responsibility of states (as opposed to – or in addition to – individual or corporate criminal responsibility) is that it would shift responsibility to states for their failure to regulate adequately and to prevent environmental harm by those actors who caused environmental damage.[99] Yet it could be argued that since states can already be held liable under the international rules on state responsibility for the payment of reparations for transboundary environmental damage,[100] the

95 *Ibid.*

96 McCaffrey, S.C., (1996) above note 76, at 1028.

97 Art. 25 (4) ICC Statute.

98 *See* 2001 ILC Articles on State Responsibility, above note 89. Under Article 4 (*'Conduct of organs of a State'*) '1. The conduct of any State organ shall be considered an act of that State under international law, whether the organ exercises legislative, executive, judicial or any other functions, whatever position it holds in the organization of the State, and whatever its character as an organ of the central Government or of a territorial unit of the State. 2. An organ includes any person or entity which has that status in accordance with the internal law of the State'. Under Article 8 (*'Conduct directed or controlled by a State'*) 'The conduct of a person or group of persons shall be considered an act of a State under international law if the person or group of persons is in fact acting on the instructions of, or under the direction or control of, that State in carrying out the conduct'.

99 See also, Rauxloh (2011), above note 24, 423–461.

100 For example, UNCLOS recognizing the liability of states for environmental damage to the marine environment and establish the obligation of states to pay 'prompt and adequate' compensation for environmental damage. See Article 235 (1) and (2) of the convention. In general, states will be liable for transboundary environmental damage if they fail to perform due diligence obligations to prevent or control pollution from economic operators operating in areas which they have jurisdictional control.

recognition of the criminal responsibility of states would have limited additional benefits from the perspective of redressing the victims of environmental harm. As can be seen in the context of international civil liability regimes, there are considerable shortcomings in relying on state liability in cases involving environmental damage. One of the limitations is that, as a general rule, only governments can bring international claims before international tribunals against another state for environmental damage.[101] And even if they are willing to proceed with such claims, finding a forum with jurisdiction will as a general rule depend on the consent of the other state.[102] An evidence of this is that, in practice, very few cases involving claims of liability for transboundary environmental damage have been handled in this way.[103] Therefore, it has been suggested that state responsibility is and should remain no more than a residual source of redress.[104]

Although it is true that the prosecution of states before international courts and tribunals would not necessarily face those similar challenges – given the central role played by the ICC prosecutor in bringing prosecutions[105] – the experience from civil liability regimes suggest that individual (and corporate) criminal responsibility would be a more effective source of redress and enforcement than would be to rely on state liability. Moreover, as international criminal law has traditionally only recognized the principle of individual criminal liability, this form of liability may also prove to be a more effective response in the context of transnational environmental crimes.

---

101 *See* A.E. Boyle, '*Globalising Globalising Environmental Liability: The Interplay of National and International Law*', Journal of Environmental Law (2005) Vol 17 No 1, 3–26.

102 *Ibid.* The jurisdiction of the ICJ is, as a rule, consensual. The ICJ only has compulsory jurisdiction if the parties to the dispute have accepted this type of jurisdiction of the court. See Article 36 of the ICJ Statute. For a list of the countries which have recognised the compulsory jurisdiction of the ICJ, see *International Court of Justice, Jurisdiction: Declarations Recognizing the Jurisdiction of the Court as Compulsory* <http://www.icj-cij.org/jurisdiction/?p1=5&p2=1&p3=3>. In contrast, ITLOS and the WTO accept the rule of compulsory jurisdiction as a general rule.

103 *Ibid.* See e.g. *Gabcikovo-Nagymoros (Hungary v Slovakia) ICJ Reports (1997); Pulp Mills case, ICJ Reports (2010).*

104 Ibid.

105 The ICC Prosecutor can initiate an investigation on the basis of a referral from any State Party or from the United Nations Security Council. In addition, the Prosecutor can initiate investigations *proprio motu* on the basis of information on crimes within the jurisdiction of the Court received from individuals or organisations ('communications').

3.5 Conceptualising the Crime of 'Ecocide'

Despite the fact that environmental damage arising in the context of peacetime activities may impact on more than one state, under international criminal law it is not possible to strictly apply the terminology 'international environmental crimes' to encompass serious cross-boundary environmental offences. International criminal law is mainly concerned with serious criminal offences that impact the peace and security of mankind, including (though not limited to) those committed in the context of an armed conflict. Although those crimes which have an impact on two or more states – including transboundary environmental crimes – could be broadly considered international crimes, environmental crimes cannot be defined as international crimes in the strict sense as understood under international criminal law. International criminal law currently only recognises war crime, crimes against humanity, genocide, torture and crimes of aggression[106] as international crimes, since other crimes of cross-boundary effects, such as drug or human trafficking or illegal movement of hazardous waste, are not susceptible to adjudication by an international criminal tribunal, such as the International Criminal Court (ICC), the International Criminal Tribunal for the Former Yugoslavia (ICTY), the International Criminal Tribunal for Rwanda (ICTR) or the Special Court for Sierra Leone.[107] According to Antonio Cassese, the existence of an international crime requires the following criteria to be met *cumulatively*: (a) violation of international customary rules; (b) the rules are intended to protect values important to the whole international community and consequently bind all states and individuals; (c) a universal interest in repressing those crimes; and (d) the perpetrator has acted in an official capacity (i.e. *de jure* or *de facto* state official).[108] There is an increasing recognition that some serious types of transnational environmental offences impact on the peace and security of mankind and violate 'customary rules' and 'universal values', and hence these crimes could satisfy the first three criteria. Significantly, the UN Security Council

---

106 Following a definition to the crime of aggression given during the ICC review conference in 2010. See Resolution RC/Res.6; adopted at the 13th plenary meeting, on 11 June 2010, by consensus.

107 Cassese, A. *International Criminal Law*, (Oxford, 2003). It has been suggested that environmental crime was not included in the Statutes of the ICTY and ICTR because the levels of environmental damage during the conflicts in the former Yugoslavia and Rwanda were not very significant. *See* Rauxloh, R. (2011) above note 24, at 433.

108 Ibid. In contrast, most crimes harmonized at the EU level – though terrorism may be one important exception – do not meet strictly the criteria set in points a-c.

recognized in 2007 that climate change poses a threat to peace and security of mankind.[109] Moreover, Natalie Klein notes that illegal, unregulated and unreported (IUU) fishing is not only an environmental concern, and should be regarded as a maritime security concern of coastal states.[110] On the other hand, the fourth criterion considerably limits the possibility for application of the rules of international criminal law to the context of environmental crime, as government officials will only in very limited circumstances be directly responsible for environmental damage (possibly, for example, in the context of environmental crimes committed by state-owned companies).[111] However, the ICC jurisdiction should not be limited to international crimes committed by state officials in a governmental capacity (although war crimes, genocide and crimes against humanity are often committed by states officials). As argued by Robert Cryer et al., with exception of the crime of aggression, the status of the perpetrator is almost always irrelevant to define international criminal responsibility.[112]

Yet 'international environmental crime' *broadly defined* (or '*latu sensu*') may include illegal trade in wildlife;[113] illegal trade in ozone-depleting substances;[114] and dumping and illegal transport of various kinds of hazardous wastes,[115] since – as will be further discussed below – there are international conventions requiring signatory parties to introduce, among other measures, penal sanctions against violations of those agreements. It is thus possible to broadly define certain

109 Following the Security Council meeting on '*Energy, Security and Climate*' held on 17 April 2007. *See Security Council Holds First-Ever Debate On Impact Of Climate Change On Peace, Security, Hearing Over 50 Speakers*, 5663rd Meeting, SC/9000, 17 April 2007. Resolution adopted by the General Assembly [without reference to a Main Committee (A/63/L.8/Rev.1 and Add.1)] 63/281. Climate change and its possible security implications, Sixty-third session, Agenda item 107.

110 *See* Natalie Klein, *Maritime Security and the Law of the Sea* (OUP, 2011) at 97.

111 This is also in clear contrast to acts by private individuals and criminal organisations subject to criminalization under EU criminal legislation, which tend to apply to crimes committed *against* or *within* states, and not 'on behalf of' the state. The EU Directive on environmental crime exempts government entities from the scope of the environmental offences under the directive (see article 2 (d) of the environmental crime directive).

112 R. Cryer. H. Friman, D. Robinson and E. Wilmshurst, '*An Introduction to International Criminal Law and Procedure*' (second ed., CUP, 2011) at 28.

113 1973 *Washington Convention on International Trade in Endangered Species of Fauna and Flora*, 27 UST 1087 (CITES).

114 1987 *Montreal Protocol on Substances that Deplete the Ozone Layer*, 1522 UNTS 3.

115 1989 *Basel Convention on the Control of Transboundary Movement of Hazardous Waste and Other Waste and their Disposal*, 1673 UNTS 126.

types of environmental damage as environmental crimes[116] '(whenever) there is movement of goods across boundaries (e.g. smuggling) or a transboundary impact to offences'.[117] These offences could be classified as 'supranational crimes' or 'transnational crimes', to be distinguished from 'crimes under international law' which are subject to the jurisdiction of an international criminal tribunal.[118] This suggests that it will be for future review conferences to decide whether international environmental crime (or other cross-national crimes, such as terrorism or drug trafficking) will be included in the ICC Statute.[119] It should be noted that illegal logging is not covered by any international convention establishing punitive measures and could not be considered 'international environmental crimes' even in this broader sense. As regards illegal fishing, although no binding international agreements require states to criminalise it, the FAO has implemented a number of initiatives in order to eliminate illegal, unregulated and unreported fishing (IUU), calling on states to adopt sanctions which are 'of sufficient severity'.[120]

Based on the codification attempts of the ILC discussed in the previous section, a combination of existing human rights documents, emerging Conventions in draft form, and various sources of soft-law, some publicists have suggested that there is a strong case for the recognition of an international crime of *ecocide* in cases involving serious environmental damage.[121] It is argued that the sheer harm caused by ecocide justifies its application during peacetime activities that destroy or damage ecosystems in a massive scale. In this vein, they have built the case that these environmental crimes could rise to the status of *jus cogens* – that is, a peremptory norm – similar to the prohibition

116 See also,. Teclaff, Ludwik A 'Beyond Restoration – The Case of Ecocide', *Natural Resources Journal* 34 (1994): 933.

117 See Hayman, Gavin and Brack, Dunkan, *Workshop Report: International Environmental Crime: The Nature and Control of Environmental Black Markets* (the Royal Institute of International Affairs, London 1998).

118 See also, R. Cryer. *et al.*, above note 112, at 4–6.

119 See A. Cassese, P. Gaeta, and J. Jones, *The Rome Statute of the International Criminal Court A Commentary* (2002), 1903.

120 See the voluntary 2001 FAO *International Plan Of Action To Prevent, Deter And Eliminate Illegal, Unreported And Unregulated Fishing:* (21) States should ensure that sanctions for IUU fishing (...) are of sufficient severity to effectively prevent, deter and eliminate IUU fishing and to deprive offenders of the benefits accruing from such fishing'. It adds that '[t]his may include the adoption of a civil sanction regime based on an administrative penalty scheme'. Therefore, the IUU International Plan of Action falls short of requiring states to introduce criminal sanctions.

121 See for example, Mark A. Gray (1996), above note 75; Ludwik A. Teclaff, (1994) *supra*.

on slavery or the general prohibition on the use of force, making it unlawful for states to derogate from that norm in future agreements.[122] It is then argued that causing severe environmental harm could lead to the breach of an *erga omnes* duty of care arising from international environmental law and human rights obligations and so to the commission of an international delict.[123] This argument is in line with Theoron Meron's view that 'there is a clear trend toward the criminalisation of international law'.[124] He further argues that this 'trend is supported by simultaneous expansion of jurisdiction to prosecute crimes arising from both international and non-international conflicts, in both international and domestic tribunals, which in turn has been spurred by recent developments in customary law'.[125]

If the rationale for criminalisation at the international level based on the seriousness of the harm or threat of harm to the environment is correct, then some of the most serious incidents of environmental damage, for example the state failure to prevent a nuclear accident,[126] significant oil spills[127] or a major industrial accident (such as *Bhopal* disaster in India),[128] arguably could be

---

122 See *ibid.* Article 53 of the *Vienna Convention on the Law of Treaties* contains the following definition of the concept of peremptory norms: '[f]or the purposes of the present *Convention*, a peremptory norm of general international law is a norm accepted and recognized by the international community of States as a whole as a norm from which no derogation is permitted and which can be modified only by a subsequent norm of general international law having the same character.' *Vienna Convention on the Law of Treaties*, opened for signature 23 May 1969, 115 UNTS 331 (entered into force 27 January 1980).

123 M. Gray, above note 75, at 267.

124 Meron, Theodor, Is International Law Moving Towards Criminalization? *European Journal of International Law* 9 (1998) 18–31.

125 *Ibid.*

126 Such as *Chernobyl* nuclear accident in 1986; or the *Fukushima* disaster in 2011. For a discussion see Malone, Linda A. 'The Chernobyl accident: a case study in international law regulating state responsibility for transboundary nuclear pollution'. *Columbia Journal of Environmental Law* 12.203 (1987).

127 This could include, for example, the *Torrey Canyon* oil spill off the coast of Cornwall, Great Britain in 1967; the *Amoco Cadiz* oil spill off the coast of Brittany, France in 1978; and the *Exxon Valdez* oil spill off the the coast of Alaska, United States in 1989.

128 The accident happened in December 1984 at the Union Carbine India Limited pesticide plant in Bophal, Madhya Pradesh. This has led 500,000 people to be exposed to methyl isocyanate (MIC) gas and other chemicals, leading to the death of at least 2,259 people. In 1989, UCC and UCIL entered into a $470 million legal settlement with the Indian Government, settling all claims arising from the incident. Between 1999 and 2007, three class action lawsuits were filed in the U.S. District Court for the Southern District of New York against UCC and former UCC Chairman based on the Alien Tort Claims Act. For an

recognised as acts of ecocide. This would be particularly the case if environmental damage could leave an ecosystem beyond repair, for example if a single nuclear disaster had the potential to leave the earth or particular ecosystems unfit to sustain human or animal and plant life.

Still, one of the challenges would be to establish the degree of *mens rea* required to establish a crime of ecocide. Many instances of environmental offences are committed without intention, including in the context of accidental oil spills or nuclear accidents. The definition of the typology of a crime of ecocide could include a *mens rea* element of 'with the intention to' or 'recklessness in' destroying the planet.[129] Yet if applied in those strict terms and high standards, examples of acts of ecocide would be rare. Indeed, most cases of environmental damage are not sufficient to destroy the planet as a whole; rather it is the accumulation of different acts of environmental damage and pollution that endangers the life in the planet.[130] An alternative approach suggested by Regina Rauxloh – borrowing from the Additional Protocol I to the Geneva Conventions – is that the offence should prohibit acts 'which are intended, or may be expected, to cause widespread, long-term and severe damage to the natural environment'.[131] Although it has been recently proposed that an international crime of ecocide should include strict liability offences,[132] most authors conceptualising the crime of ecocide have argued that intention or recklessness would be required, and that negligence or strict liability would be insufficient.[133]

Given the severe and often irreversible nature of acts of ecocide, the retributive theory should play a lesser role in justifying punishment than the role of deterrence which views the use of criminal sanctions as means to prevent environmental damage from occurring in the first place.

---

earlier analysis of the legal implications of the accident, see Abraham, C.M., and Sushila Abraham. 'The Bhopal case and the development of environmental law in India'. *International and Comparative Law Quarterly* 40.02 (1991): 334–365.

129 For a discussion of the possible features of an international crime of 'geocide', see Berat, Lynn 'Defending the Right to a Healthy Environment: Toward a Crime of Geocide in International Law' *Boston University International Law Journal* (Fall, 1993). Acts of geocide could be linked to the proliferation of nuclear weapons, especially if they were to fall in the hands of rogue states or groups.

130 Rauxloh (2011) above note 26, at 447.

131 *Ibid* at 449.

132 See the Draft Ecocide Act (2011) used at the Mock Trial in the UK Supreme Court in 2011, Art. 12, available at http://eradicatingecocide.com/the-law/ecocide-act/ (accessed on 15 February 2015).

133 See e.g. McLaughlin (2000) above note 24.

3.6 The Jurisdiction of the International Criminal Court over International Environmental Crime

Even if the legal basis for international criminal liability could be established, the question remains as to which international tribunal would have the mandate to apply criminal penalties against a state or a non-state actor for an international environmental crime. The four crimes that currently fall under the jurisdiction of the International Criminal Court (ICC) are genocide; crimes against humanity; war crimes; and the crime of aggression.[134] Despite these limited range of offences falling under the current mandate of the ICC, the ICC Rules of Procedure does not rule out,[135] and the ICC Statute expressly permits, the possibility of other international crimes coming eventually under the Court's jurisdiction.[136] This could involve an amendment to the ICC Statute[137] to extend the jurisdiction of the ICC over acts which cause widespread 'damage, destruction to or loss of ecosystems' beyond the context of an armed conflict. In this vein, it has been suggested that the ICC should create an offence of ecocide as the 5th international Crime Against Peace.[138] In 2010, Polly Higgins, a lawyer and activist, proposed that the UN Law Commission defined ecocide as the 'extensive damage to, of or loss of ecosystem(s) of a given territory, whether by human agency or by other causes, to such an extent that peaceful enjoyment by the inhabitants of that territory has been or will be severely diminished'.[139] However, this proposal was not considered by the ICC review

134 *See* Article 5, Rome Statute. The crime of aggression was defined by the ICC review conference in 2010. See Resolution RC/Res.6; adopted at the 13th plenary meeting, on 11 June 2010, by consensus.

135 See The Rules of Procedure and Evidence are reproduced from the *Official Records of the Assembly of States Parties to the Rome Statute of the International Criminal Court, First session,* New York, 3-10 September 2002 (ICC-ASP/1/3 and Corr.1), part II.A. The amendments are reflected via footnotes. 3.

136 *See* Rome Statute, Article 123 'Review of the Statute': (1.) Seven years after the entry into force of this Statute the Secretary-General of the United Nations shall convene a Review Conference to consider any amendments to this Statute. Such review may include, but is not limited to, the list of crimes contained in article 5. The Conference shall be open to those participating in the Assembly of States Parties and on the same conditions.

137 *See* Rome Statute, Article 121 'Amendments': The adoption of an amendment at a meeting of the Assembly of States Parties or at a Review Conference on which consensus cannot be reached shall require a two-thirds majority of States Parties.

138 See the 2011 proposal for a *Draft Ecocide Act*, above note 132.

139 See further, http://eradicatingecocide.com/overview/mock-trialdestruction (accessed on 15 February 2015).

conference that took place in June 2010 (i.e. 7 years after the entering into force of the ICC Statute).[140] Subsequently, a European Citizens' Initiative was discussed by the European Parliament in February 2015 with the aim to achieve a joint EU position on the crime ecocide, to provide the basis for the EU to propose an amendment to the ICC Statute.[141] Such an amendment could be proposed in a future review conference to the ICC Statute;[142] or by 'any State party' after the first review conference that took place in 2010.[143]

At present, the scope for the prosecution of environmental crime before the International Criminal Court (ICC) is very limited, given that the Rome Statute (1998) only recognises the court's jurisdiction for certain instances of environmental damage in the context of an armed conflict falling under the definition of war crimes, such as the oil spill caused by the Iraqi forces in the Persian Gulf during the Gulf War in 1991.[144] According to the ICC Statute, a war crime requires an international attack with the knowledge that it would cause 'widespread, long-term and severe *damage to the environment* which would be clearly excessive in relation to the concrete and direct overall military advantage anticipated'.[145] This provision thus mirrors Article Art. 20 (g) of the ILC Code of Offences against Peace and Security.[146] Although the ICC statute does not define 'damage to the environment', some guidance could be found in

140 Although in the years leading up to the Review Conference, many amendments were proposed and discussed (including proposals for the definition of a crime of terrorism, drug-trafficking, and other acts proscribed by international law), only two other amendments were discussed at the Conference. See http://www.haguejusticeportal.net/ (accessed on 15 February 2015). See Rome Statute, Article 123, above note 136.

141 See European Parliament to discuss End Ecocide initiative, 25th February 2015, '*The Week Ahead 23 February – 01 March 2015 Plenary and committee meetings week*' at www.europarl.europa.eu/pdfs/news/ (accessed on 15 February 2015).

142 See Rome Statute, Article 123.

143 See Rome Statute, Article 121 'Amendments 1. After the expiry of seven years from the entry into force of this Statute, any State Party may propose amendments thereto (...).'

144 *See* further, Karen Hulme, *War Torn Environment: Interpreting the Legal Threshold*, Martinus Nifhoff, 2004.

145 Rome Statute, Article 8 (2)(b)(iv) (emphasis added).

146 Art. 20 (g) states that 'in the case of armed conflict, using methods or means of warfare not justified by military necessity with the intent to cause widespread, long-term and severe damage to the natural environment and thereby gravely prejudice the health or survival of the population and such damage occurs'. See the *ILC Draft Code of Crimes Against the Peace and Security of Mankind*, above note 71.

other international agreements,[147] even though many international environmental agreements fail to define environmental damage.[148]

One study suggested that, even in the limited context of an armed conflict, the current international rules on armed conflict may be ineffective in the context of environmental crime.[149] Moreover, there is limited scope for environmental crimes to be prosecuted under the existing crimes listed in Article 5 of the Rome Statute beyond the context of an armed conflict if it they meet the requirements of the crimes of genocide and crimes against humanity. Indeed, in case there is no consensus among the parties to extend the ICC over international environmental crimes, the only possible avenue for prosecution of environmental damage before the ICC would be in connection with acts of either genocide, war crimes or crimes against humanity. However, it would be difficult for the ICC to bring effective prosecutions against environmental crime under the umbrella of the existing crimes recognized under the ICC Statute. It has been suggested that 'even if the International Criminal Court is inclined to pursue environmental damage from an internal armed conflict, the specific

147 *See Convention on International Liability for Damage Caused by Space Object*, March 29, 1972, 961 UNTS 187, Article I (1) defines 'damage' as 'loss of life, personal injury or other impairment of health; loss of or damage to property of states or persons, natural or judicial, or property of international intergovernmental organisations'. However, this narrow definition of 'damage' fails to encompass damage to the environment that do not lead to damage to human health or property.

148 In respect of state liability for environmental damage, the only definition in a treaty is provided by the 1988 Convention on Regulation of Antarctic Mineral Resources Activities (CRAMRA) (not in force), which defines environmental damage as: 'any impact on the living or non-living components of the environment or those ecosystems, including environmental harm to atmosphere, marine or terrestrial life, beyond that which is negligible or which has been assessed and judged to be acceptable pursuant to [the] Convention'. [Article 1(15)] See further, Sands and Peel (2012) at 706–707. See also, Chapter 2.

149 *See* Karen Hulme,(2004) above note 144; discussing the application of the Convention on the Prohibition of Military or Any Other Hostile Use of Environmental Modification Techniques (ENMOD) in the context of specific armed conflicts. See Convention on the Prohibition of Military or Any Other Hostile Use of Environmental Modification Techniques (ENMOD), opened for signature 18 May 1977, 31 U.S.T. 333, 1108, U.N.T.S. 151. Moreover, Article 35 (3) and Article 55 (1) of Protocol I to the Geneva Conventions explicitly outlaw 'widespread, long-term and severe damage to the natural environment'. See Protocol Additional to the Geneva Conventions of 12 August 1949, Relating to the Protection of Victims of International Armed Conflicts (Protocol I), opened for signature 12 December 1977, 16 I.L.M. 1391.

standards and norms are unclear, and the danger exists that a person might be charged for something he or she did not know was a crime'.[150] It could also be argued that this runs contrary to the principle of legality, which requires that international (criminal) norms are clearly defined.[151] Thus the principle of legality is a considerable barrier to the application of the ICC Statute to international environmental crimes committed under the umbrella of existing international crimes, such as crimes against humanity or genocide. This then arguably would strengthen the case for calls for the ICC Statute to recognise a more specific 'crime against the environment' beyond the context of an armed conflict.[152] The establishment of this crime would make the principle of criminalisation clearer to the regulated community and therefore more consistent with the legality and fair labelling principles.

The challenges in classifying environmental crime as falling under the umbrella of one of the existing crimes covered by the ICC statute can be illustrated with reference to crimes against humanity.[153] Crimes against humanity do not need to occur in the context of an armed conflict. The Rome Statute defines crimes against humanity as acts committed as part of a 'widespread and systematic attack directed against any civilian population, with knowledge of the attack'[154] and includes murder, extermination, '*or other inhumane acts of similar character intentionally causing great suffering or serious injury to body or to mental or physical health*'.[155] But could a situations involving environmental damage amount to a crime against humanity? Firstly, as per Article 7 (1) (k) of the Rome Statute, the attack to the environment would need to endanger human health in order to be recognized as a crime against humanity, thus it would leave the environment as such without effective legal protection. Moreover, the Rome Statute requires that the attack must be 'widespread or systematic'. This certainly limits the scope of this provision, as most environmental offences would not appear to meet this threshold. Yet it is not impossible to think of examples of environmental damage which are 'widespread and systematic'. One example is when a pipeline operated by Texaco Petroleum

---

150 Carl R. Bruch, 'All's Not Fair in (Civil) War: Criminal Liability for Environmental Damage in Internal Armed Conflict' (2001) 25 *Vermont Law Review* 695, at 736. See also, Rauxloh (2011) above note 24, at 446.

151 On the principle of legality, see further Chapter 5.

152 Rauxloh (2011), *supra* at 445–446.

153 See generally, Iris Haenen, 'Classifying Acts as Crimes Against Humanity in the Rome Statute of the International Criminal Court' (2013) *German Law Journal* [Vol. 14 No. 07].

154 See Rome Statute, Article 7 (1) (emphasis added).

155 Article 7 (1) (k) ibid.

Company in Ecuador continuously discharged millions of gallons of toxic waste and oil over a period of many years, causing damage to the environment and indigenous people.[156]

As regards the requirement that the act be an official policy directed at a civilian population, when the continuous and foreseeable result of the extraction of natural resources produces severe environmental damage which kills or damages the health of local populations, a policy to continue such extraction becomes tantamount to an official policy to carry out attacks against a civilian population.[157] Those conditions would appear to be fulfilled when a corporation knowingly discharges harmful pollutants into the environment with the potential to displace or injure local communities, including indigenous peoples. This threshold appears to have been met in the *Social and Economic Rights Action Center and the Center for Economic and Social Rights v Nigeria* case before the African Commission on Human Rights,[158] which concerned the negative health and environmental impacts of oil exploration in Ogoniland due to the contamination of water on indigenous land with lead and mercury affecting the communitys health, particularly that of the children. Nigeria was found to have violated several articles of the African Charter and the African Commission called on the government to ensure protection of the environment, health and livelihood of the Ogoni people.[159] Similarly, the UN Committee on Economic, Social and Cultural Rights has stated that the contamination of the areas inhabited by people by various toxic wastes is considered to be a violation of fundamental social and economic rights.[160]

---

156 *See Aguinda v. Texaco Inc.* 2000 10650, United States Court of Appeals, Second Circuit, August 16, 2002. Yet in this case the Court of Appeal concluded that the district court was within its discretion in dismissing the actions on the basis of *forum non conveniens*.

157 See P. Sharp, Prospects for Environmental Liability in the International Criminal Court (1999), *Virginia Law Journal* 217, at 239.

158 African Commission on Human and Peoples' Rights, Communication No 155/96: The Social and Economic Rights Action Center and the Center for Economic and Social Rights v Nigeria, 30th sess (27 October 2001) [56] ('Ogoni').

159 *Ibid* [68]–[69]. The Commission called for the compensation to victims of human rights violations – including relief and resettlement assistance to victims of government raids – and undertaking comprehensive clean-up of lands and rivers damaged by oil operators.

160 *See* Economic, Social And Cultural Rights, *Adverse effects of the illicit movement and dumping of toxic and dangerous products and wastes on the enjoyment of human rights*. Report submitted by the Special Rapporteur on toxic waste, Mrs. Fatma-Zohra Ouhachi-Vesely GE.01, Fifty-seventh session, E/CN.4/2001/55, 19 January 2001.

Moreover, it is possible to link environmental crimes with acts of genocide, which violate Article 2 of the UN 1948 Genocide Convention[161] and Article 6 of the Rome Statute, thus potentially attracting the jurisdiction of the International Criminal Court.[162] One evidentiary burden would be to prove certain elements of the crime of genocide, for example the requirement of '*specific intent of exterminating one ethnic group*'.[163] In particular, even if acts such as 'killing members of the group' (committed via an environmental medium) could in principle meet the *actus reus* element of the crime of genocide, it would still be challenging for the ICC prosecutor to establish that the act intended to 'destroy a group'. Hence it has been suggested that the definition of environmental crimes as crimes against humanity could prove more useful in that it covers many of the same acts that would normally fall under the rubric of genocide, but without the higher scienter element of demonstrating a 'specific intent to destroy one ethnic group'.[164] Indeed, the lower threshold of 'knowledge of the attack' is the *mens rea* required for the establishment of a crime against humanity. This appears to encompass acts committed with recklessness (and possibly even negligence), which tends to be the case with a considerable number of environmental offences. Still, one significant limitation of classifying environmental offences as crimes against humanity or genocide is that these crimes require a specific result (e.g. 'killing members of the group'), but they

161 UN Convention on the Prevention and Prohibition of the Crime of Genocide, adopted by Resolution 260 (III) A of the U.N. General Assembly on 9 December 1948.

162 See Rome Statute, Article 6.

163 *See* Article 2 (e) The Genocide Convention prohibits measures with '*intent to destroy, in whole or in part, a national, ethnical, racial or religious group*'. There have been six main ICJ cases involving the law on Genocide, *see* in particular, Application of the Convention on the Prevention and Punishment of the Crime of Genocide (Bosnia and Herzegovina v. Serbia), Judgement of February 2007, [2007] ICJ Report ('*Bosnia Genocide*' case); as well as the more recent ICJ decision in Application of the Convention on the Prevention and Punishment of the Crime of Genocide (Croatia v. Serbia), No. 118, 3 February 2015. In addition, there are several convictions for the crime of genocide before the International Criminal Tribunal for Rwanda and the International Criminal Tribunal for the former Yugoslavia. Moreover, there have been allegations of genocide in the case against President Omar Al Bashir of the Sudan. see Prosecutor v. Omar Hassan Ahmad Al Bashir, Judgement on the Appeal of the Prosecutor against the Decision on the Prosecutor's Application for a Warrant of Arrest against Omar Hassan Ahmad Al Bashir, Case No. ICC-02/05-01/09, AC 3 February 2010. For a commentary *see e.g.* Philippa Webb, *'Binocular Vision: State Responsibility and Individual Criminal Responsibility for Genocide'* in The Diversification and Fragmentation of International Criminal Law (Larissa van den Herik and Carsten Stahn eds., 2012).

164 See Sharp (1999) above note 157, at 236.

academic discourse, there has been little policy debate on enforcing environmental rights under the rubric of crimes against humanity or genocide.

Furthermore, it could also be argued that since the ICC has jurisdiction over the most serious crimes of concern to the international community, when defining the limits of those crimes, the ICC primarily intends to address human rights abuses, not environmental crimes. To quote Peter Sharp 'the Rome Statute is not an environmental document'.[168] Nevertheless, as pointed out by that author, 'current trends in the treatment of international environmental and human rights issues have begun to signal a convergence between the two bodies of law'.[169] Crucially, the importance of environmental protection to international human rights is now recognised in international environmental and human rights Conventions.[170] However, it is often not clear the exact point at which environmental damage crosses the threshold of a human rights violation.[171] Perhaps for that reason only in the past few decades the international community began to recognise the potential for using human rights norms to achieve environmental protection.[172,173]

---

168 Sharp, P. (1999) above note 157, at 217.

169 Ibid at 218.

170 Some regional agreements have incorporated a human right to a healthy environment. See e.g. Article 11 of the 1988 Additional Protocol to the American Convention of Human Rights ('Protocol of San Salvador', adopted on November 17, 1988, not yet in force); Article 24 of the African Charter on Human and People's Rights, 1520 UNTS 217, adopted on 27 June 1981; in force on 21 October 1986; and Article 37 of the Charter on Fundamental Rights of the European Union (2010/C 83/02). *See* generally e.g. Alan E. Boyle and Michael R. Anderson (eds), *'Human Rights Approaches to Environmental Protection'* (Oxford : Clarendon Press, 1996).

71 See e.g. *Hatton and Others v. the United Kingdom* [GC], *no. 36022/97, § 96, ECHR 2003-VIII; López Ostra v. Spain (judgment of 9 December 1994, Series A no. 303-C)*; *Guerra and Others v. Italy (judgment of 19 February 1998, Reports of Judgments and Decisions 1998-I)*; *Fadeyeva v. Russia (no. 55723/00, ECHR 2005-IV)*; *Moreno Gómez v. Spain (no. 4143/02, ECHR 2004-X)*; *Sporrong and Lonnroth v Sweden* (1982) 51 Eur Ct H R para 61; *Fagerskiold v Sweden* (Application No 37664/04, decision of 26 February 2008).

2 Sharp, P. (1999) supra at 219. On 16 May 1994, an international group of experts on international human rights and environmental law convened at the United Nations in Geneva and drafted the first-ever declaration of principles on human rights and the environment. See the Draft Principles on Human Rights and the Environment prepared by the UN Commission on Human Rights.

In addition, there are several civil and political rights that are relevant to the protection of the environment, including: the right to life; the prohibition of cruel and degrading treatment; freedom of expression and the right to receive information; as well as economic would not permit the prosecution for conduct which is *potentially* harmfı the environment or human health,[165] which poses challenges in particul light of the central role played by the precautionary principle in internat environmental law.[166]

So although it is in principle possible for individual criminal liability assigned for environmental damage under the existing crimes covered Rome Statute, the main limitation is that the prohibited acts of 'ecocide' amount to a serious crimes against persons, committed through envir tal means.[167] The environmental crime would hence be conceived p from an anthropocentric perspective. This helps to explain why, bey

---

165 In this vein, one common feature of domestic environmental criminal law is t of abstract endangerment offences (see Chapter 6). See also, McLaughlin (2 note 24 at 397.

166 Principle 15 of the Rio Declaration (1992) states that: 'in order to protect the e the precautionary approach shall be widely applied by states according to th Where there are threats of serious or irreversible damage, lack of full scien shall not be used as a reason for postponing cost-effective measures to pr mental degradation'. See also Article 3 of the Climate Change Conventio nises the right of the parties to take 'precautionary *measures* to anticip minimise the causes of climate change and mitigation of its adverse effe ing that 'where there are *threats of serious or irreversible damage, lack of* *tainty* should not be used as a reason for postponing such measures' (e The Seabed Disputes Chamber of International Tribunal on the Law o opined that the precautionary approach may have reached the status See ITLOS 1 February 2011, *Responsibilities and Obligations of States S and Entities with Respect to Activities in the Area* (*Request for Advisory O the Seabed Disputes Chamber*), found at:<http://www.itlos.org/fileadmi cases/case_no_17/adv_op_010211.pdf>, particularly paragraphs 131 and time that there is a clear statement from an international tribunal status of the precautionary principle. Compare it with ICJ 20 Dec *Tests Case* (*Australia v. France*), [1974] ICJ Rep. 253; WTO AB 16 Jar *Communities – Measures Concerning Meat and Meat Products*, *Hormones*); WTO DS 21 November 2006, *European Communities – Approval and Marketing of Biotech Products*, WT/DS291/R, WT/DS2 Biotech). On the precautionary principle, see e.g. N. de Sadeleer *Precautionary Principle: Approaches from the Nordic Countries, E* 2007); E. Fisher, J. Jones and R. van Schomberg (eds.), Impleme Principle: Perspectives and Prospects (Edward Elgar, 2006); M. Fit *Issues in International Environmental Law* (Edward Elgar, 2009); tionary Concept in Environmental Policy and Law: Institutional *town International Environmental Law Review* (1992) 303.

167 This is clear from the reading of e.g. Article 7 (1) (k) of the Rom

Furthermore, promoting an extension of the ICC jurisdiction over environmental crime could be regarded as premature in light of the court's recent failure to effectively bring to justice the perpetrators of some of the most recent horrific instances of human rights abuses, for example the violations of human rights in the context of the conflict in Darfur in Sudan in 2011.[174]

In line with the description of the crime of ecocide discussed above, if the ICC jurisdiction were to be extended to international environmental crime, it should take into account the *scale and severity* of the impact on the environment, for example the number of victims or the degree of harm caused to the environment. The relevance of the scale and severity of the impact of the environmental harm is also implied when the International Law Commission made reference to 'massive pollution of the atmosphere or the high seas' as possible international environmental crimes in the original version of the Draft Articles on State Responsibility.[175] That means that the ICC jurisdiction should include most issues of global environmental concerns and large-scale harm such as the depletion of the ozone layer, global warming-related damage (for example, the environmental damage caused by sea level rises) and illegal acts leading to the exhaustion of natural resources or extinction of species. Yet the identification of individual offenders would not always be easy. For example, in the case of pollution activities which arise from many sources, the identification of individual offenders could prove difficult, if not impossible.[176] In fact, the difficulties in assigning liability to specific individual offenders would be a particularly strong argument for the recognition of some form of *state* responsibility – of a civil or criminal nature – for environmental damage.

Moreover, one of the significant limitations of the ICC Statute is that it currently does not recognise the concept of criminal liability of corporations for international crimes.[177] This would represent a considerable barrier to the

---

and social rights, for example, the right to health could be defined to guarantee access to clean drinking water and no exposition to hazardous waste. See *International Covenant on Civil and Political Rights*, opened for signature 19 December 1966, 999 UNTS 171 (entered into force 23 March 1976) ('*ICCPR*'); *International Covenant on Economic, Social and Cultural Rights*, opened for signature 16 December 1966, 993 UNTS 3 (entered into force 3 January 1976) ('*ICESCR*').

174 An international arrest warrant was issued against the President of Sudan, Omar Hassan al-Bashir, but its validity was contested in light of his status as an incumbent head of state.

175 See Article 19 (3) (d) of the Draft Articles on State Responsibility, above note 82.

176 Mclaughlin, R. (2000) above note 24, at 397–398.

177 There were proposals at the Rome Conference that led to the adoption of the ICC Statute to include a regime for criminal liability of legal entities, but these proposals were

effective prosecution of international environmental crimes by the ICC, as a considerable number of environmental offences are committed by corporations. Therefore, an extension of the ICC jurisdiction would have limited scope to the context of the operations of multinational corporations and other economic operators impacting on the environment, given that they are often able to shield behind the corporate veil which represents a significant barrier to effective prosecutions. To ensure accountability for environmental offences, it is arguably necessary that corporations are held accountable under the ICC Statute. In particular, powerful international non-state actors currently face limited risk of accountability under the national laws of some host states – and limited or no liability under international law would have to act more diligently in the host countries where they operate. This would apply in particular to the operations of multinationals corporations[178] and international financial institutions.[179] However, it should be noted that not all legal systems recognise

---

rejected. *See*, Megret, Frederic 'The Problem of an International Criminal Law of the Environment' vol.36:2 *Columbia Journal of Environmental Law* (2011) at 225. See further, Andrew Clapham, The Complexity of International Criminal Law: Looking Beyond Individual Responsibility to the Responsibility of Organisations, Corporations and States, in Ramesh Thakur & Peter Malcontent (eds.), *'From Sovereignty Impunity to International Accountability: The Search for Justice in a World of States'* 233, 245 (2004); and Van den Herik, Larissa, and Jernej Letnar Černič. 'Regulating Corporations under International Law From Human Rights to International Criminal Law and Back Again'. *Journal of International Criminal Justice* 8.3 (2010): 725–743.

178 As there is currently no global investment agreement, the main sources of international investment law are regional and bilateral investment treaties, customary international law and decisions of international tribunals. There are only a few initiatives concerning the accountability of multinational enterprises. See for example the OECD' Guidelines for Multinational Enterprises (1976, updated in 2000). It establishes a system for citizens in host states to lodge complaints and settle disputes. It allows any person to lodge a complaint about a TNC's activities to a National Contact Point (NCP) of the home or host country. However, this mechanism aims for 'problem solving' rather than providing a mechanism for holding TNCs into account. See further, e.g. J. Dine, *Companies, International Trade and Human Rights* (CUP, 2010).

179 As regards the liability of financial institutions for environmental damage, in general lenders not exercising operation control are not liable for environmental damage in most legal systems. Yet, due to risk management and corporate social responsibility concerns, banks have been taking preventive steps in order to ensure that that projects that they fund are not likely to cause environmental damage. In this regard, the 'Equator Principles' is a voluntary credit risk management framework for determining, assessing and managing environmental and social risk in project finance transactions. See further, Hardenbrook, Andrew, 'Equator Principles: The Private Financial Sector's Attempt at Environmental Responsibility', 40 *Vand. J. Transnat'l L.* 197 (2007).

the criminal liability of corporations, so it would be difficult for the ICC Statute to reconcile those disparate approaches. As will be discussed in Chapter 6, those divergences in national legal systems have also posed a barrier to the recognition of corporate criminal liability in EU criminal law instruments.[180]

3.7 Criminalisation and Enforcement under Multilateral Environmental Agreements

In addition to a range of customary rules and soft-law instruments, the main mechanism used by the international community for the conservation and management of environmental and natural resources are multilateral environmental agreements, with hundreds of these in force, addressing transboundary movement of wastes,[181] dumping from oil platforms or vessels,[182] the prohibition or control of trade in endangered species[183] or for cooperation against climate change,[184] to name a few.

Some international environmental agreements contain obligations on states to introduce penal sanctions for violations thereof, but generally they do not go as far as establishing detailed mechanisms for police and judicial cooperation in criminal matters, similar to those found in international criminal law instruments. Stephen C. McCaffrey[185] notes that 'penal provisions' appear

180 For a comparative analysis of national approaches to corporate criminal liability, see Coffee, John 'Corporate Criminal Liability: an Introduction and Comparative Survey', e.d. A. Eser, G. Heine and B. Huberhttp (eds.), Criminal Responsibility of Legal and Collective Entities, (International Colloquium Berlin, 1998).

181 *See* the 1989 Basel Convention on the Transboundary Movement of Hazardous Waste, 1673 UNTS 126; 28 ILM 657 (1989).

182 *See* the 1972 Convention on the Prevention of Marine Pollution by Dumping of Wastes and Other Matter; 1046 UNTS 120 / ATS 1985 No 16 / 11 ILM 1294 / UKTS 43 (1976); 1996 Protocol to the Convention on the Prevention of Marine Pollution by Dumping of Wastes and Other Matter: 36 ILM 1 (1997); the International Convention on Civil Liability for Oil Pollution Damage (CLC) (adopted in 27 November 1992; entry into force 30 May 1996) ('Oil Pollution CLC 1992') and the International Convention on the Establishment of an international Fund for Compensation for Oil Pollution Damage (1992).

183 *See* 1978 Convention on Trade in Endangered Species, Washington, 1978. 27 UST 1087; TIAS 8249; 993 UNTS 243.

184 *See* the 1992 UN Framework Convention on Climate Change, 1771 UNTS 107; S. Treaty Doc No. 102–38; U.N. Doc. A/AC.237/18 (Part II)/Add.1; 31 ILM 849 (1992).

185 See McCaffrey (2008) above note 76, at 989.

in some fifteen multilateral agreements relating to the environment,[186] as well as several bilateral agreements between states.[187] Most commonly, these instruments require the contracting parties to take 'appropriate measures to ensure the application of the provisions of the agreement [in question] and the punishment of infractions against [those] provisions'.[188] Other approaches include requiring state parties to 'enact and enforce such legislation as may be necessary to make effective the (...) provisions (of the agreement) with appropriate penalties for violations thereof'. For example, in the context of the transboundary movement of hazardous waste, both the Basel[189] and Bamako Conventions[190] contain provisions requiring the enactment of penal measures, that is, a requirement that states take 'appropriate measures' to ensure the application of the agreement and *punishment* of violators thereof.

Other examples of international environmental treaties which contain an obligation on states to implement penal measures include the Washington Convention on Illegal Trade in Endangered Species (CITES, 1973) which requires parties to 'penalise trade in, or possession of, such specimens, or both'.[191] Under the convention on the prevention of marine pollution from

186 See discussion of some of these agreements in this section, including the Convention for the Prevention of Marine Pollution by Dumping of Wastes and Other Matter, 1971, arts. 4 and 7, and CITES (Convention on the International Trade of Endangered Species), art 8, par. 1 and the Convention for Prevention of Marine Pollution from Land-Based Sources, 1974, art 12.

187 For example, 'Agreement between Chile, Ecuador and Peru on Regulations Governing Whaling in the Waters of the South Pacific'. (1954) *See* McCaffrey, above note 76, at 990.

188 See e.g. International Convention for Regulation of Whaling (1946) art. 9; The Convention for Prevention of Marine Pollution by Dumping from Ships and Aircraft (1972) art. 15 (3); Convention on Prevention of Marine Pollution by Dumping of Wastes and Other Matter (1972) arts. 4 and 7; The Convention for the Prevention of Marine Pollution from Land-Based Sources (1978) (replaced by the OSPAR Convention) art. 12; Convention on the International Trade of Endangered Species, art 8, par. 1. See also, McCaffrey *supra*, at 1019.

189 Article 9, par. 5, reads: 'Each Party shall introduce appropriate national/domestic legislation to prevent and *punish* illegal traffic. The Parties shall co-operate with a view to achieving the objects of this Article' (emphasis added). See Basel Convention, above note 181.

190 Article 9 reads 'Each Party shall introduce appropriate national legislation for imposing *criminal penalties* on all persons who have planned, carried out, or assisted in such illegal imports. Such penalties shall be sufficiently high to both punish and deter such conduct'. (emphasis added). 1991 Bamako Convention on the Ban of the Import into Africa and the Control of the Transboundary Movement and Management of Hazardous wastes within Africa.

191 *See* Convention on the International Trade of Endangered Species, art 8, par. 1, above note 183.

ships (MARPOL),[192] the penalties specified under the law of the state parties for pollution-control shall be 'adequate in severity to discourage violations' and 'shall be equally severe irrespective of where the violations occur'.[193] Although MARPOL falls short of requiring that the penalties are of a criminal character, in practice many states have implemented the MARPOL enforcement provisions by means of criminal offences and penalties.[194] In another example, the FAO Compliance Agreement provides that '[s]anctions applicable in respect of violations shall be adequate in severity to be effective in securing compliance and to discourage violations wherever they occur and shall deprive offenders of the benefits accruing from their illegal activities'.[195] The FAO Compliance Agreement provides examples of penalties to be applied by states for non-compliance, depending on their severity. They 'shall' include provisions which may permit, inter alia, refusal, withdrawal or suspension of authorizations to serve as masters or officers on such vessels.[196] On the other hand, MEA s are not generally so prescriptive as to provide a definition for environmental offences, which sets them in contrast with multilateral criminal-law agreements concerning other serious offences.[197] Although some

192 Convention on Prevention of Marine Pollution from Ships 1973/1978 (MARPOL) (entry into force 2 October 1983).

193 Article 4 (4) *ibid.*

194 See Ilias Bantekas, *International Criminal Law* (Hart Publishing, 2010). This includes the EU Member States after the adoption of the directive on ship-source pollution, as amended in 2009 to require the EU Member States to introduce criminal offences and penalties. See e.g. Section 131 of the UK's Merchant Shipping Act 1995; see also Reg. 12. 13 and 36 of the Prevention of Oil Pollution Regulations U.S. Act to Prevent Pollution from Ships (APPS) 33 USC.

195 Article 3 (8) of the 1993 FAO Agreement to Promote Compliance with International Conservation and Management Measures by Fishing Vessels on the High Seas (in force on 14 April 2003), 2221 UNTS 91.

196 *Ibid.* See also, UN Fish Stock Agreement 34 ILM 1542 (1995); 2167 UNTS 88, Article 19 (4).

197 See e.g. UN Convention against Illicit Traffic in Narcotic Drugs and Psychotropic Substances (1988): Article 3 (1) (a) '[e]ach Party shall adopt such measures as may be necessary to establish as criminal offences under its domestic law, when committed intentionally' (a) (i) 'The production, manufacture, extraction; preparation, offering, offering for sale, distribution, sale, delivery on any terms whatsoever, brokerage, dispatch, dispatch in transit, transport, importation or exportation of any narcotic drug or any psychotropic substance contrary to the provisions of the 1961 Convention, the 1961 Convention as amended or the 1971 Convention;' (a) (ii) '[t]he cultivation of opium poppy, coca bush or cannabis plant for the purpose of the production of narcotic drugs contrary to the provisions of the 1961 Convention and the 1961 Convention as amended (...)'

MEA s require states to introduce criminal sanctions (or 'effective/dissuasive' penalties), the language employed in those agreements suggest that the enactment of criminal or similar measures would meet the legal requirement. Therefore, state parties are not required to apply criminal sanctions in individual cases, which is a question that is left to the discretion of national authorities.[198]

On the other hand, it should be noted that many international environmental agreements fail to approximate liability standards (including compensation for environmental damage), and in general they merely call on the parties to develop such liability rules at later stages through amendments or subsequent protocols to a treaty.[199] In general, there is a notable lack of political will by states to implement the provisions under international agreements calling for the establishment of civil liability regimes, which commonly lead to no effective initiatives and become 'dead letter'.[200]

There may be need for criminal provisions under MEA s in particular due to the well-known difficulties in ensuring that the standards set in MEA s are enforced. Some of the deficiencies in giving effect to international environmental obligations include the fact that multilateral or bilateral environmental treaties are directed to states,[201] and hence they rely on each state's compliance and enforcement measures. Although MEA s tend to expressly require parties to

198 Chapter 7 further discusses this point in the context of the EU environmental crime instruments, noting that although this flexibility could hinder the effective implementation and enforcement of the EU environmental crime legislation, flexibility is often regarded as a crucial aspect for effective environmental law enforcement.

199 See e.g. The Basel Convention on the Transboundary Movement of Hazardous Waste, 1989. Article 12 'Consultations on Liability:' 'The Parties shall co-operate with a view to adopting, as soon as practicable, a protocol setting out appropriate rules and procedures in the field of liability and compensation for damage resulting from the transboundary movement and disposal of hazardous wastes and other wastes'. See also, the Convention for the Protection of the Marine Environment and the Coastal Region of the Mediterranean (Barcelona Convention, 1976), Article 16.

200 See e.g. Liability Protocol to Basel Convention on transboundary waste movement (1999) (not yet in force). The Nagoya-Kuala Lumpur Protocol on Liability and Reddress (2010) (at the time of writing, not yet in force). See also, the CoE *Lugano Convention on Civil Liabiliy for Environmental Damage* (1993) (not yet in force).

201 Although there has been debate as to whether they can have direct effect and create rights for individuals. On this question, see the *Intertanko* case, ECJ C-308/06 (2008). See also, Marsden, S. 'Invoking Direct Application and Effect of International Treaties by the European Court of Justice: Implications for International Environmental Law in the European Union', 60 ICLQ July 2011 pp. 737–757.

report information on compliance to the international organisation designated by the agreement,[202] in practice actual compliance with reporting obligations under MEA s by signatory states has varied.[203] Moreover, despite some exceptions, international environmental agreements do not in general foresee the possibility of on-site visits by members of an international organisation in order to oversee the implementation and compliance with international environmental commitments.[204]

Another significant limitation in the enforcement of rights and obligations under MEA s is that they do not generally allow individual complaints to be brought by private parties who suffered environmental damage or by NGO s to an international organisation, as some human rights treaties do.[205] Hence opportunities for non-state actors to enforce international environmental law are much more limited.[206] Moreover, there is the problem of overlap and coordination among the various MEA s dealing with interrelated subjects,

---

202 See e.g. the Montreal Protocol on Substances that Deplete the Ozone Layer has an express contain reporting obligation applicable to state parties (Article 7); the United Nations Framework Convention on Climate Change (UNFCC) and the Kyoto Protocol have numerous provisions on reporting obligations. See Articles 5, 7 and 8 of the Kyoto Protocol.

203 Until recently CITES parties poorly reported on compliance measures, but in 2000 the Parties agreed to implement serious penalties – including the suspension of trade in CITES listed species – on any signatory which consistently failed to submit annual reports. This has led reporting to increase dramatically. See, *The Growth and Control of International Environmental Crime,* Chatham House, 2007 available at http://www.illegal-logging.info/uploads/Intenvcrime2007backgroundpapers.pdf (accessed on 15 February 2015).

204 One example is the Montreal Protocol which allows for on-site inspections 'with the consent of the party involved' to undertake information gathering. See Decision IV/5, Report of the Fourth Meeting of the Parties to the Montreal Protocol on Substances that Deplete the Ozone Lawyer, UN Doc. UNEP/Oz. I. Pro. 4/15 (1992). See further, Stephens, T. *'International Courts and Environmental Protection'* (CUP, 2009) at 75.

205 See e.g. the International Covenant on Civil and Political Rights (ICCPR, 1966) 999 UNTS 171. The Human Rights Committee can receive submissions of non-state actors alleging violations of the *ICCPR*.

206 Yet it should be noted that state parties to the UNECE Aarhus Convention (1998) need to provide access to justice to individuals and NGO s for enforcement of environmental rights. See Convention on Access to Information, Public Participation in Decision-Making and Access to Justice in Environmental Matters, 2161 UNTS 447; 38 ILM 517 (1999) art. 9. Moreover, to the extent that a human right to a healthy environment is recognized under some regional human rights treaties, then this would allow individual victims, as well as NGO s, to bring complaints directly to an international body. On the European Committee of Social Rights interpretation of the right to a 'healthy environment', see e.g. Marangopoulos

such as biodiversity or marine pollution, which hampers efforts for effective interstate enforcement and cooperation.[207]

Another limitation is that once transposed and implemented in national law, the enforcement of the environmental obligations under an MEA lies primarily on the public authorities and judiciary of the signatory states. Indeed, beyond overseeing compliance with reporting obligations, the Secretariats of MEA s generally lack effective enforcement powers. Although a major innovation in recent MEA s is the inclusion of non-compliance procedures, these vary in effectiveness and there are political sensitivities regarding the application of penalties under such non-compliance procedures.[208] It it is arguable that some MEA non-compliance procedures have a *penal* character because their primary aim is to punish non-compliance and deter future violations.[209] Yet one significant barrier is the limited rules on standing under non-compliance procedures, as most non-compliance procedures only allow states to initiate proceedings.[210] In this regard the Aarhus Convention Compliance Committee

Foundation for Human Rights (MFHR) v. Greece, Complaint No. 30/2005, European Committee of Social Rights (E.C.S.R.) (2006).

207 The United Nations Environmental Programme (UNEP) is entrusted with ensuring that there is better coordination between MEA s.

208 The 1987 Montreal Protocol on phasing out of ozone depleting substances established the first non-compliance procedure in a MEA. It allows the Committee to undertake information gathering in the territory of the party concerned (at the invitation of the party) and has the power to suspend specific rights and privileges under the Protocol. *Compare* it with the non-compliance procedure under Articles 258 and 260 TFEU in the European Union, discussed in Chapter 7.

209 Under the Kyoto Protocol non-compliance mechanism, the applicable penalties have a more marked punitive and deterrent character. It is made of two branches: the Facilitative Branch and the Enforcement Branch. A considerable part of the work of the Committee has been carried out through its Facilitative Branch, which aims to provide advice and assistance to parties in order to promote compliance as well as promoting 'early warning' in cases where a party is in danger of not complying with its emissions targets. The more coercive enforcement measures are exercised by the Enforcement Branch, which has the power to apply penalties to Annex I parties to the Protocol that fail to meet their commitments. The penalties include suspension of trading in the subsequent emissions trading period and making up the difference between its actual emissions and its assigned amount during the second commitment period, plus an additional penalty of 30% from its emissions reduction assigned amount. These are particularly serious penalties, and hence the *'penal'* character of the compliance mechanism. See Hoffman, L. 'Copenhagen and Beyond – How to Provide the New Climate Deal with a State-of-the-Art Non-Compliance Mechanism?' *EEELR* 2009, 192.

210 See e.g. Article 4 (1) of the Procedures and Mechanisms on Compliance under the Cartagena Protocol on Biosafety: 'The Committee shall receive, through the Secretariat,

is unique in that it allows submissions from civil society and NGO s after domestic remedies are exhausted.[211] While both the non or incorrect transposition of obligations under the MEA – as well as the non or incorrect implementation of a states' obligations under a MEA – could be subject to scrutiny by the non-compliance committees, it does not appear likely that the non-compliance procedure would be triggered against a decision of the national authorities not to pursue a particular type of enforcement action (e.g. administrative or criminal) in specific cases. Indeed, flexibility of the choice of enforcement measures in specific circumstances is often recognized as a crucial element of the enforcement theory and practice.[212]

The fact that states went as far as accepting provisions of a 'penal' character in certain international environmental conventions suggests that there is some willingness, in principle, for a wider acceptance of the need for criminal sanctions to safeguard ecological interests. This, in addition to the fact that international organisations and states have adopted resolutions calling for a degree of harmonisation and coordination of criminal sanctions in international (environmental) agreements,[213] suggests that there is an intention of states to pursue integration and cooperation in the criminal-law field to protect the environment. This provides evidence of state practice (and indeed *opiniu iuris*) which could eventually lead to the development of a rule under customary international law requiring that states accept the principle that serious infringements of provisions under multilateral environmental agreements should be subject to effective sanctions, including the possibility of

---

submissions relating to compliance from: (a) any Party with respect to itself; and (b) any Party, which is affected or likely to be affected, with respect to another Party'. *Annex,* First meeting of the Conference of the Parties serving as the Meeting of the Parties to the Cartagena Protocol on Biosafety (BS COP MOP 1), BS-I/7. See further, Mackenzie, R. (2004) The Cartagena Protocol after the First Meeting of the Parties, *Review of European Community and International Environmental Law*, 13 (3) 270.

211 Fitzmaurice, M. 'Environmental Justice through International Compliant Procedures? Comparing the Aarhus Convention and the North American Agreement on Environmental Matters' in Ebbeson and Okowa (eds) *Environmental Law and Justice in Context* (CUP, 2009) 211.

212 See Chapter 7.

213 See e.g. General Assembly Resolution 45/121; General Assembly resolution 67/189 of 20 December 2012; ECOSOC 43rd plenary meeting, 27 July 1993; Resolution 2013/40 on '*Crime Prevention and Criminal Justice Responses to Illicit Trafficking in Protected Species of Wild Fauna and Flora*' adopted by the United States Economic and Social Council on 25 July 2013, Distr.: General 17 October 2013. See also, Chapter 1.

criminal law enforcement by the national authorities.[214] Yet in light of the *ad hoc* nature and limited scope of the current developments in this field, it is doubtful that there is sufficient consistency in state treaty-making practices that would allow the development of an international customary law rule requiring states to introduce provisions of a penal nature (or of a 'deterrent and dissuasive' character) under specific MEA s. Although there is an ever-increasing number of states that have enacted criminal provisions to protect the environment,[215] as noted by Rene Provost 'even if it could be demonstrated that many states now criminalize severe environmental harm, it would not allow the conclusion that there is now an equivalent international criminal norm'.[216]

3.8 Improving Inter-agency Cooperation Against Environmental Crime

In light of the low prospects that the ICC will exercise jurisdiction over environmental crimes in the near future, and given the limited scope of harmonization of environmental criminal law under MEA s, the question arises as to the extent to which interstate multilateral and bilateral cooperation between enforcement agencies could be enhanced. It has been noted that weak coordination both between agencies and between countries represents a considerable barrier to the effectiveness of international environmental law enforcement.[217]

Following the recommendations of the 2014 *London Declaration* adopted by the conference on the illegal wildlife trade,[218] a number of countries have reported in the March 2015 progress review that they have introduced measures

214 See Art. 38 (1) (b) of the International Court of Justice Statute.

215 See 'The Role of Criminal Law in the Protection of the Environment' UN Doc. E/CN.15/1997/10. 17 February 1997; 'National Reports and Resolution of the 15th International Congress of the International Association of Penal Law, Ottawa 1994 and Rio 1995' (1994) 65; and (1995) 66 IRPL, 48–53.

216 He supports this view by noting that '[a] large number of acts constitute crimes under practically every legal systems, for example, murder or sexual assault, and yet there is clearly no accepted international crime corresponding to murder or sexual assault' Provost (1999) above note 22, at 451.

217 See Hayman, G. and Brack, D., '*Workshop Report: International Environmental Crime: The Nature and Control of Environmental Black Markets*,' the Royal Institute of International Affairs, (London, 1998).

218 Declaration of the London conference on Illegal Wildlife Trade (2014), (b), point 16, available at https://www.gov.uk/government/uploads/system/uploads/attachment_data/file/281289/london-wildlife-conference-declaration-140213.pdf (accessed on 15 February 2015).

to strengthen interstate cooperation between enforcement agencies.[219] Indeed, a number of countries have formalised interstate cooperation through bilateral agreements or Memoranda of Understanding (MoU). This includes a MoU between Indonesia and Vietnam adopted in October 2014 covering information sharing and exchange (including intelligence); public awareness; capacity building and training; enforcement coordination; and a MoU (which at the time was still in the process of being implemented) between Mozambique and South Africa for joint actions on trans-boundary environmental protection, including law enforcement, information sharing, capacity building and international cooperation to coordinate the anti-poaching efforts targeting the Great Limpopo Transfrontier Park.[220] Moreover, the 2015 progress review suggested that Indonesia and the USA have agreed on an MoU on Combating Wildlife Crime; and China has signed MoUs with neighbouring countries for cooperation in CITES implementation.[221]

INTERPOL (the International Criminal Police Organization), currently with 190 member countries, has been making efforts to combat environmental crime since 1976. It has set up an Environmental Crimes Committee in 1992, which is comprises of Working Groups on Wildlife Crime; on Pollution Crime and on Fisheries Crime.[222] The objective of the INTERPOL Environmental Crime Programme is to provide assistance to the parties and support in the effective enforcement of national and international environmental laws. As part of INTERPOL's Environmental Crime Programme, delegates from participating countries have voted unanimously in favour of a resolution encouraging greater global policing efforts against environmental crime in INTERPOL's General Assembly meeting in Doha, Qatar.[223] In order to strengthen inter-agency and inter-jurisdictional cooperation, INTERPOL has introduced a 'Ecomessage system' which allows data relating to environmental crime to be rapidly and methodically entered into the INTERPOL database where it can be

---

219 See *Kasane Conference On The Illegal Wildlife Trade – London Declaration on the Illegal Wildlife Trade: Review of Progress*, 25th March 2015, Points 52-58, available at https://www.gov.uk/government/uploads/system/uploads/attachment_data/file/415690/review-progress-kasane-conf-150317.pdf (accessed 10 April 2015).

220 *Ibid.*

221 *Ibid.*

222 See http://www.interpol.int/Crime-areas/Environmental-crime/Environmental-crime (accessed on 10 April 2010).

223 The resolution called upon national law enforcement authorities to recognise that 'environmental crime is not restricted by borders and involves organised crime networks which engage in other crime types including murder, corruption, fraud and theft.' See *ibid.*

shared with other entries.[224] Some of the benefits of the 'Ecomessage system' include the fact that it enables the reporting country to ask questions or make requests to agencies in another country – for example, it could facilitate the work of a customs agency in one country that may have seized contraband smuggled from another country.[225] In this connection, one study has recommended that 'information needs to be exchanged directly between the specialised national agencies and the Interpol General Secretariat rather than having to go through National Central Bureaus (NCB s)'.[226]

At the regional level, one notable initiative aimed at improving intestate cooperation against wildlife crime is the Lusaka Agreement on Co-operative Enforcement Operations Directed at Illegal Trade in Wild Fauna and Flora, which was adopted in 1994 and became operational in 1996.[227] The agreement aims to facilitate cross-border co-operation; exchange of information and intelligence; enhancement of wildlife law enforcement capacities; as well as investigations of crime with approval of the state parties in Africa.[228]

In the European Union context, the European Police Office (Europol) and the European Judicial Cooperation Unit (Eurojust) play important roles in coordinating the criminal policies of the Member States. The European Judicial Cooperation Unit (Eurojust), established in 2002, is responsible for facilitating coordination between judicial authorities in the Member States regarding the prosecution of serious criminal behaviour.[229] For example, in light of the instances of fraud in the European carbon markets in 2009–2011 (see Chapter 6), in 2010 Eurojust established a strategic project to enhance information exchange and judicial cooperation between Member States in cross-border VAT fraud cases, and hosted a meeting on the subject in March 2011.[230]

---

224 See Interpol's Ecomessage: A Reporting System for Environmental Crime REPIN(2006)11/Eng *Eighth Annual Meeting of the* EECCA *Regulatory Environmental Programme Implementation Network* 12–13 June 2006 (Tbilisi, Georgia) at http://www.oecd.org/dataoecd/30/15/36875899.pdf (accessed on 10 April 2015).

225 *Ibid.*

226 See Brack, D, The Growth and Control of International Environmental Crime, in *The Growth and Control of International Environmental Crime*,' (Chatham House, 2007) available at http://www.illegal-logging.info/uploads/Intenvcrime2007backgroundpapers.pdf (accessed on 10 April 2015).

227 Lusaka Agreement on Co-operative Enforcement Operations Directed at Illegal Trade in Wild Fauna and Flora. Lusaka, 8 September 1994 . United Nations, *Treaty Series*, vol. 1950, p. 35.

228 At the time of writing, there are seven state parties to the Lusuka Agreement (Congo, Kenya, Lesotto, Liberia, Uganda, Tanzania, and Zambia).

229 Art. 85 TFEU.

230 Eurojust, 'Fraud' [2011] Eurojust News, Issue No.4, July 2011, Eurojust, The Hague, The Netherlands.

The European Police Office (Europol), set up in 1992, is the European Union's law enforcement agency. Its main role is to assist Member States in their fight against serious international crime and terrorism. Europol acts to assist EU Member States through the provision of expertise and technical support, the facilitation of the exchange of information and data, and the coordination of cross-border investigations.[231] For example, Europol is involved in gathering information and data to help Member States target VAT fraudsters in the European carbon market, and has contributed to the coordination of successful investigations throughout the EU.[232] Since the 9/11 attacks, Europol has concentrated much of its activities and resources to counter-terrorism and action against organised crime.

Yet beyond the illicit trafficking in endangered animal and plant species, the original mandate of Europol did not clearly include cross-border environmental crime.[233] Under the third subparagraph of Article 2(2) of the Europol Convention,[234] the Council, acting unanimously in accordance with the procedure laid down in Title VI of the Treaty on European Union, may decide to instruct Europol to deal with other forms of crime listed in the Annex to the Convention or specific manifestations thereof.[235] The Lisbon Treaty envisaged a broader role of Europol in combatting cross-border crime in the EU, which may include any 'forms of crime which affect a common interest covered by a Union policy.'[236] Moreover, following the expert-level conference of the Augias Project held in Budapest on 24 and 25 March 2011, an informal platform for countering environmental-related crimes called 'EnviCrimeNet' was launched. 'EnviCrimeNet', supported by Europol, has as its overall aim to combat environment-related crime, including through the improvement of exchange of

231 Art. 88 TFEU. See www.europol.europa.eu/ (accessed on 10 April 2015).

232 See Nield, K. and Pereira, R., 'Fraud on the European Union Emissions Trading Scheme: Effects, Vulnerabilities and Regulatory Reform' (2011) 20 *European Energy and Environmental Law Review*, Issue 6.

233 See Council of the European Union 'Involvement of Europol in Combating Environmental Crime' Brussels, 5578/99, 1 February 1999.

234 Convention based on Article K.3 of the Treaty on European Union, on the Establishment of a European Police Office ('Europol Convention').

235 This Annex lists other serious forms of international crime, including crime against life, limb and personal freedom, crime against property, crime against public goods and fraud, illegal trading and harm to the environment. See House of Lords Session 2002-03 5th Report Select Committee on the European Union Europol's role in fighting crime, 28 January 2003. See also Europol, *Threat Assessment 2013 – Environmental Crime in the EU*, Brussels, 11 November 2013.

236 See Article 88 TFEU.

information and the gathering of criminal intelligence; training officers and exchanging best practices.[237]

However, it should be noted that neither Europol nor Eurojust have the power to bring prosecutions or start criminal investigations in the Member States, instead playing the role of coordinating the action of national authorities.

3.9 Conclusions

It is clear from the foregoing analysis that the role of the International Criminal Court for protection of the environment (beyond its current mandate primarily limited to the context of armed conflicts) would offer only limited deterrent effects against transnational environmental crime. Moreover, there is considerable fragmentation of the enforcement and penalties provisions under multilateral environmental agreements (MEA s), which calls for a more cohesive and coherent approach to implementation and enforcement under MEA s. In general, states should aim to strengthen their obligations under MEA s by aiming to enact specific penalties, including criminal penalties, for the implementation of international environmental obligations. However, MEA s should simultaneously allow flexibility in the choice of national enforcement action to be taken in individual cases.

In light of the limitations of the ICC and existing MEA s to improve the enforcement of international environmental law – and in light of the cross-border nature of many environmental offences – the improvement of inter-state cooperation through inter-agency coordination should be prioritised in multilateral and bilateral initiatives aimed at combatting environmental crime.

---

237 See Draft Council Resolution on the creation of an informal network for countering environmental crime – 'EnviCrimeNet' 8011/2/11 REV 2 ENFOPOL 70 ENV 221, Brussels, 20 May 2011.

CHAPTER 4

The Degrees of Harmonisation of Environmental Criminal Law

4.1 Introduction

This chapter starts by examining the fundamental notion of legal harmonisation in interstate relations. This is followed by an analysis of the degrees to which states may pursue harmonisation of (environmental) criminal law, assessing the merits and constrains for states to seek unification, approximation, cooperation or coordination of environmental criminal-law standards. As the experience in the European Union shows, the degrees to which states may pursue approximation of environmental criminal law are constrained by constitutional, legal and political challenges.

4.2 The Notion of Legal Harmonisation

Harmonisation of laws could be defined as a technique or method to bring about the gradual adaptation of national legal systems'.[1] Convergence means to come together, either in a single unit or to a point in which there is overlap. In linguistic terms, harmonisation can be defined as bringing two things into accordance or agreement with one another.[2] The term originates from musical composition where it defines the (aesthetically pleasant) co-existence of notes which are in accordance with one another but are not necessarily the same or even similar.[3]

As a mechanism of law reform, the notion of harmonisation of laws can be regarded as a concept, method or goal.[4] As a concept, the Oxford English

1 Tadić, F. 'How Harmonious can Harmonisation be? A Theoretical Approach towards Harmonisation of (Criminal) Law' in A. Klip, H. van der Wilt (eds.) *Harmonisation and Harmonising Measures in Criminal Law*, Amsterdam (2002) at 9.

2 Andenas, Mads, Baasch, Camilla A., Ashcroft, Ross 'Towards a Theory of Harmonisation' in M. Andenas and C. Baasch (eds.)'*Theory and Practice of Harmonisation*' Edward Elgar, 2011 at 577.

3 *Ibid.*

4 Martin Boodman, 'The Myth of Harmonization of Laws', (1991) *The American Journal of Comparative Law*, Vol. 39, at 700.

 | DOI 10.1163/9789004195882_005

Dictionary defines harmonisation – or the process of achieving harmony – as the combination or adaptation of parts, elements, or related things, so as to form a consistent and orderly whole.[5] Harmonisation may also be considered a technique or method of law reform used when problems and frictions in legal areas are (rightly or wrongly) blamed on differences between legal systems. This is often the case in the example of inter-state cooperation in criminal matters which is often hindered by differences in national penal systems.

Furthermore, harmonisation pursues specific goals. Indeed, legal harmonisation is not an objective in itself but a means of achieving specific goals.[6] Like the general notion of harmonisation, harmonisation of laws as it relates to inter-jurisdictional and international transactions cannot be justified by itself. Thus international or inter-jurisdictional legal harmonisation requires specific justification as to the desirability of harmonisation and the model upon which it is based.

It has been suggested that a word of caution is needed when globalisation is raised as the justification for harmonising of laws.[7] In particular, there are concerns over legal harmonisation undermining cultural values, customs and traditions. The literature on the harmonisation of European private law has also criticised harmonisation as a technical process devoted to market making for its disregard of the rich and deep historical roots of the national laws subject to its influence.[8] Literature criticises the fact that cultural traditions that permeate national laws are sacrificed for the benefit of the cold calculation of economic gains.

4.3 The Degrees of Interstate Harmonisation of Criminal Law

There are four main forms of interstate harmonization: unification, approximation, cooperation and coordination. Unification constitutes the strongest degree of integration and would allow states to cooperate towards the adoption not only of minimum standards, but in fact total harmonization of penal laws. This would imply that states' powers to adopt more stringent

---

5 Simpson and Weiner (ed.) *The Oxford English Dictionary* (2nd ed.) Clarendom Press, Oxford.

6 Boodman, M. *supra* at 702–703.

7 Andenas, Baasch, Ashcroft above note 2 at 573.

8 See e.g. Legrand, Pierre 'On the Unbearable Localness of the Law: Academic Fallacies and Unreasonable Observations' (2003) 10/1 *European Review of Private Law* 66.

measures would be constrained following the total harmonisation of criminal-law standards.

The term approximation denotes bringing two systems closer to each other by eliminating some of the differences between them.[9] Approximation could thus be defined as 'the action of approximating' or 'to put closer' for the 'establishment or re-establishment of contact' and evoking the 'reduction of distance between two objects'.[10] It is notable though that the European Union texts harmonizing criminal law generally fall short of defining the notion of approximation.[11]

Even though both unification and approximation tend to modify internal laws, in principle approximation preserves some flexibility and does not, as such, replace internal laws, whereas unification introduces more systematic changes and affects not only the contents but also the form of internal texts.[12] Thus while approximation allows for one element of local preferences to prevail, unification responds to the quest to systematize the national laws.

Approximation and unification constitute stronger models of legal integration than coordination and cooperation. While the former two imply adjustments of the substance of internal laws to meet specific objectives, the latter two do not aim at modifying national legislation and do not concern the norms themselves or their contents but rather the effect of the norms.[13] Coordination constitutes the weakest form of integration, but its importance cannot be underestimated: for example the lack of coordination between the EU and the Council of Europe lead to duplicated efforts to deal with the same problem and at times even inconsistent efforts to deal with the same subject.[14]

---

9 F. Tadić, (2002) above note 1, at 9.

10 A. Weyembergh, 'Le Rapprochement des Incriminations et des Sanctions Penales', (2006) 77 *Revue Internationale de Droit Penal* 185, at 187.

11 *See* A. Weyembergh, 'The Functions of Approximation of Penal Law within the European Union' (2005) 12 *Maatricht Journal of European and Comparative Law* 149.

12 *Ibid.*

13 *Ibid* at 150.

14 Compare, for example, the Council of Europe 1959 European Convention on Mutual Assistance in Criminal Matters, ETS 30 and the EU 2000 Convention on Mutual Assistance in Criminal Matters between the Member States of the European Union, OJC 197, (2000); the Council of Europe Criminal Law Convention on Corruption CETS No.: 173 and the EU Council Framework Decision 2003/568/JHA of 22 July 2003 on Combating Corruption in the Private Sector, OJ L328 (2003), at 54; OJC 195/2 (1997); OJ L279/1 (1997); OJ L358/2 (1998); the Council of Europe Convention on Cybercrime CETS no. 185 and the EU Council Framework Decision 2005/667/JHA of 24 February 2005 on Attacks Against Information Systems, OJ L69 (2005), at 67; and Council of Europe Convention on Action against

How far should the EU pursue integration in criminal matters? At one extreme side of the spectrum there is the pro-unification argument that there is no reason why, for example, one who commits the same crime in Britain and France should be convicted differently. This would imply total harmonization not only of crime definitions, but also of penalty levels. This extremist version of the pro-harmonization trend is unlikely to be accepted by the EU member states. Why should the EU be concerned about the fact that – although the human rights aspects of this could be subject to the scrutiny of the European Court of Human Rights[15] – a person convicted of murder in Britain receives a mandatory life imprisonment sentence whereas in France, say, a maximum penalty of 30 years in jail? Similarly, why should there be concern that for drink driving offences, say, one might be prosecuted summarily in France but not in Britain? Are not those examples matters of public policy that intrinsically pertain to the national, or indeed local, levels? Any attempt of the EU institutions to harmonize those aspects of the criminal law would likely be ill received by the Member States. Furthermore, in order to reach this level of complete harmonization the EU would need to become a supranational state. In my opinion it is unlikely that the EU will become a federation of states. But even in the improbability of this happening, it must be remembered – if only for the sake of the argument – that federal states often leave it to their constituent states partial or total autonomy to legislate in criminal law matters.[16] It is unlikely that the creation of a EU super-state would deviate from that rule. In fact, as will discussed in more detail in Chapter 5, under EU law the *subsidiary principle* applies and the EU should legislate in a given field only when the result cannot be achieved by the member states themselves *and* it can be better achieved at the EU level – if only to allow legislators to respond to local conditions as they arise and develop.[17]

Trafficking in Human Beings, Warsaw, 3 May 2005 (CETS No. 197) and Council Framework Decision 2002/629/JHA of 19 July 2002 on Combating Trafficking in Human Beings, OJ L2003 (2002), at 2.

15 Or the Court of Justice of the EU, since the incorporation of the Charter on Fundamental Rights (2000) into EU law following the coming into force of the Lisbon Treaty in December 2009. See Article 6 (1) TEU; *Charter on Fundamental Rights of the European Union* (2010/C 83/02).

16 A prime example is the United States. In the environmental crime context, see an early study in de Cicco, J. and Bonano, E. 'A Comparative Analysis of the Criminal Environmental Laws of the Fifty States: The Need for Statutory Uniformity as a Catalyst for Effective Enforcement of Existing and Proposed Laws', (1988) 9(4) *Criminal Justice Quarterly* 216.

17 As seen in the *Ship-Source Pollution* case, harmonization of penalty types and levels has been even more contentious than the harmonization of the principle of incrimination.

It was not totally clear from the *Environmental Crimes* and *Ship-Source Pollution* rulings whether the European Community could pursue the total harmonisation (i.e. unification) of criminal standards, so the scope for total harmonisation of environmental criminal law would have depended on the legal basis chosen for the measure. In any event, unification in the criminal-law field is more likely to be considered incompatible with the principles of necessity and subsidiarity. A clarification to this question was given by Article 83 (1) and (2) of the Treaty on the Functioning of the EU (TFEU), which provide the basis for harmonisation of substantive criminal law since the ratification of the Lisbon Treaty. Those provisions make clear that the EU can only adopt 'minimum rules' in the criminal law field. Therefore, the TFEU leaves unimpaired member states' ability to implement higher criminal-law standards than those developed by the EU. The European Commission itself has discarded the scope for *total* harmonization of criminal law, at least in environmental criminal law context.[18]

Another possibility for closer integration in criminal matters in the EU would be the drafting of a EU Criminal Code that superseded all the existing criminal laws of the member states and centralized criminal law enforcement by creating a European Criminal Court (perhaps as a division of the CJEU) and/or a European public prosecutor. In fact, the *Corpus Iuris* project, under the direction of Mireille Delmas-Marty, envisages the creation of a European Public Prosecutor (*Parquet Europeen*) under Article 18 of its final statement and the harmonization of criminal sanctions in Europe, but this project is limited to the context of Community fraud.[19] A number of recommendations of the *Corpus Iuris* project have been incorporated into the Lisbon Treaty, in particular as regards the possibility for creation of a European Public Prosecutor. Even though the creation of a European Public Prosecutor appeared a distant reality outside the context of Community fraud,[20] the Lisbon Treaty allows not only for the establishment of a European Public Prosecutor (EPP) by the unanimous

---

18 *See* Commission of the European Communities, Impact Assessment, 'Commission Staff Working Document - Accompanying Document to the Proposal for a Directive of the European Parliament and of the Council on the Protection of the Environment through Criminal Law', (2007), 51 Final; SEC/2007/0160, (hereinafter '2007 Impact Assessment') and the Commission Staff Working Paper, 'Establishing of an Acquis on Criminal Sanctions against Environmental Offences', (2001), SEC/2001/227, at 3.

19 M. Delmas-Marty (ed.), *Corpus Juris: Introducing penal provisions for the purpose of the financial interests of the European Union* (1997). For a discussion of the Corpus Iuris Project see e.g. J. Pradel and G. Corstens, *Droit Penal Europeen* (Dalloz, 2002).

20 Commission of the European Communities, Green Paper on Criminal-law Protection of the Financial Interests of the Community and the Establishment of a European

vote of the member states,[21] but also for the extension of the EPP's competence to other areas of particularly 'serious crimes' with cross-border effects other than Community fraud, for example drug trafficking or environmental crime, but this would again require the unanimous vote of the member states.[22] Moreover, under the Lisbon Treaty (as well as under the *Corpus Iuris* proposal) the Public Prosecutor would be itinerant, which means that it would rely on the criminal justice systems of the member states instead of a centralized EU criminal court.[23] Following the presentation of a proposal in 2013 for creation of a EU public prosecutor to secure the protection of the EU financial interests,[24] the European Parliament voted in favour of the proposal in March 2014,[25] but at the time of writing the Council of Ministers has not adopted the proposal.[26]

The existing rules establishing the jurisdiction of the CJEU (although a subsequent Treaty amendment could change this) do not allow for direct prosecutions to be brought before the court, although if a question of EU law arises in a criminal prosecution in a member state the CJEU may adjudicate the dispute on that specific question. As for the possibility of creation of a future EU criminal court (perhaps through the introduction of a criminal division within the European Court of Justice), this would likely be regarded as overtly intrusive and against the national interest of some Member States in maintaining the integrity of their own criminal justice systems. Yet concerns over national sovereignty and integrity of national legal systems could be partly circumvented if a future EU (criminal) court – in line with the existing EEP proposals – only had jurisdiction over a limited number of crimes in relation to the EU primary interests (such as euro-counterfeiting and fraud against the EU budget). The

---

Prosecutor, (2001), available at http://ec.europa.eu/anti_fraud/green_paper/document/green_paper_en.pdf (accessed on 10 February 2015).

21 Article 86 (1) TFEU. Although it possible for at least nine member states to pursue 'enhanced cooperation' and create the EPP for operations amongst themselves.

22 Article 86 (4) TFEU.

23 For a criticism of the itinerant character of the EPP, see S. Peers, *EU Justice and Home Affairs Law* (OUP, 2011) 13. This is interesting because medieval jurisprudence functioned in an iterant way, including the English Court system e.g. the Home Circuit.

24 *See* Proposal for a Council Regulation on the establishment of the European Public Prosecutor's Office /* COM/2013/0534 final – 2013/0255.

25 Members of the European Parliament have confirmed their support for the proposal in a plenary vote with 487 votes for, 161 against and 30 abstentions. See European Commission: Press Release. European Public Prosecutor's Office: European Parliament confirms its support, Strasbourg, 12 March 2014.

26 See http://www.statewatch.org/news/2015/jan/eppo-docs.html (accessed on 10 April 2015).

creation of such court would most certainly demand the establishment of a EU criminal prosecutor with competence over a range of crimes of special interest to the European Union budget.

More realistically, though, one could envisage the drafting of a EU Criminal Code. The idea of a 'European model penal code' was launched in 1996 by Professor Sieber's Memorandum under the supervision of the Council of Europe.[27] Yet there has been a wide range of criticism over the possibility of codification of criminal law in Europe. Cadoppi argues that a European Criminal Code would imply the unification of criminal law and the federalization of the EU member states.[28] Moreover, it is suggested that it would be difficult to reconcile the common law and civil law traditions existing in Europe. Indeed, probably the most fundamental division in the European legal culture is that between the civil law tradition (with its emphasis on codified law) and the common law tradition (with its emphasis on precedent).[29] However, the systematization of the developments in the area of EU criminal law would be welcome.[30] This is particularly so in light of the increasing activities of the EU in the criminal-law field, which has only gained further impetus since the entering into force of the Lisbon Treaty in 2009. As Weyembergh has noted,[31] the need for systematization and coherence is one of the main concerns regarding the developments in the Area of Freedom, Security and Justice (AFSJ) – the term used to encompass the developments in EU criminal law since the Amsterdam Treaty.

Most importantly, the Treaty of Amsterdam, by introducing the Framework Decision as an instrument of harmonization of criminal law, had a catalytic effect on the development of EU substantive criminal law, an area in which very little had been accomplished until then.[32] Initiatives to harmonize substantive

---

27 Sieber, U. 'Memorandum on a European Model Penal Code', (1999) 1 *European Journal of Law Reform* 445.

28 Cadoppi, A. 'Towards a European Criminal Code?', (1996) 4(1) *European Journal of Crime, Criminal Law and Criminal Justice* 2.

29 Mitsilegas, V. Monar, J. and Rees, W. *The European Union and Internal Security: Guardian of the People?* (2003), 11.

30 In this vein, Labayle and Weyembergh published in 2005 a compilation of the EU criminal law acts which had been adopted or proposed in the context of the third pillar. See H. Labayle, Henri and A. Weyembergh, *Code of Criminal law of the European Union: Texts up to January 1st, 2005* (2005); See also C. van den Wyngaert, *International Crime Law: A Collection of International and European Instruments* (2005).

31 Weyembergh, A. (2005) above note 11, at 1567.

32 For some of the few exceptions of EU criminal law measures adopted before the ToA, see e.g. the Convention on the Protection of the European Community's Financial Interests,

criminal law under the former 'third pillar' include conventions (which fell into disuse), Framework Decisions and Joint Actions in the areas of organized crime (criminal organisations,[33] terrorism,[34] money laundering[35] and drug trafficking[36]) relating to interests of the Union as such (financial interests of the Community,[37] currency,[38] unauthorized entry, transit and residence[39]) and interests that, given their potential transboundary nature, require regulation at the transnational level (corruption in the public and private sector,[40] protection of the environment,[41] ship-source pollution,[42] trafficking in human

(1995), OJC 316, at 49 and the 1998 Joint Action on Making it an Offence to Participate in a Criminal Organisation in the Member States of the European Union, OJ L351; 98/733/JHA. See also, Fletcher, Maria, Loof, Robin And Gilmore, Bill, *EU Criminal Law and Justice* (Edward Elgar, 2008) at 173.

33 Council Framework Decision 2008/841/JHA of 24 October 2008 on the Fight Against Organised Crime, OJ L300/42 (2008), repealing Joint Action 1998/733/JHA O.J. L351/1 (1998).

34 Council Framework Decision 2002/629/JHA of June 2002 on Combating Terrorism, OJ L164/3 (2002).

35 Council Framework Decision 2001/500/JHA of June 2001 on Money Laundering, the Identification, Tracing, Freezing, Seizing and Confiscation of Instrumentalities and Proceeds of Crime, OJ L166/77 (2001).

36 Council Framework Decision 2004/757/JHA of 25 October 2004 Laying Down Minimum Provisions on the Constituent Elements of Criminal Acts and Penalties in the Field of Illicit Drug Trafficking, OJ L335 (2004), at 8.

37 Convention on the Protection of the European Communities' Financial Interests, OJC 316/49 (1995).

38 Council Framework Decision 2000/283/JHA of 19 May 2000 on Increading Protection by Criminal Penalties and Other Sanctions Against Counterfeiting in Connection with the Introduction of the Euro, OJ L140/1 (2000), at 1; amended by Council Framework Decision 2001/888/JHA of 6 December 2001 Amending Framework Decision 2000/383/JHA on Increasing Protection by Criminal Penalties and Other Sanctions Against Counterfeiting in Connection with the Introduction of the Euro, OJ L329 (2001), at 3.

39 Council Framework Decision 2002/946/JHA of 28 November 2002 on the Strengthening of the Penal Framework to Prevent the Facilitation of Unauthorised Entry, Transit and Residence, OJ L328, (2002), at 1.

40 Council Framework Decision 2003/568/JHA of 22 July 2003 on Combating Corruption in the Private Sector, OJ L328 (2003), at 54; OJC 195/2 (1997); OJ L279/1 (1997); OJ L358/2 (1998).

41 Council Framework Decision 2003/80/JHA on the Protection of the Environment through Criminal Law, 27 January 2003, OJ L29 (2003) (annulled on 13 September 2005).

42 Council Framework Decision 2005/667/JHA of 12 July 2005 to Strengthen the Criminal-Law Framework for the Enforcement of the Law Against Ship-Source Pollution, OJ L255 (2005), at 67 (annulled on 23 October 2007).

beings,[43] sexual exploitation of children,[44] insider dealing and market manipulation,[45] racism,[46] fraud and counterfeiting of non-cash payment,[47] and cyber crimes)[48,49] In addition to these third pillar measures, a number of supranational criminal law measures have been adopted in the form of Directives in the aftermath of the *Environmental Crimes* and *Ship-Source Pollution* rulings;[50] as well as following the ratification of the Lisbon Treaty in December 2009 based on Article 82 and Article 83 (1) and (2) TFEU.[51]

This extensive list of EU/EC criminal law measures does not explain why some offences are singled out for harmonization or what the potential limits in the field of EU substantive criminal law are.[52] Some of those offences could be categorised as the 'core' of criminal law (that is, essentially, offences against the person and property offences) which are areas which generally fell outside the scope of the conventional EC competencies established under the former EC Treaty;[53] whereas others are connected to the traditional EU/EC objectives – including the four freedoms, non-discrimination and environmental protection – which could be thus termed

43 Council Framework Decision 2002/629/JHA of 19 July 2002 on Combating Trafficking in Human Beings, OJ L2003 (2002), at 2.

44 Council Framework Decision 2004/68/JHA of 22 December 2003 on Combating the Sexual Exploitation of Children and Child Pornography, OJ L13 (2004), at 4.

45 OJ L334/30 (1989); OJ L91/16 (2003).

46 OJ L185/5 (1996); OJC 75 E/269 (2002).

47 Council Framework Decision 2001/413/JHA of 28 May 2001 Combating Fraud and Counterfeiting of Non-Cash Means of Payment OJ L149/1 (2001).

48 Council Framework Decision 2005/667/JHA of 24 February 2005 on Attacks Against Information Systems, OJ L69 (2005), at 67.

49 *See* also W. Perron, 'Perspectives of the Humanization of Criminal Law and Criminal Procedure in the European Union', in E. Husabø and A. Strandbakken (eds.) *Harmonization of Criminal Law in Europe* (2005), 15; and Fletcher, M., Loof, R. And Gilmore, B., (2008) above note 32, at 175.

50 Directive 2008/99/EC of the European Parliament and of the Council of 19 November 2008 on the protection of the environment through criminal law, *Official Journal* L 328, 6 December 2008; and Directive 2009/123/EC of the European Parliament and of the Council of 21 October 2009 amending Directive 2005/35/EC on ship-source pollution and on the introduction of penalties for infringements; *Official Journal*, L 280/52. 27.10.2009.

51 See, for example, Directive 2014/57/EU of the European Parliament and of the Council of 16 April 2014 on criminal sanctions for market abuse ('market abuse directive'). A full list of the adopted and proposed EU criminal law measures adopted post-Lisbon can be found at http://www.eclan.eu/Default.aspx?CatID=77 (accessed on 10 April 2015).

52 Fletcher, M. et al. (2008) above note 32, at 175.

53 Post-Lisbon, these offences generally fall under the scope of Article 83 (1) TFEU.

'regulatory'.[54] Moreover, the EU legal instruments of harmonization of penal law have focused primarily on the 'special part' of the criminal law. Harmonization of the general rules and principles of criminal law are treated sparingly, falling primarily into four fields: corporate liability; liability of heads of business; the extension of criminal liability to inchoate offences i.e. conspiracy, instigation and attempts; and accomplices.[55] There has been no attempt yet in EU criminal measures to harmonize, for example, the definition of causation or the *mens rea* element of crime (for example, the definition of intention, recklessness or negligence), which are notions which are best defined under national laws.[56]

The European Commission itself has recognised that there are considerable limits to the extent to which EU/EC law could harmonise the criminal laws of the Member States. The Commission 2005 Communication suggested that the EC (thus referring to the Community legal order pre-Lisbon) could not oblige Member States to change their fundamental system of criminal law comprising, for instance, of the doctrine of criminal responsibility or the general definitions of guilt, commission of an offence, *mens rea* or complicity.[57] The Commission suggests that in these instances, the centre of gravity would lie in the improvement of judicial cooperation.[58] Given that the Lisbon Treaty gives broader powers to the EU at the supranational level to adopt measures to improve judicial and police cooperation in criminal matters, it is likely that the Commission will seek to harmonise the more detailed rules relating to criminal-law cooperation which previously appeared to fall under the scope of the third pillar (and hence outside the scope of the Community competence).[59]

In contrast, the crimes harmonized by the International Criminal Court Statute are more limited in scope – it includes genocide, crimes against humanity,

---

54 Post-Lisbon, these offences generally fall under the scope of Article 83 (2) TFEU.

55 See Kis, N. 'The Principle of Culpability in European Criminal law Systems', in M. Hollán (ed.), *Towards More Harmonised Criminal Law in the European Union* (2004) at 107. See further, Chapter 6.

56 Interestingly, in the *Intertanko* (2008) case which concerned the legality of the Ship-Source Pollution Directive, the ECJ attempted to define the standard of 'serious negligence' which appears in a number of EU criminal law instruments. See further, Chapter 6.

57 See Communication from the European Commission to the European Parliament and the Council on the Implications of the Court's Judgement of 13 September 2005 (Case C-176/03 Commission *v* Council) COM (2005) 583 final/2, 24 November 2005.

58 *Ibid* at 4. 1.

59 Indeed, the 2005 Commission Communication statement only implied that no harmonisation would be possible under the first pillar level in those areas, but it would have not prevented in principle the harmonisation of those subject areas at the third pillar level.

war crimes, and the crime of aggression.[60] However, the crimes harmonized in the ICC Statute are subject to much higher specification than is the case of EU criminal-law instruments, in particular if one considers the definitional supplement to the ICC Statute provided by the Elements of Crime.[61] The principle of legality (or legal certainty) would appear in principle to support a similar level of specification by the crimes harmonized by the EU. Yet in light of the principles of subsidiarity and proportionality, and in particular the fact that Directives or Framework Decisions harmonizing criminal law need to be transposed into national law before they create obligations on individuals, this same level of specification of the elements of crime would not be justifiable at the EU level.

4.4 Approximation or Cooperation? The Principle of Mutual Recognition in EU Criminal Law

The fact that criminals are able to exploit the differences in legislation and legal enforcement techniques in different states to their benefit has led to calls for the harmonization of both substantive and procedural criminal law. However, in order to avert fears from the part of the member states that harmonization would undermine their sovereignty in criminal matters and ultimately lead to legislative stagnation,[62] the principle of mutual recognition has been chosen as the cornerstone of police and judicial cooperation in criminal matters in the EU.[63] The principle of mutual recognition progressively replaces traditional judicial cooperation by one based on the near automatic acceptance and enforcement of all judicial decisions made during criminal proceedings taken in one member state by the appropriate authorities in all others.[64] The principle of mutual recognition in EU criminal law has been criticized

60 As was discussed in Chapter 3, whether terrorism or drug trafficking, for example, will be included in the ICC Statute will be decided in future review conferences. See further, A. Cassese, P. Gaeta, and J. Jones, *The Rome Statute of the International Criminal Court A Commentary* (2002), 1903.

61 *Ibid.*

62 V. Mitsilegas, 'Trust-Building Measures in the European Judicial Area in Criminal Matters: Issues of Competence, Legitimacy and Inter-Institutional Balance', in T. Balzacq, and S. Carrera, (eds.) *Security Versus Freedom? A Challenge for Europe's Future* (2006), 279.

63 This was stressed both at the conclusions of the Tampere European Council meeting in 1999 (see paras. 33–7) and at the 2004 Hague Programme. See I. Jegouzo, 'Le development Progressif du Principe de Reconnaissance Mutuelle des Décisions Judiciaires Pénal Dans L'Union Europeenne', (2006) 77 *Revue Internationale de Droit Penal* 97.

64 Fletcher, M. et al. (2008) above note 32, at 109.

inter alia for adapting a judicial framework developed for market regulation to the very different needs of internal security.[65]

There is intense debate on whether the principle of mutual recognition should be considered an *alternative* to harmonization or whether it should be *complemented* by it when necessary in order *inter alia* to enhance mutual trust in the criminal justice systems of the member states.[66] As put by Petter Asp, either the states involved pretend that such mutual trust exists, or they make sure that such mutual trust exists by means of harmonization.[67] Harmonization of criminal legislation could then be regarded as a means to facilitate police and judicial cooperation in criminal matters. For example, classic extradition agreements require double-criminality in both executing and issuing states, so harmonization of criminal law would facilitate the operation of those agreements because both states would have criminalized and introduced similar sanctions for similar offences.

Cooperation in criminal matters at the EU level is regarded as necessary in order to ensure that individuals do not escape prosecution simply by exercising their free movement rights. As was discussed in Chapter 3, this has been termed an *auxiliary function* of the approximation of European criminal law – that is, approximation as a tool to support judicial co-operation in the field of criminal law – which is regarded as perhaps one of the most important goals of the harmonization programme.[68] The differences in substantive and procedural criminal laws in the EU member states, in particular, undermine the principle of free movement of persons.[69] This is expressly recognised in Article 82

---

65 Mitsilegas, V. (2006) above note 64, at 10–11. The principle of mutual recognition was developed by the case-law of the Court of Justice in the context of market integration. Once a product is lawfully marketed in one member state, another member state cannot refuse the import of that product unless the refusal is based on one of the grounds for derogation provided for under the TFEU (e.g. Article 36 TFEU) or the mandatory requirements. See Case 120/78, *Rewe-Zentral* AG *v Bundesmonopolverwaltung für Branntwein* (*'Cassis de Dijon'*) [1979] ECR.

66 See Mitsilegas, V. 'The Constitutional Implications of Mutual Recognition in Criminal Matters in the EU', (2006) 43 *Common Market Law Review* 1277; and Peers, S. 'Mutual Recognition and Criminal Law in the European Union: Has the Council got it Wrong?' (2004) 41 *Common Market Law Review* 5.

67 P. Asp, 'Mutual Recognition and the Development of Criminal Law Cooperation within the European Union', in E.J. Husabø, and A. Strandbakken, (eds.) *Harmonization of Criminal Law in Europe* (2005).

68 Weyembergh, A. (2005) above note 11, at 1583.

69 *See* Commission of the European Communities, Consultation Document, Green Paper on Procedural Safeguards for Suspects and defendants in criminal proceedings throughout the European Union, (2003).

TFEU (which is the post-Lisbon legal basis for harmonisation of *procedural* criminal law) which links the harmonisation of criminal procedure to the need to support mutual recognition measures.[70] So one of the main arguments for the EU to harmonize criminal law is that, ironically, it facilitates the operation of criminal-law instruments based on the principle of mutual recognition. It is thus paradoxical that instruments of harmonisation of substantive and procedural criminal law are adopted or proposed at least partly with the aim to support mutual recognition instruments, which are themselves based on the principle of 'mutual trust' among the judicial systems of the Member States.

However, since the Treaty of Amsterdam a number of EU instruments are devoted to approximation as an autonomous goal, showing that 'approximation is slowly gaining some independence from judicial cooperation mechanisms'.[71] The Treaty of Lisbon expressly recognized the autonomous function of approximation of the penal laws of the member states, by introducing Article 83 (2) to TFEU which states that:[72]

> If the approximation of criminal laws and regulations of the Member States proves essential to ensure the effective implementation of a Union policy which has been subject to harmonisation measures, directives may establish minimum rules with regard to the definition of criminal offences and sanctions in the area concerned.

Although the principle of mutual recognition is regarded as the cornerstone of police and judicial cooperation in criminal matters in the European Union and underpins a number of initiatives in the former third pillar,[73] the successful operation of the principle requires the building of mutual trust in one

---

70 *See* Article 82 (2) TFEU: '*to the extent that is necessary to facilitate mutual recognition of judgements and judicial decisions and police and judicial cooperation in criminal matters having cross-border dimension,* the European Parliament and Council may, by means of directives adopted in accordance with the ordinary procedure, establish minimum rules' (emphasis added).

71 A. Weyembergh, 'Approximation of Criminal Laws, the Constitutional Treaty and the Hague Programme', (2005) 42 *Common Market Law Review*, at 1583.

72 This provision is equivalent to article III-270 (2) of the (now defunct) Treaty Establishing a Constitution for Europe (CT), OJC 310.

73 See, in particular, Council Framework Decision of 13 June 2002 on the European Arrest Warrant and the Surrender of Procedures between Member States, *Official Journal* L 190 18 July 2002; Council Framework Decision on the European Evidence Warrant for the purpose of obtaining objects, documents and data for use in proceedings in criminal matters, 2008/978/JHA, 18 December 2008, *Official Journal* L350/72, 30 December 2008; Council

another's legal systems, which in turn may require a degree of harmonization. For example, one judge may be hesitant to surrender a state's own national under an arrest warrant issued by another member state, if the legal system of that state does not provide minimum guarantees to the defendant in criminal proceedings. Hence in order to build mutual trust a degree of harmonization of criminal law is required. So mutual recognition is not an *alternative* to harmonization, but it is complemented by it.

It is unlikely that at the broader international level a similar system of inter-state cooperation based on mutual recognition could be developed to replace traditional mechanisms of police and judicial cooperation in criminal matters, such as extradition agreements. The safeguards contained in such instruments exist primarily in order to counterbalance the lack of trust among states and to secure certain minimum procedural rights for defendants. It appears unlikely that such safeguards could be loosed to a significant extent at the broader international level, which would be particularly challenging in the case of the international crimes covered by the ICC Statute. The numerous constitutional challenges to the EAW before the national courts[74] suggests that agreement among states on overarching fundamental human rights guarantees in order to ensure prosecutorial efficiency would be even more challenging at the global level. Hence the focus of the EU on enhancing prosecutorial efficiency,[75] which may be at odds with the protection of fundamental rights, is likely to be contested even further if applied at the broader international context.[76] In this regard,

Framework Decision 2005/214/JHA on the application of the principle of mutual recognition to financial penalties of 24 February 2005, *Official Journal* L76/16 22 March 2005.

74 See e.g. Decision of the German Constitutional Court of July 18, 2005 – European Arrest Warrant Act. and the decisions of the Polish Constitutional Court Re: Enforcement of the European Arrest Warrant, Judgement of 27 April 2005, P1/05. For a discussion see Mitsilegas, V., *EU Criminal Law* (Hart, 2009), 133.

75 This point is illustrated if one contrasts the swift adoption of the European Arrest Warrant in 2002 in the aftermath of September 11th, with the stalemate in the negotiations of a Proposal for a Council Framework Decision on certain procedural rights in criminal proceedings throughout the European Union (2004) (withdrawn by the Commission since the entering into force of the Lisbon Treaty, see Communication from the Commission to the European Parliament and the Council – Consequences of the entry into force of the Treaty of Lisbon for ongoing interinstitutional decision-making procedures /* COM/2009/0665 final).

76 However, it should be noted that a number of recent EU criminal law legislative proposals concern the protection of the defendant's or victims' procedural rights. See e.g. Directive 2012/13/EU of 22 May 2012 on the right to information in criminal proceedings; and Directive 2013/48/EU on the right of access to a lawyer in criminal proceedings and on the right to communicate upon arrest.

one question that has raised considerable debate in the context of the EAW is the possibility of surrender of a state's own nationals, which contravenes the constitutional traditions of some Member States containing the prohibition of extradition of a state's own nationals. However, it should be noted that when asked to rule in *Advocaten voor de Wereld*[77] on the question of whether the undefined offences in the 2002 EAW Framework Decision violate the principle of legal certainty or breached other fundamental rights, the ECJ ruled that the lack of a precise definition of the 'criminal offences' listed in the Framework Decision does not violate the principle of legal certainty since that Framework Decision does not seek to harmonize the constituent elements of the criminal offences in question; and that the extradition of a state's nationals is not necessarily in breach of fundamental rights.[78]

4.5 The Format of the Legal Instrument Harmonising Environmental Criminal Law: The Choice between Directives and Regulations

As the ECJ has settled in the *Environmental Crimes* decision the question of the EC competence to harmonise environmental criminal law (see further, Chapter 5), a question remained as to which supranational EC instrument – directives or regulations – should be applied for harmonisation of environmental criminal law.

One of the corollaries of the direct applicability of a EU Regulation is that it may affect individuals indirectly without the need for an implementing measure to be taken at national level.[79] According to Article 288 (2) TFEU '[a] regulation shall have general application' and '[i]t shall be binding in its entirety and directly applicable in all Member States'.[80] Even though Regulations do not require incorporation into the national legal order, in practice the adoption of national rules is frequently necessary in order for a Regulation to be fully operative. This thus allows a certain (albeit limited) degree of discretion to national authorities as regards the choice of how to implement the Regulation.[81]

Even though it is in principle possible for a Regulation to be used as an instrument of harmonisation of environmental criminal law, the Commission

77 Case C-303/05, *Advocaten voor de Wereld VZW v.Leden van de Ministerraad*, [2007] ECR 1. See also the Opinion of Advocate General Ruiz-Rabaro Colomer on 12 September 2006.

78 Advocaten voor de Wereld, para. 115.

79 Tridimas, Takis, *The General Principles of EU law* (Oxford, 2006) at 420.

80 Equivalent to former Article 249 (2) EC.

81 Prechal, Sacha, *Directives in EC Law* (Oxford, 2005) at 14.

discarded the option of adopting a Regulation to harmonise environmental criminal law since the aim of legislative action in this field would be to set minimum standards only, allowing thus the Member States to enhance on the EU standards.[82] The choice of a Directive is also in line with the Amsterdam Protocol on the Principles of Subsidiarity and Proportionality. Indeed, while paragraph 7 of the Amsterdam Protocol sets conditions for the *content* of the EU measure, paragraph 6 of the Protocol establishes guidelines as regards the *form* of the measure: '(…) [o]ther things being equal, directives should be preferred to regulations and framework directives to detailed measures'.[83]

Unlike Regulations, Directives are binding on Member States as far as the results are concerned, but not as far as the methods and instruments chosen for implementation.[84] It follows that if an instrument does not leave Member States with a certain amount of freedom of choices in the forms and methods of implementation, then it loses the character of a directive.[85] Since an instrument harmonising environmental criminal law necessarily leaves a very limited choice to Member States as regards the implementation technique – as the 'choice' of criminal law is made at the EU level – it is questionable whether such an instrument is compatible with the nature of a Directive.[86] It could be argued though that the result to be achieved by the environmental crime directive is that serious violations of EU environmental law are considered criminal offences in the Member States, and that it leaves a – albeit limited – choice of how to implement those results, for example under an existing criminal code or sparse environmental regulations. This is consistent with the nature of Directives, which may give a *detailed description* of the *result* to be achieved, provided that this is necessary for the effective realisation of the objective pursued.[87] It is clear

82 Commission Staff Working Document, Accompanying Document to the Proposal for a Directive of the European Parliament and of the Council on the Protection of the Environment through Criminal Law, *Impact Assessment* [COM (2007) 51 final SEC (2007) 160] 9 February 2007 at 35.

83 Protocol no. 30 Annexed to the Treaty of Amsterdam [1997] O.J. C340, Para. 6.

84 This is expressly stated in Article 288 (3) (ex article 249 (3) EC): 'a directive shall be binding, as to the result to be achieved, upon each member-state to which it is addressed, *but shall leave to the national authorities the choice of forms and method*' (emphasis added).

85 Prechal (2005) above note 81, at 14.

86 Faure, Michael. 'European Environmental Criminal Law: Do we really need it?' (2004) 13 *EELR* 18.

87 See Case 38/77 *Enka* [1977] ECR 2203. See Prechal, *supra* at 14. Likewise, Framework Decisions – which were used under the third pillar for the harmonisation of criminal law – were also binding as to the result to be achieved, leaving it to Member States the choice of forms and methods for implementation.

though that Article 288(3) TFEU (former Article 249 (3) EC) sets a limit to the detailed description of the result to be achieved: a Directive as a whole must leave some latitude to the Member States as far as the form and methods of implementation are concerned, but it certainly cannot oblige a Member State to introduce an exhaustive set of rules with no consideration of the law existing within the national legal order.[88] Moreover, even though under a Directive the choice of instrument of implementation is left to Member States, the ECJ has refused to accept the transposition of an environmental directive into national law by means of administrative circular or plan or other similar instruments.[89] The CJ requires a binding legislative or regulatory instrument, since that ensures legal certainty for those relying on the rights pertaining to the Directive.[90]

The choice of implementation of the Directive on environmental crime under national penal codes is consistent with the legislative practice in the Member States. Indeed, many EU Member States have introduced into their penal codes specific provisions on the protection of the environment: following the example of the German *Strafgezetzbuch* of 1980, an amendment to which introduced a chapter entitled 'Crimes against the Environment',[91] Austria (1977/97),[92] Spain (1996),[93] Portugal (1995),[94] as well as Denmark, Finland, the Netherlands, and Sweden have incorporated environmental offences into their penal codes.[95] Some European states have partially reformed their penal codes in order to incorporate, among others, environmental crimes – for example Austria and Sweden – while others have undertaken total reform of their penal codes – for example Portugal, Spain and Finland.[96] Yet the

88 *Ibid* at 15.

89 C-96/81 *Commission v Netherlands* (1982) E.C.R. 1791 at 420.

90 Kramer, L. *EC Environmental Law* (6th d. Sweet & Maxwell, 2007) at 419.

91 18 Strafrechtsanderungsgesetz (StSG) of July 1980 reformed by the 31 StAG of 1 November 1994.

92 Bundesgesetz of 23 January 1974; Strafrechtsanderungsgesetz of 1987. See Ringelmann, C. 'Recent Trends in Environmental Criminal Legislation' (1997) 5 *Eur. J. Crime L. & Crim. Just.* 393 pp. 394–395.

93 Nuevo Codigo Penal, Articles 325–331, which was promulgated on November 23 1995 and entered into force on 24 July 1996.

94 Codigo Penal of October 1995, Articles 278–281 dealing with environmental crimes.

95 *See* de Sadeleer, N. 'La Répression des Infractions en Matière de Gestion des Déchets' in Françoise Comte and Ludwig Kramer (ed.) *Environmental Crimes in Europe: Rules of Sanctions* (Groningen, 2004).

96 Ringelmann, C. supra at 395.

French *Nouveu Code Pénal* of 1994, which replaced the old Napoleonic Code, failed to introduce any criminal offences against the environment.[97]

Following the transposition deadline of the EU environmental crime directive on 26 December 2010, the Member States have reformed their legislation either by reforming their codes or by amending specific sparse environmental laws in order to incorporate environmental offences. For example, Austria and Germany have adopted federal legislation amending their criminal codes to transpose the EU environmental crime directive.[98] In contrast, the United Kingdom and Ireland, for example, which do not have a criminal code, have instead amended their sparse environmental legislation in order to implement the environmental crime directive.[99]

4.6 Direct and Indirect Effect of Environmental Crime Legislation

Directives may have direct effect on the rights of citizens of the Union whether or not the Member State has fulfilled its obligation to implement a Directive.[100] The doctrine of direct effect of Community law was affirmed by the ECJ in the *Van Gend en Los* case.[101] Direct effect allows domestic judges to apply Union law (the treaties, regulations and directives), regardless of the existence of a national transposition measure. Moreover, it allows individuals to invoke the provisions of a Directive that has not been implemented within a specific

97 *Ibid* at 395. Yet the French Environment Code (2008) lays down criminal sanctions for violations of environmental law.

98 *See* Bundesgesetzblatt for the Republic Of Austria Vintage 2011 Issued on 21 November 2011 Part I 103 Federal Law: Amendment of the Criminal Code for the prevention of terrorism and the Penal Code and the Criminal Procedure Code in 1975 to improve the criminal-law protection of the environment; NR: GP XXIV RV 674 and 1392 AB 1422 S. 124 BR: 8583 AB 8598 p 801 [CELEX number:. 32008L0099]; and German Federal Law Gazette 2011 Part I No. 64, issued in Bonn on December 13, 2011.

99 See the transposition measures communicated by Ireland and the UK to the Commission. See e.g. European Communities (Birds and Natural Habitats) Regulations 2011 (S.I. 477 of 2011) Legal act: Statutory Instrument (Regulation or Order), number: 477 of 2011; Official Journal: Iris Oifigiúl, Publication date: 27/09/2011, Entry into force: 21/09/2011; Reference: (MNE(2011)57109); Control Of Trade In Endangered Species Act, 1998 Legal act: Gibraltar Regulations, number: 1998–11; Official Journal: Gibraltar Gazette, number: 1998–11, Publication date: 29/01/1998, Entry into force: 29/01/1998; Reference: (MNE(2011)55143). On the implementation of the EU environmental crime and ship-source pollution directives, see further, Chapters 6 and 7.

100 Dine, Janet 'European Community Criminal Law?' (1993) *Crim.L.R.* 246 at 251.

101 Case 26/62 *Van Gend en Loos v. Netherlandse Administratie der Belastingen* [1963] E.C.R. 1.

time-limit against a State (vertical direct effect), but not generally by individuals against other individuals (horizontal direct effect)[102] or by a State against an individual.[103] In order to have direct effect, the provision of a directive must be 'unconditional and sufficiently precise'.[104]

In principle, a measure harmonising environmental criminal law (such as the environmental crime and ship-source pollution directives) would have direct effect on Member States, therefore allowing individuals to rely on their EU rights despite the failure of a Member State to implement the measure.[105] On the other hand, since the obligations under the directive on environmental crime are directed to the Member States *to create criminal offences* and *to apply 'effective, proportionate and dissuasive' penalties* which are connected to *existing rights and obligations under EC environmental law*, it would be difficult to establish that the directive creates any additional rights to individuals. However, this question may be put before the Court where the Directive establishes 'attenuating circumstances' for certain offences. For example in the case of the crime against protected flora and fauna specimens, the conduct does not need to be considered a crime if 'the conduct concerns a negligible quantity of such specimens and has a negligible impact on the conservation status of the species'.[106] In fact, this could be claimed by individuals raising the retroactivity of the more beneficial (Community) criminal legislation. The Court has shown willingness to foster application of the principle of retroactivity of the more beneficial (Community) legislation in the legal systems of the Member States.[107] On the other hand, it would be difficult to argue that this 'attenuating circumstance' provides a right to individuals since the Directive creates minimum standards only, allowing the Member States to enhance the EU/EC standards.[108] For the same reason it would be difficult for polluters to

---

102 See e.g. Case 91/92 *Paola Faccine Dori* [1994] ECR I-3325.

103 See e.g. Case 38/77 *Enke* [1997] ECR 2203 and Case 190/87 *Moorman* [1987] ECR 4689.

104 Case 26/62 *Van Gend en Loos,* [1963] E.C.R. I.

105 *See ibid.*

106 Article 3 (f) of the environmental crime directive.

107 See Cases C-358/93 and C-416/93 *Bordessa* [1995] E.C.R. I-361 and comments on the case in Baker, Estella 'Taking European Criminal Law Seriously' *Criminal Law Review* [1998] at 4. The guarantee of retroactivity of the more beneficial legislation is not established in Article 7 ECHR (which bans retroactive criminal legislation) and it is not accepted in the legal system of all Member States (e.g. England & Wales).

108 See Recital 12 to the Preamble of the environmental crime directive: 'As this Directive provides for minimum rules, Member States are free to adopt or maintain more stringent measures regarding the effective criminal law protection of the environment. Such measures must be compatible with the Treaty'.

raise the 'aggravating elements' of the offences under the Directive (e.g. 'serious injury' or 'serious damage') to their benefit in a criminal prosecution in the event that the national implementing measure imposes even more stringent standards.

Due to the principle of legality (*nullum crimen sine praevia lege*) a Member State that fails to implement the environmental crime and ship-source pollution directives by not criminalising the illegal activity would not be able to prosecute an individual.[109] The principle of non-retroactivity of criminal law is upheld by the Court of Justice as a general principle of law.[110] In this vein, the Court has held on a number of occasions that a Directive not transposed into national law may not be relied upon to the disadvantage of the person being prosecuted.[111] For example, in *Criminal Proceedings against Luciano Arcaro* (1996),[112] the ECJ held that the failure of the Italian government to implement a Directive regarding the discharge of cadmium into waters prevented it from prosecuting an Italian citizen who discharged the substance without authorisation. This is because, according to the ECJ, directives could only exceptionally have direct effect to the benefit of an individual, not against an individual.[113] Therefore a Member State could not take advantage of its own failure to comply with Community law in order to introduce criminal proceedings against Mr Arcaro.[114] This decision has been criticised by Ludwig Kraemer for giving less weight to the general public interest in protecting the environment than to individual rights, even though it is also suggested that administrative sanctions would have been more appropriate in that case.[115] A notable example of national implementation law which is likely to be regarded as contravening the principle of legality is Spain's legislation transposing the environmental crime directive.[116] Instead of reforming Spanish national environmental laws in order to transpose the directive, the Spanish implementation legislation simply makes a general

---

109 See e.g. Case 168/95 *Criminal proceedings against Luciano Arcaro* [1996] ECR I-4705.

110 See Case 63/83 *Kent Kirk* [1984] ECR 2689.

111 See e.g. Case 276/91 *Commission v France* [1993] ECR I-4413.

112 Case C-168/95 *Criminal Proceedings against Luciano Arcaro* ECR I–4705 [1996].

113 *Ibid.*

114 *Ibid* para. 37.

115 Kraemer, Ludwig *EU Casebook on Environmental Law*, Hart Publishing 2002, at 87.

116 *See* Ley Orgánica 5/2010, de 22 de junio, por la que se modifica la Ley Orgánica 10/1995, de 23 de noviembre, del Código Penal Legal act: Ley Orgánica, number: 5/2010; Official Journal: Boletín Oficial del Estado (B.O.E), number: 152/2010, Publication date: 23/06/2010, Page: 54811–54883, Entry into force: 23/12/2010; Reference: (MNE(2010)54213).

reference to the environmental crime directive, as if the directive itself would then become directly applicable in the Spanish legal order.[117]

It follows from the doctrine of direct effect that the invalidation of a national criminal offence for breach of a provision of the EU Treaties is only possible when that provision is 'sufficiently clear and precise' to provide citizens a right in EU law to challenge a criminal offence. A provision of a Directive may provide a defence to a criminal charge only if it is 'unconditional' and 'sufficiently clear and precise' and the date which it was due to have been implemented is passed.[118] Therefore, a Directive establishing environmental standards may have direct effect on the rights of citizens of the EU whether or not the Member State has fulfilled its obligation to implement a Directive.[119] On the other hand, Regulations will always afford a defence to a criminal charge where there is conflict between the two since Regulations are directly applicable.[120] Moreover, if a Directive or Regulation is invalid for contravening the Treaties or the general principles of EU law, an individual may challenge the validity of an implementing measure creating a criminal offence.[121]

In the EU's pre-Lisbon legal order, it was accepted that a third pillar instrument would not have direct effect on Member States.[122] However, like a first pillar measure, third pillar measures were recognized to have indirect effect following the *Pupino* decision in June 2005.[123] The doctrine of indirect effect suggests that national criminal laws must be construed so as to avoid conflict with EU law,[124] thus requiring national courts to interpret national laws in

---

117 *Ibid.* It states that 'Las modificaciones en los delitos contra el medio ambiente responden a la necesidad de acoger elementos de armonización normativa de la Unión Europea en este ámbito. De conformidad con las obligaciones asumidas, se produce una agravación de las penas y se incorporan a la legislación penal española los supuestos previstos en la Directiva 2008/99/CE de 19 de noviembre, relativa a la protección del medio ambiente mediante el Derecho penal'. ['The modifications in crimes against the environment respond to the need for regulatory harmonization in the European Union in this area. In accordance with the obligations assumed, an aggravation of sentences is produced and incorporated into the Spanish penal legislation in the cases provided for in Directive 2008/99/EC of 19 November on the protection of the environment through criminal law'. (author's translation)].

118 See Case 80/86 *Kolpinghuis Nijmegen* [1987] ECR.

119 Dine (1993) above note 100, at 251.

120 Former Article 249 EC. Dine (1993) *supra* at 251.

121 Case 38/90 *R v Lomas* [1992]64 C.M.L.R. 653.

122 As per Article 34 (2) (b) TEU (pre-Lisbon).

123 Case 105/03 *Criminal Proceedings against Pupino* [2005] ECR 5285.

124 Case 14 83, *Von Colson and Kaman* [1984] E.C.R. 1891. In the case of Directives, the duty to interpret national law in conformity with EU law arises even before the implementation

accordance with EU law. In *Pupino* the ECJ ruled that Italian criminal procedure law had to be construed in conformity with Council Framework Decision on the Standing of Victims in Criminal Proceedings (2001/220/JHA) so as to permit the testimony of young children under appropriate protective arrangements.[125] According to the ECJ, it would be very difficult for the Union to carry out its task effectively if the principle of loyal cooperation, ensuring the fulfilment of the obligations under EU law by the Member States, were not also binding in the third pillar. The Court reached this conclusion despite the fact that the TEU expressly ruled out *direct* effect to EU third pillar measures, i.e. they themselves could not be relied on by individuals (in countries which allow for private prosecutions) for the prosecution of other individuals or legal persons, until a national transposition measure is adopted.

Importantly, unlike the doctrine of direct effect, the doctrine of consistent interpretation or indirect effect is generally not restricted to cases which are favourable to citizens.[126] However, indirect effect (or consistent interpretation) would be incompatible with the principle of legality or *nulla poena sine lege* (which can be regarded as the basis for the prohibition of retroactivity of criminal law) if it effectively created a new criminal offence or aggravated the criminal liability, in contravention of Article 7 of the ECHR.[127] The same argument remains valid as regards criminal law directives adopted under a supranational (post-Lisbon) legal basis – i.e. Articles 82 and 83 (1) or (2) TFEU – consistent interpretation may not aggravate the situation of individuals or corporations in the Member States.[128]

---

date for the Directive has passed. Case C-106/89, *Marleasing* SA *v. La Commercial International de Alimentacion* SA [1990] E.C.R. 1-4135.

125 For a commentary on this decision see eg. Fletcher, Maria. 'Extending 'Indirect Effect' to the Third Pillar: The Significance of Pupino', (2005) *E. L. Rev*, 30 (6); and Mitsilegas, Valsamis 'Constitutional Principles of the European Community and European Criminal Law' (2007) *European Journal of Law Reform* 303. It has been suggested that under the pre-Lisbon EU legal order, a number of principles pertinent to the first pillar (e.g. supremacy and state liability) were applicable to third pillar (although direct effect was ruled out by virtue of Article 34 TEU). This is so in particular because of the similarities between former Article 249 EC (concerning directives) and Article 34 (2) TEU (concerning Framework Decisions) and the extension of the principle of effectiveness to the third pillar in light of *Pupino*. See Prinssen, J. 'Domestic Legal Effects of EU Criminal Law: A Transfer of EC Law Doctrines?' in Obradovic, D and Lavranos, N (eds.), *Interface between EU law and National Law* (Groningen, 2007).

126 Prechal, S. (2005) above note 81, at 205.

127 *Ibid.*

128 It could be argued that in *Pupino* the EU legislation in question – the Framework Decision on the Standing of Victims in Criminal Proceedings (2001/220/JHA) – aggravated the situation

Therefore, the principle that denies inverse or horizontal direct effect to non-implemented directives (i.e. that they are relied upon by the State against an individual, or that they create obligations upon individuals) and the principle of legality would, additionally, limit the possibility of the public authorities or individuals (in countries which allow individuals to bring prosecutions)[129] to bring prosecutions against individuals or corporations in the Member States until a Directive is transposed into national law.[130] So it is difficult to see how the direct effect of a Directive imposing criminal sanctions (as opposed to enhancing the rights of defendants in criminal proceedings, as was the case of the Framework Decision in question in *Pupino*) could benefit individual rights in the Member States.

Furthermore, it is important that the circumstances in which international (environmental or criminal law) agreements binding on the EU entail direct effect in the Union legal order are examined. International agreements which are binding on the Community/Union, and therefore part of the Community/Union legal order, have to be applied by national courts if they are directly effective. In such cases, they will override inconsistent national law – which might include national implementing legislation which transposes Union/Community legal obligations under national law.[131] For example, in the third *International Fruit Company* case,[132] the ECJ held that the legal challenge regarding the compatibility of a Community act with an international agreement is only possible if the latter is directly effective.[133] The conditions for an international agreement to have direct effect in the Community legal order are similar to those relating to direct effect of Directives as upheld in the Court's case law, i.e. the nature and the broad logic of the relevant international treaty do not preclude the examination of validity of the Community measure and, in addition, the treaty's provisions appear, as regards their content, to be

---

of the defendant. However, since this legislation relates to criminal procedural rules, the principle of non-retroactivity does not apply. Indeed, the Court held that 'these principles do not concern the extent of criminal liability of the persons concerned but the conduct of the proceedings and the means of taking evidence' (para. 46 of the judgement).

129 This includes England & Wales, Austria, Portugal, Finland and Spain. In most countries a permission of the prosecutor is not required. *See* Faure, Michael and Heine, Gunter 'Criminal Enforcement of Environmental Law in the European Union' Kluwer Law International (2005) at 50–51.

130 Joined Cases C-397/01 to C-403/01 *Pfeiffer* [2004] ECR I-8835.

131 *Ibid.*

132 Joined Cases 21 to 24/72 *International Fruit Company v Produktschap voor Groenten en* Fruit [1972] ECR 1219 Cases 21-4/72.

133 Hartley, TC, *The Foundations of European Community Law* (OUP, 2007) at 186.

unconditional and sufficiently precise.[134] Hence in order for individuals to rely on the provisions of an international agreement, they must be unconditional and sufficiently precise and the nature and broad logic of the international agreement does not preclude the examination of the Community/Union measure aimed at implementing the agreement into the domestic law. However, there are exceptions to this rule: where the Community act was intended to give effect to an obligation under the international agreement [135] or where the Community act expressly refers to the agreement.[136]

In the *Intertanko* case,[137] the ECJ examined the legality of the ship source-pollution directive in light of the 1982 UN Convention on the Law of the Sea (UNCLOS)[138] – to which, unlike MARPOL, the European Community is a party. Although the ECJ accepted that the Community was bound by UNCLOS and that it formed an integral part of the Community legal order,[139] it simultaneously upheld that the convention does not have direct effect in the Community legal order. According to the court, the nature and broad logic of UNCLOS precluded the examination of the validity of the shipping directive in light of its provisions, as UNCLOS was not directly applicable in the EU legal order as it does not aim to create rights for individuals or companies, such as shipping companies.[140] This reasoning allowed the ECJ to declare ultimately that it was not possible for it to examine the compatibility of the directive on shipping pollution with UNCLOS. On the one hand, the court was correct to hold that a provision of an international agreement must be unconditional and sufficiently precise (and must confer rights on individuals), before it can be regarded to be directly effective in the Community/Union legal order. However, the court failed to consider the exceptions to that rule recognized in previous case-law, namely in cases in which the Community/Union act aims at giving

134 *Intertanko* case, para. 45. See also Case C-344/04 *IATA and ELFAA* [2006] I-403, para. 39.

135 Case C-69/89 *Nakajima v Council* [1991] ECR I-2069.

136 Case 70/87 *Fediol v Commission* [1989] ECR 1781. See also Case C-280/93 *Germany v Council* [1994] ECR I-4973.

137 Case C-308/06 *The Queen on the Application of: International Association of Independent Tanker Owners (Intertanko), International Association of Dry Cargo Shipowners (Intercargo), Greek Shipping Co-operation Committee, Lloyd's Register, International Salvage Union v Secretary of State for Transport*, 3 June 2008 ('Intertanko').

138 UN Convention on the Law of the Sea 1833 UNTS 3 / [1994] ATS 31 / 21 ILM 1261 (1982) ('UNCLOS').

139 *Intertanko*, para. 53.

140 *Ibid.*

effect to an international agreement[141] or where the Community/Union act expressly refers to the international agreement.[142] In particular, unlike in the case of MARPOL (to which the EC is not a party), the Union/Community is bound by UNCLOS, so it is regrettable that the Court in *Intertanko* does not assess the references to that Convention in the shipping pollution directive[143] in order to establish whether it was necessary to apply the test of direct effect of international agreements or not. In other words, the Court could have assessed the legality of the shipping pollution directive in light of UNCLOS given the references in the former to the latter, regardless of whether or not UNCLOS has direct effect and confers rights on individuals.[144]

4.7 Approaches to Legislative Harmonisation

4.7.1 *Positive and Negative Harmonisation*

Prior to the ratification of the Lisbon Treaty, EC law could impact on the criminal justice systems of the Member States in a number of ways. Indeed, Community law (the 'first pillar') has had a significant impact on the criminal justice systems of the EU member states, either by requiring the member states to strike down criminal legislation incompatible with EC/EU law (negative harmonisation)[145] or by requiring them to introduce effective, proportionate and dissuasive penalties for the fulfilment of obligations arising from EC law, which needed to be at least equivalent to penalties applicable to equivalent obligations arising from national law (positive harmonisation).[146] Those developments were consistent with the view that prevailed prior to the ECJ judgement in the *Environmental Crimes* case, i.e. that the Community lacked

141 See Case C-69/89 *Nakajima v Council* [1991] ECR I-2069.

142 Case 70/87 *Fediol v Commission* [1989] ECR 1781. See also Case C-280/93 *Germany v Council* [1994] ECR I-4973.

143 See Article 3 (1) (c), Article 7 (2) and Article 9 of the ship-source pollution directive.

144 However, it is important to note that there are no references to UNCLOS in the provisions of the shipping pollution directive which were contested in this legal action (namely Article 4 and 5 (2)); and the main objective of the shipping pollution directive appears to be to implement *MARPOL*, rather than UNCLOS, standards. See also, Pereira, R. 'On the Legality of the Ship-Source Pollution 2005/35/EC Directive – the Intertanko Case and Selected Others' (2008) *European Energy & Environmental Law Review* 372.

145 See e.g. Case C-106/89, *Marleasing SA v. La Commercial International de Alimentacion SA*, [1990] 1 ECR 4135; Case 34/79 *R. v. Henn and Darby*, [1979] ECR 3795.

146 See e.g. Case 50/76 *Amsterdam Bulb*, [1977] ECR 137, paras. 32–3.

competence to prescribe criminal offences or sanctions, or to impose criminal sanctions.[147]

Whereas negative harmonisation takes full effect without the need for intervention of the national legislature (as incompatible national measures are struck down on an *ad hoc* basis by the ECJ), positive harmonisation required the instauration of the Article 258 TFEU[148] proceedings to ensure that the State concerned fulfils its obligations. So in the case of positive harmonisation the ECJ was required to establish whether or not a national sanction implementing EU law was effective on an individual basis, but Member States still retained the discretion as to the need for criminal penalties. The final task of creating the criminal sanction required by Union/Community law would remain in principle the sole competence of the national legislator with no other authority, be it a national criminal judge, the ECJ or the Commission, having a part to play.[149] As will be discussed in Chapter 5, the scope for (positive) harmonisation of both substantive and procedural criminal law in the EU has greatly increased after the ratification of the Lisbon Treaty, in light of the criminal-law legal bases inserted into the TFEU.[150]

Negative harmonisation of penal laws remains highly relevant after the ratification of the Lisbon Treaty. According to the principle of supremacy of European Community/Union law, if the law of a Member State is in conflict with Community/Union law it should be declared invalid.[151] Thus a defendant in criminal proceedings in a Member State could challenge the validity of the law creating an offence, whether or not the offence pre-dated the relevant European law.[152] In effect, since the origin of the European Communities there have been numerous cases where individuals tried to raise EC law in defence to a criminal charge.[153] For example, in the United Kingdom a conviction for a criminal offence aimed at conserving fish stocks was declared invalid as the United Kingdom was not authorised to adopt the measure without prior

147 See, for example, Sevenster, H.G. 'Criminal Law and EC Law', (1992) *CML Review* 29; and Anderson et al., *Policing the European Union* (OUP, Oxford 1995).

148 Former Article 226 EC. See further, Chapter 7.

149 Delmas-Marty, M. 'The European Union and Penal Law' (1998) 4 *European Law Journal* 1 at 90.

150 See, in particular, Articles 82 and 83 (1) and (2) TFEU.

151 Case 6/64, *Costa v. ENEL* [1964] E.C.R. 585.

152 Case C-106/89, *Marleasing SA v. La Commercial International de Alimentacion SA* [1990] E.C.R. 1-4135; Case 34/79 *R v Henn and Darby*, [1979] E.C.R. 3795; See Dine (1993) above note 102, at 246.

153 See Tobler, C. 'Case C-176/03, Commission v. Council, judgement of the Grand Chamber of 13 September 2005' (2006) *Common Market Law Review* at 845.

proper consultation with the Commission.[154] This remains relevant after the Lisbon Treaty – 'Union law' will still have a negative effect on national criminal laws by requiring a Member State to strike down national criminal laws that hinder the enjoyment of the four freedoms.[155] So Member States can be precluded from adopting criminal penalties for infringement of national laws implementing Union law on the grounds that, for example, they are excessive and thereby become an obstacle to the free movement of persons.[156] For example, in one case concerning a provision of the French Code of Criminal Procedure which restricted to French nationals the right to claim compensation if victim of a crime in France, the Court held that this provision infringed the free movement of persons in the EU.[157]

4.7.2 *Total and Minimum Harmonisation in EU Environmental Law*

EU environmental directives provide for total harmonisation in a given area when it is intended to provide for a more or less uniform European standard in a particular field, and from which derogation is precluded.[158] Total harmonisation is found above all in the fields of environmental policy where there is a definite link with the free movement of goods. It is thus not paradoxical that before the 1986 Single European Act (SEA) (which incorporated the 'environmental title' into the EC treaty), the Member States were prohibited from adopting more stringent rules in areas already affected by Community (total) harmonisation. It applied to all products put in circulation in the Community, whether they crossed a border or not. By implication, the approximation of divergent national regimes in this case pre-empted Member States' ability to derogate.[159]

---

154 Case 269/80 *R v. Robert Tymen* [1981] 2 C.M.L.R. 111.

155 See for example Case C-358/93 and C-416/93 *Bordessa* [1995] ECR I-361 concerning a prohibition under national criminal law which hindered the free movement of capital guaranteed under former Article 56 EC.

156 See e.g. Case C-193/94 *Skanavi* [1996] ECR I-929, para. 39.

157 Case 186/87 *Cowan* [1989] para. 195: '[a]lthough in principle criminal legislation and the rules of criminal procedure, among which the national provision in issue is to be found, are matters for which the Member States are responsible, the Court has consistently held [see inter alia the judgement of 11 November 1981 in Case 203/80 Casati (1981) ECR 2595] that Community law sets certain limits on their power. Such legislative provisions may not discriminate against persons to whom Community law gives the right to equal treatment or restrict the fundamental freedoms guaranteed by Community law.' See further discussion in Pradel and Corstens (2002), above note 19, at 509.

158 Jans, J. and Vedder, H. *European Environmental Law* (Groningen: 2008) at 94.

159 See Scott, Joanne 'Kith and Kine (and Crustaceans): Trade and Environment in the EU and WTO' in Weiler (ed.) *The EU, WTO and NAFTA: Towards a Common Law of International*

Yet in some circumstances total harmonisation of product standards will be the only way to ensure the free movement of the goods in question in the common market. So it was not uncommon for an internal market measure based on Article 114 TFEU (former Article 95EC) to seek total harmonisation of EC environmental law.[160] Conversely, minimum harmonisation generally is not used to harmonise product standards, in which case there is a general preference for total harmonisation.[161]

Minimum harmonisation has the advantage of allowing the EU Member States to exercise discretionary legislative powers when adopting EU environmental legislation.[162] Minimum harmonisation is thus more likely to be consistent with the principle of subsidiarity.[163] However, minimum harmonisation 'does not limit Community action to the lowest common denominator, or even the lowest level of protection established by the Member States'.[164]

Historically, environmental directives tended to contain minimum harmonisation clauses.[165] Indeed, minimum harmonisation has been used since the early 1970s well before its institutionalisation in the Treaty by the SEA 1986.[166] The move away from total to minimum harmonisation may be explained by the fact that some Member States were anxious to recuperate part of their regulatory autonomy following the exercise of the EC powers in a given field. Thus they have contested the scope for exhaustive harmonisation and have argued vehemently for a more flexible approach in relation to their remaining

Trade (OUP, 2000). Even after the coming into force of the Single European Act there was still scope for total harmonisation of European standards, although the negotiations and eventual adoption of those measures would take a number of years in light of their unpopularity with Member States whose regulatory powers are curtailed once these measures are adopted. See Barnard, Catherine. *The Substantive Law of the EU* (Oxford, 2007) at 592.

160 See e.g. Articles 3 and 6 (1) of the Cosmetics Directive 76/768 [1976] OJ L262/169, as amended.

161 Jans, J. and Vedder, H. above note 158, at 98.

162 Provided that this discretion is compressed somewhere in between the 'floor' present in the Union's secondary legislation and the 'ceiling' established in the EU Treaties, in particular Articles 34–36 TFEU. See also, Scott, J. EC *Environmental Law* (Longmans, 1998).

163 See Article 5 TEU (equivalent to ex-Article 5 EC); and *Protocol on the Application of the Principles of Subsidiarity and Proportionality*. Protocol No 30 Annexed to the Treaty of Amsterdam [1997] OJ C340. See further, Chapter 5.

164 Case C-84/95 *UK v. Council* [1996] ECR I-5755, para. 56. See Barnard, *supra*.

165 See e.g. Article 5 of Directive 85/203 on air quality standards for nitrogen dioxide, OJ 1985 L87/1, later amended.

166 Dougan, M. 'Minimum harmonisation and the internal market' (2000) 37 *CMLRev.* 853.

regulatory powers.[167] This led to the insertion by the Single European Act (1986) of Article 176 EC into the EC Treaty (post-Lisbon, Article 193 TFEU), which recognises that European environmental protection measures may only lay down minimum standards which can be enhanced by Member States.[168] According to Article 193 TFEU (former Article 176 EC), Member States are allowed to *maintain* or *introduce* more stringent protective measures, as long as they are compatible with the Treaties and the Commission is notified of the measure.[169]

This would be the case of a Member State willing to maintain or introduce stricter standards than those under the environmental crimes directive. So if a EU environmental legislation is adopted on the basis of Article 192 TFEU – as was the case with the EU environmental crime directive – it follows that the measure can apply minimum standards only. However, this restriction does not apply to the shipping pollution directive which was adopted on the basis of Article 80 EC (post-Lisbon, Article 100 TFEU) and thus it could have pursued, in principle, the total harmonisation of environmental criminal standards. This is because there is no provision equivalent to Article 193 TFEU (former Art. 176 EC) applicable to the common transport policy field.[170]

It is not totally clear from the *Environmental Crimes* and *Ship-Source Pollution* rulings whether the then Community could seek to adopt total harmonisation of criminal law[171] so the scope for total harmonisation of environmental criminal law might depend on the legal basis chosen for the measure. It is unlikely that total harmonisation of environmental criminal would be considered compatible with the principles of necessity and subsid-

167 Denmark is usually pointed as the precursor of this development.

168 Former Article 176 EC (post-Lisbon, Article 193 TFEU) states that '[t]he protective measures adopted pursuant to Article 175 EC shall not prevent any Member State from maintaining or introducing more stringent protective measures. Such measures must be compatible with this Treaty. They shall be notified to the Commission'.

169 Different notifications requirements apply depending on whether member states are maintaining or introducing a new environmental measure. See Jans, J. and Vedder, H. (2008) above note 158.

170 See Articles 90–100 TFEU on the common transport policy.

171 In para. 52 of *Environmental Crimes* the Court ruled that it was not possible for it to infer from Articles 135 and 280(4) that 'for the purposes of the implementation of environmental policy, any harmonisation of criminal law, *even as limited as that resulting from the framework decision*, must be ruled out even where it is necessary in order to ensure the effectiveness of Community law' (emphasis added). This statement possibly suggests that the Community could only adopt minimum harmonisation rules, as the Framework Decision on environmental crimes was an instrument envisaging minimum harmonisation only.

iarity.[172] In any event, the European Commission itself has been discarded the scope for total harmonisation in the context of environmental criminal law.[173]

Nevertheless, contrary to what is generally assumed, minimum harmonisation and the consequent 'right to derogate' may not necessarily correspond to a 'greener' European environment. Those Member States which have already introduced stricter environmental standards in their territories will apparently lack any incentive to force the extension of those higher standards throughout the EU.[174] So what would have been initially thought to lead to an overall improvement to the environment will in fact not necessarily contribute to extensive environmental protection in the EU. Persuasively enough, though, Tamara Joseph maintains that a Member State which has already introduced stricter legislation would still continue demanding higher 'common' standards in order to circumvent the trade competitive disadvantage caused by legislative differentiation (the 'pollution havens' effect).[175] However, as will be discussed in Chapter 7, it is not clear whether legislative differentiation in the environmental field (in particular as regards the standards of liability and enforcement of environmental law) leads to negative impacts on business competitiveness and to the migration of companies to countries with lower standards.

4.8 Conclusions

This chapter has assessed the degrees to which states may pursue the harmonisation of environmental criminal law, focusing on developments in the European Union. In particular, it has considered the merits and demerits of unification, approximation, cooperation and coordination as models for the harmonisation of environmental criminal law.

After the question of the Community competence in criminal matters was settled in the ECJ ruling in *Environmental Crimes*, the Commission was correct

---

172 See Chapter 5. Article 31 (1) (e) TEU (which was the third pillar legal basis for the harmonisation of substantive criminal law) and Article 83 (1) and (2) TFEU only allow the adoption of *minimum rules*.

173 See Impact Assessment, Commission Staff Working Document. *Accompanying Document to the Proposal for a Directive of the European Parliament and of the Council on the Protection of the Environment through Criminal Law*, COM (2007) 51 Final; and the Commission Staff Working Paper, *Establishing of an Acquis on Criminal Sanctions against Environmental Offences*, Brussels, 07.02.2001, SEC (2001) 227, p. 3.

174 *See* Joseph, Tamara: 'Preaching heresy: permitting member states to enforce stricter environmental laws than the European Community', *YJIL* (1995).

175 *Ibid.*

to seek harmonisation of environmental criminal law by means of a directive, rather than a regulation. Directives allow for more flexible implementation by the Member States and therefore are more appropriate for an instrument harmonising environmental criminal law. Yet it is not clear the extent to which directives harmonising criminal law could entail direct or indirect effects. It appears that a non-implemented directive could not be used to the detriment of individuals in the Member States, although it could exceptionally be relied on for the benefit of individuals.

EU law can impact on the environmental laws of the member states in a variety of ways, in particular through the positive and negative harmonisation of standards. Moreover, minimum harmonisation has been the principal choice of method for harmonisation of environmental law since the Single European Act, which is reflected in the text of the EU environmental crime directive which only foresees minimum harmonisation of standards.

Those legal challenges have not prevented the EU to adopt an ambitious programme aimed at enhancing police and judicial cooperation in criminal matters between the Member States. Given the sensitivities in this area, the framework of the third-pillar was used for the adoption of the relevant criminal-law measures, being intergovernmental and lacking supranational controls. In principle, environmental criminal law of the EU could have developed alongside the other developments under the third pillar, as was defended by the Council and the Member States. The question of whether and the extent to which there is scope for the harmonisation of environmental criminal law at the supranational level in order to remedy some of the deficiencies of harmonisation under the third pillar, is the one to be addressed in the next chapter.

CHAPTER 5

The Competence to Harmonise Environmental Criminal Law in the European Union

5.1 Introduction

In the European Union setting, environmental criminal law could fall into two major policy fields of activity. One of them is the EU policy on the environment which has been supranational particularly since the incorporation of the environmental title into the EC Treaty, and therefore fell in what was previously known as the 'Community method' (or 'first pillar'). On the other hand, a considerable majority of the Member States had argued that there was already a specific forum for cooperation in criminal matters – the so-called third pillar created in 1993 by the Treaty on the European Union (TEU, 1993) – and which therefore provided the correct legal basis for harmonisation of *environmental* criminal law. So before the ratification of the Lisbon Treaty in December 2009, the Member States appeared to regard co-operation in criminal matters (including legislative harmonisation) as belonging to the third pillar of the EU, being intergovernmental and hence lacking supranational controls.

Therefore, the question of deciding the correct legal basis for a measure harmonising environmental criminal law has permeated the debate on the criminal law powers of the Community/Union under the former Treaty structure of the EU. The outcome of the ECJ decisions in the *Environmental Crimes* (2005) and *Ship-Source Pollution* (2007) cases is that important limits have been set to the EC/EU competence in criminal matters, delineating the key features of the directive on environmental crimes adopted in October 2008[1] and the ship-source pollution directive (2005/2009).[2]

1 Directive 2008/99/EC of the European Parliament and of the Council of 19 November 2008 on the protection of the environment through criminal law, Official Journal L 328, 6 December 2008, pp. 28–37.

2 Directive 2005/35/EC of the European Parliament and of the Council on Ship-Source Pollution and on the Introduction of Penalties for Infringements, 7 September 2005, *Official Journal* L 255/11; 30.9.2005; and Directive 2009/123/EC of the European Parliament and of the Council of 21 October 2009 amending Directive 2005/35/EC on ship-source pollution and on the introduction of penalties for infringements; *Official Journal*, L 280/52. 27.10.2009.

 | DOI 10.1163/9789004195882_006

This chapter focuses on the question of the competence and mandate of the European Union to harmonise the environmental criminal laws of the EU Member States, in light of the limits of this competence as defined by the jurisprudence of the European Court of Justice. Moreover, it assesses the legal implications of the ratification of the Lisbon Treaty in 2009 to future attempts to harmonise environmental criminal law in the EU; and the extent to which the application and evolution of the general principles of law and EU law (including legality, effectiveness, subsidiarity and proportionality) will limit the power of the EU to adopt environmental crime legislation in future.

5.2 The Competence of the European Union in the Environmental Law Field

The classical dichotomy between environmental and social interests on one side, and economic and trade interests on the other, has been the subject of controversy in both the European Community ('EC') and on wider international levels and, not surprisingly, produced the most important body of jurisprudential authority relating to the protection of the environment.[3] Historically the EU maintained an essentially economic-centred policy when the original six Member States signed to the Treaty of Rome in 1957 and formed the *European Economic Community* (EEC).[4] However, the EEC was not merely another free trade agreement: it had profound political significance.[5] But the first, most attainable objective behind the European integration project then was clearly economic – the establishment of a common market harbouring the free movement of goods, persons, services and capital.[6] The Community has since progressively shifted from a traditionally economic to a more social-orientated policy-making, resulting in fundamental changes – more precisely after the Single European Act ('SEA') in 1987 and the Treaty of the European Union ('TEU') in 1993 – which would act as a catalyst for the transformation of the Community's role, as put by one author, 'from bastion of free trade to van-

3 Thieffy, P. *'Droit Europeen de l'Environnement',* (Dalloz, Paris 1998): *'C'est, de tres loin, la libre circulation des merchandises qui a genere le contentieux le plus important, contribuant largement a faconner le droit communautaire de l'environnement'.*

4 Joseph, Tamara: 'Preaching Heresy: Permitting Member Sates to Enforce Stricter Environmental Laws than the European Community', (1995) YJIL at 227.

5 *Ibid.*

6 *Ibid.*

guard of citizens welfare'.[7] Most significantly, the creation of the environmental Title in the EC Treaty after the enactment of the Single European Act (1987) ('SEA') has enshrined for the first time an environmental policy in the Treaty (Articles 191-193TEFU) (ex-Arts. 174–176 EC), and has defined the protection of the environment as one of the essential objectives of the Community. In particular, the Single European Act significantly accelerated the EC's regulatory making in the environmental field by expanding the scope of qualified majority voting in the Council.[8] Also significant has been the requirement that the level of environmental protection should be *high.*[9] In defining the meaning and extent of the adjective 'high' to the level of environmental protection, the ECJ has consistently held that it is for the Member States themselves to decide which level of environmental protection they consider to be appropriate, taking into account the requirements of the free movements of goods.[10] In light of the ECJ decision in the *Danish Bottles* case[11] – which indicated that the European Court of Justice (ECJ) was prepared to disregard free trade interests to uphold measures aimed at the protection of the environment[12] – both Temmink and Kraemer agree that it must be a 'reasonable' degree of protection and therefore not necessarily at the highest level.[13] High European environmental standards cannot mean 'the highest possible', especially because the Treaty itself allows Member States to adopt more stringent safeguards at the national level.[14]

Another important development was the elevation of the 'integration' principle from the Environment Title to the new article 6 EC (post-Lisbon, Article 11 TFEU), according to which environmental protection must be integrated into the implementation of other Community/Union policies[15] This provision

---

7 Dougan, Michael 'Minimum harmonisation and the Internal Market' (2000) 37 *CMLRev.* 853.

8 Vogel, David 'The Hare and the Tortoise Revisited: The New Politics of Consumer and Environmental Regulation in Europe' in Jordan, A. (ed.), *Environmental Policy in the European Union: Actors, Institutions and Processes* (2dn ed. Earthscan 2005).

9 *See* Article 191 (2) of the TFEU.

10 Ziegler, *Trade and Environmental Law in the European Community* (OUP, 1996), at 84.

11 Case 302/86 *Commission v. Denmark* (1988) ECR 4607 ('Danish Bottles').

12 The ECJ held in that case that the protection of the environment is one of the Community's essential objectives. See *ibid,* para. 121.

13 See Temmink, H. 'From Danish Bottles to Danish Bees: The Dynamics of the free movement of goods and environmental protection – a case law analysis' 2000 YEEL 61; and Kraemer, Ludwig, *EC Environmental Law* (Sweet and Maxwell, 2000).

14 See Article 193 FFEU (ex-Article 176 EC). See further, Chapter 4.

15 Article 11 TFEU (ex-Article 6 EC) states that '[e]nvironmental protection requirements must be integrated into the definition and implementation of the Union's policies and activities, in particular with a view to promoting sustainable development'.

emphasises the fundamental nature of the environmental protection objective and its extension across a range of policies and activities.[16]

The ratification of the Lisbon Treaty in 2009 was another highly important development for EU environmental law. Significantly, that Treaty incorporated the concept of sustainable development under Article 3(3) of the Treaty on the European Union (TEU).[17] The change of emphasis brought by the Lisbon Treaty amendment underlines the different dimensions of sustainable development (economic, social, and environmental). The same article also introduces specific reference to the promotion of scientific and technological progress, which are areas that have implications for environmental protection.[18] While the main principles and objectives of EU environmental policy remain largely unchanged following the ratification of the Lisbon Treaty in 2009, that Treaty reinforces the EU's commitment to sustainable development, the fight against climate change, and development of renewable energy sources. It does this, in particular, by establishing for the first time a specific legal basis for harmonization of energy policies.[19] Overall it could be said that the Lisbon Treaty establishes a more integrated Union and allows for further scrutiny by national parliaments of the EU (environmental) policies.[20]

The EU is competent to pursue any environmental policy in view of achieving the objectives pursued under the first paragraph of Article 191 TFEU.[21] These are (1) preserving, protecting and improving the quality of the environment; (2) protecting human health; (3) prudent and rational utilisation of

16 *Environmental Crimes* case, para. 42.

17 Article 3(3) of the Treaty on the European Union (TEU) states that the Union 'shall work for the *sustainable development* of Europe based on balanced economic growth and price stability, a highly competitive social market economy, aiming at full employment and social progress, and a high level of protection and improvement of the quality of the environment'. (emphasis added).

18 On the impact of the Lisbon Treaty on EU environmental law, see further Benson, D., Jordan, A. (2008) 'A grand bargain or an 'incomplete contract'? European Union environmental policy after the Lisbon Treaty.' *European Energy and Environmental Law Review*, 17, 280–290.

19 Article 194 (1) TFEU states that: 'In the context of the establishment and functioning of the internal market and with regard for the need to preserve and improve the environment, Union policy on energy shall aim, in a spirit of solidarity between Member States, to... ensure the functioning of the *energy market;...ensure security of energy supply in the Union;...promote energy efficiency and energy saving and the development of new and renewable forms of energy*; and...*promote the interconnection of energy networks*' (emphasis added).

20 See Article 12 (b) TEU.

21 Article 191 TFEU is equivalent to ex Article 174 EC.

natural resources; and (4) promoting measures at international level to deal with regional or worldwide environmental problems, and in particular combating climate change.

As can be seen from that provision, the list of objectives is very broad and allows the EU institutions considerable flexibility when selecting which areas of environmental policy to act upon.[22] In addition, the fact that there is no definition of the term 'environment' in the TFEU or TEU further broadens the mandate of the EU institutions in the environmental field. Indeed, the first objective under paragraph 1 of Article 194 TFEU – i.e. preserving, protecting and improving the quality of the environment – could be used to pursue almost every aspect of environmental policy (subject to the principles of subsidiarity and proportionality). The EU environmental crimes directive pursues all of the three first objectives under Art. 191 (1) – (3), including the protection of human health, through the requirement that Member States criminalise activities which may harm human health.[23] Moreover, both the environmental crime and ship-source pollution directives promote 'measures at international level to deal with regional or worldwide environmental problems' and hence they could be regarded as pursuing the fourth objective. Indeed, the ship-source pollution directive aims to implement MARPOL[24] in the EU legal order. In contrast, the environmental crime directive does not aim to implement one specific international environmental agreement, but a number of international environmental agreements to which the EU and/or the Member States are parties, including CITES[25] and the Basel Convention.[26]

Yet it should be noted that there is no explicit EU competence under Article 191 TFEU (ex Articles 174 EC) for measures to be adopted with the purpose of protection of the 'built environment'. It follows from Articles 191(1) and 192(2) TFEU, which are the bases for Union environmental policy, that the environment covers human beings, natural resources, land use, town and country planning, waste and water.[27] The offences listed in Article 3 of the 2008 Directive on

---

22 See also, Kraemer, L. *EC Environmental Law* (6th ed. Sweet & Maxwell, 2007) at 74.

23 See, in particular, Article. 3, paragraphs (a), (b), (d) and (e) of the environmental crime directive.

24 Convention on Prevention of Marine Pollution from Ships 1973/1978 ('MARPOL') (entry into force 2 October 1983).

25 Washington Convention on Illegal Trade in Endangered Species (CITES, 1973). 27 UST 1087; TIAS 8249; 993 UNTS 243.

26 The Basel Convention on the Transboundary Movement of Hazardous Wastes, 1989. 1673 UNTS 126; 28 ILM 657 (1989).

27 Commission Staff Working Document, *Accompanying document to the proposal for a Directive on the Protection of the Environment through Criminal Law: Impact Assessment,*

environmental crime only refer to 'persons' and 'the quality of air, soil, water, animals or plants', so they do not aim to protect the built environment.[28] The term 'environment' is also given a broad scope in EU secondary legislation, covering most aspects of environmental protection, including water and air, noise and chemicals, nature conservation, waste and some measures of a general nature.[29] Hence these expansive and broad competences recognized in the TFEU leave the European Union with a potentially far-reaching mandate in the environmental law field.

This stems from the fact that the European Union competence in the area of environmental protection is shared with the Member States.[30] Until national laws have been harmonised, Member States are free to pursue any environmental policy of their own, provided that it complies with the relevant provisions of the TFEU.[31] If the EU fails to take action to protect a given environmental objective, Member States retain the power to legislate and to decide what they find a 'reasonable' degree of environmental protection. The only specific limitations to the EU 'shared' competence in the environmental field are the TFEU and TEU (as the 'ceiling') which require that the level of environmental protection in the EU is 'high'.[32] The broad range of competences of the EU in the environmental field has enabled the EU to exercise a major influence on the environmental laws of the member states. For example, one study has estimated that 52.7% of the Austrian national laws concerning 'Agriculture & forestry, veterinary law, health, environmental protection' in force in 2003 were EU-related; while in the Netherlands 18.3% of the legislation on 'Housing and Environment' were EU-related.[33]

Regarding the sharing of competences in *maritime policy* matters with the Member States, the situation is different. As regards this policy field, some of

COM (2007) 51 SEC (2007) 161, hereinafter '2007 Directive Impact Assessment' Section 1.1., at 4.

28 This is unlike the approach taken by the Council of Europe 1998 Convention on environmental crime, which lists 'protected monuments' and 'other protected objects, property' as falling within the scope of the Convention (Article 2 (1) (b)).

29 Commission Staff Working Document, *Accompanying document to the proposal for a Directive on the Protection of the Environment through Criminal Law: Impact Assessment*, COM (2007) 51 SEC (2007) 161, hereinafter '2007 Directive Impact Assessment' at 5.

30 See Article 4 (2) (e) TFEU.

31 See Jans, Jan And Vedder, Hans. *European Environmental Law* (Groningen: 2008) at 87.

32 *See* Art. 191 (2) of the TFEU.

33 Overall, the estimates of the proportion of national laws based on EU law vary widely in other EU Member States, ranging from 6.3% to 84%. See House of Commons Library, *How Much Legislation Come From Europe?* Research Paper 10/62, 13 October 2010.

the EU competences are exclusive, which hence precludes the member states from taking independent legislative action. This exclusive competence of the EU in the maritime policy field is explained by the fact that certain policy areas have been transferred to the EU – for example in relation to conservation of marine biological resources and fisheries.[34] On the other hand, other competences are not exclusive and may be exercised by both the Member States and the EU – for example in relation to maritime transport.[35] Yet the exact borderline of these competences are not fixed – they change, in particular, in light of the case law of the ECJ.[36]

Therefore, the EU action in the fields of environmental protection and maritime transport needs to be appreciated in light of the political dynamics of the EU institutions.[37] The political philosophy of measures in those fields revolves around the division of competence between the Member States on the one hand, and the Union institutions on the other. With the ever closer integration being forged among the EU Member States, the European Commission has aimed to exercise further its mandate to initiate legislation for the EU in the environmental protection and vessel-source pollution arena, where the EU and its Member States share competence, with the correspondent displacement of Member States' competence in such matters.[38]

---

34 See Article 3 (1) (d) TFEU. See further Treves, Tullio 'The European Community and the European Union and the Law of the Sea: Recent Developments' [2008] vol. 48 *IJIL* at 1–2.

35 The EU has adopted a number of environmental protection measures on the basis of the common transport legal basis. See, for example, Directive 92/6 on the installation and use of speed limitation devices for certain categories of motor vehicles within the Community (OJ 1992 L57/27); Directive 89/629 on the limitation of noise emissions from subsonic aircraft (OJ 1989) L363/27; and Directive 2001/105/EC of the European Parliament and of the Council of 19 December 2001 of 19 December 2001 amending Council Directive 94/57/EC on common rules and standards for ship inspection and survey organisations and for the relevant activities of maritime administrations, OJ 22.01.2002.

36 *See* Treves (2008), *supra* at 1–2.

37 Khee-Jin Tan, Alan. *Vessel-Source Marine Pollution: The Law and Politics of International Regulation*, (Cambridge University Press, Cambridge 2006) at 8.

38 See Article 2 (1) TFEU: 'when the Treaties confer on the Union exclusive competence in a specific area, only the Union may legislate and adopt legally binding acts, the Member States being able to do so themselves only if so empowered by the Union or for the implementation of Union acts.' (2) 'when the Treaties confer on the Union a competence shared with the Member States in a specific area, the Union and the Member States may legislate and adopt legally binding acts in that area. The Member States shall exercise their competence to the extent that the Union has not exercised its competence. The Member States shall again exercise their competence to the extent that the Union has decided to cease exercising its competence.'

5.3 The Choice of Legal Basis for Harmonisation of EU Environmental Law

Deciding on the correct legal basis for a EU environmental policy measure is important for a number of reasons. Firstly, it is necessary in order to determine the extent of the competence in the matter in question, and thus the validity of measures taken on the basis of this competence.[39] Moreover, the choice of the legal basis has an impact the decision-making procedure to be followed when a particular environmental measure is adopted.[40] This is particularly relevant since the decision-making procedure determines the role played by the participants in the decision-making process (that is, the Commission, European Parliament and the Council). In case a EU legislative measure partly falls within the scope of one article and partly of another, both procedural requirements must be satisfied.[41]

The Court of Justice has ruled in a number of cases that the choice of the legal basis must be based on objective factors which are amenable to judicial review and include in particular the aim and content of the measure.[42] The choice of the correct legal basis thus depends on the 'main objective' of the measure[43] and the European legislature does not have discretion to decide the legal basis of a measure. Therefore, for example, if the 'centre of gravity' of a measure harmonising product standards is the internal market, Article 114 TFEU[44] would be the appropriate legal basis, whereas if the centre of gravity is the protection of the environment, decision-making under Article 192 TFEU would be applicable.[45] In this regard the Court has held that:

---

39 Jans, J. And Vedder, H. (2008) above note 33, at 10.

40 The failure to specify the legal basis is an infringement of an essential procedural requirement. See *Commission v. Council*, Case 165/87 [1998] ECR 5545 Para. 9. See also, Hartley TC *'The Foundations of European Community Law'* (Sixth ed. OUP, Oxford 2007) at 111.

41 So in *Titanium Dioxide* (*Commission v Council* Case C-300/89 [1991] ECR I-2867), the Court held that a measure intended to lay down uniform environmental-protection standards for the titanium dioxide industry had two purposes: to protect the environment – covered by former Article 175 EC and (at the time of the judgement) requiring unanimity in the Council and the consultation of the Parliament – and to promote fair competition – falling within the scope of former Article 95 EC which envisaged qualified majority voting in the Council and the co-operation procedure.

42 Case 45/86 *Commission v Council* [1987] ECR 1493, para. 11; Case C-300/89 *Commission v. Council* (TiO2) [1991] ECR I-2867, para. 10.

43 Case C-155/91 *Commission v Council* [1993] ECR I-939, Case C-187/93 *European Parliament v Council* [1994] ECR I-2857.

44 Former Article 95 EC.

45 Jans, J. And Vedder, H. (2008) above note 31, at 10.

'If examination of a Community measure reveals that it pursues a twofold purpose or that it has a twofold component and if one of those is identifiable as the main or predominant purpose or component, whereas the other is merely incidental, the act must be based on a single legal basis, namely that required by the main or predominant purpose or component'.[46]

In a similar vein, the Commission has regarded measures implementing a system of import and export licences in the trade in endangered species of wild fauna and flora and a system of notification on the import of certain dangerous chemicals as common commercial policy measures and has suggested Article 207 TFEU (former Article 133 EC) as the legal basis for such measures.[47]

In the case of environmental criminal law, the choice of the legal basis of the measure (between , for example, an environmental protection, a maritime environment or common transport policy legal bases) could have considerable legal implications. This point was at issue when the choice between ex Article 80 (2) EC (now Art 100 (2) TFEU) and ex Article 175 EC (now 192 TFEU) was made as the possible legal bases for the ship-source pollution Directive.[48] In the *Ship-Source Pollution* case, Advocate General Mazák observed that even though pollution of the sea is certainly as such an environmental concern, its reduction or prevention is at the same time an important field of Community action in maritime transport.[49] The EU has indeed adopted other measures under

46 See Case C-178/03 *Commission v. European Parliament and Council* [2006] ECR I-107, para. 42. However, following the Treaty of Amsterdam (1999), measures adopted under the 'environmental title' of the TFEU (Article 192 TFEU, ex Article 175 EC) were to follow the same procedure used for adoption of 'internal market' measures under Article 114 TFEU (former Article 95 EC) i.e. the co-decision procedure between the European Parliament and the Council and qualified majority voting in the Council (see Article 294 TFEU, ex Article 251 EC). Yet the choice of the legal basis is still very relevant in so far as it may determine the extent to which Member States are entitled to adopt more stringent environmental measures than the European standards (see Chapter 4).

47 To the extent that these policies fall within the scope of the Union's common commercial policy objectives, Article 207 TFEU (former Article 133 EC) would be the appropriate legal basis and the Community would enjoy exclusive competence to adopt such measures. For example the Commission's proposal to implement the CITES Convention (OJ 1980 C 243/16) and the Commission's proposal for the Whales Regulation (OJ 1980 C 121/5). There are a number of important judgments of the ECJ dealing with the borderline between environmental protection and the common commercial policy. See for example Case C-62/88 *European Parliament v. Council* (Chernobyl I) [1990] ECR I-1527.

48 However, the situation would be different following the ratification of the Lisbon Treaty in 2009. As will be discussed below, the criminal-law legal basis introduced to the TFEU by Lisbon might be considered *lexis specialis* and it is possible that any future harmonisation of environmental criminal law would be undertaken under those new provisions.

49 Opinion of Avocate General Mazak, *Ship-Source Pollution*, Point 127 et seq.

Art. 100 (2) TFEU to protect the environment[50] – which is in line with the integration principle enshrined in Article 11 TFEU – which requires environmental concerns to be integrated into other EU policy areas.[51] So even though a EU maritime safety policy measure may also pursue the objective of environmental protection, it does not follow necessarily that Article 192 TFEU would be the appropriate legal basis. In particular, Advocate General Mazák considered that as environmental requirements are a necessary component of the other policies of the Community, a Community measure is not to be classed as action on environmental matters merely because it 'takes account' of those requirements.[52]

The next sections discuss further challenges facing the decision on what the appropriate legal basis for harmonisation of environmental criminal law in the EU should be. It starts by discussing the specific legal framework created in 1993 by the Maastricht Treaty – the so-called 'third pillar' – for the EU member states to cooperate in criminal matters.

5.4 The Creation of an Area of Freedom, Security and Justice in the EU

The Maastricht Treaty, by creating the pillar structure, established a formal framework to allow the EU Member States to improve mutual assistance and cooperation in criminal matters through the creation for the first time of a specific forum for police and judicial cooperation in criminal matters in the EU, i.e. the third pillar. Since the entering into force of the Treaty on European Union (1993), measures concerning policing and criminal law have since been

50 See e.g. Directive 92/6 on the installation and use of speed limitation devices for certain categories of motor vehicles within the Community (OJ 1992 L57/27); and Directive 89/629 on the limitation of noise emissions from subsonic aircraft (OJ 1989) L363/27.

51 See also the second recital of Directive 2000/59/EC of the European Parliament and the Council of 27 November 2000 on port reception facilities for ship-generated waste and cargo residues (OJ 2000 L322, p. 81) which was also adopted on the basis of Article 80 (2) EC.

52 See Case C-336/00 *Huber* [2002] ECR I-7699, para. 33. *Ship-Source Pollution*, para. 60. See by analogy Case C-336/00 *Huber* [2002] ECR I-7699, para. 36. In its judgement in the *Ship-Source Pollution* case the Court has only indirectly addressed this question by holding that the integration principle enshrined in former Article 6 EC is the basis for the inclusion of environmental protection within 'the common transport policy' under former Article 80 (2) EC, thus emphasising that environmental protection is of the essential objectives of the Community. The Community legislature could hence, on the basis of former Article 80 (2) EC, decide to promote environmental protection, thus linking Community transport policy with the objective of environmental protection.

adopted under the framework of Title VI of the EU Treaty (pre-Lisbon).[53] The overall aim of the third pillar was to provide citizens with a high level of safety within an area of freedom, security and justice, by developing 'common action' in three areas: police co-operation in criminal matters, judicial co-operation in criminal matters and the prevention and combating of racism and xenophobia.[54] The initial aspiration for the AFSJ was, according to Neil Walker, 'an attempt to supply a menu of compensatory measures concerning the control of movements across the EU's external borders and the development of new capacities for the internal monitoring of populations in light of the supposed "security benefit" attendant upon the completion of an internal market in which goods, persons, services and capital should in principle move freely'.[55]

Yet the intergovernmental method applied under the third pillar was criticised for being undemocratic[56] and for the very limited political[57] and judicial[58] control over policies adopted. As a result, the harmonization of criminal law left citizens (and indeed third country nationals) particularly vulnerable to the measures adopted at the EU level, in light of the fact that executive action in this field is particularly apt to strike at their most fundamental interests.[59] Therefore the European Commission and Parliament have advanced that the AFSJ should be brought into line with the Community method that prevailed in the first pillar.[60]

The problem of establishing an appropriate legal basis for EU criminal law thus has been one of the central issues in the debate on how to improve the democratic, political and judicial control of the third pillar. The role of the ECJ

---

53 Former Article 39 TEU. *See* Peers, Steve, *Justice and Home Affairs Law* (OUP, 2006) at 5.

54 See, pre-Lisbon, former Article 29 TEU.

55 Walker, Neil. 'In Search of the Area of Freedom, Security and Justice: A Constitutional Odyssey' in Walker (ed.) *Europe's Area of Freedom, Security and Justice* (OUP, Oxford 2004) at 5.

56 Third pillar measures required unanimity in the Council and the European Parliament was merely consulted.

57 The Commission could through a scoreboard programme oversee the implementation of those third pillar instruments, but it might not institute proceedings under Art. 258 TFEU (ex. Art. 226 EC) before the ECJ for the failure of a Member State to implement a third pillar measure.

58 The Member States had the option to declare that they accepted the ECJ jurisdiction to oversee the legality of third pillar instruments in a reference for a preliminary ruling from a national Court (there were restrictions also on which national courts were able to refer questions for a preliminary ruling).

59 N. Walker (2004) *supra* at 10.

60 European Commission Communication 'Implementing the Hague Programme: The Way Forward' COM (2006) 331 final, 14.

in clarifying the competences of the EC/EU has been paramount. The next sections of this chapter examine the extent to which there is scope for harmonisation of environmental criminal law at the supranational level in the European Union legal order.

5.5 The Harmonisation of Environmental Criminal Law at the Supranational Level – Pre-Lisbon Developments

As criminal law remained outside the competence of the European Community, EC law was to a large extent implemented by national law because of the lack of an integral mechanism of execution attributed to the EC/EU. Although in a few specialist fields, such as competition law, the Commission has been given the power to apply penalties directly against economic operators, competition law regulations generally provide that, despite their punitive character, those penalties 'shall not be of a criminal nature'.[61] Similarly, in the case of EU environmental law, the EU greenhouse gas emissions trading scheme ('EU ETS') Directive (2003) specifies sanctions,[62] but they are of an administrative, regulatory nature, and do not entail penal consequences (despite their apparent punitive character). This suggests that although under primary EC law the Commission has been granted the power to apply sanctions directly and independently of the administration of justice of the Member States in relation to certain fields of EC policy, those penalties are not to be considered to be of a penal nature as such. Moreover, according to the EU legislative practice, whenever the Commission would propose an EC legislative measure containing criminal sanctions, the Council would detach the criminal provisions from the

61 See, for example, Article 23 (5) of the Council Regulation 1/2003EC on the implementation of the rules on competition laid down in Articles 101 and 102 TFEU (former Articles 81 and 82EC) [2003] OJ L1/1 (Modernisation Regulation).

62 Article 16 of the Directive 2003/87 of the European Parliament and of the Council establishing a scheme for green house gas emission allowance trading in within the Community and amending Council Directive 96/61/EC [2003] 13 Oct 2003 OJ L275/32. Operators must surrender emissions allowances (EUA) by 30 April of each year to cover their verified emissions during preceding year. Excess emissions penalty in Phase I of the EU ETS was EUR 40 and in Phase II (and subsequent periods) EUR 100 for each ton of CO2 eq. emitted but not matched with EUA s. Payment of penalty does not release operator from the obligation to surrender an amount of EUA s equal to those excess emissions in the subsequent calendar year. The EU ETS Directive 2009 amendment (regarding Phase III) requires that from 1 Jan 2013 onwards the penalty is to be in accordance with European index of consumer prices.

legislative act – and, since the creation of the third pillar, adopt the criminal part of the legislative proposal in a separate third pillar measure.[63]

The ECJ has played a crucial role in delineating the limits of the Community competence in the environmental criminal law field. Prior to the its decision in *Environmental Crimes*, the European Court of Justice had developed a cautious approach to sanctions which neither recognised nor ruled out the Community competence to lay down criminal sanctions. In the *Amsterdam Bulb* case the Court held that '*in the absence of a Community rule laying down specific penalties*, the Member States are free to adopt such penalties as appear to them to be appropriate, including criminal penalties' (emphasis added).[64] So the Court did not rule out in *Amsterdam Bulb* in principle the possibility of the Community laying down specific (criminal) penalties.

The same cautious approach is seen when the Court of Justice avoided ruling on the question of whether punitive sanctions were to be regarded as penal sanctions or which features distinguish penal sanctions from other punitive sanctions.[65] In these cases the Court has neither explicitly recognised nor excluded altogether the competence on the part of the Community to legislate in the criminal law field. For example, in *Casati* the Court stated that '[*i*]*n principle*, criminal legislation and the rules of criminal procedure are matters for which the Member States are *still* responsible'[66] (emphasis added). It appears from this statement that the Court at the time of that judgment did not rule out the potential for the competence of the Community in criminal matters altogether – in particular, it appeared that the continuing process of integration

---

63 For example Article 1 (2) of Council Regulation EEC No 2241/87 of 23 July 1987 establishing certain control measures for fishing activities and Article 31 (1) of Council Regulation (EEC) no 2847/93 of 12 October 1993 applicable to the common fisheries policy, which replaced the former, leaves within the discretion of Member States the choice of the penalty for infringements of the provisions governing that policy. On the other hand, Council Directive 91/308/EEC of 10 June 1991 on prevention of the use of the financial system for the purpose of money laundering states that the phenomenon must be combated mainly by penal sanctions (fourth recital), though there is no requirement to introduce criminal sanctions; and Council Directive 2002/90/EC of 28 November 2002 defining the facilitation of unauthorised entry, transit and residence does not contain an obligation on Member States to introduce criminal sanctions, which is present instead in the parallel Council Framework Decision 2002/946/JHA of 28 November 2002.

64 Case 50/76 *Amsterdam Bulb* [1977] ECR 137 paras. 32 and 33.

65 See e.g. Case C-240/90 *Germany v Commission* [1992] ECR I-5383, paras. 24–26.

66 Case C-203/78 *Casati* [1981] ECR 2595 para. 27 and confirmed in Case C-226/97, *Lemmens* [1998] I-3711, para. 19. See also, Weiß, Holger Tobias '*EC* Competence for Environmental Criminal Law' (Bruges, College of Europe 2006) at 11.

of the Union could lead to an eventual recognition by the Court of the Community competence in criminal matters, regardless of a formal amendment to the Treaties.

Both the European Commission and European Parliament have called for the harmonisation of criminal law to take place under the 'first pillar'.[67] They argued that harmonisation of criminal law under the first pillar would allow for enhanced supranational and democratic control of policies, including full ECJ jurisdiction (the 'Community method'). However, this view was not shared by the Council of Ministers and a considerable majority of the Member States themselves, who feared losing their sovereignty over criminal matters, often regarded as intrinsic to state sovereignty. Yet even though from the perspective of the Member States the intergovernmental model applied in the third pillar appeared preferable as it would not involve giving away their criminal-law competences to the EC, the ECJ had already started blurring the line between the pillars in a decision in June 2005 in the *Maria Pupino* case,[68] in which the ECJ held that third pillar measures have indirect effect, i.e. the national courts must interpret national criminal law in line with third pillar measures.[69] The Court reasoned that it would be very difficult for the Union to carry out its task effectively if the principle of loyal cooperation, ensuring the fulfilment of the obligations under EC law by the Member States, were not also binding in the third pillar (see Chapter 4.).[70]

---

67 Commission of the European Communities, 'Implementing the Hague Programme: The Way Forward', COM (2006) 331 final, at 14.

68 Case 105/03 *Criminal Proceedings against Maria Pupino* [2005] ECR I-5285.

69 Specifically, the Court ruled that Italian criminal procedure law had to be construed in conformity with Council Framework Decision on the Standing of Victims in Criminal Proceedings (2001/220/JHA) so as to permit the testimony of young children under appropriate protective arrangements. For commentaries on this decision see e.g. Fletcher, Maria. 'Extending 'Indirect Effect' to the Third Pillar: The Significance of Pupino', E. L. Rev, 30 (6) 2005; Mitsilegas, Valsamis 'Constitutional Principles of the European Community and European Criminal Law' *European Journal of Law Reform* 303 (2007);. Peers (2007),'Salvation Outside the Church: Judicial Protection in Third Pillar after the Pupino and Segi Judgements', *Common Market Law Review*; Herlin-Karnell (2007), 'Recent Developments in the Area of European Criminal Law',14 *Maastricht Journal of European and Comparative Law* 1; and Betlem (2007),'Beyond *Francovich*: Completing the Unified Member State and EU Liability Regime. A Comment on the Jan Jans Contribution' in Obradovic and Lavranos (eds), *Interface between EU Law and National Law*, (Europa Law Publishing).

70 Case 105/03 *Criminal Proceedings against Maria Pupino* [2005] ECR I-5285.

5.5.1 *The Environmental Crimes Case*

Given that the European Commission had proposed the adoption of a directive on environmental crimes in March 2001 (a first pillar measure) but the Council decided to go ahead and adopt instead a Framework Decision on environmental crimes (a third pillar measure) in January 2003 based on a proposal from the Kingdom of Denmark (2000), a major institutional conflict emerged. The Council did not adopt the 2001 Directive environmental crime proposal since it came to the conclusion that the majority required for its adoption in the Council could not be obtained.[71] According to the majority of the Member States represented in the Council, the 2001 Directive proposal encroached upon the Community's competence attributed to it by the Treaty establishing the European Community and that the objectives could instead be reached by adopting a Framework Decision based on the Treaty on European Union.[72]

The Council, disregarding the arguments of the other institutions, adopted the Framework Decision on 27 January 2003.[73] Even though the Council rejected the adoption of the 2001 directive proposal, it considered it appropriate to incorporate into the Framework Decision a number of the substantive provisions contained in the proposed Directive, in particular those defining the conduct which Member States must establish as criminal offences under their domestic law and the provision on penalties.[74] One of the main differences between the two instruments is that the Framework Decision did not define environmental offences by reference to pieces of EC environmental legislation. Rather, it tied the definition of offences to aggravated breaches of national legislation.[75]

On 15 April 2003 the European Commission, supported by the Parliament, sought an annulment of the Council Framework Decision on environmental crimes.[76] The Council was supported by eleven of the then fifteen EU Member

---

71 Recital 7 to the 2003 Framework Decision on environmental crime.

72 Specifically, under Title VI of the TEU, Article 34.

73 2003/80/JHA of 27 January 2003 OJ L 29/55 (5.2.2003). The legal basis for the measure was Article 29, *Article 31* (e) and Article 34 (2) (b), as worded prior to the coming into force of the Treaty of Nice on 1 February 2003. Subsequently, former Article 31 (e) TEU was worded as Article 31 (*1*) (e) TEU.

74 EU Council 13421/02, DROIPEN 73 ENV 602. See Recital 5 to the Framework Decision.

75 See also, Walsh, 'Protecting the Environment through Criminal Law' (2005) 17 *ELM* at 204.

76 Under Article 36 (6) EU (pre-Lisbon), the ECJ had jurisdiction to review the legality of Framework Decisions and Decisions in actions brought by a Member State or the

States – thus reflecting the constitutional importance of the case – who have broadly concurred with the arguments presented by the Council.[77] The Commission challenged the choice of the legal basis for Articles 1 to 7 of the Framework Decision,[78] claiming that the purpose and content of the latter are within the Community competence relating to the environment.[79] Further, the Commission argued that the correct legal basis for a measure harmonising environmental criminal law in the European Union would be under the 'environmental title' of the EC Treaty.[80]

In its decision handed down on 13 of September 2005,[81] the Court was generally persuaded by the arguments raised by the Commission and held that the Community had the power under the first pillar to require Member States to introduce criminal sanctions in the case of serious violations of EC environmental

---

Commission on grounds of lack of competence, infringement of an essential procedural requirement, infringement of the EU Treaty or any other rule of law relating to its application, or misuse of powers, subject to a declaration made by a Member State accepting the Court's jurisdiction to review the legality of Framework Decisions.

77 Denmark, Germany, Greece, Spain, France, Ireland, the Netherlands, Portugal, Finland, Sweden and the United Kingdom. The only EU-15 Member States that did not intervene in this action were Austria, Belgium, Italy and Luxembourg. However, it should be noted that Austria and Belgium did intervene in support of the Council in the subsequent *Ship-Source Pollution* case, discussed below. The Netherlands, on the other hand, supported the objectives sought by the Council but presenting a different reasoning. Whilst supporting the Council's position that the content and purpose of the Framework Decision is the harmonisation of criminal laws and hence that the third pillar provided the correct legal basis, the Dutch government contended that the Community may, in exercising the powers conferred on it by the Treaty, require the Member States to provide for the possibility of punishing certain conduct under national criminal law, provided that the penalty is inseparably linked to the relevant substantive Community provisions and that it can actually be shown that imposing penalties under criminal law in that way is necessary for the achievement of the objectives of the Treaty in the area concerned. See Paragraph 16, the Netherlands' submission. See Case C-240/90 *Germany v Commission* [1992] ECR I-5383. *Environmental Crimes*, para. 36.

78 Specifically, Article 34 EU, in conjunction with Articles 29 EU and 31 (e) EU. Articles 1 to 7 of the Framework Decision on environmental crimes related to the definition of environmental criminal offences, penalties for natural persons, the liability of legal persons and sanctions.

79 *Environmental Crimes*, para. 18.

80 Specifically, under Article 175 (1) EC (equivalent to Article 192 (1) TFEU post-Lisbon).

81 Case 176/03 *Commission v. Council* [2005] ECR I-7879; [2005] 3 CMLR 20.

law. In a statement with far-reaching consequences, the Court ruled that 'as general rule, neither criminal law nor the rules of criminal procedure fall within the Community's competence',[82] but added that 'the last-mentioned finding does not prevent the Community legislature, when the application of effective, proportionate and dissuasive criminal penalties by the competent national authorities *is an essential measure* for combating *serious environmental offences*, from *taking measures which relate to the criminal law* of the Member States which *it considers necessary* in order to ensure that the rules which it lays down *on environmental protection are fully effective*'. (emphasis added).[83]

The *Environmental Crimes* ruling is thus fundamentally motivated by the concern to ensure the full effectiveness of Community law.[84] It has been observed that the Court's emphasis on the principle of effectiveness to establish the Community competence is striking.[85] In particular, criminal law is regarded by the Court as a view to an end, rather than a special field of law where special rules must apply.[86] Moreover, it has been suggested that the notion of effectiveness is very imprecise for the purposes of competence monitoring.[87] Since the Court linked the Community competence in criminal matters to the effectiveness of an EC policy area, the Court would need in future to device reliable tests to define 'an essential measure' and 'effectiveness'.[88] The express conferral of supranational powers to the EU in criminal matters post-Lisbon does not solve this imprecision. As will be discussed below, *the exercise* of this criminal law competence is still dependent post-Lisbon on the notion of effectiveness.

---

82 *Ibid*, para. 47.

83 *Ibid*, para. 48.

84 See paras. 48 and 52 of *Environmental Crimes*.

85 Mitsilegas, Valsamis 'The Competence Question: The European Community and Criminal Law', in Guild, Elspeth and Geyer, Florian (ed.) *Security versus Freedom? Police and Judicial Cooperation in the European Union* (Ashgate, 2008) at 154.

86 *Ibid.*

87 *See* Ross, Malcom 'Effectiveness in the European Legal Order(s): Beyond Supremacy to Constitutional Proportionality' *European Law Review* 30 (6) (2005); Weatherill, S. 'Better Competence Monitoring' 30 *European Law Review* 23 (2005); and Weatherill, S. 'Competence Creep and Competence Control' 23 *Yearbook of European Law* 1 (2004).

88 White, Simone 'Harmonisation of Criminal Law under the First Pillar' (2006) *E.L.Rev*, 31 (1) (2006) at 91.

The Court then focused on the fact that environmental protection constitutes *one of the essential objectives of the Community,*[89] recalling that (ex) Article 2 EC[90] promoted 'a high level of protection and improvement of the quality of the environment'.[91] The ECJ found that the main objective of the Framework Decision was the protection of the environment and hence the measure could have been properly adopted under former Article 175 EC (post-Lisbon, Article 192 TFEU).[92] The Court finally ruled that 'the entire framework decision, *being indivisible*, infringed [ex-]Article 47 EU as it encroached on the powers in environmental matters which [ex-]175 EC [Article 192 TFEU] confers on the Community'.[93] Therefore, the ECJ ultimately dismissed and considered to be ill-founded the argument of the Council that the Framework Decision harmonising criminal law needed to be adopted under the former TEU (third pillar) legal basis.

By extending the Community powers to (environmental) criminal matters, the Court has effectively bypassed the negative Dutch and French referenda on the Constitutional Treaty (CT) in the summer of 2005 which, had it been ratified, would have provided a clearer Treaty basis for the Community/Union to harmonise the criminal laws of the Member States.[94] Yet the decision is not inconsistent with the court's own case-law, in which the Court has consistently held, interpreting the loyal-cooperation principle enshrined in ex-Article 10 of the EC Treaty,[95] that sanctions for the non-implementation of EC law must be 'effective, proportionate and dissuasive' (see, for example, the *Greek Maize* case)[96] and even that a State's failure to prosecute could amount to a

89 See Case 280/83 *ADBHU* [1985] ECR 531, para. 13; Case 302/86 *Commission v Denmark* [1998] ECR 4607, para. 8.

90 Repealed and replaced, in substance, by Article 3 TEU.

91 *Environmental Crimes*, para. 41.

92 *Ibid*, paras. 47 and para. 48.

93 *Ibid*, para. 53.

94 See Treaty Establishing a Constitution for Europe (CT), OJC 310, art. III-270 (2).

95 Post-Lisbon, repealed and replaced, in substance, by Article 4, paragraph 3, TEU, which states that: '[p]ursuant to the principle of sincere cooperation, the Union and the Member States shall, in full mutual respect, assist each other in carrying out tasks which flow from the Treaties. The Member States shall take any appropriate measure, general or particular, to ensure fulfilment of the obligations arising out of the Treaties or resulting from the acts of the institutions of the Union. The Member States shall facilitate the achievement of the Union's tasks and refrain from any measure which could jeopardise the attainment of the Union's objectives'.

96 Case 68/88 *Commission v. Hellenic Republic* [1989] ECR 2965.

violation of former Article 10 EC (see *Greek Maize*;[97] *Spanish Strawberries*).[98] The principle of loyal cooperation has been interpreted in this expansive fashion by the court despite the fact that the prosecutorial activities in some countries are ruled by the opportunity principle, i.e. there is no duty for the relevant authorities in those countries to bring a prosecution in individual cases.[99] Moreover, despite the fact that there was no explicit reference to the Community competence in criminal matters in the EC Treaty[100] and the third pillar appeared to offer the framework for Member States' co-operation in criminal matters, the Court restated in *Environmental Crimes* the rule under former Article 47 of the TEU[101] that nothing in the Treaty on the European Union would affect the Community competence under the EC Treaty.[102] Hence former Article 47 TEU effectively created a 'border' between the first pillar and the other two.[103]

---

97 *Ibid.*

98 Case 265/95 *Commission v. France* [1997] ECR 6959.

99 For example, Belgium, the UK and the Netherlands. See Faure, Michael And Heine, Gunter, *Criminal Enforcement of Environmental Law in the European Union* Kluwer Law International (2005), at 60.

100 In fact, the Council and some Member States argued in *Environmental Crimes* that the effect of Arts. 135 EC and 280 (4) (post-Lisbon, Articles 33 and 325 TFEU), which *excluded* the Community competence to lay down rules concerning the application of national criminal law or the national administration of justice in the cases of customs cooperation and fraud to the financial interests of the Community, would be to rule out the criminal law competence of the Community in relation to other policy areas as well. This argument was however rejected by the Court in *Environmental Crimes*. Yet one cannot help but notice an anomaly in that in two areas which are often regarded as fundamental to the operation of the EU (customs cooperation and the Community budget), the Community competence in criminal matters would have appeared to be limited or excluded, while in the case of other essential objectives of the EC (i.e. environmental protection) the same limitation would not apply. This anomaly is corrected in the Lisbon Treaty under the new wording of Articles 33 and 325 TFEU, which provide that the EU is competent to seek the harmonization of criminal law against fraud to the EU budget and as regards customs cooperation.

101 Since Lisbon replaced by Art. 40 TEU. Given that the Lisbon Treaty abolished the third pillar, this article no longer governs the distribution of competences between the first and third pillars.

102 Ex-Art. 47 TEU (replaced by Art. 40 TEU) literally stated that 'nothing in [the TEU Treaty] shall affect the Treaties establishing the European Communities or the subsequent Treaties and Acts modifying or supplementing them'.

103 Peers, Steve, (2006) above note 53, at 7.

The *Environmental Crimes* judgment was based on the doctrine of 'implied powers' according to which the Community (now Union) enjoys the powers or means necessary to achieve a given objective or task attributed to it.[104] That is, the EC environmental protection objective would be deprived of its *effet utile* if the EC legislature did not have the power to adopt the criminal law measures necessary to ensure that the rules which it lays down on environmental protection are fully effective.[105] The doctrine of implied powers is thus an exception to the principle of conferral of powers according to which the Community was only competent to act in the fields for which powers have been attributed to it.[106]

Following an appraisal of the Court's case-law on penalties,[107] one commentator suggested that the Court's line of reasoning in *Environmental Crimes* is 'convincing'[108] and argued that although there is no implicit transfer through former Article 175 EC of Member States' power in criminal law, the EC Treaty did not contain a catalogue of negative competences and thus 'there are no fields where Community action or the influence of Community law would be ruled out absolutely and categorically'.[109]

Yet the Court has left many questions unanswered in the *Environmental Crimes* case, in particular whether the power of the Community in criminal matters extended beyond the environmental field or not, and whether the Community had the power to approximate the definition of offences and the

---

104 Cases 281, 283–5, 287/85 [1987] ECR 3203. See Hartley, T (2007) above note 40, at 104–110.

105 See Joined Cases 281/85, 283/85 to 285/85 and 287/85 *Germany v Commission* [1987] ECR 3203, para. 28. See also, the Opinion of Advocate General Mazak in the *Ship-Source Pollution* case (discussed below), Points 89–90.

106 Article 5 EC stated that 'the Community shall act *within the limits of the powers attributed to it* [by this Treaty] and of the objectives assigned to it therein' (emphasis added). This provision is equivalent to Article 5 TEU (post-Lisbon) which states that: '(1.) The limits of Union competences are governed by the principle of conferral. The use of Union competences is governed by the principles of subsidiarity and proportionality. (2.) Under the principle of conferral, the Union shall act only within the limits of the competences conferred upon it by the Member States in the Treaties to attain the objectives set out therein. Competences not conferred upon the Union in the Treaties remain with the Member States'.

107 In particular, Case 14/83 *von Colson and Kamann v. Land Nordrheim Westfalen* [1984] ECR 1891 and Case C-271/91 *Marshall v Southampton and South-West Hampshire Area Health Authority* (Marshall II) [1993] ECR I-4367, para. 25.

108 Tobler, C. 'Case C-176/03, Commission v. Council, judgement of the Grand Chamber of 13 September 2005' (2006) *Common Market Law Review* 845, at 849.

109 *Ibid* at 851.

types and levels of criminal penalties (for example to establish minimum levels of fines or terms of imprisonment, as was already the practice in the third pillar). Indeed, the Court's ruling allowed the Community legislature to take '*measures* which relate to the criminal law of the Member States which it considers necessary in order to ensure that the rules which it lays down on environmental protection are fully effective'[110] (emphasis added). The judgment hence fell short of defining what type of criminal law measures could be defined by the Community and must be introduced by Member States in order to achieve the objective of environmental protection. So even though the decision indicated that the nature of the sanction to implement EC law could be established at EC level (i.e. criminal or administrative), it was not clear whether this power extended to the definition of specific offences and penalties.[111]

The Commission itself took the view that the Community had the power to harmonise criminal offences and penalties, as can be seen in its Communication of November 2005 outlining its interpretation of the September 2005 ruling[112] as well as from its second proposal for a directive on environmental crimes of February 2007. Yet many Member States feared that the power of the Community to define criminal offences and the types and levels of criminal penalties would undermine the coherence of their own national legal systems and their powers to properly label offences and grade corresponding sanctions according to their severity. Although this view was supported by Advocate General Colomer in his Opinion in *Environmental Crimes*,[113] the question of harmonisation of criminal penalties is not directly addressed by the ECJ in that case. The ECJ had the opportunity to rule on this question in the follow-up *Ship-Source Pollution* case, which is discussed next.

110 *Environmental Crimes* case, para. 48.

111 See 42nd Report of Session 2005–2006, House of Lords, European Union Committee, 'The Criminal Law Competence of the European Community. Report with Evidence' 28 July 2006, 21–23. However, as regards the Community competence to harmonise criminal offences, Professor Peers considered that the Community 'must at least have the power to define what criminal offences must be prosecuted by Member States' as 'paragraph 48 [of the judgement] ...does not rule out the Community being relatively specific and being very, very prescriptive as to what precisely Member States should ban' (21–22).

112 Communication from the European Commission to the European Parliament and the Council on the Implications of the Court's Judgment of 13 September 2005 (Case 176/03 Commission v. Council), COM(2005)583 final/2, 24 November 2005.

113 Case 176/03, Opinion of Advocate General Ruiz-Jarabo Colomer, Points 83 to 87.

5.5.2 *The Ship-Source Pollution Case*

Fuelled by the Court's findings in the *Environmental Crimes* ruling, the Commission brought an annulment action in November 2005 against the Council challenging the third pillar legal basis of the Framework Decision on shipping pollution crimes.[114] The Commission was supported by the European Parliament, while the Council was supported by the governments of twenty Member States.[115] This indicates the constitutional significance of this dispute.[116] As was the situation in *Environmental Crimes*, this case concerned the distribution of competences between the first and third pillars of the European Union as well as between the EC and the Member States in the area of criminal law.

One of the important differences between the shipping pollution Framework Decision and the Framework Decision on environmental crimes is that the former contained detailed rules on penalties.[117] Hence it was expected that the Court would clarify in this case its position in relation to the Community competence to establish specific types and levels of penalties.[118] In *Environmental Crimes* the powers of the Community to harmonise the criminal laws of the Member States were defined narrowly and in direct relation to the facts of the case, rather than in the form of a principle, which accounts for the difficulty of distinguishing the underlying rationale from its concrete application.[119] Indeed, it was not clear from *Environmental Crimes* the extent to which the Community competence in criminal matters only applied to environmental protection and 'serious environmental offences' or whether it might in principle be applicable to other common policy areas, such as the EC transport policy. As put by AG Mazak in the *Ship-Source Pollution* case, the *Environmental Crimes* ruling left 'delicate questions to be considered as to the circumstances in which the Community has competence to oblige the Member States to provide for criminal penalties, and the precise extent to which that competence may be exercised'.[120]

114 This was possible because this annulment action was brought just under two months after the adoption of the shipping pollution framework decision.

115 They are: Belgium, the Czech Republic, Denmark, Estonia, Greece, France, Ireland, Latvia, Lithuania, Hungary, Malta, the Netherlands, Austria, Poland, Portugal, Slovakia, Finland, Sweden and the United Kingdom and Slovenia. It is notable that nine of those Member States have joined the EU in May 2004. The only new (EU-25) Member State that did not intervene in support of the Council was Cyprus.

116 Mitsilegas, V. (2008) above note 85, at 159.

117 *See* Articles 4 and 6 of the Framework Decision on ship-source pollution (2005).

118 See 42nd Report of Session 2005–2006, House of Lords, European Union Committee, 'The Criminal Law Competence of the European Community'. Report with Evidence' 28 July 2006.

119 Opinion of *Mazak* AG, para. 89.

120 *Ibid*, para. 4.

Although Advocate General Mazak opined that there is no sound basis for limiting the EC power to provide for criminal measures to the environmental law field, the significance of this objective had been emphasised by the Court and Advocate General Colomer in *Environmental Crimes*.[121] In particular, the *raison d'etre* for the Community criminal-law powers lied with the general principle of effectiveness underlying Community law.[122] So the Advocate General was prepared to accept the Community competence in criminal matters in order to ensure the effectiveness of Community law without any link with environmental protection.[123]

Yet the ECJ in *Ship-Source Pollution* decided to stay very close to the facts of the case (again focusing on 'environmental protection') rather than making a broader statement of principle on the extent of the competence of the EC to protect its regulatory schemes by means of criminal law.[124] The Court held that: 'since Articles 2, 3 and 5 of the Framework Decision 2005/667 are designed to ensure the efficacy of the rules adopted in the field of maritime safety, non-compliance with which may have serious consequences, by requiring Member States to apply criminal penalties to certain forms of conduct, those articles must be regarded as being essentially aimed at improving maritime safety, *as well as environmental protection*, and could have been validly adopted on the basis of Article 80(2)'[125] (emphasis added). So while the Commission received a confirmation of the existence of a (limited) Community competence in criminal matters, the extent to which the Community remained competent to harmonise the criminal laws of the Member States remained unclear after the *Ship-Source Pollution* case.[126]

121 He elaborated that the EC criminal law powers could be extended to other essential objectives of the Community enshrined in former Articles 2 EC and 3 EC and could extend to other Community policy areas such as transport (*Mazak* AG, Point 94). He dismissed the argument raised by Member States that environmental protection is the only horizontal policy enshrined in the EC Treaty in light of the integration principle established in Article 6 EC. He suggests that this attribute is applicable to other areas too (e.g. non-discrimination, Article 12 EC) (Point 96 of the Opinion).

122 *Mazak* AG, Point 99.

123 *Ibid.*

124 Fletcher, Maria, Loof, Robin And Gilmore, Bill, *EU Criminal Law and Justice*, Edward Elgar (2008) at 180.

125 *Ship-Source Pollution*, para. 69.

126 See also, 10th Report of Session 2007–2008, House of Lord, European Union Committee, '*The Treaty of Lisbon: an Impact Assessment*' Volume I: Report 13 March 2008 Chapter 6; and Peers, S (2008) 'The European Community's Criminal Law Competence: the Plot Thickens' *European Law Review* 399 at 407.

The Court appears to share the Council's view that the Community competence in criminal matters was linked to the exceptional nature of the subject matter, i.e. environmental protection. So if the protection of the environment is a transversal objective of EC action, criminalisation in legislative action would be allowed in all fields of EC action with an environmental objective, such as sea transport.[127]

Like the Advocate General, the court upheld the principle of effectiveness as the main criterion to establish the Community competence to harmonise environmental criminal law. So the court confirms its position in *Environmental Crimes* that the existence of the Community competence in criminal matters was linked to the principle of effectiveness of Community law. However, the Court does not elaborate why criminal sanctions are effective in the context of ship-source pollution. In this regard, the Advocate General observed that establishing a benchmark of effectiveness is particularly difficult since 'effectiveness is in several respects an imprecise criterion on the basis of which to establish competence for the adoption of measures relating to criminal law' or to establish when rules in a specific field are not sufficiently or not 'fully effective', thus necessitating an instrument of criminal law.[128] Moreover, according to the Advocate General it may be too simple to assume that criminal law is always the appropriate remedy for a lack of effectiveness and 'policy considerations behind the use of criminal penalties in a given community go well beyond the mere question of effective enforcement'.[129]

The Court however approached the issue of effectiveness of Community law more cautiously than the Advocate General. The Court restates its position in *Environmental Crimes*[130] that while neither criminal law nor criminal procedure fall within the Community's competence, when the application of effective, proportionate and dissuasive criminal sanctions by the competent national authorities is an essential measure for combating serious environmental offences, the Community legislature may require the Member States to introduce such penalties in order to ensure that the rules which lays down in that field are fully effective.[131] So the Court dispensed in this case (as it had done in *Environmental Crimes*) with any specific analysis of the effectiveness

127 See also, Fletcher, et al (2008), above note 124, at 182.

128 *Mazak* AG, Point 115 et seq.

129 *Mazak* AG, Point 117–118.

130 *Environmental Crimes*, par. 47.

131 *Ship-Source Pollution*, para. 66.

of environmental criminal law.[132] In sum, if the Council considers an action to be necessary, 'the Court will not second-guess it'.[133]

Given the political sensitivities in this area, and the possible link between the effectiveness of criminal law with the types and levels of penalties available to the national authorities,[134] in perhaps the most significant statement in the judgement the Court held univocally that 'the determination of the type and level of criminal penalties to be applied does not fall within the Community's sphere of competence'.[135] This statement fails to elaborate on why the Community lacked competence to adopt specific types and levels of criminal sanctions. The court then swiftly moved on to rule that since Articles 4 and 6 of the Framework Decision 2005/667 relate to the types and levels of criminal penalties, they were not adopted in infringement of the Community competence.[136] It is not clear why the Court does not elaborate on the question of the lack of Community competence to adopt criminal penalties – it has been suggested that this may have been due to political reasons in light of the negotiation process of the EU Reform/Lisbon Treaty.[137] In particular, perhaps due to the criticisms for alleged 'judicial activism' that the court had received following the *Environmental Crimes* ruling,[138] the court decided in *Ship-Source Pollution* to limit the Community competence to the definition of criminal offences, but not to the harmonisation of criminal penalties.

Unlike the ECJ decision, the Opinion of Advocate General Mazák has provided reasons to substantiate his position that the Community legislature should be entitled to require Member States to introduce criminal penalties and to prescribe that they are 'effective, proportionate and dissuasive', but not

---

132 Indeed, the Court referred in the 2005 ruling to criminal law measures which the Community legislature '*considers* necessary' and established that 'the Council *took the view* that criminal penalties are essential'. See *Environmental Crimes*, paras. 48 and 50 (on the necessity test, see further discussion below). Similarly, in this instance the recitals to the shipping Directive and Framework Decision appear to show that both the Council and the Commission are of the view that criminal sanctions are necessary to ensure compliance with Community rules on maritime safety. See Opinion of AG Mazak in *Ship-Source Pollution*, Point 119; *Ship-Source Pollution*, para. 67.

133 Fletcher, M.(2008) above note 124, at 182.

134 See Chapter 6.

135 *Ship-Source Pollution,* para. 70.

136 *Ship-Source Pollution.* para. 71.

137 Peers, S (2008) 'The European Community's Criminal Law Competence: the Plot Thickens' *European Law Review* 399 at 407.

138 See Dawson, Mark, De Witte, Bruno; Muir, Elise, *Judicial Activism at the European Court of Justice* (Edward Elgar, 2013).

to specify the penalties to be imposed.[139] According to AG Mazák, the harmonisation of the types and levels of penalties raises not only concerns as to the internal consistency of the criminal law of the Union but also as to the coherence of each national penal system.[140] Since each criminal code reflects a particular ranking of legal interests which it seeks to protect (property, the person, the environment, and so on) and the penalties vary accordingly, the determination by the Community legislature of the type and level of penalties to be imposed could lead to the fragmentation and compromise the coherence of national penal systems. Further, he argues that the seriousness of a criminal penalty, its effectiveness and dissuasiveness, cannot be viewed in isolation from the other criminal penalties provided for under national law and the manner in which penalties are employed in a given Member State as an instrument of enforcement. For example, a given level of fine can send out very different messages in different Member States regarding the seriousness of the offence in question. The principle of subsidiarity also played a central role in the AG's argument rejecting the Community powers to adopt criminal penalties. He suggests that in accordance with the subsidiarity principle, the Member States are as a rule better placed than the Community to 'translate' the concept of 'effective, proportionate and dissuasive' criminal penalties into their respective legal systems and societal contexts.[141]

Yet the argument raised by the Advocate General regarding the coherence of each national legal system is perhaps not so strong if one takes into account that the harmonisation of criminal penalties was already taking place under the third pillar, and it must be remembered that those third pillar legislative measures are legally binding and even, after the *Pupino* decision in June 2005, had indirect effect. Moreover, the subsidiarity principle does not appear to be a strong enough justification to restrict the Community competence to adopt *minimum* levels of *maximum* criminal penalties, in line with the Justice and Home Affairs Council conclusions on penalties.[142] Moreover, it could be argued that the imposition of the requirement of criminalisation in the first place – which, under the qualified

139 *Mazak AG*, Point 103 et seq. This view had also been supported by Advocate General Colomer in his Opinion in *Environmental Crimes*, though as discussed above the question of harmonisation of criminal penalties is not directly addressed by the ECJ in that case. See *Colomer AG*, Points 83 to 87.

140 *Mazak AG*, para. 111.

141 *Mazak AG*, para. 108.

142 Justice and Home Affairs Council conclusions, April 2002. See also, Peers (2008) above note 137, at 407.

voting system which was applicable to the first pillar, meant that Member States could be outvoted – arguably constitutes a greater challenge to State sovereignty and the exercise of power in the criminal law sphere, than is the dictation of specific criminal sanctions.[143]

The effect of the *Ship-Source Pollution* judgement is that an EC measure harmonising environmental criminal could require Member States to criminalise certain conduct and lay down specific offences, but it could not specify the types and levels of criminal penalties. Therefore, the limits of the Community criminal-law powers recognized in the *Ship-Source Pollution* judgment would allow eco-criminals to exploit the differences in the environmental criminal legislation of the Member States (as one Member State may apply a small criminal fine and another a long prison sentence for the same offence), unless it could be established that any criminal sanctions set at a low level are not 'effective, proportionate and dissuasive' enough,[144] which is difficult to establish in individual cases. Moreover, at the level of police and judicial co-operation in criminal matters a certain level playing field for criminal penalties would have been desirable, given that some EU criminal law measures which apply to environmental crimes, such as the 2002 European Arrest Warrant (EAW) and the 2005 European Evidence Warrant (EEW), require a certain minimum penalty threshold for their operation without the requirement of double criminality.[145]

Despite the limitations to the Community criminal law competence set by the ECJ ruling in the *Ship-Source Pollution* case, the Lisbon Treaty – discussed in the next section – has expanded the EU powers in criminal matters by establishing a clear legal basis for the Union to harmonise at the supranational level not only criminal offences but also penalties.

---

143 Mitsilegas, Valsamis, 'Trust-Building Measures in the European Judicial Area in Criminal Matters: Issues of Competence, Legitimacy and Inter-institutional Balance' in Balzacq, Thierry and Carrera, Sergio (ed.) *Security Versus Freedom? A Challenge for Europe's Future* (Datmouth: Ashgate 2006) at 307–308.

144 There is a general requirement under EU law – based on the principle of loyal cooperation – that penalties for failure to comply with EU legislation must be 'effective, proportionate and dissuasive'. The same requirement is inserted in many pieces of EU legislation, including the EU directives on environmental crime and ship-source pollution.

145 As was discussed in Chapter 2 and will be further analysed in Chapter 7, the issuing of an EAW is only possible (unless the sentence has already been passed) for acts punishable in the issuing state by a custodial sentence or a detention order of at least 12 months. In the case of environmental crime, issuing the EAW without the condition of dual criminality requires that the offence is punishable in the issuing Member State by a maximum of at least three years imprisonment.

5.6 The Lisbon Treaty and the Future of EU Environmental Criminal Law

5.6.1 *Overview of changes to AFSJ*

Despite the above discussed litigation in which a considerable majority of the Member States sided with the Council against criminal-law powers being transferred to the EC, the Member States themselves recognized the deficiencies under the third pillar by aiming to ratify a treaty that would bring police and judicial cooperation in criminal matters to the supranational level. Following the failed attempt to ratify the Constitutional Treaty in 2005, the Lisbon Treaty was signed on 13 December 2007 by the heads of government and state of the member states and was ratified in November 2009, following the Irish second referendum[146] and the Czech and Polish ratifications. It entered into force in December 2009.

Under Lisbon, the intergovernmental third pillar is abolished and two separate bodies of law are generated: an amended version of the Treaty on the European Union (TEU) and the Treaty on the Functioning of the Union (TFEU), which replaces the Treaty establishing the European Community (TEC).[147] Hence the dispute relating to the EU pillar structure and legal basis for the harmonization of criminal law, highlighted in the ECJ cases discussed above, will no longer be as relevant following the ratification of the Treaty of Lisbon.

The Treaty of Lisbon completes the absorption of the remaining third pillar aspects of Justice and Home Affairs Law – i.e. police and judicial cooperation in criminal matters – into the 'first pillar'. This means that measures under all aspects of the Area of Freedom, Security and Justice are determined by the ordinary legislative procedure of qualified majority voting and co-decision between the Council and European Parliament, unless otherwise specified. Moreover, subject to transitional, and in the case of the UK, Ireland and Denmark, opt-in arrangements, pre-existing third pillar acts would fall after a five-year transitional period within the jurisdiction of the ECJ.[148] As this five-year transitional period expired in 1 December 2014, all criminal law

146 The Irish 'no vote' on the Treaty on 12 June 2008 had shed doubt on whether the Treaty of Lisbon would indeed be ratified by all member states.

147 S. Carrera, and F. Geyer, 'The Reform Treaty and Justice and Home Affairs: Implication for the Common Area of Freedom, Security and Justice', in E. Guild and F. Geyer (eds.) *Security versus Justice: Police and Judicial Cooperation in the European Union* (2008), at 291.

148 Art. 10 of the *Transitional Protocol*. See 10th Report of Session 2007–2008, House of Lord, European Union Committee, *'The Treaty of Lisbon: an Impact Assessment'* Volume I: Report 13 March 2008.

measures adopted under the third pillar currently fall under the jurisdiction of the CJEU.

Another innovation introduced by the Lisbon Treaty in the context of criminal law is that it allows a member state to pull the 'emergency brake' when a legislative proposal would bring about fundamental changes to its national criminal justice system. The matter is then referred to the European Council and the ordinary legislative procedure is suspended. If the European Council arrives at a consensus within four months, the matter is then referred back to the Council of Ministers for continuation of the legislative procedure.[149] If no agreement is reached, this would then allow a number of member states (at least nine of them) to initiate enhanced cooperation in order to implement a criminal law proposal to be applicable among themselves. They need to notify the European Parliament, the Commission and the Council and authorization for enhanced cooperation is deemed to have been granted. However, although perhaps a necessary compromise which has arisen in the negotiations of the Lisbon Treaty, this process of enhanced cooperation could be criticized for creating a 'two-speed' Europe. It has been argued that the 'emergency brake' is unlikely to be frequently used in practice, but that it is likely to impact on negotiations in the Council through the possibility of its use.[150]

5.6.2 *Possible Amendments to EU Environmental Crime Legislation Post-Lisbon*

It is possible that the criminal law measures adopted under the first pillar in the aftermath of the *Environmental Crimes* and *Ship-Source Pollution* rulings (i.e. the Environmental Crimes Directive adopted in October 2008 and the Ship-Source Pollution Directive adopted in 2005/2009) will be amended with the view of harmonising specific penalties (e.g. minimum levels of maximum prison sentences and fines), and perhaps also other measures on police and judicial cooperation in criminal matters, such as prosecutorial and jurisdictional rules.[151] The Commission had indicated that it would propose such amendments when launching the Action Plan to implement the Stockholm

149 *Ibid*, at 118.

150 See *Ibid*. On the relevance of the British and Irish opt outs in light of the new 'emergency brake' rules, see Peers (2008), above note 137. It must be noted that the emergency brake does not apply to mutual recognition measures or Eurojust – only to substantive criminal law and domestic criminal procedure. See also, Peers, S. 'Mission Accomplished? EU Justice and Home Affairs after the Lisbon Treaty' (2011) 48 *Common Market Law Review*, 661–639.

151 If an amendment to those Directive(s) is proposed along the lines described above, they would have to be based on a dual legal basis, since the amending act would be based on a criminal law provision (as discussed below, quite possibly Article 83 (2) TFEU) while the

Programme in April 2010, which sets out the priorities of EU criminal law for the next five years.[152] However, the Commission has so far not proposed amendments to the environmental crime and ship-source pollution directives, but has instead commissioned two studies on the implementation of the environmental crime directives in the EU, which may inform its decision on whether or not to seek further harmonisation of environmental criminal law.[153]

According to Recital 15 of the preamble to the Environmental Crimes Directive, '[w]henever subsequent legislation on environmental matters is adopted, it should specify where appropriate that this Directive will apply. Where necessary, Article 3 [which defines the criminal offences] should be amended'. The directive thus allows for any future pieces of EU environmental legislation to themselves prescribe criminal sanctions by reference to the environmental crime directive. Alternatively, the Commission may propose in future an amendment to the environmental crime directive to amplify the list of offences or, possibly, the list of EC/Euratom secondary legislation which appear in Annexes A and B to the environmental crime directive. But given the significance of these amendments, they would most certainly require the 'ordinary legislative procedure' between the Parliament and Council of Ministers.[154] However, recent legislative practice does not suggest that the Commission will

---

Directives are based on a environmental protection (i.e. Article 192TFEU) or the common transport policy (i.e. Article 100 (2) TFEU) legal bases.

152 See European Commission, Communication From the Commission to the European Parliament, the Council, the European Economic and Social Committee and the Committee of Regions, Delivering an Area of Freedom, Security and Justice for Europe's Citizens: Action Plan Implementing the Stockholm Programme, COM(2010) 171 final: *Legislative proposals supplementing Directive 2008/99/EC on the protection of environment through criminal law and Directive 2009/123/EC on ship-source pollution, Commission 2012.*

153 Under Service Contract 2011 144–238006 (contract notice of 29 July 2011) the Commission launched an open procedure to award a contract on the implementation of the environmental crime directive, and to provide the basis for the Commission to assess whether improvements to the legislation is necessary. Moreover, the Commission has commissioned in 2012 another broader study concerning environmental crime in the EU. See http://efface.eu (accessed on 15 February 2015).

154 Through the comitology procedure, the Commission may seek to adopt complementary measures to EU legislation via delegated acts (Article 290 TFEU) and implementing acts (Article 291 TFEU) without having to seek broader agreement through the EU co-decision procedure (which also involves Council of Ministers and the European Parliament) through the use of the comitology procedure whichh allows. See e.g. Commission Decision 2008/689/EC and Commission Decision 2010/115/EU amending Annex II of Directive 2000/54/EC of the European Parliament and of the Council on end-of-life vehicles.

seek necessarily to insert criminal provisions in future EU environmental legislation.[155] In general, this approach is commendable since the adoption of criminal penalties in future EU environmental legislation (without a formal amendment to the environmental crime directive) could lead to the fragmentation of environmental criminal law in the EU; and thus could be problematic from the perspective of the principle of legality, given that criminal offences and penalties would be found not in one or two pieces of EU environmental legislation, but in several ones.

5.6.3 *The Legal Basis of Future Acts of Harmonisation of Environmental Criminal Law in the EU*

5.6.3.1 The Scope of Article 83(1) and (2) TFEU

Under the TFEU, the European Union gains competence at the supranational level to define minimum rules (approximation) regarding the definition of criminal offences as well as penalties. Paragraph 1 of Article 83 of the Treaty on the Functioning on the European Union (which replaces the EC Treaty) states that:

> The European Parliament and the Council may, by means of directives adopted in accordance with the ordinary legislative procedure, establish minimum rules concerning the *definition of criminal offences and sanctions* in the areas of particularly *serious crime* with a *cross-border dimension* resulting from the nature or impact of such offences or from a special need to combat them on a common basis.
>
> These areas of crime are the following: terrorism, trafficking in human beings and sexual exploitation of women and children, illicit drug trafficking, illicit arms trafficking, money laundering, corruption, counterfeiting of means of payment, computer crime and organised crime.
>
> On the basis of developments in crime, the Council may adopt a decision identifying other areas of crime that meet the criteria specified in this paragraph. It shall act unanimously after obtaining the consent of the European Parliament (emphasis added).

The list of offences under paragraph 1 of Article 83 is exhaustive, and it does not include environmental crime. This is perhaps surprising considering the

---

155 See e.g. Directive (EU) 2015/412 of the European Parliament and of the Council of 11 March 2015 amending Directive 2001/18/EC as regards the possibility for the Member States to restrict or prohibit the cultivation of genetically modified organisms (GMO s) in their territory (Text with EEA relevance). This directive does not prescribe criminal sanctions.

above discussed institutional litigation before the ECJ emphasising the seriousness of environmental offences. However an unanimous decision of the Council might bring environmental crime into the scope of that provision, so ultimately it is not impossible that Article 83 (1) TFEU will be used in future to amend the environmental crime directive in order to, for example, harmonise specific criminal penalties for environmental offences.

The approximation of criminal law is also possible under paragraph 2 of Article 83 TFEU:

> If the approximation of criminal laws and regulations of the Member States *proves essential* to ensure *the effective implementation of a Union policy* in an area which has been subject to harmonisation measures, directives may establish minimum rules with regard to the definition of *criminal offences and sanctions* in the area concerned. Such directives shall be adopted by the same ordinary or special legislative procedure as was followed for the adoption of the harmonisation measures in question, without prejudice to Article 76 (emphasis added).

This provision has a broader scope than paragraph 1 of Article 83 TFEU, and it could be used to ensure the effective implementation in principle of any Union policy, including the EU laws and policies aimed at environmental protection. Some commentators consider that paragraphs (1) and (2) of Article 83 TFEU may be *lex specialis* in relation to one another, which would then allow the adoption of a proposal for an amendment to the environmental crime directive, for example, under paragraph 2 only.[156] That is, since the harmonization of criminal law would be sought as a means to ensure the effective implementation of a Union policy, it is suggested that any future harmonization of environmental criminal legislation would have to be based on Article 83 (2) TFEU. So it would not be possible for the Commission to seek harmonisation of environmental criminal law under either paragraphs 1 or 2 of Article 83, as paragraph 2 is to be regarded as *lex specialis*.[157] In this regard, it should be noted that in some instances an environmental criminal law measure would be based on a dual legal basis, depending on whether, for example, it includes rules on jurisdiction and prosecution.[158]

---

156 See Peers (2008) above note 137, 516–517.

157 *Ibid.*

158 At its meeting of 20 September 2010 the Committee on Legal Affairs accordingly decided with one abstention to recommend that the Proposal for a Directive of the European Parliament and of the Council on preventing and combating trafficking in human beings, and protecting victims, repealing Framework Decision 2002/629/JHA, should be based on

5.6.3.2 Does Article 83 (2) TFEU Prevail over the other TFEU Legal Provisions?

Arguably, there may be still scope for the EU to harmonise environmental criminal law under Article 192 TFEU i.e. under the environmental title of the TFEU, rather than para. (2) of Article 83 TFEU. Although Article 83 (2) TFEU allows for the adoption of minimum criminal rules in order to ensure the effective *implementation of a Union policy* (which clearly includes environmental policies), the *Environmental Crimes* and *Ship-Source Pollution* rulings had clarified that there was scope for harmonisation of criminal sanctions under a EC Treaty article belonging to other policy areas (e.g. Article 175EC on environmental protection or Article 80EC on transport policy). This interpretation would potentially have important consequences as the UK, Ireland and Denmark have secured in Protocols 21 and 22 to the Lisbon Treaty the option to opt out from the EU initiatives in criminal law only.[159] This means that the British, Irish and Danish opt outs will be irrelevant if the criminal policy finds its legal basis as a means to enforce other policy areas of the TFEU (e.g. environmental, transport or consumer protection). Moreover, as discussed above any Member State may pull the 'emergency brake' to prevent a criminal law measure from being adopted by the Council, but this only applies to measures based Article 83 (1) or (2) TFEU, not to measures adopted under other TFEU provisions such as Article 192 TFEU.

On the other hand it has been argued that Article 83 TFEU is *lex specialis* in relation to other Treaty provisions, and hence the correct legal basis for the future harmonisation of (environmental) criminal law.[160] This appears to have been the intention of the Member States when negotiating the provisions on police and judicial cooperation under the Lisbon Treaty, in particular when negotiating the provisions on the 'emergency brake'. Recent law-making practice in the EU appears to confirm this view. For example, the legal basis for

---

the legal basis of Articles 82(2) and 83(1) of the Treaty on the functioning of the European Union. See also, Opinion on the legal basis of the proposal for a Directive of the European Parliament and of the Council on preventing and combating trafficking in human beings (repeal of Framework Decision 2002/629/JHA) (COM(2010)0095 – C7-0087/2010 – 2010/0065(COD)). In the light of the foregoing, it was considered that there is no justification for adding the legal basis of Article 79(2) TFEU.

159 See Peers (2007) *Statewatch Analysis*, EU Reform Treaty Analysis no. 4: British and Irish Opt-Outs from EU Justice and Home Affairs Law, 26 October 2007, available online at http://www.statewatch.org [accessed on 10 February 2015]. Obviously those countries also have opt outs in other policy areas under the EC Treaty, e.g. Title IV on immigration and asylum, and they would retain the right to opt out in those areas post-Lisbon.

160 See Peers, S. (2008) above note 137.

the second EU market abuse directive (MAD II)[161] was Article 83 (2) TFEU, and not Article 114 TFEU (former Article 95 EC) which was the internal market legal basis used for adoption of the first Market Abuse Directive (MAD I).[162]

5.6.3.3 A Common 'European Environmental Criminal Law'?

One of the important differences between the original 2007 proposal for a directive on environmental crime, and the final compromise text of the directive adopted in 2008, is that under the latter only violations of EC/EU environmental law, not national environmental law, may be criminalised at the EC level, in line with the *Ship-Source Pollution* case.[163] Hence the directive contains an Appendix listing over 70 pieces of EC environmental legislation which relate to the environmental offences defined in the directive. Thus no 'autonomous environmental offences' (i.e. criminalising national environmental law, regardless of whether or not they violate EU environmental legislation) is present in the directive.[164]

It is possible, though perhaps unlikely, that the Commission may wish to amend the environmental crime and ship-source pollution directives to create a common 'European environmental criminal law', so that violations of national environmental law could also be criminalised, a possibility which was ruled out under the first pillar by the ECJ *Ship-Source Pollution* ruling.[165] There would be difficulties in securing such an amendment, though. Firstly, it is not clear whether the criminal law provisions of the Lisbon Treaty permit the harmonisation of purely domestic environmental law, as the two possible legal bases for such harmonisation, i.e. paragraphs 1 and 2 of Article 83 of the TFEU, appear to rule out the possibility of harmonisation of purely domestic environmental law. Paragraph 1 requires a *transnational* element for harmonisation of criminal law. So unless a transnational link with the offence could be made, it would not appear possible for the EU to seek to harmonise purely national

161 Directive 2014/57/EU of the European Parliament and of the Council of 16 April 2014 on criminal sanctions for market abuse ('market abuse directive'). See also, Regulation (EU) No 596/2014 of the European Parliament and of the Council of 16 April 2014 on market abuse ('market abuse regulation' or 'MAR').

162 Directive 2003/6/EC of the European Parliament and of the Council of 28 January 2003 on insider dealing and market manipulation (market abuse).

163 Case 440/05, para. 66: '[...] the Community legislature may require the Member States to introduce such penalties in order to ensure that *the rules which it lays down in that field* are fully effective' (emphasis added).

164 See Article 3 of the environmental crime directive. For a discussion of the harmonisation of autonomous environmental offences in Europe, see Chapter 6.

165 *Ship-Source Pollution*, para. 66, *supra*.

environmental law under Article 83 (1) TFEU. As for paragraph 2 of Article 83 TFEU, it only permits the harmonisation of criminal law in order to ensure the effective *implementation of a Union policy* in an area which has been subject to harmonisation measures, so it would not enable the Commission to seek the harmonisation of purely national environmental law.[166]

Some of the advantages of an amendment to the environmental crime directive to harmonise purely national environmental law would be that the list of Community/Euratom Acts (contained in Annexes A and B to the Directive on environmental crime, which themselves relate to the environmental criminal offences defined in Article 3 of the Directive) could be discarded, and potentially the definition of some of the offences in the Directive could be simplified. This could improve the accessibility and potentially facilitate the implementation of the Directive. However, given that the Member States would have already transposed the environmental crime directive into their national legal system by the time such an amendment act became effective, it is difficult to envision the additional real benefits that the harmonisation of purely national environmental criminal law would bring. Moreover, as discussed above, a considerable proportion of the environmental legislation in the Member States is in any event based on EU environmental law.

5.6.3.4 The British, Danish and Irish Opt-outs

If there is an amendment to a EU criminal law measure in future, the UK and Ireland (though Denmark's arrangements differ to some extent) secured in Protocols 21 and 22 to the Lisbon Treaty the possibility to opt out from that measure. As for the other Member States, a transitional period of five years would be applicable until a pre-existing criminal-law legislative measure is subject to full ECJ jurisdiction.[167] Yet that does not apply to the environmental crime or ship-source pollution directives, as the Protocol applies to third-pillar measures which preceded the Lisbon Treaty only, not to the environmental crime or ship-source pollution directives which were adopted under the first pillar. So the UK and Ireland may not be able to opt out from the environmental crime and shipping pollution directives (which were adopted prior to Lisbon)

166 However, as discussed above, it is possible – though perhaps unlikely – that other TFEU legal bases outside the criminal cooperation title of the TFEU could be used for the harmonisation of environmental criminal law, which could allow the EU in principle to criminalise violations of purely national environmental law.

167 See also, Peers (2007) *Statewatch Analysis*, EU Reform Treaty Analysis no. 4: British and Irish Opt-Outs from EU Justice and Home Affairs Law, 26 October 2007, available online at http://www.statewatch.org (accessed on 15 February 2015).

after (and if) they are eventually amended to harmonise for example criminal penalties based on a post-Lisbon criminal-law legal basis.

5.7 Legal Principles Limiting the Future Harmonisation of Environmental Criminal Law in the EU

Beyond the division of competences between the EU/EC treaties and the EU and the Member States, there are further constitutional challenges to the definition of the competence of the EU to harmonise environmental criminal law, which will be examined in this section. Some of the legal principles discussed in this section have been developed in particular by the jurisprudence of the European Court of Justice. These principles could be regarded as at times legitimising and other times limiting the competence of the EU in the environmental criminal law field.

5.7.1 *The Principle of Legality*

The principle of legality (*nullum crimen, nulla poena sine lege*), which underlines the constitutional traditions of the Member States, is a specific expression of the principle of legal certainty, and requires criminal offences and penalties to be clearly defined.[168] Legal certainty requires that the effect of Community/Union legislation must be clear and predictable[169] with the aim of 'ensur[ing] that situations and legal relationships governed by Community law remain foreseeable'.[170]

In the *Environmental Crimes and Ship-Source Pollution* cases, the ECJ overlooks the question of the extent to which a EU/EC legislative measure on environmental crimes could breach the principle of legality. But in his Opinion in the *Environmental Crimes* case, AG Colomer suggested that the criminalisation of offences by the EC would not breach the legality principle if the Community harmonisation initiative requires the intervention of the national parliaments for the final incorporation of the EU/EC legislative provisions into their legal systems.[171] Indeed, as was discussed in Chapter 4, Directives criminalising certain prohibited activities do not entail direct effect, so a non-implemented

168 See Case C-303/05 *Advocaten voor de Wereld* [2007] ECR I-3633, para. 49 and 50.

169 Case C-316/93 *Vaneetveld v SA Le Foyer* [1994] ECR I-763.

170 Tridimas, Takis, *The General Principles of EU law* (OUP, 2006) at 242.

171 See Case 80/86 *Kolpinghuis Nijimegen*, European Court Reports, 1987, para. 13 and Case C-60/02, *X*, ECR 2004 p.I-651, para. 61.

Directive could not be relied upon to the detriment of an individual in a criminal prosecution.[172]

A similar interpretation is given by the Court in the *Intertanko* case, in which the ECJ ruled that the lack of definition of the concept of 'serious negligence' in the shipping pollution Directive does not breach the principle of certainty, as a national implementing measure was required before the Directive could be relied upon against an individual.[173] Moreover, the ECJ suggested that common features relating to the term could be found in the legal systems of all Member States. The Court found that serious negligence is to be taken to mean an unintentional action or omission by which the person responsible commits a *patent* breach of the duty of care which he should have and could have complied with in view of his attributes, knowledge, abilities and individual situation.[174] Furthermore, the court suggested that as the shipping pollution directive only lays down minimum standards, in case there is legal uncertainty as to the content of the minimum standard, questions could be referred to the ECJ for clarification.[175]

A similar conclusion was reached by the ECJ as regards the extent to which EU mutual recognition instruments could breach the principle of legality. In *Advocaten voor de Wereld* the ECJ ruled that the lack of a precise definition of the 'offences' listed in the 2002 EAW Framework Decision[176] does not violate the principle of legal certainty since the EAW Framework Decision does not seek to harmonise the constituent elements of the criminal offences in question.[177]

5.7.2 *The Principles of Proportionality and Subsidiarity*

The ability of the Commission to propose harmonisation of criminal sanctions is limited by other general principles of EU law, such as proportionality and subsidiarity.[178] The principle of subsidiarity restricts the EU competence to those areas in which the relevant results cannot be sufficiently achieved by the

172 See e.g. Case 80/86, *Kolpinghuis Nijmegen* [1987] E.C.R. 3969.

173 Case C-308/06 International Association of Independent Tanker Owners (*Intertanko*) v Secretary of State Lloyds Rep 260 88 [2009] para. 74–76.

174 *Ibid.*

175 *Ibid.*

176 Council Framework Decision of 13 June 2002 on the European Arrest Warrant and the Surrender of Procedures between Member States, *Official Journal* L 190 18 July 2002.

177 Case C-303/05, *Advocaten voor de Wereld*, judgement of 3 May 2007, paras. 52–53. See also the Opinion of Advocate General Ruiz-Rabaro Colomer on 12 September 2006.

178 See, for example, Case 157/79 *R v Stanislaus Pieck* [1980] 3 C.M.L.R 220.

Member States themselves *and* can be better achieved at the Union level.[179] So the two requirements are cumulative – it is not sufficient that Member States cannot achieve the results by themselves, but it is necessary that they can be better achieved by the Union. The Lisbon Treaty has strengthened the role of national parliaments in monitoring observance of the principles of subsidiarity and proportionality.[180]

The test of proportionality adds the condition that a EU measure may not go beyond what is necessary to achieve the result sought. Under Article 5 (4) TEU (former Article 5 (3) EC) '(...) the content and form of Union action shall not exceed what is necessary to achieve the objectives of the Treaties'. According to Takis Tridimas, this provision forms part of a system of provisions that aims to control the expansion of EU legislative action.[181] In this vein, according to Article 7 of the Protocol on the *Application of the Principles of Subsidiarity and Proportionality*,[182] EU measures 'should leave as much scope for national decision as possible' and should respect 'well established national arrangements and the organisation and working of Member States' legal systems'. The sanctions adopted under national law for implementation of EU law must also abide by the principle of proportionality.[183]

In the *Environmental Crime* and *Ship-Source Pollution* cases the ECJ does not address the question of whether the test of subsidiarity (or proportionality) for adoption of a first pillar measure on environmental crimes is met by the legislative initiatives under scrutiny in those actions. This is despite the fact that the Member States had raised broader concerns in *Ship-Source Pollution* case of loss of sovereignty in criminal matters and in relation to the principles of subsidiarity, attributed powers and proportionality, the 'margin of appreciation' remaining to the Member States, and the system set up by the Treaty on the European Union which would be undermined if the arguments of the Commission were upheld.[184]

This omission in addressing subsidiarity and proportionality by the court is unfortunate. Indeed, the court could have attempted to establish whether, given the scale and effects of the proposed action, the objective in question could be better achieved by the Community and could not be achieved individually by the Member States, for example by taking into consideration the

179 Article 5 TEU (equivalent to former Article 5 EC).

180 See Article 12 (b) TEU.

181 Tridimas, Takis, (2006) above note 170, at 176.

182 Protocol No 30 Annexed to the Treaty of Amsterdam [1997] OJ C340.

183 See Case 157/79 *R v Stanislaus Pieck* [1980] 3 C.M.L.R 220, in which it was held that the failure to obtain residence permit was not to be punishable with imprisonment.

184 AG *Mazak*, Point 42.

transnational aspects of certain environmental crimes.[185] It is another example of the lack of analysis or distinct reasoning on the part of the ECJ when dealing with the subsidiarity argument.[186]

Yet despite not explicitly referring to the principles of subsidiarity and proportionality, the ECJ subjected the EC competence in the criminal-law field to a 'necessity test' as the Community could only take measures 'which it considers *necessary* in order to ensure that the rules that it lays down on environmental protection are fully effective'.[187] It should be noted that the principle of necessity – discussed further below – is regarded as a manifestation of the principles of subsidiarity and proportionality.

The proportionality principle plays a significant role in relation to penalties applied by Member States. Indeed, the free movement of goods, persons, services and capital in a common market is placed at risk if the penalties incurred for breaches of the rules relating to intra-EU movement are much higher than the penalties imposed in the event of a comparable breach of the rules governing internal movement.[188] Thus the Court has held that 'a system of penalties should not have the effect of jeopardising the freedoms provided for by the EEC Treaty. That would be the case if a penalty were so disproportionate to the gravity of the offence that it became an obstacle to the freedom guaranteed by Community law'.[189]

It is also recognized that when the ECJ is asked to review the legality of a Union measure, it should not substitute the assessment of the EU legislature with its own evaluation, though it is open to the Court to assess whether the view of the EU legislator applying the tests of comparative efficiency and scale to a measure is correct.[190] The greater the degree of interference with national criminal justice systems, the higher the standard of reasoning for the adoption of a harmonisation measure.

The principle of proportionality is also incorporated by implication in the principle of subsidiarity. However, while the latter comes into play at an earlier stage by defining whether or not action must be taken at the Union level, the

185 *See* para 5 of the Amsterdam Protocol.

186 See also Case C-491/01 *The Queen v Secretary of State for Health ex p British American Tobacco Ltd.* [2002] ECR I-11453.

187 *Environmental Crimes*, para. 48.

188 Corstens, Geert And Pradel, Jean, *European Criminal Law* (Kluwer Law International, 2002) at 510.

189 See Case 193/94 *Skanavi and Chryssanthakopoulos* [1996] p. I-929-955; and Case 299/86 *Drexl* [1988] ECR 1213.

190 See Case C-377/98 *Netherlands v Parliament and Council* [2001] ECR I-7079. Tridimas (2006) above note 170, at 186.

former comes into play only once it is decided that EU action is necessary.[191] Once action at EU level is considered necessary, the proportionality principle seeks to define its scope.[192] The Amsterdam protocol adds that the reasons for concluding that the EU objective can be better achieved by the Community (now Union) must be based on qualitative and, wherever possible, quantitative indicators.[193]

As with subsidiarity, the ECJ does not tend to go into in-depth analysis of proportionality issues.[194] Indeed, the ECJ tends to interpret narrowly the proportionality test as a limit to the competences of the EU legislator.[195] Moreover, the Court has resisted attempts to restrict the scope of application of the fundamental freedoms on the basis of subsidiarity,[196] which may be explained by a perception of subsidiarity as a primarily political principle. That said, the Court cannot employ a high degree of scrutiny when examining subsidiarity issues because of the political responsibilities involved. Yet subsidiarity is a legally binding rule, compliance with which is subject to review by the Court.[197] It has been suggested that subsidiarity may have greater potential as a procedural ground than a ground of substance – the Union act has often to explain in substance, in the statement of reasons, why the EU legislature considers that the measure is necessary and satisfies the test of subsidiarity.[198] This is the case of the environmental crime and ship-source pollution directives, both of which refer to the principles of subsidiarity and proportionality in their Recitals.[199]

---

191 See *ibid.*

192 See Estella, Antonio, *The EU Principle of Subsidiarity and its Critique* (OUP, Oxford 2002); and *ibid* at 176.

193 Protocol No 30 [1997] OJ C340, para. 4.

194 For example Case C-377/98, *The Netherlands v Parliament and Council* [2001] ECR I-7079 paras. 30 et seq.

195 See, for example, Case C-434/02, *Arnold Andre* [2004].

196 See e.g. Case C-415/93 *Bosman* [1995] ECR I-4921, para. 8.

197 Tridimas, T., (2006) above note 170, at 185.

198 *Ibid.* Yet it is not necessary for the statement of reasons to refer expressly to the principle of subsidiarity. It is sufficient if the reasoning of the legislature can be derived by implication from the preamble of the measure. See Case C-233/94 *Germany v Parliament and Council* [1997] ECR I-2405.

199 *See* Recital 14 of the preamble of the environmental crime directive states that '[s]ince the objective of this Directive, namely to ensure the more effective protection of the environment, *cannot be sufficiently achieved by the Member States* and can therefore, by reason of the scale and effects of this Directive, *be better achieved at Community level,* the Community may adopt measures, in accordance with the principle of subsidiarity as set out in Article 5 of the Treaty. In accordance with the principle of proportionality, as set out in that Article, this Directive does not go beyond what is necessary in order to achieve

5.7.3 *The Principle of Necessity*

Not only the Commission, but also the Council and the European Parliament, agree on the need for criminal sanctions for environmental protection in the EU. They share the view that approximation of environmental criminal law would allow the development of stronger cooperation among the Member States in the fight against environmental criminality – in particular in the case of environmental crimes with cross-boundary effects – and to more effective enforcement of environmental law in the EU. They therefore support action at the European level to harmonise the criminal laws in Member States for the protection of the environment – although, as has been discussed above, there was an institutional dispute as regards the appropriate legal basis for the relevant harmonisation measure.

The question of necessity of harmonisation of (environmental) criminal law is left to the Community (now Union) political institutions to decide and thus is not itself a question amenable to judicial review. So in both *Environmental Crimes* and *Ship-Source Pollution* the Court implied that the necessity of the measure was satisfied by the fact that the Council had unanimously agreed on the relevant measures harmonising environmental criminal law, that is, the Framework Decisions on environmental crimes and ship-source pollution.[200] According to the court, it is sufficient that the Community institutions 'consider' criminal measures necessary for the purposes of the effectiveness of EC law, not that they prove it to be necessary.[201] Therefore once a measure has been agreed by the Council, the Court implies that the measure is necessary and there is no further judicial scrutiny on this point. Arguably it would amount to excessive interference with the political process and could jeopardise the institutional balance of the Union if the Court were to rule on the specific question of the necessity of the measure (for example to decide whether criminal sanctions are effective or not in the environmental field), though the court might still review the legality of the measure in light of, for example, the other principles of EU law discussed above, such as proportionality, the Treaty provisions or the failure to follow certain procedural requirements. It has been suggested that this lack of judicial review of 'necessity' may be especially problematic in the case of a criminal law measure adopted by the

---

that objective'. (emphasis added). In a similar vein, see recital 15 of the preamble of Directive 2005/35 on ship-source pollution.

200 See *Environmental Crimes.* para. 46; *Ship-Source Pollution*, para. 67.

201 See also Tobler (2006) who suggests that although this means that the Community must reasonably consider such measures necessary, 'it would nevertheless seem that it is very easy to pass this test'. Tobler (2006) above note 108, at 847–848.

Council in which a Member State is outvoted, as there would not be consensus among the Member States that criminal law is necessary in the field.[202]

The Court referred in *Environmental Crimes* ruling to criminal law measures which the Community legislature '*considers* necessary' and to the fact that 'the Council *took the view* that criminal penalties are essential'.[203] In this regard, the recitals to the shipping Directive and (annulled) Framework Decision on ship-source pollution suggest that both the Council and the Commission share the view that criminal sanctions are necessary to ensure compliance with Community rules on maritime safety.[204] According to Advocate General Mazak, one must assume that it is the view of the Community legislature that the adoption of criminal measures is necessary for effective protection of the marine environment and that such measures are essential to combat serious pollution offences in the seas.[205] Thus the Advocate General, having initially broadened the Community competence in criminal matters by extending it potentially to any Community policy, tries to establish some limits to it by stating that the necessity of Community criminal law does not stem only from the objective criterion of the existence of a legal basis in the EC Treaty, but also from a degree of judgement by the institutions involved.[206]

The Council Model Provisions (2009) defined a number of conditions to be taken into account when defining the necessity of a criminal-law measure. Under the heading '*Assessment of the need for criminal provisions*', the Council agreed in defining the necessity of the measure by applying a similar criteria to those adopted under the Article 83 (1) and (2) TFEU and the ECJ case-law.[207] Criminal law provisions should be introduced when they are considered

202 Fletcher, M. et al (2008) above note 124, at 177.

203 *Environmental Crimes*, paras. 48–50 ;and Opinion of AG Mazak in *Ship-Source Pollution*, Point 119.

204 *See Ship-Source Pollution*, para. 67.

205 *Mazak* AG, Point 136.

206 Mitsilegas, V. (2008) above note 85, at 163.

207 See Council Conclusions on model provisions, guiding the Council's criminal law deliberations *2979th Justice and Home Affairs Council meeting, Brussels, 30 november 2009*: (1) Criminal provisions should be adopted in accordance with the principles laid out in the Treaties, which include the principles of proportionality and of subsidiarity, to address clearly defined and delimited conduct, which cannot be addressed effectively by less severe measures: (a) in the areas of particularly serious crime with a cross-border dimension resulting from the nature or impact of such offences or from a special need to combat them on a common basis; or (b) if the approximation of criminal laws and regulations of the Member States proves essential to ensure the effective implementation of a Union policy in an area which has been subject to harmonisation measures.

'essential' in order for the interests to be protected. Moreover, the Council Model Provisions add that, as a rule, criminal law should be used only 'as a last resort'.[208]

Further, the Council Model Provisions linked the need for criminal sanctions with the results of the impact assessment made prior to the legislative proposal.[209] In this regard, arguably one of the deficiencies of the impact assessment accompanying the Commission's 2007 environmental crime directive proposal is that the Commission does not examine whether a third pillar instrument could not achieve the same results envisaged without the need for a first pillar instrument.[210] Moreover, the Commission did not consider it necessary to carry out an impact assessment in the context of the 2005/2009 shipping pollution directive(s) in order to demonstrate the necessity of criminal measures in that field, since the Council had already unanimously agreed on the 2005 Framework Decision on ship-source pollution.

5.7.4 *The Principles of Equivalence and Effectiveness*

The principle of effectiveness has been recognised by the Court of Justice as a general principle of EC/EU law.[211] There are two main requirements arising from this principle: the effective protection of EU rights; and the effective enforcement of EU law in national courts. The principle does not originate in the law of the Member States but from the distinct characteristics of Union law, particularly primacy and direct effect. The principle derives from the interpretation techniques of the Court which aim at ensuring the *effet utile* of the Treaty provisions.[212] The Court developed the principle of effectiveness of Community law in particular in light of the fact that the Community order was based on a decentralised system of justice and national courts are the principal venue for the assertion of Community rights.[213]

---

208 *Ibid.*

209 'When there seems to be a need for adopting new criminal provisions the following factors should be further considered, while taking fully into account the impact assessments that have been made'. *Ibid.*

210 Commission Staff Working Document. *Impact Assessment: Accompanying Document to the Proposal for a Directive of the European Parliament and of the Council on the Protection of the Environment through Criminal Law* COM (2007) 51 Final.

211 See for example Joined Cases C-46 and C-48/93 *Brasserie du Pecheur v Germany and the Queen v Secretary of State for Transport, ex p Factortame Ltd* [1996] ECR I-1029, para. 95; Tridimas, T. (2006) above note 170, at 418.

212 *Ibid* at 419.

213 *Ibid.*

Effectiveness is reflected in the overall structure of the EU with the aim of ensuring that European legal systems are integrated, consistent and expedient. It suggests that Member States effectively implement and enforce EU law. So the Court has recognised that, in order to ensure the full effectiveness of EU law, 'the executory force of community law cannot vary from one State to another in favour of domestic legislation without endangering the achievement of the treaty goals'.[214]

The principle of effectiveness is a corollary of the principle of loyal co-operation, which itself contains two related principles.[215] Firstly, effectiveness relates to the principle of *assimilation* which holds that while retaining the choice of sanctions, [the Member States] should in particular ensure that breaches of Community/Union law are sanctioned on conditions, substantive and procedural, analogous to those applying to breaches of national law of a similar nature and importance.[216] The second principle developed by the court is the obligation of *efficacy* of sanctions, which the ECJ has found needs to be 'effective, proportionate and dissuasive'.[217] In this vein, in the famous *Greek Maize* case[218] the Court recognised that even though the Member States retain the discretion over which sanctions to apply for the enforcement of Community obligations, the sanction chosen had to be of a certain minimum level that ensured the effectiveness of Community law and they needed to be equivalent to sanctions applied for similar violations of national legislation.[219] So the principle of equivalence (or assimilation) ensures that Community/Union rights receive the same protection as domestic ones, and hence is complementary to the principle of effectiveness.[220]

As was discussed above, Article 83 (2) TFEU also links the EU powers to harmonise criminal law to the effective implementation of a Union policy. Therefore, it is expected that effectiveness will continue to play a significant role in future initiatives to harmonise environmental criminal law in the EU.

---

214 Case 6/64 *Costa ENEL* [1994] ECR 1141.

215 Delmas-Marty, M. 'The European Union and Penal Law' (1998) 4 *European Law Journal* 1 at 89–90.

216 Tridimas, above note 170, at 424–425.

217 See Ward, Angela. 'Effective Sanctions in EC Law: A Moving Boundary in the Division of Competence' (1995) 1 *European Law Journal* 205.

218 Case 68/88 *Commission v Greece* [1989] ECR 2965.

219 *Ibid* para. 24.

220 Tridimas, *supra* at 425.

5.7.5 *The 'Seriousness' Requirement*

The principle of effectiveness is qualified by the requirement set by the Court that the environmental offence subject to EU harmonisation needs to be 'serious'. Indeed, the Court in *Environmental Crimes* linked the Community competence to harmonise environmental criminal law to the 'seriousness' of environmental offences.[221] This is important given that criminalisation at the supranational level – and the same could be said about criminalisation at the domestic level – for the sake of effectiveness or efficiency alone could lead to unfair results.

An interesting analysis in this context was that developed by Advocate General Colomer in *Environmental Crimes* who linked the seriousness of environmental offences with the attribution of competence to the EC to harmonise environmental criminal law. He suggested that there is no obstacle to the view that the appropriate response to, for example, attempted murder or corruption of minors, must be criminal, and consequently, if the legal interests protected in such offences were one of the objectives of the Community, no one would dispute the ability of its law-making bodies to require Member States to prosecute in criminal law.[222] He also alludes to the right to healthy environment as developed by the case law of the ECHR.[223] After noting that a number of countries have resorted to penal protection of the environment, AG Colomer suggests that '[i]t seems reasonable that Community law, through the powers entrusted to the institutions in order to achieve those ends, must in certain cases avail itself of criminal penalties as the only "effective, proportionate and dissuasive response."'[224] Yet the Court itself does not follow the same line of reasoning of AG Colomer, despite the fact that it does emphasise that environmental protection is one of the Community's essential objectives and that it linked the Community competence to the seriousness of environmental offences.

Unlike Article 83 (2) TFEU which subjects the harmonisation of criminal law mainly to a test of 'effectiveness', the Article 83 (1) legal basis requires that EU criminal law addresses 'particularly *serious crime*'.

5.8 Conclusions

Although a convenient choice for the Member States, the pillar structure which underpinned integration in criminal matters in the EU between 1993–2009 can

221 *Environmental Crimes*, para. 48.

222 *Colomer AG*, Point 50.

223 *Lopez Ostra v Spain*, ECHR judgement of 9 December 1994, Series A No. 303-C, p. 55; ECHR, judgement of 19 February 1998, Series A No 735/932.

224 *Colomer AG*, Point 72.

hardly be considered a model for interstate cooperation and integration in criminal matters. This is not only because of the general criticism that criminal law measures adopted under the third pillar lacked democratic legitimacy and were deficient from the perspectives of accountability and legal enforcement, but because the exact borderline between the pillars was ill-defined and hence constantly subject to legal dispute.

Before the ratification of the Lisbon Treaty, it appeared that the only way for the Commission to seek harmonisation of environmental criminal law would be to combine supranational and intergovernmental components, the principle of criminalisation and the main prohibitions contained in a directive on environmental crime, while the criminal penalties and measures to foster cooperation between the police and judicial authorities in the Member States would be harmonised at the third pillar level.

Since the ECJ had already settled in 2005 the most controversial question regarding the competence of the Community (EC) to criminalise environmental offences, the Council and Member States must welcome the reforms introduced by the Lisbon Treaty which will allow them adopt further, more effective measures to combat environmental crime in the EU.

Yet historically the hesitancy of the Court to recognise a competence of the Community in criminal matters is justifiable in light of the lack of express conferral of powers attributed to the Community in the EC Treaty in criminal law matters. It was to be expected that the court would be accused of judicial activism by recognising the implied powers of the Community in criminal matters. Still, it has not been uncommon for the court throughout its history to employ an activist stance for example when recognising the principles of supremacy and direct effect of Community law. It is thus perhaps not so surprising that the court eventually came to recognise criminal-law powers to the Community. In particular, the principle of effectiveness of Community law (combined with the doctrine of implied powers) was a strong weapon that allowed the Court eventually to recognise the competence of the Community in criminal matters, driving further the process of integration of the EU member states in criminal matters even before the ratification of the Lisbon Treaty.

The *Environmental Crimes* and *Ship-Source Pollution* judgments suggest that the ECJ is ready to continue to influence the development of the Union legal order and to contribute towards the constitutionalisation of the Treaties through an expansive interpretation of the competence of the EU institutions.[225] This is so despite the fact that the Court appeared prepared to adopt a less expansive interpretation of the Community powers, for example by holding in other cases

225 See Weatherill, S. 'Competence Creep and Competence Control' (2004) *YEL*.

that the EC was not competent to accede to the ECHR[226] or to adopt internal market measures which pursue the objective of protection of public health.[227] So despite the fact that those earlier judgements reversed a long trend towards the expansive interpretation of the Community's competence, in *Environmental Crimes and Ship-Source Pollution* the Court returns to an interventionist stance interpreting generously the powers of the Community under the Treaties. Hence those judgements are relevant not only from an environmental protection perspective but also from a broader EU constitutional law perspective.

Moreover, the *Environmental Crimes* and *Ship-Source Pollution* judgments have been criticised as the ECJ appears to regard criminal law as a means to an end, rather than a separate Community policy or objective. So it is suggested that criminal law is regarded by the court as another field of law (along with civil law, administrative law) which is there to serve a Community objective.[228] According to Valsamis Mitsilegas, this approach towards criminal law may be of concern to the extent that it disregards the special place of criminal law in domestic legal systems and the extensive safeguards surrounding criminal law at the national level.[229]

The clarification given by the court in those two cases had the overall positive effect in allowing the Council and Parliament to adopt the directive on environmental crimes and ship-source pollution (amending) directive under the co-decision procedure. However, there will be considerable constitutional and legal challenges if the Commission seeks further harmonisation of environmental criminal law beyond the measures already adopted. In addition to the challenges surrounding the choice of legal basis of the measure, this stems from the fact that the EU competence in (environmental) criminal matters is limited by the general principles of EU law; as well as by the parameters relating to this competence set by the ECJ in the *Environmental Crimes* and *Ship-Source Pollution* rulings. Before such eventual amendments to the existing EU environmental crime legislation become effective, the limitations recognised by the Court regarding the Community competence to lay down specific types and levels of criminal penalties – as is reflected in the final text of the Directives – leave important questions open as far as the effectiveness of harmonisation of environmental criminal law in the EU is concerned.

---

226 Opinion 2/94 *Accession to the ECHR* [1996] ECR I-1759. The ECJ thus interpreted narrowly Article 308 EC.

227 Case 376/98 *Germany v Parliament and Council* (*Tobacco Advertisement Directive*) [2000] ECR I-8419, para. 83.

228 Mitsilegas, V., *EU Criminal Law* (Hart, 2009) at 110.

229 *Ibid.*

CHAPTER 6

The Harmonisation of Substantive Environmental Criminal Law and Penalties

6.1 Introduction

As has been seen in the previous chapters, the harmonisation of EU environmental criminal law has taken place under the supranational level following the ECJ *Environmental Crimes* and *Ship-Source Pollution* rulings. In this respect, the adoption of the Environmental Crimes Directive on 24 October 2008 marks a significant step in the Union's process of integration, given that for the first time a 'criminal law' measure was adopted under the former 'first pillar'. But the Directive, which was adopted exactly one year after the *Ship-Source Pollution* ruling, necessarily does not define specific types and levels of penalties or any rules on prosecution or jurisdiction, since the ECJ either ruled out the Community competence in the area – in the case of penalties – or did not clarify whether such competence exists – in the case of rules on police and judicial cooperation.

The objective of this chapter is to assess the methods applied for harmonisation of substantive environmental criminal law adopted under the European Union and the Council of Europe instruments on environmental crime. Moreover, this chapter analyses the extent to which those instruments aim to implement specific international environmental agreements. Specifically, this chapter assesses the specific provisions of those instruments and discusses the legal implications of the different models of harmonisation of environmental criminal law standards in the following areas: criminal offences (including inchoate offences); complicity; corporate criminal liability; jurisdictional and prosecutorial rules; and criminal penalties.

6.2 Criminal Offences

6.2.1 *The Classification of Offences*

The principal classification of criminal offences in the national legal systems of the EU Member States is according to their gravity. In the UK there are three categories of offences: indictable-only offences (more serious offences), summary offences (minor offences) and triable-either-way offences. Also in France,

 | DOI 10.1163/9789004195882_007

Belgium, Greece and Luxembourg there are three categories of offences: serious crimes (*crimes*), major offences (*délit*) and minor offences (*contraventions*). Austria, Germany and Italy have only recognized traditionally two categories of offences according to their gravity: serious offences (*Verbrechen/delitti*) and other (minor) offences (*Vergehen/contravvenzioni*).[1] The classification of the offences according to their gravity may determine the maximum punishment which may be imposed[2] and under which national court the offence is tried.[3]

The environmental crime directive and shipping directive (as amended in 2009) require Member States to consider certain violation of environmental law as 'criminal offences'.[4] Even though those Directives do not impose any particular classification of offences on Member States, a purposive or teleological reading of those instruments appears to indicate that the Commission (as well as the Council and the Parliament) considers the offences contained therein to be particularly serious and hence that they should be considered indictable/serious crimes, or at least 'major offences' in countries with a tripartite classification. Yet since those Directives do not impose a minimum level of penalties on Member States, they are left with considerable discretion on how to classify those offences under national law, so long as they are considered 'criminal'.[5] The creation of quasi-criminal offences[6] does not satisfy the requirements of those Directives, as that would defeat many of the purposes envisaged by the Commission when proposing those measures;[7] and they are not strictly speaking criminal offences.

---

1 Summary of Replies to the Questionnaire on the Approximation of Sanctions (9402/1/01 DROIPEN 50 REV 1) 5 October 2001 at 3–4.

2 For example, in Ireland summary offences are punishable by a maximum of 1 year imprisonment and or a fine of up to EUR 3000. *Ibid.*

3 For example, in England and Wales summary offences are tried in the magistrate's court and indictable offences in the Crown Court.

4 See Article 3 of the environmental crime directive; and Article 5 (a) of the ship-source pollution directive.

5 As was discussed in Chapter 2, the European Court of Human Rights applies an autonomous definition of criminal offences.

6 For example, Germany and Austria have a well-established system of administrative criminal sanctions (*Ordnungwidrigkeiten*). As was discussed in Chapter 2, quasi-criminal sanctions represent a hybrid system of enforcement which lies in between administrative and criminal law. See also, Milieu & Huglo Lepage 'Summary Report: Study on Measures other than Criminal Ones in Cases where Environmental Community Law has not been Respected in the EU Member States', 20 September 2004, at 52. (B4-3040A/2003/369724/MAR/A.3).

7 The Commission argues that the criminal law secures an extra guarantee of impartiality and secures the better cooperation between the Member States to deal with cross-border environmental crimes. See further, Chapter 7.

6.2.2 *The Types of Offences*

There is a close relationship between administrative and criminal law in the environmental law systems of many countries, including in the EU Member States.[8] Administrative regulations often determine the extent of permissible pollution and acceptable risks in specified areas, while criminal law attaches criminal liability to aggravated forms of violations of environmental regulations. This is at times called 'accessoriarity' or dependency between environmental administrative law and penal law. However, certain environmental criminal offences are not dependent on a violation of administrative law (autonomous offences) and the degree of dependency between the two may vary according to whether the endangerment offence relates to a concrete harm or an abstract harm.

6.2.2.1 Autonomous Offences

There are certain violations of environmental law which are so serious that they require criminalisation regardless of whether the operator holds a licence or not. Accordingly, an interstate instrument of harmonisation of environmental criminal law should arguably criminalise those activities regardless of whether or not they are lawful under national environmental law.

There is only one autonomous offence in the Council of Europe Convention on environmental criminal law. State parties must criminalise this offence irrespectively of whether it is illicit ('unlawful') or not within their legal systems. This autonomous offence relates to the intentional 'discharge, emission or introduction of a quantity of substances or ionising radiation into air, soil or water [which either] causes death or serious injury to any person, or creates a significant risk of causing death or risk of serious injury to any person'.[9] This offence must be criminalised regardless of its unlawfulness under national law, i.e. the infringement of the law, an administrative regulation or a decision taken by a competent authority.[10] The objective of this provision is not to leave it to the discretion of the national regulatory bodies the prerogative to grant licences which may risk the life or physical health of humans. The Explanatory Memorandum confirms the autonomous status of the offences under Article 2

---

8 See Milieu & Huglo Lepage 'Summary Report: Study on Measures other than Criminal Ones in Cases where Environmental Community Law has not been Respected in the EU Member States', 20 September 2004, at 52. (B4-3040A/2003/369724/MAR/A.3); and Faure, Michael and Heine, Günter '*Criminal Enforcement of Environmental Law in the European Union*' IMPEL Network, July 2000.

9 Article 2 (1) (a) of the Council of Europe Convention on environmental crime. Convention on the Protection of the Environment through Criminal Law, Council of Europe, ETS No. 172.

10 See the definition of 'unlawful' under Article 1 (a) of the Council of Europe Convention.

(1) (a), by emphasising that 'compliance with environmental administrative law cannot always preclude criminal liability'.[11] An administrative permit or consent is considered irrelevant in such cases.

As for the other criminal offences under the CoE Convention, it is necessary that they are considered 'unlawful' under national administrative law. This considerably limits the harmonisation potential of the convention. Indeed, for all the other offences in the Convention other than the autonomous offence under Article 2 (1) (a), it is necessary that the activity is considered 'unlawful' under national law before a state's obligation to criminalise the offence arises. So if there is no breach of national administrative environmental regulations of a party to the Convention, there would be no obligation on the part of that state to introduce criminal sanctions against violations of the other offences listed under Article 2 (1) of the convention.[12]

This confirms the strong 'accessoriaty' or dependency between criminal law and administrative law, and ultimately leaves it to the discretion of each State party to indicate in its internal laws the tolerable levels of pollution and the acceptable risks caused by dangerous activities.[13] Hence the requirement of 'unlawfulness' considerably limits the reach and application of the offences under the Convention, given that it is left to the discretion of the national authorities to decide whether and the conditions upon which those activities would be prohibited. On the other hand, it should be noted that the 'unlawfulness' requirement is not determined only by national law, given that a number of offences under the Council of Europe convention relate to prohibitions established in international and/or EU law.

Unlike the Council of Europe Convention, the EU environmental crime directive does not contain any autonomous offence. Under the directive, the 'unlawfulness' of the activity is a requirement for all offences.[14] Therefore, a

11 '(...) A permit may legalise certain acts, but does not grant absolute rights to the polluter. Administrative consent must not be available, or if granted, irrelevant in those cases where environmental use causes death or serious injury to any person or which creates a significant risk thereof. There is a consensus among member States that the concrete endangerment of life and of physical integrity of natural persons should, at least in certain areas, constitute a criminal offence. An "autonomous" offence should accordingly be established (...)' Point II, Explanatory Memorandum to the Council of Europe Convention on environmental crime.

12 See also, Comte, F., 'Criminal Environmental Law and Community Competence', 12 EELR 5, 2003.

13 Dandachi S.A., 'Convention sur la Protection de L'Environnement', *Revue Juridique de L'Environnement* n. 2/2003, at 283.

14 *See* Article 3 of the environmental crime directive.

licence granted to an operator *may* constitute a defence to *all* criminal offences under the Directive. As was discussed in Chapter 5, the ECJ rulings in *Environmental Crimes* and *Ship-Source Pollution* linked the Community competence in criminal matters to the effective implementation of an EC policy, so it was not possible for the European Union institutions to seek the harmonisation of purely national environmental law under the previous legal framework of the European Communities.[15] However, it is possible that the Commission may seek to amend the environmental crime directive to harmonise national environmental criminal law based on a TFEU legal basis.[16]

It should be noted that under the EU environmental crime directive there is also a strong dependency between the criminal offences and violations of a number of pieces of EC/EU environmental legislation listed in Appendices A and B to the directive. According to Article 2 (a) of the environmental crime directive, 'unlawful' is defined as the infringement of: (i) the legislation adopted pursuant to the EC Treaty and listed in Annex A; or (ii) with regard to activities covered by the Euratom Treaty, the legislation adopted pursuant to the EURATOM Treaty and listed in Annex B; or (iii) a law, an administrative regulation of a Member State or a decision taken by a competent authority of a Member State that gives effect to the Community legislation referred to in (i) and (ii). This suggests that the environmental offences under the directive are accessory to both EU environmental law and national environmental law. This accessoriarity or dependency relates to violations of both EU and national environmental laws, thus not permitting the harmonisation of purely national environmental law determining, for example, the conditions for validity of a licence to operate. This approach to harmonisation is in line with the overall objective of the

15 This led the EU institutions to delete the autonomous offence present in the original 2007 environmental crime proposal. This offence prohibited under Article 2 (a): 'the discharge, emission or introduction of a quantity of materials or ionising radiation into air, soil or water, which *causes* death or serious injury *to any person*' (emphasis added). The term 'unlawful' is *not* used as a qualifying element of this offence. This offence carried the highest level of (minimum) maximum fine for legal persons (EUR 750,000–1,500,000) and the highest (minimum) maximum prison sentence for individuals (5 to 10 years) under the 2007 directive proposal. This offence was inspired by the autonomous offence established in Article 2 (1) (a) Council of Europe 1998 Convention which was also independent of the infringement of any national administrative regulation or licence; and which is also linked to the harm to human health. See also, Article 2 (a) of the annulled 2003 Framework Decision on environmental crimes.

16 Yet as was discussed in Chapter 5, it does not appear likely that Article 83 (1) and (2) TFEU allow for the harmonisation of purely national environmental law.

environmental crime directive which is to strengthen the implementation of EC/EU environmental law.

Autonomous offences, such as that under Article 2 (1) (a) of the Council of Europe instrument on environmental criminal law, could be criticised for adopting an anthropocentric philosophy in that it aims to protect human health primarily, while the environment is only protected indirectly. Yet it could be contended that environmental offences which have a significant impact on human health are arguably *more* serious because of the additional impact on human health, and on that basis possession of a licence should not be considered a defence to a criminal charge in such circumstances. The principle behind this autonomous offence is that the assignment of criminal responsibility is justifiable because an administrative permit or licence cannot be a defence to a concrete harm or a significant risk of harm to human life or health. Thus, in such cases the illegality of the activity is no longer a prerequisite for criminal liability.[17] In this vein, reflecting the consolidation of the right to health as a human right under international law,[18] there is an even stronger case for the criminalisation of certain pollution offences which cause harm to or endanger the lives of human beings.

On the other hand, this anthropocentric approach could be criticised as a licence should not be considered a defence to a criminal charge in the case of polluting activities which cause large scale environmental harm, even if they do not impact on or endanger human health. Moreover, pollution incidents which cause death or serious harm to human health are likely to be covered by other offences against the person (for example, assault or battery) prohibited under national legal systems. Additionally, the existence of a civil liability regime providing (substantial) damage awards to the parties injured by the polluting activity could provide a strong deterrent that could act to prevent economic activities from causing damage to human health through an environmental means or media.[19]

6.2.2.2 Concrete Endangerment Offences

Most offences under the EU environmental crime directive require a concrete endangerment to the environment or human health. They require that the unlawful activity 'causes or [that it] *is likely to cause* death or serious injury to

---

17 Faure, M. and Visse, M. 'How to Punish Environmental Pollution? Some Reflections on the Various Models of Criminalisation of Environmental Harm' (1995) 3 *European Journal of Crime, Criminal Law and Criminal Justice* at 341.

18 See Chapter 2.

19 On the role of civil liability regimes, see Chapter 2.

any person or substantial damage to the quality of air, the quality of soil or the quality of water, or to animals or plants' (emphasis added).[20] In those cases the minimum standard is that of a concrete harm to the environment (or significant risk of causing harm) and an abstract endangerment is not sufficient to establish an offence.[21]

Similarly, the Council of Europe environmental crime convention aims to establish 'result' or 'concrete endangerment' offences. The offences under Article 2 (1) of the convention must be criminalised when they 'cause or create a significant risk of causing' death or serious injury to any person.[22] Moreover, the offence under Article 4, paragraph (f) requires a specific result or 'concrete endangerment': 'the causing of changes detrimental to the natural components of a national park, nature reserve, water conservation area or other protected areas'; as does the offence in Article 4, paragraph (g): 'the damaging and killing of protected species'. The occurrence of actual damage to the environment, humans or property is not required for all concrete endangerment offences, but the '*significant risk* of harm' would suffice.[23]

Since it is the administrative agency that generally establishes permissible pollution levels, for example by setting the emission standards, concrete endangerment offences are defined by the strong accessoriarity or dependency between administrative law and criminal law. That is, it will generally be the administrative authorities which will set the allowable levels of pollution and hence what a 'significant risk of harm' to the environment or human health is. In such cases, the continental European literature on environmental criminal law, in particular, tends to speak of the existence of an 'absolute dependency' between environmental law and administrative law.[24]

---

20 See Article 3 (a), (b), (d) and (e).

21 See for example Article 3 (h) of the environmental crime directive: 'any conduct *which causes* the significant deterioration of a habitat within a protected site' (emphasis added); The offences against protected specimens (f-g) and protected habitat (h) also apply a specific damage threshold.

22 The French version speaks of 'd'atteinte a "des personnes"', though the explanatory memorandum explains (which is confirmed by the English version) that acts directed at *any* person (so at least one person) is sufficient to constitute an offence.

23 See for example Article 2 (1) (a) ii of the CoE environmental crime convention: 'the discharge (...) of substances or ionising radiation into air, soil or water which creates a *significant risk of causing* death or serious injury to any person' (emphasis added). Although there is no specific harm caused by such activities, they create a significant risk of harm to humans thus calling for the criminalisation of such activities.

24 See, for example, Ringelmann, C. 'Recent Trends in Environmental Criminal Legislation' (1997) 5 *Eur. J. Crime L. & Crim. Just.* 39; Faure, M. and Visse, M (1995) above note 17, at 341;

This inter-dependency between environmental criminal law and administrative law has been criticised in the literature. Focusing on developments in the United States, Richard Lazarus even suggested that environmental law may be inherently antithetical to criminal law.[25] In particular, two characteristics of environmental law – its evolutionary nature and aspirational quality – may be incompatible with the maximum certainty which is required by the criminal law. Lazarus suggests that the evolutionary nature of environmental law means that environmental regulations need to be constantly altered in order to adapt to new scientific evidence or societal imperatives either downgrading or upgrading an environmental threat. Moreover, he argues that environmental law is marked by its aspirational quality, that is, environmental standards are set in many instances at a level higher than what is actually required to achieve an environmental objective. The reason for the agencies to set this high threshold is to secure at least the minimum level of protection needed to prevent serious harm to the environment. In other words, at least in the U.S. experience, environmental agencies have established particularly stringent pollution control standards which are arguably to ensure that, at a minimum, the desired level of environmental protection is accomplished and that it produces a behavioural change in businesses. Richard Lazarus argues that both the evolutionary and aspirational qualities of environmental law could run contrary to the principle of legality (*nullum crimen, nulla poena sine lege*), a general principle of law recognised in virtually all legal systems.[26]

Yet far from suggesting that criminal law should be discarded altogether for the enforcement of environmental law, Lazarus' criticisms of the evolutionary nature and aspirational quality of environmental law serve to show the importance for businesses to co-operate with administrative agencies and to constantly familiarise themselves with changes in environmental standards and properly comply with environmental regulations.[27]

Hans-Jorg Albrecht And Seppo Leppa, 'Criminal Law and the Environment', Proceedings of the European Seminar held in Lauchhammer, Land Brandenburg,, Germany, April 1992.

25 Richard Lazarus, 'Meeting the Demands of Integration in the Evolution of Environmental Law: Reforming Environmental Criminal Law', 83 *Georgetown Law Journal*, 1995 at 2428/2429.

26 See *ibid.* On the principle of legality, see also chapter 5.

27 In the UK context, the Environment Agency has suggested that between 70% and 75% of small and medium size enterprises (SME s) are not actually aware of their environmental obligations or of environmental legislation. 'Greener Business is Good Business: Spotlight on Business, Environmental Performance in 2003', Environment Agency and House of Commons Environmental Audit Committee, '*Corporate Environmental Crime*'. Second Report of Session 2004–2005' (2005) at 14.

6.2.2.3 Abstract Endangerment Offences

Administrative infringements can be classified as substantial infringements or technical/formal infringements. Substantial infringements may constitute typical crimes against the environment since they affect or may affect elements of the environment (e.g. waste dumping or discharges of dangerous substances into water).[28] Those types of infringements could be classified as autonomous or concrete endangerment offences, as discussed above. In contrast, technical or formal infringements include violations of the terms of a permit (e.g. failure to supply monitoring reports to the competent authority) or carrying out an activity without a permit (which need not cause any environmental damage).[29] The mere violation of the permit, or carrying out the activity without one, is sufficient for the commission of the offence. Abstract endangerment offences are sometimes called 'formal offences' as they incriminate conduct which is potentially dangerous, independently of the result.[30]

The Council of Europe Convention on environmental crime envisages abstract endangerment offences under Article 4, paragraphs (a) to (e), given that they do not require a specific result or environmental damage. This includes the 'unlawful operation of a plant' and the 'unlawful causing of noise'. Since those abstract endangerment criminal offences are not common to all legal systems, the drafters of the Convention left it to the discretion of the signatory states to determine whether such offences are of a criminal or administrative nature.[31]

There are only two abstract endangerment offences in the EU environmental crime directive. The illegal shipment of waste contrary to Regulation (EC) No. 1013/2006 on shipments of waste,[32] which includes the shipment carried out without the notification or consent of the competent authorities;[33] and the 'production, importation, exportation, placing on market or use of ozone-depleting

28 'Study on non-criminal measures in EU-15' above note 8, at 20.

29 Other technical infringements include the failure to notify certain information to the authorities; falsification of documents; obstruction to controls and inspections; or financial infringements (e.g. to pay environmental levies). *ibid* at 21.

30 Dandachi S.A., above note 13, at 284.

31 *Ibid.*

32 Regulation (EC) No. 1013/2006, OJ L 190, 12.7.2006.

33 Article 3 (c) of the environmental crime directive refers to Article 2 (35) of the Regulation on shipments of waste. This later provision defines illegal shipment as those shipments carried out under certain circumstances including (a) without notification to all competent authorities concerned pursuant to this Regulation; or (b) without the consent of the competent authorities concerned pursuant to this Regulation.

substances'.[34] All the other offences require at least a concrete endangerment to the environment or human health.[35] This cautious approach to criminalisation of abstract endangerment offences is in line with the Council Model Provisions (2009) which suggest that EU criminal legislation, as a general rule, should refrain from criminalising an abstract danger.[36]

Abstract endangerment offences generally aim to protect the interests of the administrative authority in the proper enforcement of environmental law (the environment being protected indirectly).[37] Yet although the main rationale behind these offences is to serve the interests of the administration in controlling the industrial activity, there is a presumption that an intolerable endangerment to the environment has occurred.[38] So the aim of the use of criminal law is to target the abstract endangerment of the environment, irrespective of any specific damage or direct threat of environmental harm. Thus in potentially serious cases of endangerment to the environment, the economic activity carried out without a permit may constitute not only an administrative infringement but also a crime.[39]

6.2.2.4 Omission Offences

There are three forms of omission which may lead to a criminal offence: direct liability for omissions or the breach of a statutory duty (e.g. failure to submit a tax return); derivative liability for omissions, which represents extensions of offences that are typically committed by affirmative conduct (the so-called' commission by omission' offences);[40] and direct liability for negligently causing harm. In the

---

34 Article 3 (h) of the environmental crime directive.

35 As discussed above, the offences in the environmental crime directive generally require the prohibited activity 'to cause' or '[to be] *likely to* cause' damage or injury to a person or the environment. See Article 3 (a), (b), (d), (e). The offences against protected specimens (f-g) and protected habitat (h) also apply a specific damage threshold.

36 Paragraph (4) states that 'The criminal provisions should focus on conduct causing actual harm or seriously threatening the right or essential interest which is the object of protection; that is, avoiding criminalisation of a conduct at an unwarrantably early stage. Conduct which only implies *an abstract danger* to the protected right or interest should be criminalised only if appropriate considering the particular importance of the right or interest which is the object of protection' (emphasis added). Council Conclusions on model provisions, guiding the Council's criminal law deliberations 2979th JUSTICE and HOME AFFAIRS Council meeting, Brussels, 30 November 2009.

37 Faure, M. and Visse, M. (1995) above note 17, at 320.

38 'Study on non-criminal measures' above note 8, at 20.

39 Interestingly, Denmark and Spain (in the waste sector) allow for a *de facto* legalisation of an activity carried out without a licence, by granting a licence *a posteriori*. *Ibid* at 21.

40 Fletcher, G. *Rethinking Criminal Law* (OUP, Oxford 2000) at 585.

latter case there is a breach of a duty of care in managing an activity rather than a duty to intervene and prevent harm.[41]

Despite the fact that no specific provision on liability for omissions is present in the Council of Europe environmental crime convention, the Explanatory Memorandum states that it applies to both acts and omissions, at least in the context of the 'intentional offences' under Article 2 of the convention.[42] As for the EU Directive on environmental crime, it expressly covers offences committed by 'serious negligence' so it applies to at least this form of direct liability for omissions (e.g. the breach of a duty to close a gate which would stop pollutants from being released into a stream that lead to one of the offences listed under Article 3). Moreover, as regards legal persons the EU environmental crime directive requires that they are liable where the 'lack of supervision or control' has made possible the commission of an offence, potentially expanding the scope of liability for omission offences.[43]

A broader scope for liability for omissions is present in the recital to the environmental crime directive which appears to cover other forms of (derivative) liability for omission. Recital 6 states that:

'Failure to comply with a legal duty to act can have the same effect as active behaviour and should therefore also be subject to *corresponding penalties*'. (emphasis added).[44]

Since the recital of the Directive contains substantive provisions which are addressed to Member States, it could be considered a legally binding interpretative tool of the provisions of the directive; and if so, Member States are required to criminalise omission offences. The use of 'corresponding penalties' in Recital 6 seems to imply that omissions would need to be subject to the same penalties as the positive act. This suggests that if a Member State applies a system which reduces the penalty in the case of liability for omissions (for example by one third or two thirds of the penalty applicable to the positive act), at least for the environmental offences in the Directive, the same (or 'corresponding') penalty for positive acts and omissions would need to be applicable. Yet it would be difficult to reconcile this line of reasoning with the principles of subsidiarity and

41 *Ibid* at 587.

42 Commentary III, Section II, of the explanatory memorandum states that Article 2 covers the most serious environmental offences which, whether by an act or an omission, are committed 'intentionally'.

43 However, as will be discussed below, it is not necessary that the liability of the legal person is of a criminal nature under the environmental crime directive.

44 There is no corresponding provision in the ship-source pollution directive, which hence does not require the criminalisation of omission offences, or at least not for the so-called 'commission by omission' offences.

proportionality, and also the ECJ case law regarding the limitations of the competence of the Community to adopt the types and levels of criminal penalties.[45]

It has been suggested that since no EU/EC measures rule out the criminalisation of omissions in principle, the Court will leave it to the discretion of Member States to determine how to define omissions.[46] The 2011 Italian legislation implementing the environmental crime directive, for example, has not been consistent on this point – it recognises the liability for omissions for certain offences;[47] while requiring the commission of an offence for others.[48]

6.2.2.5 Inchoate Offences

According to the Council Model Provisions (2009), when adopting EU criminal law legislation, the criminalisation of inciting, aiding and abetting the intentional offences should normally follow the criminalisation of the main offence.[49] This section discusses the extent to which EU environmental crime legislation incorporates inchoate offences. In contrast, the Council of Europe on environmental criminal law only requires the criminalisation of inchoate offences as regards one of the 'intentional' offences under Article 2 (1) of the convention.[50]

---

45 Indeed, as the Community (pre-Lisbon) legislation could not prescribe specific types and levels of criminal penalties, the term 'corresponding penalties' in Recital 6 of the directive (adopted prior to the ratification of the Lisbon Treaty) may not have the effect of equating the punishment for omissions with that for positive acts.

46 Peers, S. *EU Justice and Home Affairs Law* (OUP, 2006) at 416.

47 Article 260-bis of Legislative Decree April 3, 2006 # 152, after paragraph 9 the following is added: '9-a [whoever] violates with an act or omission the various provisions referred to in this Article (…). The same penalty applies to those who commit acts or omissions (…)' (author's translation). 'Attuazione della direttiva 2008/99/CE sulla tutela penale dell'ambiente, nonché della direttiva 2009/123/CE che modifica la direttiva 2005/35/CE relativa all'inquinamento provocato dalle navi e all'introduzione di sanzioni per violazioni'. Legal act: Decreto legislativo, number: 121; Official Journal: Gazzetta Ufficiale della Repubblica Italiana, number: 177, Publication date: 01/08/2011, Entry into force: 01/08/2011; Reference: (MNE(2011)56553) 'DECREE: Implementation of Directive 2008/99/EC on criminal law protection of the environment, as well of Directive 2009/123/EC, amending Directive 2005/35/EC on ship-source pollution and on the introduction of penalties for violations'.

48 *See* Article. 2 (Amendments to the Decree of 8 June 2001, n. 231) Article 25 (Environmental Crimes) '1. In relation to the commission of offenses under the Criminal Code, (…) the following penalties shall apply (…).'

49 Council Conclusions on model provisions, guiding the Council's criminal law deliberations 2979th JUSTICE and HOME AFFAIRS Council meeting, Brussels, 30 November 2009.

50 Art. 2 (2) of the Council of Europe convention states that each party shall adopt such appropriate measures as may be necessary to establish as criminal offences under its

6.2.2.5.1 *Attempts*

There are different approaches in the EU Member States regarding the penalties applicable to an attempt to commit a crime.[51] Some Member States apply lighter sanctions for an attempt to commit an offence[52] while in others the same penalty as for a completed offence is applied,[53] though it may be accepted as an attenuating circumstance.[54] In some countries the attempt to commit certain categories of crimes is not punishable.[55]

There is no requirement under the environmental crime directive for Member States to criminalise an attempted crime. In contrast, most other EU criminal law instruments require the criminalisation of attempts.[56] They are thus consistent with the Council Model Provisions.[57]

---

domestic law aiding or abetting the commission of any of the offences established in accordance with paragraph 1 of this article.

51 Summary of replies to the questionnaire on the approximation of sanctions (9402/1/01 DROIPEN 50 REV 1) 5 October 2001 (29.20) 12531/01. pgs. 8–9.

52 For example, Belgium, Finland, Greece, Italy, Luxembourg, the Netherlands (reduction of one-third of maximum penalty), Portugal, Italy (reduction of between one-third and two-thirds for certain crimes or *delitti*), Spain (generally one or two degrees less severe than for the completed offence). Pradel, J. and Corstens, G. *Droit Penal Compare,* (Dalloz, 2002) at 284.

53 For example, Denmark, France, Germany, Ireland, and the United Kingdom (with one exception in Section 4 (5) of the Criminal Attempts Act). Under Article 11 bis of the *Corpus Juris* project, an attempted offence was to be punishable by the maximum penalty applicable to the completed offence. See also, Summary of replies to the questionnaire on the approximation of sanctions (9402/1/01 DROIPEN 50 REV 1) 5 October 2001 (29.20) 12531/01.

54 Pradel, J. and Corstens, G. *Droit Penal Compare* (Dalloz, 2002).

55 In Portugal the crime itself must carry a maximum penalty of more than 3 years in prison; in France an attempt to commit a minor offence or *contravension* is never punishable. *Ibid.*

56 For example Art. 3 (2) of the Framework Decision in counterfeiting currency; Art. 5 of the Framework Decision on counterfeiting non-cash instruments; and Art. 4 of the Framework Decision on terrorism; and Article 3 of the Directive on preventing and combatting trafficking in human beings and protecting its victims. See also, Peers, S. (2006) above note 46, at 414–415.

57 According to the Council 2009 Model Provisions '[a]ttempts to commit an intentional offence should be criminalised if it is necessary and proportionate in relation to the main offence. Consideration should be given to the different regimes under national law'. Moreover, EU criminal law instruments do not require the criminalisation of an attempted crime if the conduct is not intentional, which is a reflection of the fact that the law on attempts in a number of countries only criminalise an attempted crime which is committed intentionally. Thus the Council Model Provisions states that Member States shall criminalise attempts according to the following formula: '2. Each Member State shall ensure that attempting the *intentional* conduct referred to in Article (Article on Criminal

6.2.2.5.2 *Conspiracy*

Conspiracy is a distinct offence which is consummated when two or more parties enter into an agreement to commit a criminal offence. In the UK and Germany there is a special crime of conspiracy. Other EU Member States criminalise certain types of preparatory acts, despite not calling them 'conspiracy'.[58]

Neither the environmental crime directive nor the shipping source pollution directive require Member States to criminalize conspiracy. However, as will be further discussed below, participation in criminal organizations are covered by the EU Framework Decision on organised crime (2008),[59] provided that a certain minimum penalty threshold applicable to the underlying criminal offence is met.

6.2.2.5.3 *Incitement*

The environmental crime directive requires Member States to ensure that inciting the intentional conduct referred in Article 3 is punishable as a criminal offence. As there is a strong accessorial link between the incitee and incitor, the analysis of 'complicity' (discussed below) also applies to incitement. One of the corollaries of this strong accessorial link is that in case the incitee does commit a criminal offence, under the law of a number of countries the incitor will no longer be liable for incitement but as an accessory to the criminal offence committed.[60]

In this regard, the environmental crime directive follows the standard that was later followed under the 2009 Council Model Provisions which suggests that EU criminal law legislation should criminalise inchoate offences such as incitement. In the context of environmental crime, incitement could occur, for example, if a company were to promote fly-tipping offences in its website.

6.3 Complicity

There are two ways in which an actor can be derivatively liable for the crime of a perpetrator (or 'principle'): she can aid or abet the criminal act, in which event

Offences) is punishable as a criminal offence (emphasis added). *See* Council Conclusions on model provisions, guiding the Council's criminal law deliberations 2979th JUSTICE and HOME AFFAIRS Council meeting, Brussels, 30 November 2009.

58 Eser, Albin, 'Harmonization of Penal Sanctions in Europe Comparative Typology of Convergences and Divergences' in Delmas-Marty (ed.) *'L'Harmonisation des Sanctions Pénales en Europe'* (2003), at 408. For example, preparatory acts (not sufficient to establish an attempted crime) are generally punishable in Sweden.

59 Council Framework Decision on the Fight Against Organised Crime of 24 October 2008 (O.J. L300/42, 11.11.2008).

60 In the context of English criminal law, see discussion in Allen, Michael. *Textbook on Criminal Law* (8th ed. OUP, Oxford 2005).

she occupies a subsidiary status in the criminal enterprise, or she can instigate or solicit the criminal act, which renders her status closer to that of a full partner in the crime.[61] Co-principles are punished alike in most legal systems.

There are two main models in Europe as regards the participation in criminal offences. In the so-called unitary model of participation, all participants are equally punishable, though there may be some differentiation in the sentencing stage.[62] Hence in a minority group of countries which include Austria, Ireland and France, accomplices incur the same penalties and are liable for the same offence as the principle, although differing penalties may be applied at the sentencing stage.[63] One of the arguments in the French literature for punishing accomplices and perpetrators alike is that some accomplices are instigators, and at least this group of accomplices deserve the same punishment as full perpetrators.[64]

In contrast, the 'differentiation model' distinguishes between perpetrators and accessories (instigator/accomplice). The dominant tradition within the EU Member States is to distinguish between the different forms of participation at the level of attribution, i.e. between direct perpetration, co-operation, perpetration by means, instigation and complicity. Hence the majority of the EU Member States foresee different penalties depending on the degree of participation of a person in the commission of an offence.[65] The Member States following the differentiation model can be divided into two groups: countries in which the mitigation of the penalty to the accessories to crime is obligatory (e.g. Belgium, Germany and Spain), while in others the mitigation of the penalty is at the discretion of the court (e.g. Poland and Sweden).[66]

The Council of Europe 1998 Convention contains an obligation for states to criminalise complicity in relation to the intentional offences listed in Article 2 (1) only.[67] So it is not necessary for state parties to criminalise complicity

---

61 Fletcher, G. (2000) above note 40, at 640.

62 Esser, Albin, 'Harmonization of Penal Sanctions in Europe Comparative Typology of Convergences and Divergences', in Delmas-Marty (ed.) '*L'Harmonisation des Sanctions Pénales en Europe*' (2003) at 409.

63 Ambos, K. 'Is the Development of a Common Substantive Criminal Law for Europe Possible?', 12 MJ 2 (2005) p. 183.

64 For a discussion see Fletcher (2000), above note 40, at 645.

65 Summary of replies to the questionnaire on the approximation of sanctions (9402/1/01 DROIPEN 50 REV 1) 5 October 2001 (29.20) 12531/01.

66 *Ibid.*

67 See Article 2 (2) of the 1998 Convention on the Protection of the Environment through Criminal Law: 'Each Party shall adopt such appropriate measures as may be necessary to establish as criminal offences under its domestic law aiding or abetting the commission of any of the offences established in accordance with paragraph 1 of this article'.

in the case of the offences listed in Article 4 (which may be of a criminal or administrative nature) nor in relation to the negligent offences under Article 3.

In the course of the decision-making leading to the adoption the EU environmental crime directive, the European Parliament rejected the original proposal for the criminalisation of complicity in the case of non-intentional offences.[68] This is in light of the fact that in some Member States non-intentional (secondary) participation in a criminal offence is not punishable.[69] Hence Article 4 of the 2008 environmental crime directive states that 'Member States shall ensure that (...) aiding and abetting the *intentional conduct* referred to in Article 3 is punishable as a criminal offence' (emphasis added).[70] Similarly, Article 1 (3.2.) of the original 2008 (amending) shipping directive proposal required that 'aiding and abetting' the offence of ship-source discharges 'is punishable when committed with intent, recklessness or serious negligence', but this provision was modified in the final text of the directive adopted in October 2009 so that only participation in *intentional* offences need to be criminalised.[71]

The adopted final text of the environmental crime directive differs from Article 4 of the original 2007 proposal, under which the Member States would have been required to consider 'participation in' the conduct referred to in Article 3 as a criminal offence. Indeed, the use of the term 'aiding and abetting' in the final text of the Directive is narrower than 'participation in' used in the original 2007 directive proposal. The latter would cover forms of participation other than aiding and abetting (e.g. counselling or soliciting). Since that original proposal envisaged the harmonisation of criminal penalties, it could have required, in

68 *See* Report on proposal for a directive of the European Parliament and of the Council on the protection of the environment through criminal law, A6-0154/2008 of 15 April 2008 (COM(2007)0051 – C6-0063/2007 – 2007/0022(COD)) European Parliament, Committee on Legal Affairs, Rapporteur: Hartmut Nassauer, at 17.

69 For example in English criminal law the *mens rea* for secondary participation (aiding, abetting, counselling or procuring) is intention. The accomplice must intend her own contribution as well as appreciate the nature of the perpetrator's action (i.e. she must foresee the elements of the offence). *See* Simester, A.P. and Sullivan, G.R. *Criminal Law: Theory and Doctrine* (3rd ed. Hart Publishing, Oxford 2007) at 207.

70 In a similar vein, see Article 4 of the (annulled) Framework Decision on environmental crimes, which required the criminalisation of 'participation in' the intentional offences set out in Article 2 only.

71 See Article 5.2 of the final text of the 2009 shipping pollution amending directive. This amendment was suggested in a draft Report of the European Parliament Committee on Transport and Tourism on the proposal for a directive of the European Parliament and of the Council amending Directive 2005/35/EC on ship source pollution and on the introduction of penalties for infringements (COM(2008)0134 – C6-0142/2008 – 2008/0055(COD)).

principle, that Member States adopted the 'unitarian' or 'differentiation' model of participation in a criminal offence. However, any attempt to do this would hardly be consistent with the principles of subsidiarity and proportionality.

6.4 General Structure of the Criminal Offences

6.4.1 *The Mens Rea Requirement*

Under the Council of Europe environmental crime convention, offences are differentiated on the basis of the *mens rea* requirement. For example, while 'intentional' unlawful transport and disposal of hazardous waste endangering human and animal life fall under article 2 (1) (c) of the convention – in relation to which signatory parties *must* introduce criminal sanctions – the 'unlawful disposal, treatment, storage, transport, export or import of waste' (so non-hazardous wastes or other wastes that are not likely to endanger human and animal life) fall under Article 4 (c) when committed 'intentionally or with negligence', leaving it to the discretion of national Parliaments the choice between criminal or non-criminal sanctions. So the contracting parties to the convention are obliged, in relation to the 'hard core' 'intentional offences' under Articles 2, to classify them as 'criminal'.[72] Moreover, paragraph (1) of Article 3 extends criminal liability to negligent offences. Yet paragraph (2) of Article 3 allows contracting parties, when ratifying the Convention, to limit liability for Article 2 offences to those committed with 'gross negligence'.[73]

Under the EU environmental crime directive, Member States are required to criminalise a number of prohibited activities committed intentionally or with 'at least' serious negligence.[74] It should be noted, however, that under English criminal law the concept of *serious* negligence does not exist. Indeed, the standard of criminal liability for negligent acts is '*gross* negligence'. The Council Model Provisions has recommended that EU criminal legislation should, as a general rule, only prescribe penalties for acts which are committed intentionally.[75] Moreover, it suggests that '[n]egligent conduct should be criminalised when a

72 Those offences should usually carry at least as an alternative sanction of imprisonment. See Article 6, 2nd sentence of the convention.

73 The Council of Europe convention refers to 'gross negligence', rather than 'serious negligence' applied in the EU environmental crime instruments.

74 See 'caput' of Article 3 of the environmental crime directive.

75 Point 6, Council Conclusions on model provisions, guiding the Council's criminal law deliberations 2979th JUSTICE and HOME AFFAIRS Council meeting, Brussels, 30 November 2009.

case-by-case assessment indicates that this is appropriate due to the particular relevance of the right or essential interest which is the object of protection, for example in cases of serious negligence which endanger human life or cause serious damage'.[76] Yet the Council Model Provisions make it clear that the criminalisation of an act that has been committed without intention or negligence (i.e., strict liability), should not be prescribed in EU criminal legislation.[77] The position of the Council on this question is not surprising, given that strict liability standards are not widely accepted under the national criminal laws of all member states.[78]

Under the shipping pollution (amended) directive Member States are required to criminalise certain polluting activities committed intentionally, recklessly or with serious negligence.[79] It thus covers both operational (or 'deliberate') and accidental ('reckless or seriously negligent') discharges, for example if it can be shown that pollution arose out of damage to the ship or its equipment which can be traced to serious negligence or recklessness in operation or maintenance. In effect there is no distinction under the Directive between the illicit activities of rogue operators and maritime accidents. However, though recent maritime disasters have focused the attention on accidental oil pollution,[80] the main threat still comes from deliberate operational discharges, for example tank-cleaning operations.[81]

By introducing the standard of liability of serious negligence under Article 4, the shipping pollution directive could be in conflict with the right of innocent passage enshrined in UNCLOS. This Convention states that passage is no longer innocent *inter alia* when '*wilful* and serious pollution' is caused.[82] It could be argued that, if the pollution is caused by a seriously negligent act (i.e. non-intentional), the passage is still innocent and the coastal state might not exercise its enforcement jurisdiction against the vessel (e.g. apprehension). Yet

---

76 Point 7, *ibid.*

77 Point 8, *ibid.*

78 See generally, Fletcher, G. (2000) above note 40.

79 See Article 4 (1) and Article 5a (3) of the ship-source pollution directive.

80 See generally Wang Hui 'The EU Marine Oil Pollution Prevention Regime – Recent Developments' [2004] EELR 292; and Faure, Michael and Wang, Hui, 'Liability for Oil Pollution: Recent Developments' [2004] vol. 12 Environmental Liability no. 2.

81 Veronica Frank 'Consequences of the Prestige Sinking for European and International Law' [2005] 20 *The Int J Mar Coast Law* 44.

82 Article 19 (2) (h) UNCLOS.

some legal commentators tend to regard the list of non-innocent passages listed in Paragraph 1 of Article 19 UNCLOS as non-exhaustive.[83]

However, when prompted to address this question in the *Intertanko* case, the ECJ held that it could not examine the compatibility of the shipping pollution directive with international law, including the right of innocent passage under UNCLOS (see Chapter 4).[84] On the other hand, the ECJ in *Intertanko* did examine the compatibility of the term 'serious negligence' under Article 4 of the shipping pollution directive with the principle of legality. The ECJ found that there were common features relating to the term which could be found in the legal systems of all Member States. Somewhat surprisingly, the Court went on to define the concept of serious negligence. It found that serious negligence is to be taken to mean an unintentional action or omission by which the person responsible commits a *patent* breach of the duty of care which he should have and could have complied with in view of his attributes, knowledge, abilities and individual situation.[85] The Court added a 'subjective' element to the definition of serious negligence, in that the personal characteristics of the defendant and individual situation could be taken into account. Moreover, the Court referred to a 'patent' breach of a duty of care, which is consistent with though perhaps not the same as an 'obvious' breach of a duty of care as required by the English Courts in order to establish 'gross' negligence.[86] Yet there is no suggestion that the definition of serious negligence provided by the Court in *Intertanko* aims at harmonising the law of the Member States. Rather, the Court appeared simply to be pointing out to common features of the law on (criminal) negligence of the Member States to substantiate its findings that no conflict between the shipping pollution directive and the principle of legal certainty existed.

---

83 See e.g. Tanaka, Y. *The International Law of the Sea* (Cambridge, 2012) at 86. This is because the last paragraph (l) of Article 19 (2) mentions 'any other activity not having a direct bearing on passage' as possibly rendering the passage non-innocent.

84 Case C-308/06 *The Queen on the Application of: International Association of Independent Tanker Owners (Intertanko), International Association of Dry Cargo Shipowners (Intercargo), Greek Shipping Co-operation Committee, Lloyd's Register, International Salvage Union v Secretary of State for Transport*, 3 June 2008 ('Intertanko').

85 *Intertanko*, paras. 74–76.

86 See, for example, *Adomako* [1994] UKHL 6. Therefore, unlike the Advocate General who tried to construe the concept of serious negligence as 'recklessness in the knowledge that damage would probably result' as regards accidental discharges outside the territorial sea so as to avoid conflict with MARPOL, the Court did not see the need to follow this narrow interpretation of the term – perhaps because it had found that the legality of the ship-source pollution Directive could not be assessed in light of UNCLOS or MARPOL.

6.4.2 *The Threshold of Harm*

The harm principle – as was discussed in Chapter 2 – needs to be taken into account not only in the decision to criminalise, but also in relation to how offences are labelled and penalties are graduated. The rationale behind this is the assumption that individuals or companies will only assimilate the moral wrongfulness of the offence, and therefore respect the criminal law system, if offences are graduated according to their harmfulness. The degree of harm is, alongside culpability, a determinant of the seriousness of an offence.[87] Hence in order to graduate offences legislators must evaluate the interests affected, the degree of harm inflicted or potentially inflicted, and culpability (the mental element).

It is difficult to create a general rule reflecting the relative degree of harm of the wrongdoing when it comes to ranking criminal offences.[88] The challenges in creating a reliable system that graduates offences according to their seriousness and the level harm caused or likely to be caused can be illustrated if the penalties for a minor bodily injure (a physical offence to the person) is contrasted with the robbery of a million pounds (a property offence).[89]

The approach under the Council of Europe Convention on environmental crime is to establish the need for criminalisation relative to the degree of harm or potential harm. The contracting states to the convention are obliged to criminalize the 'hard core', 'intentional offences' under Article 2, all of which specify a specific degree of harm such as 'death or serious injury to any person or substantial damage to the quality of air, soil, water, animals or plants.'

Arguably one of the deficiencies of the Council of Europe Convention from the perspective of legislative harmonisation is that it requires criminalisation of activities which cause or are likely to cause *substantial damage* of some kind.[90] Although the requirement of 'substantial damage' is justifiable as it contributes to defining the 'seriousness' element required for the criminalisation of environmental offences, it simultaneously introduces an evidential hurdle that is particularly

---

87 Ashworth, A. *Principles of Criminal Law* (OUP, 2006) at 38.

88 On the ranking of criminal offences according to their seriousness see A. von Hirsch and N. Jareborg 'Gauging Criminal Harms: a Living Standard Analysis' (1991) 11 *Oxford JLS* 1, who assess the seriousness of crimes (with individual victims) according to the interests violated: (1) physical integrity, (2) material support, (3) freedom from humiliation and (4) privacy and autonomy. Since their study only applies to crime with individual victims, it only applies to a limited number of environmental crimes, i.e. those which affect human beings.

89 In many countries sentencing guidelines serve as a guide for judges to impose relatively predictable sentences for similar offences See e.g. Federal sentencing guidelines manual 2012, United States Sentencing Commission – 2013.

90 See also, Hedemann-Robinson, Martin. *Enforcement of European Union Environmental Law: Legal Issues and Challenges* (Routledge-Cavendish, 2007) at 517.

difficult for the prosecution to overcome. This problem is further complicated by the fact that there is no guidance in the Convention, nor in the Explanatory Memorandum to it, as to the meaning of the aggravating elements leading to the requirement of criminalisation, such as 'substantial', 'serious' or 'significant' damage/risk.[91] This leaves considerable room for discretion to national authorities in implementing those provisions. Indeed, the Council of Europe Convention has been criticised for allowing significant variation of implementation by national parliaments; as well as by courts regarding the interpretation of some terms under the convention once the measures are transposed into the national legal systems.[92] Hence the actual level of protection of the environment can be compromised depending on the definition and judicial interpretation given to such terms as 'serious negligence', 'serious injury' or 'significant damage' and other terms which are undefined under the convention.[93] Those terms shall be interpreted in light of the traditions and legal system of each Member State.[94] Yet these undefined notions may be too vague to bring fundamental changes in the levels of environmental protection and enforcement in practice.[95]

As was discussed above, most offences in the environmental crime directive require a specific result, i.e. that they cause or are likely to cause harm to persons or the environment (air, soil, water, animals or plants). This in line with the Council of Justice and Home Affairs' model provisions on criminal offences.[96] The EU environmental crime directive also contains vague notions of harm such as 'substantial damage', 'serious injury', 'significant deterioration' and 'negligible impact' in its definitions of offences.[97] Yet as the directive only

91 See e.g. 'serious' injury (art 2 (1) [a – e]); 'substantial' damage (art 2 (1) (a) (d)) and 'significant' risk (art 2 (1) (a) (i)).

92 See e.g. Selin, C., 'Your Money or Your Life: A Look at the Convention on the Protection of the Environment through Criminal Law' RECIEL 10 (1) 2001; Comte, Françoise, 'Protection of the Environment through Criminal Law: Destiny of the Various European Union's Initiatives' in Odina, Marco (ed.) *Europe and the Environment* (Groningen, 2004).

93 Selin (2001), *supra* at 110.

94 *See* also, Comte (2004), *supra* at 8.

95 *See* Kramer, Ludwig. 'Case Law Analysis: Environment, Crime and EC Law', (2006) 18 (2) *Journal of Environmental Law* 277, commenting on Article 2 of the annulled 2003 Framework Decision on environmental crime which also contained undefined terms such as 'substantial damage'.

96 See Point 5 of the Council Conclusions on model provisions, guiding the Council's criminal law deliberations *2979th Justice And Home Affairs Council meeting, Brussels, 30 November 2009:* '[t]he criminal provisions should focus on conduct causing actual harm or seriously threatening the right or essential interest which is the object of protection'.

97 See Article 3, (a)-(h) of the environmental crime directive.

imposes minimum standards, Member States may adopt higher standards and criminalise even less serious activities which do not cause or are likely to cause 'substantial damage', 'serious injury' or 'significant deterioration'. Therefore, those terms do not need to be transposed literally into national law as long as the standard adopted is equal or higher than that under the directive (for example, the term 'damage' or 'injury' may be transposed without the 'substantial' or 'serious' qualifying elements). Yet certain terms under the Directive, such as 'hazardous waste', must be transposed literally by national law, since linguistic differentiations may have not only legal consequences, but may also affect monitoring, surveillance, statistics, customs, police controls and other administrative matters.[98] It should be noted that if a Member State adopts or maintains more stringent standards than the EU environmental crime directive, under Article 193 TFEU they are required to notify the Commission.[99] The Austrian national implementing legislation appears to apply a higher threshold (but lower environmental protection standards) for establishing the criminal offences relating to trade in endangered species,[100] as it requires that a 'significant amount of species' ('*eine erhebliche Menge von Exemplaren einer geschützten wildlebenden Tierart*') are affected, whereas the environmental crime directive requires that 'more than a negligible quantity' of species are affected ('*eine unerhebliche Menge dieser Exemplare betrifft*'). Thus, the Austrian legislation applies a higher threshold of harm and thus makes it more difficult for prosecutors to establish that a criminal offence has been committed, and hence is arguably incompatible with the environmental crime directive.[101]

It is clear that in both the Council of Europe and EU instruments on environmental criminal law, the seriousness of the violation of environmental law is paramount to establish a benchmark for criminalisation. In fact, 'seriousness' is a condition for the establishment of the EC/EU competence to lay down environmental offences.[102] This is reflected in the final text of the adopted

---

98 See Kramer, L. *EC Environmental Law*, (6th ed. Sweet & Maxwell, 2007) at 421.

99 Article 193TFEU (former Article 176EC) states that '[t]he protective measures adopted pursuant to Article 175 EC shall not prevent any Member State from maintaining or introducing more stringent protective measures. Such measures must be compatible with this Treaty. They shall be notified to the Commission'. See chapter 4.

100 Article 3 (g) of the environmental crime directive.

101 See § 181f. (1), *Bundesgesetz: Änderung Des Strafgesetzbuches Zur Verhinderung Von Terrorismus Und Des Strafgesetzbuches Und Der Strafprozessordnung Im Jahr 1975 Den Strafrechtlichen Schutz Der Umwelt Zu Verbessern,* Jahrgang 2011 Ausgegeben am 21. November 2011 Teil I.

102 See Chapter 5. Prior to the ratification of the Lisbon Treaty, as the Community was competent to lay down criminal offences for 'serious' violations of EC environmental law in

2008 directive, as all offences under the directive (other than the 'abstract endangerment offences') are linked to a threshold of serious harm, either actual or potential. Indeed, it is doubtful that a supranational or intergovernmental instrument of harmonisation of environmental criminal law should aim to criminalise activities which do not carry at least the risk of serious harm to the environment or humans. As was agued in Chapter 2, only serious violations of environmental law should be criminalised (although criminal sanctions should also be available for the failure to comply with administrative decisions).

It is interesting to note that the Commission's first proposal for a directive on environmental crimes adopted in 2001 reduced the discretion left to the national authorities in the Member States by requiring the criminalisation of activities which infringed specific Community legislation regardless of any degree of harm,[103] for all offences but one.[104] While this approach had the advantage of restraining the ability of the national authorities in the Member States to circumvent the objectives of the Directive proposal by applying a narrow interpretation of the offences contained therein, it would have created simultaneously a particularly low threshold for criminalisation which is probably not consistent with the principle that only serious violations of environmental law should be criminalised.

There is an additional requirement under the shipping directive as regards the threshold of harm for commission of the offence. Illicit ship-source discharges of polluting substances should be regarded as a criminal offence as long as they result in *'deterioration in the quality of water'*. So less serious cases of illicit ship-source pollution discharges that do not cause deterioration in the quality of water need not be regarded as criminal offences – these are thus regarded under the directive as 'minor infringements'.[105] However, to ensure a high level of safety and protection of the environment in the maritime transport sector and in line with the polluter-pays principle, the directive requires that

light of the *Environmental Crimes* case, it appears that by virtue of Article 47 EU the Council was precluded from prescribing the definition of environmental offences for even less serious violations of environmental law by applying a third pillar legal basis under Title VI of the former TEU.

103 According to the Explanatory memorandum to the 2001 directive proposal, '[c]ommunity law considers such activities harmful or particularly dangerous to the environment. For this reason, these activities should also be considered criminal offences, as the risk for the environment lies in the activity as such, independently from an eventual damage that it causes'. See Section 3 (b), at 4.

104 The offence of '*significant deterioration* of a protected habitat' (emphasis added) under Article 3 (e) of the 2001 directive proposal.

105 Article 5 (a) (2) of the shipping pollution directive.

repeated minor cases, which do not individually but in conjunction result in deterioration in the quality of water, should be regarded as a criminal offence.[106] Still, it will be particularly challenging for law enforcement bodies to monitor and to establish the existence of 'repeated minor offences' which 'in conjunction result in the deterioration in the quality of water' so as to establish the criminal liability of the operator.[107]

6.5 The Range of Offences in the European Environmental Crime Legislation

The range of offences under the Council of Europe Convention on environmental crime is more comprehensive than under the environmental crime directive. In particular, the CoE convention protects additional forms of environmental media, such as offering legal protection in relation to the unlawful causing of 'noise',[108] specific legal protection to 'national parks, national reserve, water conservation or other protected areas',[109] as well as to 'protected monuments' and 'other protected objects [and] property'.[110] Hence, unlike the EU environmental crime directive and ship-source pollution directive which aim to protect 'any person' and 'air', 'soil', 'water', 'animals' or 'plants',[111] the CoE Convention also aims at protecting 'property' and other elements of the 'built environment'. As was discussed in Chapter 2, this reflects the fact that there is no explicit EU/EC competence under Articles 191 TFEU (former Article 174EC) for the Union to harmonise environmental measures for the protection of the 'built environment', although it should be noted that Article 192 TFEU recognises the scope for harmonisation of measures affecting 'town and country planning' so long as the Council of Ministers unanimously votes in favour of the measure – a threshold which would be particularly difficult to achieve.[112]

106 Article 5 (a) (3) *ibid.*

107 However, it should be noted that under Article 4 of the ship-source pollution directive 'minor cases of such discharges' are to be regarded as 'infringements' if committed with intent, reckless of serious negligence, even if not amounting to a criminal offence.

108 Article 4 (b) of the CoE environmental crime convention.

109 Article 4 (f) *ibid.*

110 Article 2 (1) (b) *ibid.*

111 See Article 3 of the environmental crime directive.

112 See Article 192 (2) TFEU. Likewise, the offences listed in Article 3 of the 2007 Directive proposal and the (annulled) January 2003 Framework Decision on environmental crime only referred to 'persons' and 'the quality of air, soil, water, animals or plants', so they did not aim to protect elements of the build environment.

Aside from considerations over considerations over the level of harm (as discussed above), it is not always clear why the CoE environmental crime convention 'downgrades' certain offences to Article 4 (in relation to which there is no obligation to penalise). This is a considerable weakness of the Convention, as some potentially very serious environmental offences with transboundary impacts, in particular the 'unlawful trade, possession, damaging (...) of protected wild flora and fauna species',[113] only fall under Article 4 and thus there is no obligation on state parties to criminalise such offences. In this respect, it appears that the Convention follows an 'anthropocentric' approach, since 'wildlife' and 'natural habit protection' crimes (i.e. 'possession (...) or trading of or in protected (...) species' or 'changes detrimental to natural components of a national park, natural reserve (...) and other protected areas'), even when committed intentionally, would not necessarily entail criminal sanctions.[114]

The definition of the criminal offences in the final text of the environmental crime directive corresponds largely to the definitions set out in the annulled 2003 Framework Decision on environmental crimes, while taking into account the amendments suggested by the Parliament to the 2001 directive proposal and accepted by the Commission after first reading.[115] The Commission had decided to introduce in its 2007 directive proposal on environmental crime the list of offences unanimously agreed by the Member States in the (annulled) Framework Decision on environmental crime, which itself shares similarities with the list of offences of the 1998 Council of Europe Convention. Two offences have been added to the Directive other than the ones set out in the 2003 Framework Decision on environmental crime: the unlawful significant deterioration of a protected habitat; and the illegal shipment of waste.

Most offences under the original 2007 directive proposal have been retained (including the 'significant deterioration of a habitat' and 'illegal waste shipment') with relatively minor amendments in the final text of the directive adopted in 2008. Indeed, the offences under the 2008 environmental crime directive of discharge of materials or ionising radiation,[116] waste shipment,[117] dangerous operation of a plant,[118] and production/disposal of nuclear materials or other

113 Article 4 (g) of the Council of Europe environmental crime convention.

114 *Compare* Article 4 (f) and (g) with the offences under Article 2 of the convention, all of which recognise the protection of 'any person' in addition to the protection of elements of the natural environment and/or property.

115 Explanatory Memorandum, 2007 directive proposal, point 5 (1), p. 7.

116 Article 3 (a) of the directive corresponds to Article 3 (b) of the proposal.

117 Article 3 (c) of the directive corresponds to Article 3 (e) (except for the 'for profit' requirement which was deleted in the final text).

118 Article 3 (d) of the directive corresponds to Article 3 (e) of the proposal.

hazardous radioactive substances[119] correspond closely to the offences envisaged in the 2007 proposal, with only a few amendments and modifications.

This section examines in further detail the substantive provisions of the environmental offences under the EU environmental crime directive and Council of Europe environmental crime convention. It also discusses the substantive provisions and main prohibitions under international environmental agreements particularly relevant to field of environmental criminal law. The offences are discussed according to the following broad categories: (a) pollution-control offences; (b) biodiversity-related offences; (c) trade in hazardous wastes and dangerous substances or organisms; (d) international organised crime; and (e) financial crimes in environmental markets.

6.5.1 *Pollution-Control Offences*

A number of global conventions have been adopted aimed at controlling, combatting and preventing pollution from both direct and diffuse sources and impacting on different types of environmental media. This includes the 1979 UNECE Convention on Long-Range Transboundary Air Pollution;[120] and its 1999 Gottenburg Protocol[121] which aims to abate acidification, eutrophication and ground-level ozone, covering four main pollutants: sulphur, nitrogen oxides, volatile organic compounds, and ammonia.

The pollution offences under Article 3 of the environmental crime directive include discharge of materials or ionising radiation,[122] dangerous operation of a plant[123] and the production/disposal of nuclear materials or other hazardous radioactive substances.[124] These pollution-control offences largely aim at ensuring the effective implementation of EC secondary legislation listed in Appendices A and B of the environmental crime directive, particularly the integrated pollution and control (IPPC) Directives.[125] It should be noted though

---

119 Article 3 (e) of the directive corresponds to Article 3 (f) of the proposal (apart from the addition of 'handling', 'disposal' and 'holding'; and the deletion of 'manufacture and treatment' and inclusion of 'production and processing' instead).

120 1979 UNECE Convention on Long-Range Transboundary Air Pollution TIAS 10541; 1302 UNTS 217; 18 ILM 1442 (1979).

121 The 1999 Gothenburg Protocol to Abate Acidification, Eutrophication and Ground-Level Ozone to the 1979 UNECE Convention on Long-Range Transboundary Air Pollution, entered into force on 17 May 2005.

122 Article 3 (a) of the directive.

123 Article 3 (d) *ibid.*

124 Article 3 (e) *Ibid.*

125 Directive 2008/1/EC of the European Parliament and of the Council of 15 January 2008 concerning integrated pollution prevention and control, OJ L 24, 29.1.2008, p. 8; and IPPC Directive 96/61/EC.

that the IPPC directives were repealed since January 2014 by the EU Industrial Emissions Directive (IED).[126] Although the IED does not establish criminal offences or penalties, it states that sanctions for violations thereof shall be 'effective, proportionate and dissuasive'.[127]

Another important aspect affecting the implementation of the environmental crime directive relates to the use in certain provisions of the terms 'nuclear materials' and 'ionising radiation'. In the Draft Report of the Committee on Legal Affairs of the European Parliament of 2 February 2008, Rapporteur Hartmut Nassauer suggested that the reference to 'nuclear material' or 'ionising radiation' under Article 3 (a) and (e) of the environmental crime directive did not mean that a EURATOM legal basis[128] was required for adoption of that directive.[129] In contrast to the (annulled) 2003 Framework Decision on environmental crime, the 'radioactive-related' pollution-control offences under the final text of the Directive on environmental crime refer to 'material' instead of 'substance' as the Commission regards the former as a more comprehensive term.[130]

The pollution-control offences in the environmental crime directive borrow a number of elements from the pollution discharges offences under the Council of Europe convention on environmental crime. However, the Council of Europe convention requires the criminalisation only of concrete endangerment pollution-control offences (i.e. those that cause or are likely to cause damage) when committed intentionally or negligently,[131] but not generally in relation to abstract endangerment pollution-control offences (such as the 'unlawful operation of a plant'), which hence may be regarded as criminal or administrative offences by state parties.[132]

126 Directive 2010/75/EU of the European Parliament and of the Council of 24 November 2010 on industrial emissions (integrated pollution prevention and control) ('Recast'). This Directive had to be transposed into national law in the Member States by 7th January 2013.

127 Article 79 of the IED states that 'Member States shall determine penalties applicable to infringements of the national provisions adopted pursuant to this Directive. The penalties thus provided for shall be effective, proportionate and dissuasive. Member States shall notify those provisions to the Commission (...)'.

128 With regard to activities covered by the Euratom Treaty, the legislation adopted pursuant to the Euratom Treaty is listed in Annex B to the environmental crime directive.

129 He referred to the ECJ decision in *Environmental Crimes*, as the environmental crime directive aims to cover infringements of any Community legislation concerning the protection of the environment irrespective of the legal basis on which they have been adopted. See Draft Report on the Directive on the Protection of the Environment through Criminal Law. European Parliament, Committee on Legal Affairs, Rapporteur: Hartmut Nassauer, 26 February 2008. On this question see also the Opinion of the Council's Legal Service (10260/07) JUR 218 DROIPEN 55 ENV 304.

130 Explanatory Memorandum to the 2007 directive proposal.

131 See Articles 2 and 3 of the CoE environmental crime convention.

132 Article 4 (d) *ibid.*

Ship-source Pollution

As regards pollution discharges from vessels, MARPOL[133] is currently the main international legal framework aimed at the prevention of pollution from ships.[134] Although at first sight the Council of Europe environmental crime convention does not appear to cover ship-source pollution, the explanatory memorandum to the convention clarifies that the pollution-control offences under Article 2 of the convention apply to pollution in the seas in violation of UNCLOS, MARPOL and related anti-dumping treaties.[135]

The purpose of the EU shipping pollution directive (as amended in October 2009) is to implement MARPOL in the EU legal order through the approximation of the definition of ship-source pollution offences committed by natural or legal persons; and the scope of their liability and the criminal nature of penalties that can be imposed for such criminal offences.[136] The EU shipping pollution directive forms part of the broader EU maritime policy programme which, as was highlighted in the 2002 Sixth Environment Action Programme, comprises seven main areas, including 'conservation of marine environment', with special attention is to be given to areas of high biodiversity value.[137]

---

133 IMO *International Convention for the Prevention of Pollution from Ships 1973/1978* ('MARPOL').

134 MARPOL, which was adopted in 1973 and significantly amended in 1978 in order to facilitate its entry into force. Annexes I and II regulate carriage of oil and chemicals respectively.

135 CoE Convention Explanatory report '*Art. 2 Paragraph 1/a* The polluting conduct is described as "the discharge, emission or introduction of a quantity of substances or ionising radiation" into one of the three environmental media (cf. also the definition of "pollution" by reference to the introduction of substances in Article 1 (4) of the UN Convention on the Law of the Sea – UNCLOS – and the definition of "discharge" in Article 2 (3) (a) of the International Convention for the Prevention of Pollution from Ships, 1973). It also includes cases of dumping. The enumeration of different alternatives, even if they may overlap, shall guarantee that all sorts of polluting activities are included. They are different in form, depending on the state of substances (solid, liquid or gaseous) and on the media they enter. "Ionising radiation" is added, because not in all cases substances which are discharged etc. are its source'.

136 Under Article 4 (4) of MARPOL the penalties specified under the law of the contracting state shall be '*adequate in severity to discourage violations* of the present Convention' and shall be equally severe irrespective of where the violations occur.

137 See the 2002 Sixth Environment Action Programme; the 2002 EU Commission Marine Strategy Communication; the 2006 EC Commission Green Paper on Maritime Policy and the 2007 Communication on Integrated Marine Policy for the European Union. See also Directive 2008/56/EC of the European Parliament and of the Council of 17 June 2008 establishing a framework for community action in the field of marine environmental policy (Marine Strategy Framework Directive).

As was discussed above, under the shipping pollution directive, illicit ship-source discharges of polluting substances should be regarded as a criminal offence as long as they have been committed with 'intent, recklessly or with serious negligence' and result in 'deterioration in the quality of water'. The directive requires Member States to introduce in their domestic law the specific offence of illegal discharge of polluting substances – which, according to an Appendix to the Directive, includes oil and oily and other noxious substances listed in two Appendices to MARPOL.[138] Moreover, the Directive – following the 2009 amendment[139] – obliges Member States to provide in their national legislation for 'effective, proportionate and dissuasive' *criminal* penalties in respect of those illegal pollution discharges.

The shipping pollution directive recognises a number of exceptions or 'defences' available to the shipping industry. The objective of those defences is primarily to define the standard of care to be met in order to establish that a criminal offence is committed. Article 5 (2) of the shipping pollution directive incorporates a defence of 'due diligence' for pollution discharges: 'A discharge of polluting substances into the [straits, EEZ and the high seas] shall not be regarded as an infringement for the owner, the master or the crew when acting under the master's responsibility if it satisfies the conditions set out in Annex I, Regulation 11 (b) (...)'. This provision aims to implement MARPOL which itself contains an exception for discharges resulting from damage to a ship or its equipment (e.g. following a collision), so that the owner, the master or the crew are to be held accountable only if they acted with intent to cause damage to the ship or with 'recklessness with the knowledge that damage would probably result'.[140] However, this defence under the shipping pollution directive only applies to pollution discharges in international straits, the EEZ of a Member State or the high seas, but not for discharges in the territorial seas. Therefore, by making the defence of 'due diligence' unavailable in the case of discharges in the territorial sea, the shipping pollution directive could be in conflict with MARPOL.[141]

---

138 See Article 6 of the shipping pollution directive.

139 Directive 2009/123/EC of the European Parliament and of the Council of 21 October 2009 amending Directive 2005/35/EC on ship-source pollution and on the introduction of penalties for infringements; *Official Journal,* L 280/52. 27.10.2009.

140 See Regulation 11 of Annex I to MARPOL. Those provisions are equivalent to those under Regulation 6, Annex II to MARPOL (which however deal with noxious liquid substances in bulk, rather than oil or oily mixtures).

141 Moreover, under the Directive acts of all persons (including the crew) could give rise to liability for accidental discharges, whereas the liability for similar discharges under MARPOL is limited to the master or owner.

Furthermore, under the shipping pollution directive the EU member states must prescribe criminal sanctions against serious illegal pollution discharges not only in European waters, but also in the high seas.[142] These are 'prescriptive' standards set by the Directive, and not 'enforcement' standards (despite a few exceptions). So the enforcement powers of the EU member states in the high seas to control pollution remain restricted by the principle of exclusive flag state jurisdiction, but not their prescriptive power to introduce environmental criminal offences for discharges occurring in the high seas (therefore, the Member States can enforce the EU regulatory standards for pollution offences occurring in the high seas if the vessel voluntarily docks in a EU port).[143]

6.5.2 *Biodiversity-Related Crimes*

Trade in Endangered Species

The Convention on Biological Diversity (CBD) was negotiated since 1988 and concluded in the Rio conference on Environment and Development ('the Earth Summit' in 1992, UNCED)[144] with the main objectives to ensure the conservation of biodiversity as well as the sustainable use of biological resources (both *in situ* and *ex situ*)[145] and the access to and benefit sharing of genetic resources. It entered into force on 29 December 1993 and has presently virtual universal participation.[146]

As it was adopted in the form of a 'framework convention', the CBD largely leaves it to individual states to determine how best to implement its legal provisions. This technique is unlike that deployed in other biodiversity-related agreements, such as the Convention on International Trade in Endangered Species of Fauna and Flora (CITES, 1973).[147] CITES regulates international

142 See Article 3 (1) (e) *ibid.*

143 This position is confirmed in the *Aviation Emissions* case (C-366/10, judgement of 21 December 2011), in which the CJEU held that the European Union has the power to apply higher environmental standards in the high seas than international law, despite the lack of consensus in the assigned international organisation (ICAO) to harmonise aviation emissions standards (see paras. 106, 108 and 126).

144 Convention on Biological Diversity (1992) 1760 UNTS 79; 31 ILM 81.

145 See Articles 8 and 9, *CBD*.

146 With 196 parties – although the United States has still not yet ratified it – the CBD is one of the most widely ratified international environmental agreements. The Unites States initially refused to sign it for threatening to delay development of biotechnology and for not sufficiently protecting ideas. President Clinton signed the Convention but the US congress has not ratified it. See further, Birnie et al., *International Law & the Environment* (OUP, 2009).

147 Convention on International Trade in Endangered Species of Fauna and Flora 27 UST 1087; TIAS 8249; 993 UNTS 243. CITES was signed in Washington DC by 21 countries on 3 March 1973 and entered into force on 1 January 1975.

trade in specimens of species of wild fauna and flora with specific trade restrictions and requirements for specific lists of species, i.e., export, re-export and import of live and dead animals and plants and of parts and derivatives thereof, based on a system of permits and certificates which can be issued if certain conditions are met. It establishes a permit system for species listed in three appendices which aims to ensure that listed species of wild fauna and flora are not subject to unsustainable exploitation linked to illegal cross-country trade.[148] Depending on which annex a species feature, trade is either prohibited, restricted or permissible under certain conditions.[149] Significantly, there is an express requirement under CITES for states to enforce its provisions through criminal penalties.[150]

The Council of Europe convention requires state parties to establish as 'criminal or administrative offences' the 'unlawful possession, taking, damaging, killing or trading of or in protected wild flora and fauna species'.[151] So one of the significant weaknesses of the CoE environmental crime convention, as was discussed above, is that it relegates the biodiversity-related offences to Article 4 (in relation to which there is no obligation for states to penalise).[152]

The obligations of the EU Member States under the Convention on Trade in Endangered Species were implemented under the CITES EU Regulation 338/1997.[153] This Regulation calls on Member States to impose sanctions for a

---

148 See http://www.cites.org/eng/app/appendices.php (accessed on 15 February 2015).

149 Trade of Annex I species is forbidden as they are threatened with extinction. Appendix II species are those not threatened with extinction but which may become if trade is not controlled and monitored. A licence from the exporting state is required. Appendix III includes all species identified as subject to regulation in their jurisdiction and requiring interstate cooperation to control trade. See *ibid.*

150 Under Art 8, par. 1,; the parties to CITES must 'penalise trade in, or possession of, such specimens, or both' and to 'provide for the confiscation or return to the State of export of such specimens'. Moreover, CITES requires state parties to take appropriate measures to enforce its provisions.

151 Article 4 (g) of the CoE environmental crime convention.

152 See Article 4 (f) of the CoE Convention: 'unlawful trade, possession, damaging (...) of protected wild flora and fauna species'; and Article 4 (g) of the convention: 'changes detrimental to natural components of a national park, natural reserve (...) and other protected areas'. This is despite the fact that the Explanatory Memorandum recognises, in relation to Paragraph (g) that ['c]onducts described in this paragraph are in virtually all member States an offence sanctioned at least by fines but often by criminal measures, though in this case they may require additional qualifying elements (e.g. that the protected animal is threatened by extinction or that the perpetrator acted in a professional manner with the aim to make illegal profits)'.

153 Council Regulation (EC) No 338/97 of 9 December 1996 on the Protection of Species of Wild Fauna and Flora by Regulating Trade Therein and Commission Regulation (EC) No

series of infringements.[154] It specifies that specimens listed in Annex B or C 'must be seized' if they arrive at an entry point without 'the appropriate valid permit or certificate'.[155] These measures 'shall be appropriate to the nature and gravity of the infringement'[156] and shall include provisions for seizure and 'where appropriate, confiscation of specimens'.[157] Although Article 16 (2) of the Regulation calls on the Member States to adopt 'appropriate sanctions', it falls short of requiring that member states introduce criminal sanctions (as required under CITES). This is unsurprising as the Regulation was adopted in 1997 under the former EC 'first pillar', so before powers in criminal matters were recognized to the EC. Moreover, although Regulations are directly applicable in all EU Member States (see Chapter 4), the necessary enforcement provisions of the CITES Regulation, including penalties, must be transposed into national laws for enforcement of its provisions by the national authorities.

Under the EU environmental crime directive, the offence of 'possession/damaging specimens of protected wild fauna and flora species' present in the 2007 environmental crime directive proposal[158] was 'split' into two separate offences in the final text of the directive adopted in 2008. The first offence under the final text of the Directive is the 'killing, destruction, possession or taking' of specimens;[159] and the second is the 'trading in' specimens.[160] Only in the latter case ('trading in') are Member States required to criminalise conduct affecting 'parts or derivatives' of protected specimens. This division did not appear in the original 2007 environmental crime directive proposal, which hence provided more extensive protection for 'parts or derivatives' of protected wild fauna or flora species against '[killing], possession or taking'.[161] The main reason for this 'split' is that each of those offences relates to different pieces of Community legislation which provide for different definitions of and protection for 'wild

939/97 of May 1997 laying down detailed rules concerning the implementation of Council Regulation (EC) No 339/97 was adopted. See also, Commission Regulation (EU) No 1320/2014 of 1 December 2014 amending Council Regulation (EC) No 338/97 on the protection of species of wild fauna and flora by regulating trade therein.

154 See Article 16 (1) of the EU CITES Regulation, *ibid.*

155 Article 16 (4) *ibid.*

156 Article 16 (2) *ibid.*

157 *Ibid.*

158 Article 3 (f) of the 2007 environmental crime proposal.

159 Article 3 (f) of the environmental crime directive.

160 Article 3 (g) of the environmental crime directive Article 3 (d) of the proposal.

161 Moreover, the final text added 'destruction' of the specimens and did not retain 'damaging' thereof, which was present in the 2007 directive proposal.

fauna and flora species'.[162] Indeed, 'trading in' species (falling under Article 3 [g] of the environmental crime directive) concerns the EU obligations to comply with the enforcement provisions under CITES;[163] while the offence under Article 3 (f) of the environmental crime directive relate to violations of other EU biodiversity laws, in particular the Habitats Directive[164] and Birds Directive.[165]

Moreover, there is a requirement for a specific threshold of environmental damage for those offences under the Directive.[166] That is, under the final text of the Directive those activities need not be criminalised if 'the conduct concerns a negligible quantity of such specimens and has a negligible impact on the conservation status of the species'.[167] Given the vagueness of the terms 'negligible quantity' and 'negligible impact', it is expected that there will be considerable differences in the way national administrative and judicial authorities in the Member States will interpret those criminal offences. Yet the national implementing measure may adopt stricter standards and criminalise even conduct which has a negligible impact on the conservation status of species. Alternatively it could be argued that the Directive creates rights for individuals (in this case the polluter or smuggler) and they might potentially have a defence based on the Directive against the prosecution for negligible environmental damage to protected species.[168] However, this line of reasoning would be difficult to reconcile with the general objective that the directive

---

162 See Article 2 (b) of the environmental crime directive: '[f]or the purposes of Article 3 (f), "protected wild fauna and flora species" are those listed in Annex IV to Council Directive 92/43/EEC of 21 May 1992 on conservation of natural habitats and of wild fauna and flora (OJ 206, 22.7.1992, p. 7) and Annex I, and referred to in Annex 4 (2) of, Council Directive 79/409/EEC of 2 April 1979 on the conservation of wild birds (OJ L 103, 25.4.1979, p.1) whereas for the purposes of Article 3 (g) they are listed in Annex A or B of Council Regulation (EC) No 338/97 of 9 December 1996 on the protection of species of wild fauna and flora by regulating trade therein (OJ L 61, 3.3.1997, p. 1.)'.

163 Council Regulation (EC) No 338/97 of 9 December 1996 on the protection of species of wild fauna and flora by regulating trade therein (OJ L 61, 3.3.1997, p. 1).

164 Council Directive 92/43/EEC of 21 May 1992 on conservation of natural habitats and of wild fauna and flora (OJ 206, 22.7.1992, p. 7).

165 Council Directive 79/409/EEC of 2 April 1979 on the conservation of wild birds (OJ L 103, 25.4.1979, p.1).

166 As suggested by the Council Working Group on Substantive Criminal Law 5587/08 DROIPEN 3 ENV 30 CODEC 78, 28 January 2008 p. 6.

167 See Article 3 (f) and (g). Under the annulled Framework Decision on environmental crime, this conduct did not need to be criminalised if the protected species are not '*threatened with extinction as defined under national law*'. See Article 2, (f).

168 See Chapter 4.

adopts minimum standards only.[169] As was discussed in chapter 4, the Austrian 2011 implementing law fails to implement Article 3 (f) and (g) of the EU environmental crime directive correctly by requiring that a 'significant amount of species' are affected, rather than allowing for a defence in case the activity has 'a negligible impact on the conservation status of species'. It should be noted that neither the EU CITES Regulation, nor the the Habitats or Birds directives themselves contain an exception for activities which have a 'negligible impact on species', so such activities could still remain prohibited under EU environmental law, albeit not amounting to a criminal offence.

Offences against Protected Habitats

The EU Habitats Directive,[170] together with the Birds Directive,[171] form the cornerstone of Europe's nature conservation policy. The Habitats Directive is based on a system of 'Designation of Special Areas of Conservation (SAC)' with view of setting a coherent European ecological network of such areas under the Natura 2000.[172] It includes two Appendices listing the sites of Community interest and those habitats that require protection. The Habitats and Birds Directives could be regarded as a reflection of the standards found in the Council of Europe Bern Convention on the Conservation of European Wildlife and Natural Habitats.[173] It should be noted that the first international agreement to protect one specific habitat was the Ramsar Convention on Wetlands.[174]

The EU environmental crime directive requires the criminalisation of 'any [unlawful] conduct which causes the significant deterioration of a habitat within a protected site'.[175] 'Habitat within a protected site' is defined under the environmental crime directive as any habitat of species in an area which is classified as a special protection area pursuant to Article 4 (1) or (2) of the Birds Directive (Directive 79/409/EEC), or any natural habitat or a habitat of species

169 See Recital 12 of the environmental crime directive.

170 Council Directive 92/43/EEC of 21 May 1992 on conservation of natural habitats and of wild fauna and flora (OJ 206, 22.7.1992, p. 7).

171 Directive 2009/147/EC of the European Parliament and of the Council of 30 November 2009 on the conservation of wild birds (codified version); Council Directive 79/409/EEC of 2 April 1979 on the conservation of wild birds (OJ L 103, 25.4.1979, p.1).

172 Art 3 (1) *ibid.*

173 Convention on the Conservation of European Wildlife and Natural Habitats CETS No.:104 ('The Berne Convention'). The EC is not a party to this convention.

174 Convention on Wetlands of International Importance especially as Waterfowl Habitat, 996 UNTS 245; TIAS 11084; 11 ILM 963 (1972).

175 Article 3 (h) of the environmental crime directive.

in relation to which a site is designated as a special area of conservation pursuant to Article 4 (4) of the Habitats Directive (Directive 92/43/EEC).[176]

The corresponding offence under the original 2007 environmental crime proposal did not contain the conditions relating to 'any conduct' or 'which causes'.[177] It appears that, with the addition of 'any conduct' under the final text of the environmental crime directive, omissions would not need to be criminalised. Moreover, the addition of 'which causes' suggests that Member States are not required to criminalise endangerment activities (i.e. conduct which 'is likely to cause' environmental damage).

One considerable shortcoming of both the EU and CoE environmental crime instruments is that they not address directly forestry crimes in the context of illegal logging. This is a considerable deficiency of those environmental crime instruments in light of the fact that, at present, there is no global legally finding treaty which directly addresses illegal logging. The 1994 International Timber Organisation (ITO) Tropical Timber Agreement, as amended in 2006, is a commodities agreement (among others relating to trade in natural resources) rather than a treaty aimed at preventing illegal logging.[178] However, the EU FLEGT Action Plan was adopted in 2003 in order to prevent the import of illegally sourced timber into the EU.[179] At the regional level, one positive development concerning intestate cooperation against illegal logging is the Lusaka Agreement on Co-operative Enforcement Operations Directed at Illegal Trade in Wild Fauna and Flora, which was adopted in 1994 and became operational in 1996 (see also, chapter 3).[180] The convention aims to facilitate cross-border co-operation; exchange of information and intelligence; enhancement

176 Article 2 (c) *ibid.*

177 The offence under Article 3 (h) of the 2007 directive proposal is 'the unlawful significant deterioration of a protected habitat'.

178 International Tropical Timber Agreement, 2006, United Nations Conference on Trade And Development, Distr. General Td/Timber.3/12 1 February 2006. See also the United Nations Conference for the Negotiation of a Successor Agreement to the International Tropical Timber Agreement (1994) Fourth Part Geneva, 16–27 January 2006. Its main principle is that forests should be managed and conserved by national authorities. It also provides for financial incentives for sustainable forest management (Preamble (f)).

179 Brussels, 21.5.2003 COM (2003) 251 Final Communication from the Commission to the Council And The European Parliament Forest Law Enforcement, Governance and Trade (FLEGT) Proposal for an EU Action Plan.

180 Lusaka Agreement on Co-operative Enforcement Operations Directed at Illegal Trade in Wild Fauna. and Flora. Lusaka, 8 September 1994 . United Nations, *Treaty Series*, vol. 1950, p. 35.

of wildlife law enforcement capacities; as well as investigations of crime with approval of the state parties in Africa.[181]

Illegal, Unreported and Unregulated (IUU) Fishing

Another shortcoming from the perspective of biodiversity protection is that neither the EU environmental crime directive nor the CoE Convention on environmental crime require state parties to criminalise illegal fishing. In the EU, the competence to legislate on common fisheries policies belongs exclusively to the EU, and so it is not shared with the member states.[182] On the basis of the principle of loyal cooperation, member states must implement 'effective, proportionate and dissuassive' penalties for implementation of EU fisheries laws. Moreover, illegal fishing poses significant challenges for international regulation. The UN Food and Agriculture Organisation (FAO) has been particularly engaged in seeking to adopt international measures to combat illegal, unregulated and unreported fishing (IUU) fishing. In 2001 the FAO adopted an Action Plan to control illegal, unregulated and unreported fishing. This action plan calls on states to adopt sanctions which are 'of sufficient severity'.[183] However, this Action Plan is non-binding. Although the subsequent 2009 FAO Agreement on Port State Measures to control, deter and prevent IUU[184] is a promising mechanism – as it gives powers to ports to reject vessel engaged in IUU – this Agreement is unlikely to be ratified by flag-of-convenience states.[185] In this

181 At the time of writing, there are seven state parties to the Lusuka Agreement (Congo, Kenya, Lesotto, Liberia, Uganda, Tanzania, and Zambia).

182 Article 3 (1) (d) TFEU.

183 See the voluntary 2001 FAO *International Plan Of Action To Prevent, Deter And Eliminate Illegal, Unreported And Unregulated Fishing:* (21) States should ensure that sanctions for IUU fishing (...) are of sufficient severity to effectively prevent, deter and eliminate IUU fishing and to deprive offenders of the benefits accruing from such fishing'. It adds that '[t]his may include the adoption of a civil sanction regime based on an administrative penalty scheme'. Therefore, the FAO IUU Action Plan falls short of requiring states to adopt criminal sanctions.

184 2009 FAO Agreement on Port State Measures to Prevent, Deter and Eliminate Illegal, Unreported and Unregulated Fishing.

185 The FAO Port State Measures agreement is not yet in force. At the time of writing, there are 11 parties to it (25 ratifications are required for it to enter into force). The main problem with relying on flag state enforcement is that some states offer open registries (and are commonly known as 'flag of convenience' states) thus allowing foreign vessels to register to evade the higher regulatory standards found elsewhere. The International Tribunal on the Law of the Sea (ITLOS) has failed to rule that these open registries are per se illegal. See the *Saiga N. 2* case in which ITLOS interpreted generously the requirement under UNCLOS that the vessel must have a *'genuine link'* with the flag State. The Tribunal could not see in this

regard, one encouraging initiative is the 1993 FAO's Compliance Agreement on Fishing Vessels in the High Seas (in force since 2003)[186] which establishes a number of flag state responsibilities for their fishing vessels in the high seas.[187] In particular, it aims to prevent vessels from re-flagging by establishing that 'no Party shall authorize any fishing vessel previously registered in the territory of another Party that has undermined the effectiveness of international conservation and management measures to be used for fishing on the high seas (…)'.[188] It also states that '[s]anctions applicable in respect of such contraventions shall be of sufficient gravity as to be effective in securing compliance with the requirements of this Agreement and to deprive offenders of the benefits accruing from their illegal activities' and that '[s]uch sanctions shall, for serious offences, include refusal, suspension or withdrawal of the authorization to fish on the high seas'.[189]

A promising recent measure to combat illegal fishing is the EU Regulation to control IUU[190] which, like the FAO IUU Action Plan, also focuses on on port state measures.[191] Article 44 (2) of the Regulation requires Member States to take action against their nationals if they are found to be involved in IUU fishing and apply the maximum sanction of at least five times the value of the fishery products obtained by IUU fishing. Yet the Regulation leaves it to Member States the choice of introducing either administrative or criminal penalties, as long as they are 'effective, dissuasive, and proportionate'.[192] Two studies conducted for the European Parliament on sanctions against IUU published in 2014 suggested that the actual penalties provided by the Member States against illegal fishing vary, with some EU Member States dealing with violations of fisheries laws primarily under the criminal law[193] while others,

---

requirement a ground for other states to contest the nationality of a vessel. See The M/V 'SAIGA' (No. 2) Case (Saint Vincent and the Grenadines v. Guinea).

186 1993 Agreement to Promote Compliance with International Conservation and Management Measures by Fishing Vessels on The High Seas, 2221 UNTS 91.

187 Article 3 *ibid.*

188 Article 3 (5) (a) *ibid.*

189 Article 3 (8) *ibid.*

190 Council Regulation (EC) No 1005/2008 of 29 September 2008 establishing a Community system to prevent, deter and eliminate illegal, unreported and unregulated fishing, amending Regulations (EEC) No 2847/93, (EC) No 1936/2001 and (EC) No 601/2004 and repealing Regulations (EC) No 1093/94 and (EC) No 1447/1999.

191 It requires the EU member states to designate specific ports in which a minimum of at least of 5% of landing and transhipments must be inspected (Article 9 (1) *ibid*).

192 See Article 44 (1) and (4).

193 Belgium, Finland, Ireland, Italy, Netherlands, Sweden; and the United Kingdom (which applies a mixed system of sanctions). Blomeyer & Sanz (2014). *The CFP- infringement procedures and*

such as France, supplement these with administrative sanctions.[194] Some Member States apply predominantly administrative and civil sanctions against IUU.[195] Overall, it has been noted that in most Member States, administrative authorities impose sanctions for fisheries infringements, while some apply criminal procedures in cases involving serious infringements.[196] In a 2001 Green Paper the European Commission considered the harmonisation of penalties against IUU across the EU,[197] but no specific proposals were adopted.[198]

6.5.3 *Trade in and Illegal Disposal of Hazardous Wastes and other Dangerous Substances or Organisms*

Waste Offences

The Basel Convention on the Transboundary Movement of Hazardous Waste is the main global agreement concerning the transboundary movement of hazardous wastes,[199] while a number of other treaties address the dumping of wastes into the oceans.[200] In this context, both the global Basel Convention on the Transboundary Movement of Hazardous Waste and the regional Bamako Convention[201] contain

---

imposed sanctions throughout the EU, at 37, available at: http://www.europarl.europa.eu/RegData/etudes/note/join/2014/514003/IPOL-PECH_NT(2014)514003_EN.pdf (accessed on 15 April 2015).

194 See M. Beke, and R. Blomeyer, *Illegal, Unreported and Unregulated Fishing: Sanctions in the EU: Study* (2004) at 51, available at http://www.europarl.europa.eu/RegData/etudes/STUD/2014/529069/IPOL_STU%282014%29529069_EN.pdf (accessed on 15 April 2015).

195 Bulgaria, Croatia, Cyprus, Denmark, Estonia, France (mixed), Germany, Greece, Latvia, Lithuania, Malta, Poland, Portugal, Romania, Slovenia, and Spain. Blomeyer & Sanz (2014) *supra* at 37.

196 *Ibid* at 31.

197 'A third element in this package would be to explore ways of improving the dissuasiveness of penalties for infringement, including "administrative" penalties such as loss of fishing quota, withdrawal of licences or repayment of financial aid for vessels which infringe fisheries regulations'. See *Green Paper On The Future Of The Common Fisheries Policy* /* COM/2001/0135 final.

198 '(...) proposals to strengthen Community rules and to increase the powers of Community inspectors did not obtain agreement from the Member States'. *Ibid.*

199 *See* the 1989 Basel Convention on the Transboundary Movement of Hazardous Waste (entry into force on 5 May 1992) United Nations, *Treaty Series*, vol. 1673, p. 57.

200 *See* in particular, the 1972 London Convention on the Prevention of Marine Pollution by Dumping of Wastes and Other Matter 1046 UNTS 120 / ATS 1985 No 16 / 11 ILM 1294 / UKTS 43 (1976) and the 1996 Protocol to the London Convention on the Prevention of Marine Pollution by Dumping of Wastes and Other Matter 36 ILM 1 (1997).

201 1991 Bamako Convention on the Ban of the Import into Africa and the Control of Transboundary Movement and Management of Hazardous Wastes Within Africa.

competitors is met by a firm response from the public and judicial authorities. This firm response shall include the possibility of imprisonment, substantial fines and licence revocation, in particular in the case of rogue operators.

Furthermore, is suggested that there should be no *a priori* hierarchy between the different penalties available to public authorities (discussed in Chapter 6) or the enforcement strategies discussed in this chapter. The use of criminal, administrative or civil enforcement must be based on specific criteria such as the seriousness of the environmental harm, culpability and recidivism. It is thus not necessary for the regulator to exhaust all the conciliatory strategies and administrative measures before it seeks a criminal prosecution as a form of back-up enforcement mechanism. Otherwise companies would have little incentive to abide by the rules if 'carrots' were always offered before the 'sticks'. However, the gradual law enforcement (according to which the criminal sanction is only applied when all other measures have been exhausted) may be established in the law of some Member States, that is, less severe sanctions must be applied prior to the more stringent ones.[116] Moreover, as will be further discussed below, the environmental crime directive or ship-source pollution directive do not affect the enforcement choices of the Member States, as there is no obligation for the authorities in the Member States to bring prosecutions in individual cases.

Finally, it should be noted that the studies discussed in this chapter provide evidence of the difficulties faced by each mechanism for environmental law enforcement which raises procedural law questions that go beyond the effectiveness of substantive law. Since the Directive on environmental crimes focus on the harmonisation of substantive criminal law and it does not affect the enforcement choices of the Member States, it is doubtful that it could remedy to a significant extent all the problems of legal enforcement which were highlighted in this chapter.

7.8 Assessing the need for *Harmonisation* of Environmental Criminal Law

The objectives of the directive on environmental crimes, according to the Commission, are to ensure a high level of environmental protection throughout the Community/Union and to improve the implementation and enforcement deficit of EC environmental law; to improve police and judicial cooperation in criminal matters in the EU; and to create a level playing field for

116 For example in Poland and Lithuania. See 'Study on non-criminal measures in Candidate Countries' above note 4, at 14.

businesses that comply with environmental legislation and avoid safe-havens for criminals in the Community/Union.[117]

This section discusses whether the harmonisation of environmental criminal law in the EU would enable the accomplishment of those objectives.

7.8.1 *The Improvement of the Implementation Deficit of EU Environmental Law*

The need to establish effective enforcement mechanisms to give effect to obligations related to the environment remains one of the major challenges in the area of international and European environmental law. The development of rules of international and European law concerning the protection of the environment is of very little relevance if not accompanied by effective means of enforcement and compliance.[118]

The Commission points out that although the responsibility for implementation of EU environmental legislation rests primarily with the Member States, it is the essential task for the Commission under Article 17 (1) TEU[119] as the guardian of the Treaties, to ensure the full application, enforcement and implementation of all existing Community legislation, which was a strategic priority highlighted in the both the 6th Environment Action Programme[120] and the 7th Environment Action Programme which will be guiding EU environmental policy until 2020.[121]

One of the central goals of the environmental crime directive is to ensure a more effective application of EU environmental law.[122] The lack of satisfactory implementation of EC environmental law was one of the facts that triggered the Commission's proposal. The Explanatory Memorandum of the Directive proposal on environmental crimes states that:

> Experience has shown that the sanctions currently established by the member states are not always sufficient to achieve full compliance with Community law. Not all member states provide for criminal sanctions

117 2007 Impact Assessment, above note 49, at 3.

118 See McLaughlin, R. 'Improving Compliance: Making Non-State International Actors Responsible for Environmental Crimes', 11 *Colorado Journal of International Law and Policy* (2000) at 377.

119 Article 17 (1) TEU is equivalent to former Article 211 EC.

120 See 2007 Impact Assessment, above note 49, at 23.

121 See Decision No 1386/2013/EU of the European Parliament and of the Council of 20 November 2013 on a General Union Environment Action Programme to 2020 'Living well, within the limits of our planet', Priority Objective 4, Point 57.

122 See Article 1 of the environmental crime directive.

> against the most serious breaches of Community law protecting the environment.[123]

The Fourth Annual Survey (2002) and 6th Annual Survey (2004) on the implementation and enforcement of Community environmental law suggested that complaints for breaches of environmental law accounted for over one third of all infringement cases investigated by the Commission.[124] As a result of those complaints, the Commission brought 65 cases in 2002 against Member States before the Court and issued 137 reasoned opinions on the basis of Article 258 TFEU (ex-Article 226 EC). Moreover, according to the 29th annual report on monitoring the application of EU law,[125] in 2009 alone there were 451 infringement cases related to Union environment legislation, with a further 299 reported in 2011 together with an additional 114 new proceedings being initiated,[126] which makes the environment *acquis* the area of Union law with most infringement proceedings.[127] In a similar vein, in a 2008 Communication on the implementation of EC environmental law the Commission has expressed concerns over the lack of of implementation of key pieces of EC environmental legislation.[128]

7.8.1.1 The Enforcement Powers of the European Commission and Court of Justice

The European Union institutions are not marked by any rigid separation of powers.[129] The European Commission exercises administrative, executive, legislative and even judicial powers.[130] The powers of the Commission are set out in Article 17 (1) TEU[131] which aim to ensure that the provisions of the Treaty and measures taken by the institutions are applied. The general powers of

---

123 Explanatory Memorandum, *Proposal for a Directive on the Protection of the Environment through Criminal Law*, 2007/0022 (COD).

124 See Commission Staff Working Paper, SEC 2003 804.

125 29th annual report on monitoring the application of EU law (2011) (COM(2012) 714).

126 *Ibid.*

127 7th Environment Action Programme, above note, Point 56.

128 See Communication from the Commission to the European Parliament, the Council, the European Economic and Social Committee and the Committee of the regions on Implementing European Community Environmental Law. Brussels, 18.11.2008 COM (2008) 773 final.

129 See Craig, P. and de Burca, G., *EU Law: Text, Cases and Materials* (Oxford, 2007) at 59.

130 For example, in the context of EU competition law.

131 Equivalent to Article 211 EC.

enforcement actions that may be brought against Member States for breach of EU law are set out in article 258 TFEU:

> If the Commission considers that a member state has failed to fulfil an obligation under the Treaty, it shall deliver a reasoned opinion on the matter after giving the state concerned the opportunity to submit its observations. If the State concerned does not comply with the opinion within the period laid down by the Commission, the latter may bring the matter before the Court.

It follows from the foregoing that the Commission cannot apply sanctions directly against Member States who fail to implement or breach Community law, as proceedings need to be instituted before the Court of Justice. The Commission starts Article 258 TFEU proceedings either in response to a complaint from an individual in a Member State, or on its own initiative.[132] The Commission relies heavily on third parties to bring complaints to its attention (e.g. injured parties, NGOs). The individual complaints from individuals constitute a significant source for the detection of infringements, but it is not intended to provide individuals with a means of redress but rather to ensure compliance with EU law.[133] Moreover, the Commission must institute proceedings before the CJEU on the basis of the Article 258 TFEU (ex Article 226 EC) procedure against the Member State for its failure to implement EU environmental law, rather than the individual polluter. This indirect application of sanctions is arguably not very effective to ensure compliance with EU environmental law.[134] But the procedure introduced under Article 260 TFEU (ex Article 228 EC) by the 1992 Maastricht Treaty, which allows the Commission to seek financial penalties against Member States that fail to comply with an Article 258 TFEU judgement, can indeed provide a strong incentive for compliance.[135] On the other hand, the Commission has discretion as to whether to institute proceedings under Articles 258 or 260 TFEU;[136] and the CJEU is reluctant to

---

132 Craig, P. and de Burca, G, above note 129, at 398.

133 *Ibid* at 389.

134 Lee (2005), above note 28, at 55.

135 See Case C-304/02 of 12 July 2005, in which the European Court of Justice (ECJ) ordered France to pay an unprecedented sum of €20 million and a periodic 6-month penalty of €57,761,250 running from that day, for failing to comply with a 1991 Court ruling on serious failings in its enforcement of fisheries rules.

136 See Davies, P. *European Union Environmental Law: an Introduction to Key Selected Issues*, Ashgate (2004) at 83. See also, Pal Wenneras, A *New Dawn for Commission Enforcement under Articles 226 and 228 EC: General and Persistent Infringements, Lump Sums and*

allow private parties to challenge the Commission's discretion to bring action under article 258 TFEU.[137] Yet the Commission does have a duty under Article 17 (1) TEU to ensure that the Treaties are applied.[138]

Although the fines applied by the CJEU can potentially be very high, they have not been frequently applied in practice.[139] This can be explained by the fact that the Member State can negotiate with the Commission under Article 258 TFEU before the judicial proceedings are instituted. Most cases tend to be settled at that stage, given the Commission's strong negotiating position and the threat of judicial proceedings and fine. This could be a disincentive for compliance *ex ante*, given that a fine may only be sought and applied after this negotiating phase.[140] Under the reforms brought by the Lisbon Treaty to Articles 258 and 260 TFEU, a second reasoned opinion from the Commission is no longer necessary,[141] which is expected to enhance to a certain degree the speed of the Article 260 proceedings.[142] Another innovation brought by the Lisbon Treaty is paragraph 3 to Article 260 TFEU, which regulates the imposition of financial penalties for a Member State's failure to transpose EU legislation.[143]

Penalty Payments, Common Market Law Review 43, 2006, 31; Kilbey, *'Financial Penalties under Article 228 (2): Excessive Complexity?',* Common Market Law Review 44, (2007); Wenneras, *The Enforcement of EC Environmental Law* (OUP, 2007); Hedemman-Robinson, *Enforcement of European Union Environmental Law: Legal Issues and Challenges* (Routledge, 2006).

137 See e.g. Case 247/87 *Star Fruit v. Commission* [1989] ECR 291–302.

138 Horspool, M. and Humphreys, M. *European Union Law* (OUP, Oxford 2006) at 230.

139 It has been suggested that before the end of 2010, the ECJ had applied fines in infringement proceedings fewer than 15 times. See Smith, M., 'Inter-institutional dialogue and the establishment of enforcement norms: A decade of financial penalties under Article 228 EC', (2010) 16 *European Public Law*, 4.

140 See *ibid.* See also, Pereira, R. 'Compliance and Enforcement in International, European and National Environmental Law' in Makuch, K. and Pereira, R. (eds.) *Environmental and Energy Law* (Wiley-Blackwell, 2012).

141 See 260 (2) TFEU.

142 See some of the CJEU decisions post-Lisbon on the basis of Article 260 TFEU: Commission v France C-121/07; Commission v Belgium (C-533/11); Commission v Luxembourg (C-576/11); *Commission v Ireland* (C-374/11).

143 On the application of Articles 258 and 260 TFEU after the ratification of the Lisbon Treaty, see Smith, M. (2010), above note 139; Peers, S. 'Sanctions for Infringement of EU law after the Lisbon Treaty', (2012) 33 *European Public Law*; Andersen, S. *The Enforcement of EU Law: The Role of the European Commission* (OUP, 2012). Jack, B. *'Enforcing Member States Compliance with EU Environmental Law: A Critical Evaluation of the Use of Financial Penalties'*, Journal of Environmental Law 23:1, 2010; Sibylle Grohs, 'Articles 258/260 TFEU Infringement Procedures: The Commission Perspective in Environmental Cases' in Marisa Cremona (ed.) *Compliance and the Enforcement of EU Law* (OUP, 2012).

As regards the implementation of EU ship-source pollution legislation, the Commission has issued reasoned opinions to a number of Member States (including Malta, Cyprus, Estonia, France, Portugal, Finland, Luxembourg and the UK) on 28 November 2007 which had not implemented the 2005 shipping pollution directive under national law by the transposition deadline.[144] In its decision in Case C-557/08 in 9 July 2009,[145] the court ruled that 'by failing to adopt the necessary laws, regulations and administrative provisions necessary to comply with the directive, the United Kingdom has failed to fulfil its obligations under that directive'.[146] In June 2011, the Commission brought infringement proceedings against eight Member States (Czech Republic, Finland, Greece, Italy, Lithuania, Portugal, Romania and Slovakia) which had failed to implement the 2009 ship-source pollution (amending) directive by the November 2010 deadline.[147] The Commission subsequently dropped the infringement proceedings against Finland, Slovakia and Romania for non-implementation of the 2009 ship-source pollution amending directive.[148]

As regards the implementation of the EU environmental crime directive, the Commission has released reasoned opinions in June 2011 to eight Member States (Cyprus, the Czech Republic, Germany, Greece, Lithuania, Malta, Portugal and Slovenia); and subsequently to Austria, Finland, and the UK in October 2011 for failing to transpose the EU environmental crime directive correctly by the December 2010 deadline.[149] The Commission later dropped the cases brought against Italy and Romania for the non-implementation of the environmental crime directive.[150] In March 2012, the Commission brought infringement proceedings against Cyprus,[151] but subsequently dropped the cases against Greece and Finland who have communicated complete transposition of the environmental crime directive.[152]

144 See ECSA Newsletter, European Community's Shipowners' Association n. 7/07. www.ecsa.be/newsletters/077.pdf (accessed on 10 April 2015).

145 See Judgment of the Court (Fifth Chamber) of 9 July 2009 – Commission of the European Communities v United Kingdom of Great Britain and Northern Ireland (Case C-557/08).

146 *Ibid* para. 10.

147 See *Environmental crimes: Commission asks 12 Member States to implement EU rules*, Press Release, Brussels, 16 June 2011.

148 See *Environmental crimes: Commission continues legal action against Member States*, Press Release, Brussels, 27 October 2011.

149 *ibid.*

150 *Ibid.*

151 See *Environmental Crimes: Commission takes Cyprus to Court for failing to transpose EU rules*, Press Release, Brussels, 22 March 2012.

152 *Ibid.*

In practice there are many other documented difficulties faced by the Commission in ensuring that EU environmental law is properly implemented by Member States, for example the fact that the DG Environment is understaffed and the sharing of competence between some Member State's central government and the regions, which means that the Commission does not have to deal with only one piece of legislation but several ones.[153]

7.8.1.2 Enforcement of EU Environmental Law by the Member States

There is scope for the Member States to bring action before the CJ against other Member States for their non-compliance with EU environmental law (even if there is no direct violation of a right or interest of the former). This is recognised under Article 259 TFEU (ex Article 227 EC), which allows a Member State to take enforcement action against another member state for breach of EU law before the CJEU. However, such actions have been rare because of the likely political ramifications, and Member States generally prefer to rely on the Commission to take action for the non-compliance of other member states that do not affect their direct interests.[154]

There has been academic debate on whether Member States were required under the original proposal of the environmental crime directive not only to introduce criminal sanctions for serious violations of EC environmental law but also to *apply* them in individual cases. This question has obvious implications for the implementation of the directive and is connected to that of prosecutorial discretion in bringing prosecutions for environmental offences, as will be further analysed below. Commenting on the March 2001 directive proposal, Michael Faure argued that it did not leave room for states to apply sanctions other than criminal ones for the crimes listed in Article 3[155] and that Member States needed not only to introduce but also apply criminal sanctions, and a more differentiated approach in which they could apply either criminal or administrative sanctions in individual cases would not be possible. This view was shared by Corstens who asserted that the 2001 Commission's directive proposal left no room for Member States to deal with environmental offences committed intentionally or with serious negligence by means other than the criminal law.[156] According to Maria Lee, such an approach 'would be

153 See Davies, P. *European Union Environmental Law: an Introduction to Key Selected Issues*, (Ashgate, 2004) at 68.

154 One of the few examples of such actions is Case 141/78 *France v United Kingdom* [1979].

155 Faure (2004) above note 9, at 27.

156 Corstens, G.J.M., 'Criminal law in the first pillar?' (2003) *European Journal of Crime, Criminal Law and Criminal Justice*, 11/1 at 137.

a major step back for environmental law, flying in the face of decades of research on the flexibility of effective law enforcement'[157] and could 'ultimately (...) be corrosive of the stigmatising power of the criminal law'.[158] However she points out that 'sole reliance on criminal law is probably not a necessary interpretation of the Commission's proposal, and is certainly nowhere stated'.[159] The February 2007 environmental crime directive proposal stated that 'Member States shall ensure that the commission of the offences referred to in Articles 3 and 4 is *punishable* by effective, proportionate and dissuasive criminal sanctions'[160] (emphasis added), which seems to allow for flexible implementation by Member States as regards the choice of applying either administrative or criminal sanctions in individual cases.[161] This provision was maintained in the final text of the Directive,[162] although without specifying the types and levels of penalties. Moreover, Recital 10 of the environmental crime directive makes it clear that '[the] Directive creates no obligations regarding the *application* of [criminal penalties], or any other available system of law enforcement, in individual cases' (emphasis added), which should leave no further doubt as to the discretionary enforcement powers left to the national authorities in the Member States.[163]

A similar interpretation is applicable to the Council of Europe environmental crime convention, which requires the criminalisation of serious environmental offences, rather than requiring the application of criminal sanctions in individual cases.[164]

157 Lee, M. (2005) above n. 28, at 72.

158 *Ibid.*

159 *Ibid.* In fact, the Explanatory Memorandum to the 2001 directive proposal stated that '[i]t is up to the judicial authorities in the Member States to decide whether the offences according to Article 3 must be prosecuted in any individual case or whether they provide for possibilities to refrain from imposing criminal penalties in minor cases, where the impact on the environment is insignificant'. So it does not appear that Commission's intention ever was to intervene so heavily with the national environmental enforcement mechanisms in individual cases. See Section 3 (c) p. 4 of the proposal.

160 2007/0022 (COD), art 5 par. 1.

161 It should be noted that the *electa una via* principle may restrict the ability of national enforcement agencies to apply both administrative and criminal sanctions for the same act (see Chapter 2).

162 Article 5 of the environmental crime directive.

163 Recital 10 was inserted into the directive as a suggestion of the Report of the European Parliament, Committee on Legal Affairs, Rapporteur: Hartmut Nassauer, 15 February 2008 at 7.

164 See Article 2 (1) of the CoE environmental crime convention.

7.8.1.3 The Legislative Procedure and CJ Jurisdiction

The procedures for adoption of EU environmental legislative measures and regarding the CJ jurisdiction under the former 'first pillar' framework remains largely unchanged following the ratification Lisbon Treaty. Post-Lisbon the ordinary legislative procedure (formerly 'co-decision procedure') is applicable for the adoption of EU criminal law measures, which implies the use of qualified majority voting in the Council and co-decision with the Parliament; in place of the rule of unanimity in the Council with consultation with the Parliament applicable to the third pillar.[165] Therefore these reforms will prevent one Member State from exercising veto powers in the Council; and will allow the Commission and CJ to exercise full enforcement powers for the implementation of EU criminal law measures. This is thus a considerable improvement in relation to the former third pillar from the perspectives of accountability, enforcement and implementation of EU environmental law.[166] Hence the transfer of criminal-law matters which previously fell under the third pillar to the supranational framework of the EU have the potential to improve the democratic deficit and enforcement of EU (environmental) criminal law.

7.8.1.4 Differences in Criminal Procedural Laws in the Member States

Another potential problem that may impact on the effective implementation of the environmental crime and shipping directives is the existing variations in the criminal procedure laws and legal enforcement practices in Member States. For example, in some EU Member States, individuals may not bring a prosecution (e.g. Portugal and Germany), which could lead to less effective enforcement in those states. Moreover, as was discussed above, some Member States are governed by the 'opportunity principle' and there is no duty to prosecute (e.g. Belgium, the UK and the Netherlands).[167] Hence in some countries the prosecution may decide to be tolerant of minor technical breaches of environmental law or, where the chances of securing a conviction are low, it could

165 Peers, S. *EU Justice and Home Affairs Law* (OUP, 2011) at 665.

166 The adoption of third pillar measures required unanimity in the Council with the Parliament merely being consulted, hence they lacked the democratic legitimacy of a first pillar instrument. Moreover, there was limited judicial or political control of implementation by Member States of third pillar measures. As was discussed in chapter 5, Member States had the option to declare that they accepted the ECJ jurisdiction to oversee the legality of third pillar instruments in a reference for a preliminary ruling from a national court. Moreover, the Commission could through a scoreboard programme oversee the implementation of those third pillar instruments, but it could not institute proceedings under former Article 226 before the ECJ for the failure of a Member State to implement a third pillar measure.

167 See IMPEL Network Report, above note 1, at 60.

be decided that it is not realistic or practical to bring a prosecution.[168] It could be argued that the discretion as to whether to prosecute may diminish levels of compliance with environmental regulations if prosecutions are rare. However the ECJ has consistently held that a failure to prosecute a violation of Community law could constitute a breach of the principle of loyal cooperation enshrined in former Article 10 EC[169] and a Member State can be challenged before the Court for its failure to prosecute.[170] In *Spanish Strawberries* the Court of Justice noted that 'only a very small number of the persons who participated in those serious breaches of public order has been identified and prosecuted'[171] and that 'the measures adopted by the French Government were manifestly inadequate to ensure freedom of intra-Community trade in agricultural products on its territory by preventing and effectively dissuading the perpetrators of the offences in question from committing and repeating them'.[172]

There are a number of initiatives adopted by the Council under the third pillar – and, post-Lisbon based on Article 82 TFEU – envisaging the approximation of Member States' law in specific areas of criminal procedure.[173] Prior to the ratification of the Lisbon Treaty, one of the main constitutional challenges to EU action in the area of criminal procedure is that there was no explicit legal basis in the former TEU for the harmonisation of criminal procedure in the EU.[174] Since under the Lisbon Treaty the pillar structure of the European Union is abolished, approximation of both substantive and procedural criminal law are

168 *Ibid* at 86.

169 Repealed and replaced, in substance, by Article 4, paragraph 3, TEU.

170 Case C-265/95, *Commission v France* (*Spanish Strawberries*) [1997]. In an exceptional case, under Article 194 of the Euratom Treaty - which regulates the protection of Euratom secrets - it is provided that the expediency principle (i.e. the principle that the prosecutor has a discretion of whether or not to prosecute) does not apply in the case of protection of Euratom secrets.

171 *Ibid* paras. 50–52.

172 *Ibid.*

173 See e.g. Framework Decision on the Standing of Victims in Criminal Proceedings, O.J. 2001, L 82/1; Framework Decision on confiscation of crime-related proceeds, instrumentalities and property, O.J. 2005, L. 2005. Post-Lisbon, see e.g. Directive 2012/13/EU of 22 May 2012 on the right to information in criminal proceedings; and Directive 2013/48/EU on the right of access to a lawyer in criminal proceedings and on the right to communicate upon arrest.

174 See Mitsilegas, V. 'Trust-building Measures in the European Judicial Area in Criminal Matters: Issues of Competence, Legitimacy and Inter-institutional Balance' in S. Carrera and T. Balzasq (eds.) *Security versus Freedom: A Challenge for Europe's Future* (Datmouth: Ashgate 2006). The Commission had put forward Article 31 (1) (c) EU as the appropriate legal basis for the adoption of the Framework Decision on certain minimum procedural rights (2004).

adopted at the supranational level, and Article 82 TFEU provides a clear legal basis for the harmonisation of criminal procedural law.[175] But it would certainly entail a great effort on the part of the Commission if it wished to approximate all the aspects of Member States' criminal procedure that could affect the effective implementation of EU environmental (criminal) law. In fact, most proposals in this field have focused on the procedural rights of suspects or victims in the criminal proceedings,[176] perhaps as a means to give more weight to the 'freedom' aspect of the AFSJ, which has been criticised for its 'repressive orientation' as developed in mutual recognition instruments.[177] Moreover, EU criminal procedural measures need not relate necessarily to judicial or police cooperation, as demonstrated by Directive 2010/64 on the right to interpretation and translation in criminal proceedings, which applies to all criminal proceedings in the Member States.[178]

Therefore, it is paramount that an area of Freedom, Security and Justice requires not only approximation of the criminal law protecting citizens against crimes, but also to ensure that national procedural criminal law is developed to protect citizen's from the excessive application of criminal-law powers by states. In this vein, the Vienna Action Plan aimed to give EU citizens a 'common' sense of justice and that the criminal procedural rules and guarantees should be 'similar' in all Member States.[179] It should be noted that one of the few third-pillar measures that target directly the improvement of the effectiveness of national criminal procedure (as opposed to improving judicial fairness) is the Framework Decision on confiscation of crime-related proceeds,

---

175 Art. 82 (1) concerns inter alia mutual recognition rules as such, whereas art. 82 (2) concerns procedural harmonisation in order to facilitate inter alia mutual recognition (Peers, 2011, above note 165, at 668).

176 Post-Lisbon, see e.g. Directive 2012/13/EU of 22 May 2012 on the right to information in criminal proceedings; and Directive 2013/48/EU on the right of access to a lawyer in criminal proceedings and on the right to communicate upon arrest. Pre-Lisbon, see e.g. the Proposal for a Council Framework Decision on certain Procedural Rights in Criminal Law Proceedings throughout the European Union (COM (2004) 328 final) (withdrawn in 2009). For a criticism of this proposal, see Loof, Robin 'Shooting from the Hip: Proposed Minimum Rights in Criminal Proceedings throughout the EU' 12 *European Law Journal* 421 [2006].

177 See also Weyembergh, A. 'Approximation of Criminal Laws, the Constitutional Treaty and the Hague Programme' (2005) *Common Market Law Review* 42 at 1569.

178 See Klip, A. *European Criminal Law* (Intersetia, 2012) at 226.

179 Council and Commission Action Plan of 3 December 1998 on how best to implement the provisions of the Treaty of Amsterdam on the creation of an area of freedom, security and justice, paras. 15 and 19.

instrumentalities and property.[180] However, it has been suggested that efficiency of prosecution plays a predominant role in the criminal justice of the EU, in particular in the mutual recognition instruments.[181] On the other hand, improving procedural fairness appears to have played a significant role in EU criminal procedure initiatives so far, as can be seen from recent EU criminal procedural law initiatives aimed at improving judicial fairness, including the 2013 proposal for a directive on procedural safeguards for children suspected or accused in criminal proceedings;[182] and the 2013 proposal for a directive on certain aspects of the presumption of innocence and of the right to be present at trial in criminal proceedings.[183]

It is perhaps due to the above discussed complexities pertaining to the criminal enforcement of environmental law that some commentators have suggested that the harmonisation of environmental criminal law in the European Union should not be used as a means to improve the implementation deficit of EU environmental law.[184] On the other hand, if the deterrent effects of criminal sanctions are considered, then the argument that the harmonisation of environmental criminal law could lead to the improvement of the implementation deficit of EC environmental law becomes stronger, despite any deficiencies in the enforcement practices by the judicial authorities in the Member States and the Commission.

7.8.1.5 The Consistency in Implementation of the Environmental Crime Directive in the Member States

The approximation of environmental criminal law standards in the Member States is regarded by the Commission as an advantage as it could provide a

180 Framework Decision on confiscation of crime-related proceeds, instrumentalities and property, O.J. 2005, L. 2005.

181 Fletcher, M. et al., *EU Criminal Law and Justice*, Edward Elgar (2008) at 127. This view is also supported by the failure of the EU institutions to adopt the 2004 Proposal for a Framework Decision on certain procedural rights applying in proceedings in criminal matters in the European Union (withdrawn in 2009).

182 COM (2013) 822/2 Proposal for a Directive of the European Parliament and of the Council on procedural safeguards for children suspected or accused in criminal proceedings {SWD(2013) 480} {SWD(2013) 481}.

183 COM (2013) 821/2 Proposal for a Directive of the European Parliament and of the Council on the strengthening of certain aspects of the presumption of innocence and of the right to be present at trial in criminal proceedings {SWD(2013) 478} {SWD(2013) 479}.

184 See e.g. Heine, G. and Ringelmann, C. 'Approximation of European Environmental Criminal Legislation', in Comte, F. and Kramer, L. *Environmental Crime in Europe: Rules of Sanctions* (Groningen, 2004). See also, Faure (2004) above note 9.

deterrent against transboundary crimes.[185] Several studies provide evidence of the disparate approaches in relation to the constitutive elements and penalties applicable for environmental offences in all EU Member States.[186]

In its impact assessment accompanying the February 2007 proposal for a directive on the protection of the environment through criminal law,[187] the Commission showed the disparity that existed in the choice of sanctions in Member States implementing the EC Regulation on the protection of species of wild fauna and flora[188] and EC Regulation 1013/2006 on shipments of waste.[189] For example, regarding the trade in endangered species, the factor between the lowest defined maximum fine applied in Poland (€1,293) and the highest in the Netherlands (€450,000) was 348, and maximum prison sentences differed from 6 months in Luxembourg to 8 years in Lithuania, the Czech Republic and Slovakia.[190]

Another study on environmental crime in the EU-27 Member States[191] published in 2007 (hence before the adoption of the EU environmental crime directive) also suggested that there were considerable differences as regards the types and levels of penalties for the specific offences envisaged in the 2007 environmental crime directive proposal. As regards the offence of waste shipment, some Member States provided for a prison sanction for this offence only where the act concerns hazardous waste[192] and/or only if it led to environmental damage.[193] When environmental damage is caused, the prison penalty

185 Explanatory Memorandum, Proposal for a Directive on the Protection of the Environment through Criminal Law, 2007/0022 (COD) p. 3.

186 Particularly those organised by the Max Planck Institute and the Institute METRO (Masstricht European Institute for Transnational Legal Research), those of the group Hugle-Lepage, and those of the Unity of Comparative Law under the supervision of M. Delmas-Marty. See e.g. Faure, Michael and Heine, Günter, *Final Report: Criminal Penalties in EU Member States Environmental Law*, Maastricht 4 October 2002. See also, Bayle, M. 'Systems of Sanctions in the Field of Environmental Criminality', in Comte, F. and Kramer, L. (eds.) *Environmental Crimes in Europe: Rules of Sanctions* (2004) at 53.

187 Commission Staff Working Document, *Accompanying document to the proposal for a Directive on the Protection of the Environment through Criminal Law: Impact Assessment*, COM (2007) 51 SEC (2007) 161, p. 3.

188 Council Regulation (EC) No. 338/97, *Official Journal* L 061.

189 Regulation (EC) No 1013/2006 of the European Parliament and of the Council of 14 June 2006 on shipments of waste, OJ L 190, 12.7.2006, pp. 1–98.

190 2007 Impact Assessment, above note 49, at 17.

191 Huglo Lepage & Partners, *Study on environmental crime in the 27 Member States*, JLS/D3/2006/05 Final Report (5 April 2007).

192 Czech Republic, Estonia and Latvia. *Ibid.*

193 Greece, Spain, Hungary, Latvia, Lithuania, Poland, Slovakia (*ibid*). As was discussed in Chapter 6, Member States are required under the Directive on environmental crimes to

could be high (up to 7–8 years).[194] The lowest prison sentence for this offence was applied in Luxembourg (from 8 days to 6 months). As regards legal persons, the study suggested that there were significant differences regarding the maximum levels of fines applied. The lowest criminal fines for this offence were applied in Portugal and Bulgaria[195] and the highest were present in Ireland and Estonia.[196] Other Member States only applied administrative penalties[197] or no fine at all.[198]

Subsequent to the adoption of the environmental crime directive and its implementation deadline expired in December 2010, it appears that considerable differences remain as regards the choice of types and levels of criminal penalties for specific environmental offences in the Member States. The Estonian legislation implementing the environmental crime legislation[199] criminalises the illegal transboundary waste shipment 'in significant quantities' with a (unspecified) pecuniary penalty for legal persons or up to one year of imprisonment for individuals.[200] The Austrian implementing legislation[201] criminalizes illegal waste shipments 'in large quantities' by up to one year imprisonment or a fine of up to 360 punishing daily rates (a lower penalty applies to grossly negligent offences).[202] The Polish implementing legislation[203] requires the criminalisation of those acts of whoever 'stores, removes, processes, performs recovery, disposes of or transports waste or substances (…) shall be punished by imprisonment of 3 months to 5 years'.[204]

Regarding the offence of damage to a natural habitat, the 2007 Huglo Lepage & Partners study had similarly suggested that there were important differences in the choice of criminal penalties in the Member States. It was noted that

make waste shipment an abstract endangerment offence, i.e. regardless of any degree of harm.

194 *Ibid* at 10.

195 Maximum of €3,000 and €5000 respectively. ibid.

196 Maximum of €15,000,000 and €16,000,000. ibid.

197 Austria, Czech Republic, Germany, Spain, Sweden. Austria has the lowest maximum fine (€7,270). ibid.

198 Luxembourg, Poland, Slovenia and Spain. ibid.

199 2011 Penal Code Amendment Act, RT I, 11.03.2011, Entry into force: 21/03/2011; Reference: (MNE(2011)52275).

200 § 368 (1) and (2) *ibid.*

201 2011 Amendment of the Criminal Code, Bundesgesetz, number: I Nr. 16/2010; Official Journal: Bundesgesetzblatt für die Republik Österreich (BGBL.), number: I Nr. 16/2010, Publication date: 16/03/2010.

202 Clause 6 *ibid*: 'In § 181b is added after paragraph 2, the following paragraph 3: (…)'.

203 The Criminal Code and certain other laws, Journal of Laws No. 88, item. 553, 25 March 2011.

204 Clause 2 *ibid*: 'Article. 183 § 1 shall be replaced by the following (…):'.

although most Member States had already created a criminal offence concerning this act, the average criminal penalty was relatively low (maximum of up to 3 years.).[205] The prison penalties ranged from a maximum of 6 months[206] to 6 years.[207] There was no criminal sanction for that offence in Italy or Romania. As regards legal persons, there were significant differences between the lowest maximum fines applied in Belgium[208] and the highest applied Estonia and Slovakia.[209]

The German legislation implementing the environmental crime directive[210] is one of the most stringent when it comes to the choice of criminal penalties for protection of natural habitats: in the case of serious damage to protected habitat, it imposes imprisonment for up to five years or a fine;[211] or if committed recklessly, a penalty of imprisonment of up to three years or a fine.[212] Under the Austrian implementing law,[213] the criminal offence against protected habitat 'shall be punished with imprisonment up to two years or with a fine up to 360 daily rates'[214] (a lower penalty is applicable in the case of grossly negligent conduct).[215] A lower penalty for the same offence is foreseen in the Italian implementation legislation,[216] which creates a punishment of imprisonment of up to eighteen months and a fine of not less than 3,000 Euros.[217] In contrast, the Dutch government has communicated to the Commission a correlation table between its existing environmental crime legislation and the EU environmental crime directive, suggesting that it would maintain the same definition of the offence against protected habitats and the applicable punishment that existed prior to the coming into force of the environmental crime directive.[218]

205 Huglo Lepage & Partners (2007) above note 191, at 11.

206 Belgium (Walloon district); France and United Kingdom (except in Northern Ireland where there was no prison penalty). *Ibid.*

207 Latvia and Sweden (in the case of large scale damage or particularly dangerous act). Germany applied a maximum penalty of 5 years imprisonment. *Ibid.*

208 Brussels €125; Wallon District €300. *Ibid.*

209 €16,000,000 and 2,168,818 respectively. *Ibid.*

210 Federal Law Gazette 2011 Part I No. 64, issued in Bonn on December 13, 2011.

211 Clause 7 '§ 329 is amended as follows (...):'.

212 *Ibid* '(c) the following paragraph 6 is added (...)'.

213 Bundesgesetz, number: I Nr. 103/2011.

214 § 181 h. (1) and (2) *ibid.*

215 § 181 i. *ibid.*

216 Gazzetta Ufficiale della Repubblica Italiana, number: 177, Publication date: 01/08/2011, Entry into force: 01/08/2011.

217 Article 733-bis, *ibid.*

218 Netherlands: Announcement of Implementation Directive 2008/99/EC of the European Parliament and of the Council of 19 November 2008 on the protection of the environment

As for the offence of illegal trade in ozone depleting substances, prior to the adoption of the environmental crime directive there was no corresponding criminal offence in a number of EU Member States[219] and no prison penalty existed for this offence in others.[220] Moreover, the maximum levels of criminal fines applicable to legal persons were particularly low in a number of Member States.[221]

The Estonian 2011 implementing legislation[222] lays down an offence of manufacturing, importing, exporting, marketing or using of prohibited substances that deplete the ozone layer, making it punishable by a (unspecified) pecuniary punishment or imprisonment of up to one year of imprisonment (if committed by a legal person – punishable by a pecuniary punishment only).[223] Moreover, the offence is aggravated if it poses a danger to the life or health of persons or creates a threat of injury to the environment.[224] Under the Austrian implementing legislation,[225] the same offence is punishable with imprisonment up to one year or a fine of up to 360 daily rates (a lower penalty is applicable if committed by a grossly negligent conduct).[226] In turn, the Polish implementing legislation[227] imposes a fine or deprivation of liberty of 2 years for the same offence.[228]

As was discussed in Chapter 6, the February 2007 environmental crime directive proposal aimed at correcting the disparate approaches in the Member States as regards the constitutive elements and level of sanctions applicable for environmental offences. It specified types and levels of sanctions to be applied for specific offences. However, as has been seen, the rules on penalties have not been maintained in the final text of the Directive agreed on 21 May 2008; and

through criminal law (OJ L 328) Appendix: Correlation Of Directive No. 2008/99/EC. It correlated Article 3, (h) on the offence of protected habitats with Articles 19c and 19d of the Nature Conservation Act 1998.

219 Bulgaria, Czech Republic, Greece, Latvia, Romania, Sweden. See Huglo Lepage & Partners (2007) above note 191.

220 United Kingdom, Austria, Luxembourg, Portugal. *Ibid.*

221 Belgium (Flanders) €300; Estonia €3,250; Malta 2,300; Ireland €3,000. *Ibid.*

222 RT I, 11.03.2011, above note 199.

223 § 368 (1) and (2), *ibid.*

224 In this respect, the the Estonian legislation imposes higher standards than the environmental crime directive, as the offence of handling ozone depleting substances under the directive is an abstract endangerment offence and so harm or risk of harm does not aggravate the liability of the defendant. See Chapter 6.

225 Bundesgesetz, number: I Nr. 16/2010, above note 214.

226 § 177e. and § 177d *ibid.*

227 The Criminal Code and certain other laws, Journal of Laws No. 88, above note 216.

228 Art 47a. 1 *ibid.*

neither does the 2009 shipping (amending) directive contain minimum types and levels of penalties, in line with the *Ship-Source Pollution* ruling. They only contain a general obligation that the offences envisaged therein are punishable by effective, proportionate and dissuasive penalties.[229] Hence harmonisation of environmental criminal law under the above directives may not be sufficient to prevent certain Member States from becoming pollution havens due to lax environmental regulation, especially in view of the most recent enlargements of the EU eastwards (May 2004; January 2007 and June 2013).[230] Moreover, although the directives on environmental crime and ship-source pollution require Member States to implement 'effective, proportionate and dissuasive' sanctions, it would be difficult to establish whether the implementation by the Member States meet this threshold. Hence eco-criminals would still be able to exploit the differences in the environmental criminal legislation of the Member States (as one Member State may apply a small criminal fine and another a high prison sentence for the same offence).

Yet it is not only the harmonisation of penalties which could have an impact on the implementation and enforcement of EU environmental law. The Commission acknowledges that a consistent sentencing policy in the Union would require consideration of four main issues: (a) the level of penalties and the range of penalties available (e.g. custodial sentences, alternative sanctions, fines etc.) (b) the rules governing prosecution (discretionary or mandatory prosecution, priorities of criminal policy etc.) (c) the general rules of criminal law (participation, attempts, aiding and abetting, instigation, aggravating circumstances, recidivism etc.) and (d) rules and practices regarding enforcement (conditional release, remission and reduction of sentence, amnesty, pardon, rehabilitation, involvement of judicial authorities in enforcing sentences etc.).[231] In addition to the harmonisation of offences, the directive on environmental crimes only covers point (c) (see Chapter 6). It is questionable whether the harmonisation of all the above points would be possible without an excessive intrusion in matters pertaining to national legal traditions and enforcement choices. Moreover, as was discussed in Chapter 6, certain concepts present in the environmental crime and ship-source pollution directives

229 See Article 5 of the 2008 environmental crime directive and Article 1 (6.1) of the 2009 shipping pollution (amending) directive.

230 See also, Hedemann-Robinson, M., *Enforcement of European Union Environmental Law: Legal Issues and Challenges* (Routledge-Cavendish, 2007) at 517.

231 European Commission Green Paper on the 'Approximation, Mutual Recognition and Enforcement of Criminal Sanctions in the European Union', Brussels 30.04.2004 COM (2004) 334 final.

that form part of the definition of the offences, such as 'intention' or 'gross negligence', are not state-of-the-art concepts and there will be variations in the way the national courts will apply them.[232]

7.8.2 *The Creation of a Level-playing Field in the Common Market*

The diversity of national penal systems allows criminals to select the system that is regarded as least effective and use it as sanctuary or safe haven. The diversity of offences, sanctions and levels of efficiency of criminal procedures are even harder to justify in the case of the so-called Euro-crimes.[233] Thus it has been suggested that the existing legal diversity between legal systems constitutes a 'weapon' in the hands of criminals.[234] Modern technical means of communications allow criminals to choose at a distance where to commit certain types of offences according to the standard of incrimination and level of penalties. In accordance with the Tampere conclusions criminals must not find ways of exploiting differences in the judicial systems of the Member States.[235]

The completion of an internal market requires the creation of a level-playing field for competitors.[236] Differences between national sanctions may impact on the costs of non-compliance with environmental regulations and hence distort competition. Thus in order to ensure the establishment of a common market a system ensuring undistorted competition within the Community is needed.[237] Penalties that vary in nature (administrative or criminal) or severity (fine or imprisonment) can create distortions in the application of the underlying rules and even distort competition.[238] The Commission suggests that businesses established in certain Member States with low levels of criminalisation and penalties are placed in a competitive advantage in relation to

---

232 See also, Hedemann-Robinson, M. (2006) above note 230, at 517.

233 Weyembergh, A. 'The Functions of Approximation of Penal Law within the European Union' (2005) 12 *Maatricht Journal of European and Comparative Law* 2 at 164.

234 *ibid.*

235 Point 5 of the Presidency Conclusions to the Tampere European Council 15 And 16 October 1999. See also, Communication from the Commission to the Council and the European Parliament – Area of Freedom, Security and Justice: Assessment of the Tampere programme and future orientations (COM/2004/0401 final).

236 See e.g. Case C-300/89, *Commission v Council* ('*Titanium Dioxide*') [1991] ECR I-2867 para. 15; and Case C-350/92, *Spain v Council* [1995] ECR I-1985 para. 32.

237 This was recognized in Article 3 EC. However, famously this provision was repealed (and replaced by Articles 3 to 6 TFEU) by the Lisbon Treaty (largely due to insistence of the French government). Article 3 (1) (b) TFEU states that EU has exclusive competence for the establishing of the competition rules necessary for the functioning of the internal market.

238 Corstens, G. And Pradel, J., *European Criminal Law* (Kluwer Law International, 2002) at 514.

their competitors based in other Member States with more stringent liability regimes, as they may violate certain rules without risking the costs of fines or other criminal sanctions.[239] The Commission then suggests that only a minimum degree of harmonisation of criminal offences and penalties can ensure fair competition.[240]

Furthermore, the Commission asserts that environmental crimes can affect the economic viability of lawful businesses that comply with environmental regulations, since these businesses have made investments into new technology that the non-complying competitors did not make.[241] Hence the Commission argues that action at EU/EC level is necessary to extend the scope of liability and approximating the definitions of offences and the level of sanctions. Moreover, the Commission considered that this would not create any additional costs for economic operators, as it does not create any new obligations, but would serve instead to improve the application of the existing rules.[242]

It questionable though that the Commission would be able to rely on the argument of eliminating distortions in the internal market alone as the main justification for a Directive on environmental crimes. The ECJ emphasised in the *Tobacco Advertising* case, which related to the legality of the Tobacco Directive,[243] that the Community could not rely on the need to eliminate distortions of competition in the tobacco advertisement or sale sectors for adoption of that measure, since the lawfulness of a Directive based on Article 114 TFEU (former Article 95 EC) is dependent on whether the distortions of competition which the measure purports to eliminate are *appreciable*.[244] Although the Court accepted that advertising agencies and producers based in Member States with fewer restrictions are at an advantage in terms of economies of scale and profitability, the effects of such advantages on competition are remote and indirect and do not constitute appreciable distortions. The court reached that conclusion despite the fact that it had accepted that some appreciable distortions were identifiable, since the prohibition of tobacco sponsorship in some Member States led to the relocation of some sporting events such as Formula One.

The literature on the harmonisation of European private law has also criticised harmonisation as a technical process devoted to market-making for the disregard of the rich and deep historical roots of the national laws subject to its

239 2007 Impact Assessment, above note 49, at 24.

240 *Ibid.*

241 *Ibid*, Section 5.3. at 29.

242 *Ibid.*, Section 5.3.2.

243 Directive 98/43 OJ 1998, L 213/9.

244 Case C-376/98 *Germany v Parliament and Council*, [2000] ECR I-8419, para. 107.

influence.[245] Their criticism is *inter alia* based on the argument that the ornate strands of cultural tradition that permeate national laws are sacrificed by harmonisation because of the cold calculation of economic gains.[246] This helps to explain the restrictive approach applied by the ECJ in the *Tobacco Advertising* ruling.

7.8.2.1 Environmental Regulation and Business Competitiveness

There is widespread concern that free trade with countries with lower environmental standards lead to a shift of production activity from home countries with higher environmental standards to foreign countries with lower ones. Connected to that is the fear that countries with higher standards would be forced to lower their standards if capital and jobs also migrated to exploit lower standards and therefore cheaper conditions abroad (the so-called 'race to the bottom').[247] There is an instinctive tendency to view environmental regulation stringency as directly related to business decisions to relocate across countries or within specific jurisdictional areas in a given country. Thus, common sense would lead to the conclusion that the tougher the environmental regulations of a country, the less attractive that country would be for investors. The acknowledgement of this raises the fears that some developing countries could become pollution heavens for the world's dirty industries.[248] However, economists generally contend that the effects of environmental regulation on business location ought to typically be small, compared to other variables such as wages.[249] The fact that stringent environmental regulations has played a small role in management decisions to allocate firms across countries may be explained by the fact that environmental investments are only a small fraction of the total costs of production for most firms other than the heavily polluting ones.[250] Yet it is exactly the heavily polluting industries that should be

---

245 See also, Chapter 4.

246 Legrand, Pierre 'On the Unbearable Localness of the Law: Academic Fallacies and Unreasonable Observations' (2003) 10/1 *European Review of Private Law* 66.

247 See also, Pereira, R. 'Environmental Regulation, Business Competitiveness and Corporate Responsibility', in Makuch, K. and Pereira, R. (eds.) *Environmental and Energy* (Wiley-Blackwell, 2012).

248 Five sectors emerge as leading candidates for environmentally sensitive goods: iron and steel, nonferrous metals, industrial chemicals, pulp and paper, and non-metallic products. Those sectors incur in some of the highest expenditures on pollution abatement and control. See *ibid.*

249 See e.g. T. Bartick, 'The Effects of Environmental Regulation on Business Location in the United States', *Growth and Change* (1988) at 37.

250 Karen Palmer, Wallace E. Oates, and Paul R. Portney. 'Tightening Environmental Standards: The Benefit-Cost or the No-Cost Paradigm?' (1995) 9 *Journal of Economic Perspectives* 4, 119 at 130. This is also so because there is a perception that tighter environmental regulations

the focus of most attention given their potentially higher adverse impact on the environment.[251] For those industries, it seems that the effects of environmental regulation on business location could potentially be much higher.[252]

However, other studies have suggested that even in the case of pollution-intensive industries the degree of aversion to stringent states could be small. Studies carried in other jurisdictions demonstrate that environmental regulation may have little impact on business location. Levinson summarises the findings of those studies:

> After examining trends in US direct investment abroad and US imports from pollution-intensive industries, Leonard (1988) finds no evidence that establishments in robust domestic industries have moved abroad in order to avoid US pollution regulations. Similarly, Grossman and Krueger (1991) conclude that differences between the US and Mexico's environmental regulations 'play at most a minor role in guiding intersectoral resource allocations'. Low and Yeats (1992) show that developing countries have gained a greater share of total world exports of pollution-intensive products, but that industrialized countries continue to be by far the largest exporters of these goods.[253]

There are possible explanations for this apparent lack of correlation between environmental regulations and manufacturer location. It might be that firms manufacturing products in a variety of jurisdictions find it most cost effective to operate according to the most stringent regulations, eliminating the necessity of designing a different production process for each location.[254] It might also be that the most heavily polluting industries tend to be well regulated in most countries anyway and that environmental compliance costs have a tendency to converge to a uniform level across countries.[255] Since those studies only focus on the stringency of the underlying legal rules, rather than the

---

in developing countries is inevitable, and that it is less expensive to invest initially in state-of-the-art abatement technology than to retrofit later.

251 Levinson, *infra* points out that the pollution-intensive industries in his study spent about 4 percent and sometimes 5 percent or more of their investments on pollution abatement equipment, and that one industry (petrol and coal) spent 16 percent (at 26).

252 Bartick (1988), above note 249, at 37.

253 A. Levinson, 'Environmental Regulation and Manufactures' Location Choices: Evidence of the Census of Manufactures', (1996) *Journal of Public Economics*, 62, at 6.

254 *Ibid.*

255 *Ibid* at 26. His study also suggests that larger branch plants are more sensitive to local environmental regulation stringency than smaller ones (id.).

enforcement practices or liability regimes applied in the countries under study, it would be difficult in any event to make a strong case that businesses would necessarily relocate to Member States with less stringent environmental enforcement on the basis of the findings of those studies.[256]

In this regard, the 2007 impact assessment to the environmental crime directive proposal stated that eliminating the illegal options in the market would encourage more investments in legal businesses.[257] For example, if illegal waste dumping becomes too risky and costly due to the introduction and application of criminal sanctions by the authorities, investment in state of the art waste treatment becomes more viable. So it is perhaps not so surprising that some European business groups declared themselves to be favourable to the 2007 environmental crime directive proposal.[258]

7.8.3 *The Facilitation of Police and Judicial Cooperation in Criminal Matters in the Context of Trans-frontier Environmental Crime*

Cooperation in criminal matters at EU level is regarded as necessary in order to ensure that individuals do not escape prosecution simply by exercising their free movement rights. This has been termed an *auxiliary function* of the approximation of European criminal law – that is, approximation as a tool to support judicial co-operation in the field of criminal law-and is regarded as perhaps one the most important goals of the harmonisation programme.[259] The differences in in both substantive and procedural criminal laws in the EU Member States, in particular, undermine the principle of free movement of persons since 'people travelling abroad should be confident that existing

256 It should be noted that, despite the findings of the above studies, the recent statements of some European industries that they would relocate in case the EU adopts very stringent emission targets for the implementation of the Kyoto Protocol and the 2009 Commission Directive to amend the European Emissions Trading Scheme which attempts to address the problem of 'carbon leakage' by providing preferential treatment for certain industries when allocating allowances, seems to show that the stringency of environmental standards does have an impact on industry location choices. See Directive 2009/29/EC of the European Parliament and of the Council of 23 April 2009 amending Directive 2003/87/EC so as to improve and extend the greenhouse gas emission allowance trading scheme of the Community.

257 2007 Impact Assessment, above note 49.

258 *The Financial Times* 'EU "green crime" laws raise sovereignty fears' 8 February 2007. However, the shipping industry was strongly opposed to the shipping pollution directive for imposing higher standards than MARPOL and UNCLOS, as was seen in the *Intertanko* case C-308/06, discussed in Chapters 4, 5 and 6.

259 Weyembergh, A. 'Approximation of Criminal Laws, the Constitutional Treaty and the Hague Programme' (2005) 42 *Common Market Law Review* at 1583. See further, Chapter 4.

standards [in criminal proceedings] offer equivalent protection whatever the Member State so as not to impede their free movement for fear of encountering a system operating lower standards'.[260]

The 1999 Tampere European Council concluded that better compatibility and more convergence between the legal systems of the Member States must be achieved and that '[c]riminals must find no ways of exploiting the differences in the judicial systems of Member States'.[261] Moreover, approximation of penal law is sometimes regarded as necessary to enhance the levels of mutual trust among the criminal justice systems of the Member States and therefore as a means to provide legitimacy for the EU criminal law programme based on the principle of mutual recognition. In this regard, it has been suggested that the 2004 Hague Programme had 'taken a step backwards' by recognising the function of harmonisation as a tool to facilitate mutual recognition only.[262]

The level of sanctions often has a significant impact on the investigation methods available to the law enforcement authorities. Hence it could have a significant impact on the effectiveness of police and judicial cooperation in the European Union. For example, the use of technical surveillance in Finland requires that the investigation is linked to a crime with a maximum sanction of at least six months imprisonment and in Portugal the interception of mail is possible only for crimes punishable with imprisonment for a term exceeding three years.[263] Moreover, in Austria mutual assistance for the interception, recording and tracing of telecommunications requires that the request for mutual assistance relates to an international offence punishable by imprisonment for a term exceeding twelve months. The link between a certain sanction threshold and specific investigation techniques could hinder the cooperation between Member States in the investigation of cross-border environmental crime. Hence the Commission suggests that approximation of minimum maximum penalties would imply in some Member States an increase of the level of sanctions, thereby providing the authorities with additional important investigation tools.[264]

A number of Member States experience problems relating to transfrontier pollution.[265] One of the most famous examples is the Mox-Plant nuclear power plant based in Sellafield, Cumbria in the UK, which has been criticised by

260 Consultation Document, European Commission's Green Paper on 'Procedural Safeguards for Suspects and defendants in criminal proceedings throughout the European Union' COM (2003) 75 final, 19 February 2003.

261 Tampere European Council Conclusions, 15–16 October 1999, para. 5.

262 See Weyembergh, A. (2005) above note 259.

263 2007 Impact Assessment, above note 50, Section 1.3.2. at 13.

264 *Ibid.*

265 See Impel Network Report (2005), above note 1, at 68.

Ireland due to concerns over the release of radioactive substances into the Irish Sea. This has led Ireland to bring proceedings against the UK before the International Tribunal on the Law of the Sea[266] and before the OSPAR Commission,[267] as well as to one case brought by the Commission against Ireland before the European Court of Justice.[268] In another example, in 30 January 2000 a company based in Romania contaminated a river system with cyanide-rich tailing waste, causing environmental damage to Hungary estimated at around EUR120 million.[269] The 2000 IMPEL study on the criminal enforcement of environmental law found that the differences in the definition of offences did raise some problems in transfrontier incidents,[270] although it suggested that the problems relate less to substantive criminal law than to rules intrinsic to police and judicial cooperation. If so, then the answer to the question of the improvement of police and judicial cooperation in criminal matters lies less in the harmonisation of substantive rules but those relating to police and judicial cooperation in criminal cooperation in criminal matters; as well as relating to the operation of such bodies as Interpol, Europol and Eurojust (see Chapter 3), and the extent to which they are able to effectively coordinate their activities and cooperare with the Member States.

Although there is currently no centralised binding mechanism of jurisdiction allocation in criminal matters in the European Union,[271] as was discussed in Chapter 6, mechanisms and criteria for the allocation of jurisdiction do exist in the EU Framework Decision on conflicts of jurisdiction (2009) as well as in sectoral third pillar instruments. Jurisdictional rules to facilitate judicial cooperation were also present in the annulled Framework Decisions on environmental crime and ship-source pollution, but those instruments were annulled by the ECJ.

Moreover, there is strong indication that the harmonisation of the levels of penalties could facilitate the use of the European Arrest Warrant (EAW)[272] and

266 The MOX Plant Case (Ireland v. United Kingdom), Provisional Measures, Case n. 10.

267 See the 2003 OSPAR Radioactive Substances Committee Progress Report on the More Detailed Implementation of the OSPAR Strategy with Regard to Radioactive Substances.

268 Judgment of the Court (Grand Chamber) of 30 May 2006. Commission of the European Communities v Ireland (Case C-459/03).

269 Gyula, Bandi 'Liability and Sanctions, Criminal Liability in Hungary' in Comte, Françoise and Kramer, Ludwig (eds.) *Environmental Crime in Europe: Rules of Sanctions* (Europa Law Publishing, Groningen 2004) at 129.

270 Impel Network Report (2005), above note 1, at 69.

271 See also, Mitsilegas, V. 'The Transformation of Criminal Law in the "Area of Freedom, Security and Jusctice"' (2007) 26 *YEEL* 1 at 28.

272 Council Framework Decision of 13 June 2002 on the European Arrest Warrant and the Surrender of Procedures between Member States, OJ 2002 L 190.

other EU criminal law instruments based on the principle of mutual recognition.[273] Even though the EAW is based on the principle of mutual recognition (or 'mutual trust' in the European space) and therefore does not require 'double criminality' in the issuing and executing states for a list of 32 offences (including environmental crimes),[274] the issuing of an EAW is only possible (unless the sentence has already been passed)[275] for acts punishable in the issuing state by a custodial sentence or a detention order of at least twelve months. In the case of environmental crime,[276] issuing the EAW without the condition of dual criminality requires that the offence is punishable in the issuing Member State by a custodial sentence or a detention order for a maximum of at least three years imprisonment. The EAW was used for the first time by the Environment Agency in the UK in a case involving illegal waste dumping in which the defendant had flown to Ireland.[277] The successful operation of the European Arrest Warrant, as well as other more recent similar developments in the area of European judicial and police cooperation in criminal matters (e.g. the European Evidence Warrant, which follows the same sanction threshold as the EAW for the abolition of the dual criminality principle[278]), could arguably be weakened by the present disparate sanctions presently adopted by Member States for implementation of EU environmental law. In fact, the Commission suggests that the legislation of the Member States in many cases would not meet this three-year threshold.[279] Therefore, the dual criminality

273 E.g. Council Framework Decision 2005/214/JHA on the application of the principle of mutual recognition to financial penalties of 24 February 2005, *Official Journal* L76/16 22 March 2005 and Council Framework Decision on the European Evidence Warrant for the purpose of obtaining objects, documents and data for use in proceedings in criminal matters, 2008/978/JHA, 18 December 2008, *Official Journal* L 350/72, 30 December 2008.

274 See Alegre S. and Leaf, M. 'Mutual Recognition in European Judicial Cooperation: A Step too Far too Soon? Case Study – The European Arrest Warrant', *European Law Journal*, (2004) 10.

275 In this case the threshold is of at least four months.

276 As was discussed in Chapter 2, the term 'environmental crime' is not defined in EU mutual recognition instruments, apart from the express reference to 'illicit trafficking in endangered animal species and in endangered plant species and varieties'.

277 As a result of a three-year investigation codenamed '*Operation Huron*', the Environment Agency found that between January 2003 and June 2004, the two defendants had masterminded an elaborate operation in London and Essex of illegally dumping over 14,600 tonnes of waste – equivalent to around 750 lorry loads – on at least 15 different sites. See http://www.environment-agency.gov.uk/news (accessed on 10 April 2015).

278 See generally, Vervaele, J.A.E. *European Evidence Warrant: Transnational Judicial Inquiries in the EU*, Intersentia 2005.

279 '2007 Directive Impact Assessment', above note 49, at 14.

principle would apply in many instances of cross-border environmental crime, hence defeating one of the main objectives of those instruments which is to facilitate cross-border cooperation between the Member States.[280]

The Directive on environmental crime – unless it is amended in light of the coming into force of the Lisbon Treaty – might not be able to enhance the levels of police and judicial cooperation in criminal matters in the European Union, since it necessarily does not prescribe specific types and levels of penalties or jurisdictional and prosecutorial rules. However, the harmonisation of offences under the directive could lead to a certain improvement in the levels of police and judicial cooperation. In particular, as the environmental crime directive requires the criminalisation of a number of environmental offences in all Member States, double criminality should not pose a significant barrier to the operation of the EAW. However, a barrier to the operation of the EAW (and other mutual recognition instruments) would remain if a Member State implements the directive with a custodial sentence or a detention order of less than twelve months or with pecuniary penalties only.

The studies commissioned by the Commission showed that there are discrepancies in the legislation of Member States as regards the choice between criminal or administrative law to address environmental damage. In this vein, it has been suggested that the large use of administrative sanctions in Germany explains at least partly the reluctance of administrative bodies to cooperate with criminal enforcement bodies and the fact that multilateral agreements rarely deal with mutual assistance and cooperation between administrative authorities.[281] Hence if environmental damage is not criminalised in some Member States, then it is less likely that mechanisms of cross-border cooperation would be available to facilitate the prosecution or investigation of environmental crimes.[282] As put by Guild, 'the use of borders as mechanisms for differentiation of legal orders becomes problematic when only the enforcement

---

280 *Ibid.*

281 See Gallas, A. and Werner, J. 'Transboundary Environmental Crimes: German Experiences and Approaches', Fifth International Conference on Environmental Compliance and Enforcement, vol. 1 INECE, 1998 at 377.

282 Some of the few instruments dealing with the cross-border co-operation between administrative authorities in the EU are the EC Regulation No. 515/97 on Mutual Assistance between the Administrative Authorities of the Member States and Co-operation between the Latter and the Commission to ensure the Correct Application of the Law on Customs and Agricultural Matters (1997); and Convention on Mutual Assistance and Co-operation between Customs Administrations (1997) *Official Journal* C 24 of 23.01.1998.

mechanisms of criminal law are given equal status across them'.[283] So a certain harmonisation of the definition of offences (as in the environmental crime and ship-source pollution Directives) could facilitate in some circumstances the prosecution of an operator in a Member State who causes environmental damage in another Member State. Accordingly, Recital (4) to the directive on environmental crime states that 'common rules on criminal offences make it possible to use effective methods of investigation and assistance within the Member States'. This is in line with the principle developed in the *Trail Smelter* arbitration between the United States and Canada in 1939–41 and enshrined in Principle 21 of the 1972 Stockholm Declaration on Human Environment and Principle 2 of the 1992 Rio Declaration on the Environment and Development regarding State liability for cross-border environmental damage – but applied in order to hold individual polluters criminally liable.

It should be noted that due to the principle of separation of powers, the public prosecutor in charge of the preliminary investigation may not give orders to the enforcing bodies, although a duty to co-operate may be laid down in the rules of criminal procedure or administrative law in some countries.[284] In this regard, the Council of Europe Convention on environmental crimes – unlike the EU environmental crime directive – creates an obligation on the parties to introduce measures to ensure the cooperation between the administrative and judicial authorities.[285]

One related problem is that the lack of a common definition of crime may have an impact on crime statistics, as the collection of data and statistics depends on the legal categorisation given by each legal system and the comparability of the figures may be compromised by variations. According to Harding, that constitutes one of the main justifications for legal harmonisation, since the comparability of legal norms is fundamental for an effective transnational crime control.[286]

Moreover, the Commission suggested that 'citizens no longer run the risk of double convictions under administrative and criminal law for core environmental

283 Guild, Elspeth, 'Crime and the EU's Constitutional Future in an Area of Freedom, Security, and Justice' (2004) 10 *European Law Journal* 2, at 219.

284 See Impel Network Report, above note 49, at 48.

285 See Article 10 of the 1998 Council of Europe environmental crime convention. This was also the case with the original 2000 Danish proposal for a Framework Decision on environmental crimes.

286 Harding, C. 'European Regimes of Crime Control: Objectives, Legal Bases and Accountability' 7 *MJ* 3 (2000) p. 227. The Commission set up an expert group to remedy the lack of EU statistics on crime and criminal justice (Press Release, IP/06/1089) (8 August 2006). See also, Chapter 3.

crimes if they are considered as such crimes in all Member States'.[287] However, it is not clear whether this is indeed the case, since the Directive on environmental crime does not require the *application* of criminal sanctions in individual cases but simply the criminalisation of certain violations of EU environmental law. Moreover, when interpreting the *ne bis in idem* rules contained in Article 54 of the Schengen Implementing Agreement (incorporated into EU law by the Treaty of Amsterdam)[288] the Court of Justice focuses on the result for the individual, not the form adopted by the Member State.[289] So the title that a State gives to a form of punishment will not be decisive of whether it is the same or different from the act which has justified punishment in another Member State.[290]

7.9 Conclusions

The harmonisation of environmental criminal law at the supranational level is expected to provide stronger political and judicial control of the implementation of environmental criminal law by the Member States. Yet it is not clear whether the harmonisation of environmental criminal law will necessarily enhance the implementation and enforcement of EU environmental law since it concerns the harmonisation of *substantive* rules only and there is no duty on a state to *apply* criminal law in individual cases, although the presence of a criminal justice system to enforce those rules could indeed provide a strong deterrent. Moreover, it is likely that the creation of a level playing field could erase certain distortions in competition connected to the lax enforcement of environmental law in some Member States, but it would be difficult to support market integration alone as a justification for criminalisation of environmental offences in the EU member states. Moreover, despite the lack of penalties or jurisdictional rules in the environmental crime or shipping pollution (amending) directives, the criminalisation of environmental infringements could provide a certain degree of improvement in the levels of police and judicial cooperation in criminal matters between the Member States. This is because mechanisms

287 2007 Impact Assessment, above note 49, at 29.

288 It states that '[a] person whose trial has finally been disposed of in one Contracting Party may not be prosecuted in another Contracting Party for the same acts provided that, if a penalty has been imposed, it has been enforced, is actually in the process of being enforced or can no longer be enforced under national laws'. See Mitsilegas (2007) above note 271, at 9.

289 C-187/01 & C-385/01 *Gozutok & Brugge* [2003] ECR I-1345.

290 Guild, E. (2004) above note 283, at 230–231. See also the Commission's proposal on *the ne bis in idem* throughout Europe (COM (2005) 696 final).

of interstate cooperation against transnational crime tend to require double-criminality in both states. However, the EU mutual recognition instruments do not require double criminality for environmental offences as long *as a minimum penalty threshold* is met. So although enhancing the types and levels of environmental criminal penalties could be considered an objective in itself (i.e. to improve environmental enforcement in the member states), it could also be regarded as necessary to improve police and judicial cooperation in the EU.

CHAPTER 8

Concluding Remarks

The seriousness of certain environmental offences demands an effective response from the State and from international and regional organisations, such as the European Union. Criminal sanctions, alongside civil and administrative penalties, are crucial tools in the enforcement of environmental law. It is desirable that all three main systems of sanctions – civil, administrative and criminal – are made available in the environmental field in order to optimise enforcement. Moreover, additional measures should be established in order to foster cooperation between the administrative and judicial authorities.

Although there are strong arguments for advancing the jurisdiction of the International Criminal Court over environmental crime (particularly in the context of transnational environmental crime), it is not clear whether an eventual ICC jurisdiction would provide an effective response and have strong deterrent effects against environmental crime. Although there would be important symbolic reasons to extend the ICC jurisdiction over international environmental crime, it appears that the jurisdiction of the ICC requires further testing before it could be established as the forum for prosecution of transnational environmental crime. Perhaps one indication of the challenges that the ICC would face is the failure of other initiatives aimed at introducing effectively an Environment Chamber to hear environmental disputes into other international tribunals, in particular the ICJ.

It is argued that the current state of fragmentation of the enforcement and penalties provisions under multilateral environmental agreements (MEAs) calls for a more cohesive and coherent approach to implementation and enforcement of MEAs. This reinforces the case for a global environmental crime convention which could require the criminalisation of serious environmental offences and envision deterrent penalties against the most serious forms of environmental crime. Such global agreement could have a number of benefits, such as strengthening interstate cooperation against environmental crime, creating reporting and information exchange mechanisms, establishing annual review procedures for parties to assess progress in implementation and, perhaps most significantly, it could act to improve the awareness globally of the seriousness of environmental offences. Yet, as the experience with existing MEAs demonstrate, it would be difficult for any such global environmental crime convention to require state parties to apply criminal penalties in individual cases, given that the flexibility in the choice of national enforcement action is often regarded as a crucial element in the theory of environmental law enforcement. For this reason,

 | DOI 10.1163/9789004195882_009

neither the environmental crime directive nor the ship-source pollution (amending) directive require Member States to necessarily apply one type of sanction in individual cases. This means that ultimately the levels of environmental protection will be left to the enforcement choices of national authorities, thus hindering the effectiveness of a global or regional agreement on environmental crime.

In some ways, the Council of Europe environmental crime convention already provides a template for a global agreement on environmental crime. Indeed, the CoE convention permits, in principle, accession by countries outside the Council of Europe. Yet the many deficiencies of the CoE environmental crime convention suggestions that it could hardly be the model for a global convention. This is because the Council of Europe environmental crime convention was drafted in the European setting, and many areas of environmental criminality which currently pose major challenges and concerns to the global community (particularly wildlife crime) are not adequately addressed in the CoE convention. Moreover, there is a certain degree of contradiction that it is specifically in the area of pollution-control offences that the CoE convention makes crimininalisation mandatory, as it is exactly in this area that academic studies have suggested that criminal sanctions may not be effective (or as effective as civil or administrative sanctions). On the other hand, if other serious environmental crime (typically committed by criminal organisations, such as wildlife crime) were to be criminalised in a global treaty, but not pollution-control offences (typically committed by companies), then it would be questionable whether the enforcement system does not unfairly favour white-collar criminals over blue-collar criminals. This analysis suggests that it would be particularly difficult to draft a comprehensive global environmental criminal law agreement that encompasses all the most serious environmental offences.

There appears to be strong public opinion in support for state intervention to tackle serious violations of environmental law, including for the adoption of harmonisation measures. For example, a 2008 Eurobarometer survey in the 27 Member States suggests that 82% of the respondents regard harmonisation of environmental law at the EU level as necessary; and the highest proportion of respondents (37%) supported the introduction of heavier fines for offenders as an effective way to tackle environmental problems.[1] In another survey, 81% of respondents supported action at the EU level in the fight against organised crime and trafficking.[2]

1 Eurobarometer, 'Attitudes of European Citizens Towards the Environment', March 2008, at 40 available at http://ec.europa.eu/public_opinion/archives/ebs/ebs_295_en.pdf (accessed on 15 February 2015).

2 Eurobarometer, 'The Role of the European Union in Justice, Freedom and Security Policy Area', June 2008 at 3 available at http://ec.europa.eu/public_opinion/archives/ebs/ebs_290_en.pdf (accessed on 15 February 2015).

The harmonisation of rules on substantive environmental criminal law (as in the environmental crime directive) could improve the implementation deficit of EU environmental law to a limited extent, i.e. in so far as criminal sanctions are recognised to have stronger deterrent effects than those of an administrative or civil nature. Although the creation of a level playing field in a common market is an important aspect of harmonisation of environmental criminal law, market integration should not be considered a determinant element for the establishment of necessity of a measure harmonising environmental criminal law. It also appears that the facilitation of police and judicial cooperation in the EU would be limited without a regime harmonising penalties and jurisdictional and prosecutorial rules.

As regards the harmonisation of criminal penalties for environmental crimes following the ratification of the Lisbon Treaty, the concerns of two Advocate Generals regarding the consistency and coherence of the internal penal systems of the Member States need to be given due consideration. This point is also highlighted in the Commission's 2005 Communication, which emphasises that the EC criminal law measures must also respect the 'overall *consistency* of the Union system of criminal law' so as to ensure that criminal provisions do not become 'fragmented and ill-matched' (emphasis added).[3] It is thus necessary that there is reflection and rationalisation for the establishment of a real programme of harmonisation that goes 'beyond mere reactions to events and to introduce continuity in the EU legislative actions'.[4] Moreover, the programme of harmonisation of EU substantive criminal law must be accompanied by other initiatives such as common judicial training and exchange programmes, which have emerged as an important means of promoting knowledge and trust between national judicial authorities.[5] Despite the fact that there are differences in the penalties introduced by Member States for transposition of the environmental crime directive, thus far no enforcement proceedings were brought by the Commission before the Court of Justice against Member States for failure to implement the environmental crime directive with 'effective, proportionate and dissuasive' penalties, despite their criminal nature. Moreover, although reasoned opinions were issued to a

3 Communication from the European Commission to the European Parliament and the Council on the Implications of the Court's Judgement of 13 September 2005 (Case C-176/03 Commission v Council) COM (2005) 583 final/2, 24 November 2005, para. 13.

4 Weyembergh, A. 'Approximation of Criminal Laws, the Constitutional Treaty and the Hague Programme' (2005) 42 *Common Market Law Review* at 1587.

5 Fletcher, M., Loof, R. And Gilmore, B. EU *Criminal Law and Justice*, (Edward Elgar, 2008), at 108. Eurojust plays an important role in this regard.

number of Member States for non-implementation of the environmental crime and ship-source pollution directives, so far Article 260 TFEU has not been triggered to apply financial penalties for non-implementation of those directives.

The foregoing remarks show the complexity of achieving even a minimum level of harmonisation of environmental criminal law. That does not mean that States should shy away from the efforts of doing so, especially given the transboundary nature of many environmental offences, and in particular the limited border controls within the European Union, which allows criminals to easily operate across borders. In this context, it is called upon the EU to ensure that the sanctions against eco-criminals are consistently enforced in all Member States in light of the strong deterrent effect of criminal law. However, it is also crucial that the EU programme of harmonisation of environmental criminal law is not overtly intrusive and that the minimum standards applied allow for an element of local preferences and enforcement choices to prevail. Since there appears to be strong grounds for the more serious violations of environmental law to be criminalised, the key question that will continue permeating the debate on future harmonisation of environmental criminal law in the EU is the political question of whether those matters should be dealt with by the EU or the Member States.

Bibliography

Abott, C., *'Enforcing Pollution Control Regulation: Strengthening Sanctions and Improving Deterrence'* (Hart Publishing, 2009).

Abraham, C.M., and Sushila Abraham. 'The Bhopal case and the development of environmental law in India.' *International and Comparative Law Quarterly* 40.02 (1991): 334–365.

Adler, Freda. 'Offender-Specific vs. Offense-Specific Approaches to the Study of Environmental Crime.' In Environmental Crime and Criminality: Theoretical and Practical Issues, Sally M. Edwards, Terry D. Edwards, Charles B. Fields (Garland Pub, New York 1996).

Albrecht, Hans-Jorg and Leppa, Seppo (ed.) *Criminal Law and the Environment*, Proceedings of the European Seminar held in Lauchhammer, Land Brandenburg,, Germany, April 1992.

Alegre S. and Leaf, M. 'Mutual Recognition in European Judicial Cooperation: A Step too Far too Soon? Case Study – The European Arrest Warrant', *European Law Journal*, (2004) 10.

Allen, Michael. *Textbook on Criminal Law* (8th ed. OUP, Oxford 2005).

Alvazzi, A. and Norberry, J. ed., *Environmental Crime, Sanctioning Strategies and Sustainable Development*, 1993.

Amendola, Gianfranco 'Need for a Strengthening of Criminal Environmental Law? The Italian Case' in Comte, Françoise and Kramer, Ludwig (eds.) Environmental Crime in Europe: Rules of Sanctions (Europa Law Publishing, Groningen 2004).

Ambos, K. 'Is the Development of a Common Substantive Criminal Law for Europe Possible?' 12 *MJ* 2 (2005).

Anja Gauger, Mai Pouye Rabatel-Fernel, Louise Kulbicki, Damien Short and Polly Higgins, *'Ecocide is the Missing 5th Crime Against Peace'* July 2012, Human Rights Consortium, School of Advanced Study, University of London.

Andenas, Mads, Baasch, Camilla A., Ashcroft, Ross 'Towards a Theory of Harmonisation' in M. Andenas and C. Baasch (eds.)*'Theory and Practice of Harmonisation'* Edward Elgar, 2011.

Andenas, Mads, Baasch, Camilla A (eds.) *'Theory and Practice of Harmonisation'* Edward Elgar, 2011.

Anderson et al, *Policing the European Union* (OUP, Oxford 1995).

Andersen, S. *The Enforcement of EU Law: The Role of the European Commission* (OUP, 2012).

Ashworth, Andrew, *Principles of Criminal Law* OUP (Fifth ed. OUP 2006).

Asp, P. 'Mutual Recognition and the Development of Criminal Law Cooperation within the European Union,' in *Harmonization of Criminal Law in Europe*, Husabø, E.J. and Strandbakken, Asbjørn.

Arlen, J and Kraakman, R. Controlling Corporate Misconduct: An Analysis of Corporate Liability Regimes, (1997) *New York University Law Review.*

Bandi, Gyula 'Liability and Sanctions, Criminal Liability in Hungary' in Comte, F. and Kramer, L. (eds.) Environmental Crime in Europe: Rules of Sanctions (Europa Law Publishing, Groningen 2004).

Bayle, M. 'Systems of Sanctions in the Field of Environmental Criminality', in Comte and Kramer (eds.) *Environmental Crimes in Europe: Rules of Sanctions* (2004).

Barber, M. Diane, 'Fair Warning: The Deterioration of Scienter Under Environmental Criminal Statutes', 26 *Loy. L.A.L.Rev.* 105 (1992).

Bantekas, I. 'The Legal Nature of Transnational Financial Crime' in Bantekas, I. and Keramidas, G. (ed.) *International and European Financial Criminal Law* (Butterworths, 2006).

Bantekas, Ilias, *International Criminal Law* (Hart Publishing, 2010).

Baker, Dennis, *The Right not to be Crimininalised: Demarcating Criminal Law's Authority*, (Ashgate, 2011).

Baker, Estella 'Taking European Criminal Law Seriously' *Criminal Law Review* [1998].

Barnett, Jon. *The Meaning Of Environmental Security: Ecological Politics And Policy In The New Security Era*. Zed Books, 2001.

Bartick, T. 'The Effects of Environmental Regulation on Business Location in the United States,' *Growth and Change* (1988).

Barrios, P. 'The Rotterdam Convention of Hazardous Chemicals: A Meaningful Step toward Environmental Protection', 16:4 *Georgetown International Environmental Law Review* (2003), 679.

Becker, G. 'Crime and Punishment: An Economic Approach' 76 *Journal of Political Economy* (1968) 161.

Berkman, 'Sacrificed Sovereignty? Dutch Soft Drug Policy in the Spectre of Europe Without Borders' *Boston College International and Comparative Law Review* vol. xix, no. 1, (1996) 173–185, 180.

Beccaria, Cesare *Beccaria On Crimes and Punishments and Other Writings.* Cambridge Texts in the History of Political Thought (1764).

Beke, M. and Blomeyer, R. *Illegal, Unreported and Unregulated Fishing: Sanctions in the EU: Study* (2004) at 51 available at http://www.europarl.europa.eu/RegData/etudes/STUD/2014/529069/IPOL_STU%282014%29529069_EN.pdf (accessed on 15 April 2015).

Bell, Stuart and Mcgillivray, Donald, *Environmental Law*, (sixth ed., OUP 2006).

Benson, D., Jordan, A. (2008) A grand bargain or an 'incomplete contract'? European Union environmental policy after the Lisbon Treaty. *European Energy and Environmental Law Review*, 17, 280–290.

Bentham, J. 'An Introduction to the Principles of Morals and Legislation' Oxford: Clarendon Press, 1996.

Berat, Lynn, 'Defending the Right to a Healthy Environment: Toward a Crime of Geocide in International Law' *Boston University International Law Journal* (Fall, 1993).

Bericht; Der Interministeriellen Arbeitsgruppe 'Umwelthaftungs – Und Umwelt-strafrecht', 19 Dezember 1998.

Betlem, G 'Beyond *Francovich*: Completing the Unified Member State and EU Liability Regime. A Comment on the Jan Jans Contribution' in Obradovic, D and Lavranos, N (ed), *Interface between EU law and National Law*, (Europa Law Publishing, Groningen 2007).

Betreuungsgesellschaft Für Umweltfragen (BFU), *Final Report: Organised Crime in the EU Member States*, Kassel 15 May 2003; http://ec.europa.eu/environment/legal/crime/pdf/organised_member_states.pdf.

Betreuungsgesellschaft Für Umweltfragen (BFU), *Final Report: Organised Crime in a Few Candidate Countries*, Kassel 10 September 2003; http://ec.europa.eu/environment/legal/crime/pdf/organised_candidate_countries.pdf.

Birnie, P. and Boyle, A. 'International Law and the Environment' 2nd edition, (OUP, 2002).

Birnie, P., Boyle, A. and Redgwell, C., 'International Law and the Environment' 3nd edition, (OUP, 2009).

Blanco, E. and Razzaque, J., *Globalisation and Natural Resources Law*, Edward Elgar, 2011.

Boeles, P. 'Introduction: Freedom, Security and Justice for All' in *Implementing Amsterdam: Immigration and Asylum Rights in EC Law* in Guild, E. and Harlow, C. ed. (Hart Publishing, Oxford 2001).

Boodman, Martin, 'The Myth of Harmonization of Laws', 39 *American Journal of Comparative Law.*

Boyle, A.E. '*Globalising Globalising Environmental Liability: The Interplay of National and International Law*', Journal of Environmental Law (2005) Vol 17 No 1, 3–26.

Boyle, A and Anderson, M. *Human Rights Approaches to Environmental Protection*, (Clarendon, Oxford 1998).

Brack, D, The Growth and Control of International Environmental Crime, in '*The Growth and Control of International Environmental Crime*' (Chatham House, 2007).

Brickey, Kathleen F. 'Environmental Crime at the Crossroads: the Intersection of Environmental and Criminal Law Theory', Tulane Law Review (1996).

Brito, B. & Barreto, P. Enforcement against Illegal Logging in the Brazilian Amazon. In: Kotze, L., Paddock, L., Qun, D., Markell, D.L., Markowitz, K.J., Zaelke, D. & Kotze, L.J. (eds.) *Compliance and Enforcement in Environmental Law: Toward More Effective Implementation* Edward Elgar Pub, (2011).

Bruch, Carl R, 'All's Not Fair in (Civil) War: Criminal Liability for Environmental Damage in Internal Armed Conflict' (2001) 25 *Vermont Law Review* 695, at 736.

Byam, John T. 'The Economic Inefficiency of Corporate Criminal Liability', J. Crim. L. & Criminology 582 (1982).

Buente, David T. 'The Civil Implications of Environmental Crime', 23 Envtl. L. Rep. (Oct. 1993).

Burrows, Paul; Ogus, Anthony I.; Richardson, Generva *Policing Pollution: A Study of Regulation and Enforcement Policing Pollution: A Study of Regulation and Enforcement* (Oxford, 1982).

Cadoppi, A. 'Towards a European Criminal Code?' 4 *European Journal of Crime, Criminal Law and Criminal Justice* 2 (1996).

Cassese, A. Gaeta, P. and Jones, J., *The Rome Statute of the International Criminal Court A Commentary* (2002).

Cassese, Antonio. *International Criminal Law* (OUP, Oxford 2003).

Carrera, Sergio and Geyer, Florian 'The Reform Treaty and Justice and Home Affairs: Implication for the Common Area of Freedom, Security and Justice' in Guild and Geyer (ed.) *Security versus Justice: Police and Judicial Cooperation in the European Union.*

Cicco, John and Bonano, Edward 'A Comparative Analysis of the Criminal Environmental Laws of the Fifty States: The Need for Statutory Uniformity as a Catalyst for Effective Enforcement of Existing and Proposed Laws' (1988) *Criminal Justice Quarterly* 9 (4) 216.

Cho, Byung-Sun, 'Emergence of an International Environmental Criminal Law?' Ucla *J. Envtl. L. & Pol'y* 11, (2000/2001).

Christopher D. Stone, 'Should trees have standing? Toward legal rights for natural objects', in *Should Trees Have Standing?* Oceana Publications, (1996).

Clapham, Andrew, The Complexity of International Criminal Law: Looking Beyond Individual Responsibility to the Responsibility of Organisations, Corporations and States, in Ramesh Thakur & Peter Malcontent (eds.), *'From Sovereignty Impunity to International Accountability: The Search for Justice in a World of States'* 233, 245–226 (2004).

Clifford, M. *Environmental Crime: Enforcement, Policy and Social Responsibility* (Gaitherburg: Aspen, 1998).

Coffee, John 'Corporate criminal liability, and introduction and comparative survey' in Criminal responsibility of legal and collective entities, Max Planck Institute, 1999.

Coffee, John 'No Soul to dawn: no body to kick: an unscandalized inquiry into the problem of corporate punishment', *MichLR*, 1980–1981.

Cohen, Mark A., 'Criminal Law: Environmental Crime and Punishment: Legal/Economic Theory and Empirical Evidence on Enforcement of Federal Environmental Status', 82 *J. Crim. L. & Criminology* 1054, (Winter, 1992).

Commission Staff Working Paper, *Establishing of an Acquis on Criminal Sanctions against Environmental Offences*, Brussels, 07.02.2001, SEC (2001) 227.

Commission Staff Working Document. *Impact Assessment: Accompanying Document to the Proposal for a Directive of the European Parliament and of the Council on the Protection of the Environment through Criminal Law* COM (2007) 51 Final.

Commission Communication to the European Parliament and the Council on the Implications of the Court's Judgement of 13 September 2005 (Case C-176/03 Commission v Council) COM (2005) 583 final/2, 24 November 2005.

Commission Green paper on conflicts of jurisdiction and the principle of *ne bis in idem* in criminal proceedings (COM (2005) 696, 23 Dec. 2005).

Commission Green Paper on the 'Approximation, Mutual Recognition and Enforcement of Criminal Sanctions in the European Union', Brussels 30.04.2004 COM (2004) 334 final.

Commission Green Paper on 'Procedural Safeguards for Suspects and defendants in criminal proceedings throughout the European Union' COM (2003) 75 final, 19 February 2003.

Commission Green Paper on criminal-law protection of the financial interests of the Community and the establishment of a European Prosecutor (COM (2001) 715 final), 11 December 2001.

Commission Communication 'Implementing the Hague Programme: The Way Forward' COM (2006) 331 final, 14.

Commission 'Impact Assessment, Next Steps? In Support of Competitiveness and Sustainable Development' SEC (2004) 1377, October 21, 2004.

Commission (DG Environment) '*Study on Criminal Penalties in a Few Candidate Countries' Environmental Law'*: Final Report' 6 October 2003.

Commission (DG Environment) '*Study on Measures other than Criminal Ones in Cases where Environmental Community law has not been respected in a few candidate countries: Summary Report,'* 30 September 2004. (B43040/2003/369100/MAR/A.3) http://ec.europa.eu/environment/legal/crime/pdf/cd_summary_report.pdf.

Comte, Françoise 'Environmental Crime and the Police in Europe: A Panorama and Possible Paths for Future Action' (2006) 15 *EELR* 190 at 198.

Comte, Françoise and Kramer, Ludwig (eds.) *Environmental Crime in Europe: Rules of Sanctions* (Europa Law Publishing, Groningen 2004).

Comte, Françoise, 'Protection of the Environment through Criminal Law: Destiny of the Various European Union's Initiatives' in Odina, Marco (ed.) *Europe and the Environment* (Groningen, 2004).

Comte, Françoise, 'Criminal Environmental Law and Community Competence,' (2003) *European Environmental Law Review*, 147.

Comte, Françoise, 'European Environmental Criminal Law – Recent Developments'. [2005] vol. 4 *YEEL* 209.

Corsterns, G.J.M., 'Criminal Law in the First Pillar?' (2003) *European Journal of Crime, Criminal Law and Criminal Justice*, 11/1.

Corstens, Geert and Pradel, Jean, *European Criminal Law* (Kluwer Law International, 2002).

Craig, Paul and De Burca, Graig, *EU Law: Text, Cases and Materials* (Fourth ed. OUP, Oxford 2007).

Grohs, Sibylle 'Articles 258/260 TFEU Infringement Procedures: The Commission Perspective in Environmental Cases' in Marisa Cremona (ed.) *Compliance and the Enforcement of EU Law* (OUP, 2012).

Crowford, Adam 'The Governance of Crime and Insecurity in an Anxious Age: The Trans-European and the Local' in (Crowford ed.) *Crime and Insecurity: The Governance of Safety in Europe,* (2002).

Cryer, R., Friman, H., Robinson, D. and Wilmshurst, E. 'An Introduction to International Criminal Law and Procedure' (second ed., CUP, 2011).

Council of Europe, European Committee on Crime Problems, *Report on Decriminalisation,* Strasbourg: Council of Europe (1980) 275.

Council of Europe Recommendation No. R.(88) 18 of the Committee of Ministers to Member States *concerning Liability of Enterprises having Legal Personality for Offences committed in the Exercise of their Activities*, 20 October 1998.

Darroch, Fiona and Harrison, Peter. *Environmental Crime* (London, 1999).

Davies, P. *European Union Environmental Law: an Introduction to Key Selected Issues,* Ashgate (2004).

Dawson, Mark, De Witte, Bruno; Muir, Elise, *Judicial Activism at the European Court of Justice*, (Edward Elgar, 2013).

De Baere, Geert, *EU External Action*, in Catherine Barnard and Steve Peers (eds.) *European Union Law* (OUP, 2014).

De Cicco, John and Bonano, Edward 'A Comparative Analysis of the Criminal Environmental Laws of the Fifty States: The Need for Statutory Uniformity as a Catalyst for Effective Enforcement of Existing and Proposed Laws' (1988) *Criminal Justice Quarterly* 9 (4) 216–294.

De Sadeleer, N. 'La Répression des Infractions en Matière de Gestion des Déchets' in Françoise Comte and Ludwig Kramer (ed.) *Environmental Crimes in Europe: Rules of Sanctions* (Groningen, 2004).

De Sadeleer, N. (ed.), *Implementing the Precautionary Principle: Approaches from the Nordic Countries, EU and USA* (Earthscan, 2007).

Delmas-Marty, Mireille, *Towards a Truly Common Law* (Cambridge University Press, Cambridge 2002).

Delmas-Marty, M. and Vervaele, J.A.E. (eds.), *The Implementation of the Corpus Juris in the Member States, Penal Provisions for the Protection of European Finances.* Intersentia (2000).

Delmas-Marty, M. 'The European Union and Penal Law' (1998) 4 *European Law Journal* 1.

Denza, Eileen. *The Intergovernmental Pillars of the European Union* (OUP, 2002).

De Prez, Paul 'Excuses, Excuses: The Ritual Trivialisation of Environmental Prosecutions' 12 *Journal of Environmental Law* 1.

Dine, Janet. 'European Community Criminal Law?' (1993) *Crim.L.R.* 246.

Dine, Janet, Companies, International Trade and Human Rights (CUP, 2010).

Drumbl, Mark A., 'International Human Rights, International Humanitarian Law, and Environmental Security: Can the International Criminal Court Bridge the Gaps?' *ILSA Journal of International and Comparative Law*, (Spring, 2000).

Dworkin, R., *A Matter of Principle* (Harvard University Press, 1985).

Dougan, 'Minimum harmonisation and the internal market' (2000) 37 *CMLRev.* 853.

Douma and Hartmanova 'EC or EU pillar – Criminal Enforcement of European Environmental Law' 11 European Law Reporter (2005).

Dunphy, A. Griffiths and S Benn, *'Organizational Change for Corporate Sustainability'* (Routledge, 2003).

Durkheim, E., The Evolution of Punishment, in Lukes and Scull (eds.) Durkheim and the Law (Oxford: Martin Robertson 1983).

Elsen, C (2007) 'From Maastricht to the Hague: the Politics of Judicial and Police Cooperation' *ERA Forum* 13.

Elkins, P. and S Speck, The impacts of environmental policy on competitiveness: the theory and evidence, in Baker, T. and Kohler (eds.) *International Competitiveness and Environmental Policies*, (Edward Elgar, 1998).

Emberland, Marius, *The Human Rights of Companies: Exploring the Structure of ECHR Protection* (OUP, Oxford 2006).

Estella, Antonio, *The EU Principle of Subsidiarity and its Critique* (OUP, Oxford 2002).

Esser, Albin, Harmonization of Penal Sanctions in Europe Comparative Typology of Convergences and Divergences in Delmas-Marty (ed.) *'L'Harmonisation des Sanctions Pénales en Europe'* (2003).

European Parliament Resolution on the consequences of the judgement of the Court of 13 September 2005 (C-176/03 *Commission v Council*) (2006/2007 (INI)) Committee on Legal Affairs (Rapporteur Giuseppe Gargani).

European Parliament Draft Report of the European Parliament Committee on Transport and Tourism on the proposal for a directive of the European Parliament and of the Council amending Directive 2005/35/EC on ship source pollution and on the introduction of penalties for infringements (COM(2008)0134 – C6-0142/2008 – 2008/0055(COD)).

European Parliament Report of June 21, 2000 on the initiative of the Kingdom of Denmark with a view to the adoption of a Council Framework Decision on combating environmental crime, rapporteur G. Di Lello Finuoli, A5 0178/2000 (Committee on Citizen's Freedoms and Rights, Justice and Home Affairs).

European Parliament Opinion on the Initiative of the Kingdom of Denmark with the view of Adopting a Framework Decision on Combating Serious Environmental Crime 07.07.2000, OJ 24.04.2001 C121/494.

European Parliament recommendation on criminal sanctions and Community law (OJ C 140 E/524 13.6.2002, T5 – 0147/2002, Bull.2002/4, point 1.4.53).

Faure, Michael. 'European Environmental Criminal Law: Do we really need?' (2004) 13 *EELR* 18.

Faure, Michael and Heine, Gunter, *Criminal Enforcement of Environmental Law in the European Union* Kluwer Law International (2005).

Faure, Michael and Heine, Günter, *Final Report: Criminal Penalties in EU Member States Environmental Law*, Maastricht 4 October 2002; http://ec.europa.eu/environment/legal/crime/pdf/criminal_penalties1.pdf.

Faure, Michael and Heine, Günter 'Criminal Enforcement of Environmental Law in the European Union' IMPEL Network, July 2000.

Faure, Michael and Heine, Gunter, *Environmental Criminal Law in the European Union. Documentation of the Main Provisions with Introductions* (Freiburg, 2000).

Faure, M. and Visse, M. 'How to Punish Environmental Pollution? Some Reflections on the Various Models of Criminalisation of Environmental Harm' (1995) 3 *European Journal of Crime, Criminal Law and Criminal Justice.*

Fisher, D.E., 'Environmental protection and the Criminal Law' *Crim. L.J.* (1981).

Fisher, E., Jones, J. and Van Schomberg, R. (eds.), Implementing the Precautionary Principle: Perspectives and Prospects (Edward Elgar, 2006).

Feinberg, J. *The Moral Limits of the Criminal Law: Harm to Others*, Oxford University Press, 1984.

Fletcher, Maria, Loof, Robin and Gilmore, Bill, *EU Criminal Law and Justice* (Edward Elgar, 2008).

Fletcher, G. *Rethinking Criminal Law* (OUP, Oxford 2000).

Foucault, M. *Discipline and Punishment: The Birth of the Prison*, 1977.

Francioni, Francesco (ed.), '*The 1972 World Heritage Convention, Oxford Commentaries on International Law*', (OUP, 2008).

Gallas, Andreas and Werner, Julia 'Transboundary Environmental Crimes: German Experiences and Approaches' Fifth International Conference on Environmental Compliance and Enforcement, vol. 1 INECE, 1998 at 377.

Galligan, D.J. *Due Process and Fair Procedures: A Study of Administrative Procedures* (Clarendon Press, Oxford 1996).

Garoupa, Nuno and Stephen, Frank H. 'Why Plea-Bargaining Fails to Achieve Results in So Many Criminal Justice Systems: A New Framework for Assessment' (2008) 15 (3) *M.J.* 323.

Gaynor, Kevin A. and Bartman Thomas R., 'Criminal Enforcement of Environmental Laws', *Colorado Journal of International Environmental Law and Policy*, (Winter, 1999).

Gray, Mark A., 'The International Crime of Ecocide', *California Western International Law Journal*, (1996).

Gobert, James and Punch, Maurice, *Rethinking Corporate Crime,* (Butterworths, 2003).

Gobert, James 'Controlling Corporate Criminality: Penal Sanctions and Beyond' (1998) *Web Current Journal of Legal Issues.*

Gormley, 'Free Movement of Goods and the Environment' in Holder (ed.) Impact of EC environmental law in the United Kingdom (Wiley 1997).

Gidi, Antonio 'Class Actions in Brazil – A Model for Civil Law Countries' (2003) *American Journal of Comparative Law* 311.

Gilbert, G. 'The Criminal Responsibility of States' (1990) 39 *I.C.L.Q* 345.

Guild, Elspeth and Geyer, Florian (e.d.) Security versus Justice? Police and Judicial Cooperation in the European Union (Ashgate, 2008).

Guinchard, Audrey 'Human Rights in Financial Services: the Boundaries between Discipline and Crime' (2007) 15(2) *European Journal of Crime, Criminal Law and Criminal Justice* 2007 pp 173–203.

Guinchard, Audrey 'Fixing the Boundaries of the Concept of Crime: the Challenge for Human Rights', International and Comparative Law Quarterly, vol. 54, (July 2005).

Guinchard, Audrey, *Les Enjeux du Pouvoir de Repression en Matiere Penale Du Modele Judiciaire a L'Attraction d'un Systeme Unitaire,* L.G.D.J. 2003.

Hadish, Sanford, 'The Crisis of Overcriminalisation' (1967) 374 *The Annals of American Academy of Political and Social Science.*

Haenen, Iris, Classifying Acts as Crimes Against Humanity in the Rome Statute of the International Criminal Court, (2013) *German Law Journal* [Vol. 14 No. 07].

Hall, Matthew, *Victims of Environmental Harm: Rights Recognition and Redress under National and International Law,* (Routledge, 2013).

Hafner, G. 'Pros and Cons Ensuing from Fragmentation of International Law', (2004) 25 *Michigan Journal of International Law* 849.

Hanley, N., Shogren, Jason and White, Ben, *Introduction to Environmental Economics,* (OUP 2001).

Hardin, G. (1968), 'The Tragedy of the Commons', *Science,* 162 (1968).

Harding, C. 'European Regimes of Crime Control: Objectives, Legal Bases and Accountability' 7 *MJ* 3 (2000).

Hayman, Gavin and Brack, Dunkan, *Workshop Report: International Environmental Crime: The Nature and Control of Environmental Black Markets* (the Royal Institute of International Affairs, London 1998).

Hartley TC, *The Foundations of European Community Law* (Sixth ed. OUP, Oxford 2007).

Hardenbrook, Andrew, 'Equator Principles: The Private Financial Sector's Attempt at Environmental Responsibility' 40 *Vand. J. Transnat'l L.* 197 (2007).

Hans-Jorg Albrecht and Seppo Leppa, 'Criminal Law and the Environment', Proceedings of the European Seminar held in Lauchhammer, Land Brandenburg, Germany, April 1992.

Hawkins, K. *Environment and Enforcement: Regulation and Social Definition of Pollution* (Oxford, 1984).

Hawke, Neil *Corporate Liability* (London: Sweet & Maxwell, 2000).

Hedemann-Robinson, Martin The European Union and Environmental Criminal Liability: A Legal Analysis in the Light of the Recent Ruling of the European Court of Justice on EC Competence (Case C-176/03 European Commission v Council). (2005) *Environmental Liability*, 13 (6).

Hedemann-Robinson, Martin *Enforcement of European Union Environmental Law: Legal Issues and Challenges* (Routledge-Cavendish, 2007).

Hedemann-Robinson, Martin The emergence of European Union environmental criminal law: a quest for solid foundations – Part II (2008) *Environmental Liability*, 16 (4).

Hedemann-Robinson, Martin The emergence of European Union environmental criminal law: a quest for solid foundations – Part I. (2008) *Environmental Liability*, 16 (3).

Hedemann-Robinson, Martin, The EU and Environmental Crime: The Impact of the ecj's Judgment on Framework Decision 2005/667 on Ship-Source Pollution, (2008) *Journal of Environmental Law.*

Heine, Gunter 'Environmental Protection and Criminal Law' in Owe Lomas ed. *Frontiers of Environmental Law* (Chancery Law Publishing, 1991).

Heine, G. and Ringelmann, C. 'Approximation of European Criminal Legislation', in Comte, F. and Kramer, L. *Environmental Crime in Europe: Rules of Sanctions* (Groningen, 2004).

Herlin-Karnell, Ester (2007) 'Recent Developments in the Area of European Criminal Law' 14 *Maastricht Journal of European and Comparative Law* 1.

Herlin-Karnell, Ester. '"Light Weapons" and the Dynamics of Art 47 EU – The ec's Armoury of Ever Expanding Competences' [2008] 71 (6) *M.L.R.* 998.

Hey, E. 'The Precautionary Concept in Environmental Policy and Law: Institutionalizing Caution', 4:2 *Georgetown International Environmental Law Review* (1992).

Hey, E. *Reflections on an International Environmental Court*, Martinus Nijhoff Publishers, 2000.

Hitchcock, Teresa and Trounson, Noy 'Green Crimes: the EU Proposal for an Environmental Crimes Directive' (2007) 19 *ELM* 119.

Hoare, Alison (ed.), *'The Growth and Control of International Environmental Crime',* (Chatham House, 2007) available at http://www.illegal-logging.info/uploads/Intenvcrime2007backgroundpapers.pdf (accessed on 10 April 2015).

Hoffman, L. 'Copenhagen and Beyond – How to Provide the New Climate Deal with a State-of-the-Art Non-Compliance Mechanism?' *EEELR* 2009.

Hoffmeister, Frank 'The Contribution of EU Practice to International Law' in Marisa Cremona (ed.), *'Developments in EU External Relations Law'* (OUP, 2008).

Horspool, M. and Humphreys, M. *European Union Law* (OUP, Oxford 2006).

House of Lords, European Union Committee, 'The Treaty of Lisbon: an Impact Assessment' Volume I: Report 13 March 2008. 10th Report of Session 2007–2008.

House of Commons Select Committee, the Twenty-Third Report on the Amending Ship-Source Pollution Directive (29560) 7616/08 COM (08) 134.

House of Lords, European Union Committee, 42nd Report of Session 2005–2006 'The Criminal Law Competence of the European Community. Report with Evidence' 28 July 2006.

House of Commons Environmental Audit Committee, Second Report of Session 2004–2005, 'Corporate Environmental Crime' (2005) HC 136.

House of Commons Environmental Audit Committee, Ninth Report of Session 2003–04, 'Environmental Crime: Fly-tipping, Fly-posting, Litter, Graffiti and Noise', HC445.

House of Commons Select Committee on European Scrutiny of the UK Parliament 13th Report of the, 'Draft Directive on the Protection of the Environment through Criminal Law' April 2001.

House of Commons, Research Paper. Judicial Review: A Short Guide to Claims in the Administrative Court, 0644 (2006). http://www.parliament.uk/commons/lib/research/rp2006/rp06-044.pdf.

Hulme, Karen, *War Torn Environment: Interpreting the Legal Threshold*, Martinus Nijhoff Publications, 2004 (Volume 7 International Humanitarian Law Series).

Huglo Lepage & Partners, *Study on Environmental Crime in the 27 Member States*, JLS/D3/2006/05 Final Report April 2007; http://ec.europa.eu/environment/legal/crime/pdf/report_environmental_crime.pdf.

Husak, Douglas. 'The criminal law as last resort.' *Oxford Journal of Legal Studies* 24.2 (2004).

Husak, Douglas, Overcriminalisation: *The Limits of the Criminal Law* (New York: Oxford University Press, 2008).

Jack, B. *Enforcing Member States Compliance with EU Environmental Law: A Critical Evaluation of the Use of Financial Penalties*, Journal of Environmental Law 23:1, 2010.

Jans, Jan and Vedder, Hans. *European Environmental Law* (Groningen: 2008).

Holder, Jane and Lee, Maria. *Environmental Protection, Law and Policy* (Cambridge University Press, Cambridge 2007).

Jegouzo, Isabelle. 'Le development Progressif du Principe de Reconnaissance Mutuelle des Décisions Judiciaires Pénal Dans L'Union Europeenne' *Revue Internationale de Droit Penal*, 1/2 Trimestres 2006.

José M. Borrero Navia (ed) *Control social y política criminal en medio ambiente: memorias: encuentro regional celebrado en la Universidad del Cauca*, Popayán, 1997.

Joseph, Tamara: 'Preaching heresy: permitting member states to enforce stricter environmental laws than the European Community,' YJIL (1995).

Farkhanda Zia-Mansoor, 'International Regime and the EU Developments for Preventing and Controlling Vessel-Source Oil Pollution', (2005) *EELR* 165.

Fisse, Brent 'Reconstructing Corporate Criminal Law: Deterrence, Retribution, Fault and Sanctions', 56 *A. Cal. L. Rev.* 1141 (1983).

Fisse, Brent and Braithwaite, John 'Corporations, Crime and Accountability' (Cambridge University Press, Cambridge 1993).

Fitzmaurice, M. *International Legal Problems of the Environmental Protection of the Baltic Sea*, (Springer, 1992).

Fitzmaurice, M. *Contemporary Issues in International Environmental Law* (Edward Elgar, 2009).

Fitzmaurice, M. 'Environmental Justice through International Compliant Procedures? Comparing the Aarhus Convention and the North American Agreement on Environmental Matters' in Ebbeson and Okowa (eds) *Environmental Law and Justice in Context* (CUP, 2009).

Fitzmaurice, M. 'Natural Resources Management: Protecting Fisheries in the 21st Century', in E. Blanco and J. Razzaque (eds.), *Natural Resources and the Green Economy: Redefining the Challenges for People, States and Corporations*, Martinus Nijhoff/BRILL, 2012.

Fletcher, George, *Basic Principles of Criminal Law* (OUP USA, 1998).

Fletcher, Maria, Loof, Robin and Gilmore, Bill. *EU Criminal Law and Justice*, Edward Elgar (2008).

Frank, Veronica 'Consequences of the Prestige Sinking for European and International Law' [2005] 20 *The Int J Mar Coast Law* 44.

Friedman, Lawrence. 'Questions of Intent: Environmental Crimes and "Public Welfare" Offences' *Vill. Envtl. L.J.* (1999).

Kadish, Sanford H., 'Some Observations on the Use of Criminal Sanctions in Enforcing Economic Regulations', 30 U.Chi.L.Rev. 423 (1963).

Kalas, Peggy Rodges 'Internartional Environmental Dispute Resolution and the Need for Access by Non-State Entities', *Colorado Journal of International Environmental Law & Policy* 1996.

Kellett, P. 'Is the Better Regulation Agenda Producing Better Regulation?' (2008) 20 *Environmental Law & Management* 5, 210.

Kecse-Nagy et al, *Study on the Enforcement of the EU Wildlife Trade Regulations in the EU-25: Final Report*, November 2006. http://ec.europa.eu/environment/legal/crime/pdf/cites_report.pdf.

Kis, Norbert 'The Principle of Culpability in European Criminal law Systems' in *Towards More Harmonised Criminal Law in the European Union* (Miklos Hollan Budapest 2004).

Klein, Natalie, *Maritime Security and the Law of the Sea* (OUP, 2011).

Kostenniemi, M. Martti and Leino, P. 'Fragmentation of International Law? Postmodern Anxieties', (2002) 15 *LJIL* 553.

Khee-Jin Tan, Alan. *Vessel-Source Marine Pollution: The Law and Politics of International Regulation* (Cambridge University Press, Cambridge 2006).

Khanna, V.S. 'Corporate Criminal Liability: What Purpose Does it Serve?' (1996) 109 *Harvard Law Review* 7.

Kharlamov, O., Kharlamova, G., Kirillova, N. and Fomenko, V, 'Persistent Organic Pollutants (Pops) at Nanotechnology and Their Impact on People Health', in: E. Mehmetli and B. Koumanova (eds.), *The Fate of Organic Pollutants in the Environment* (Springer, 2008).

Kraakman, Reinier H., 'Corporate Liability Strategies and the Costs of Legal Controls', 93 Yale L.J. 857 (1984).

Kramer, L. *EC Environmental Law* (6th ed. Sweet & Maxwell, 2007).

Kramer, Ludwig. 'Case Law Analysis: Environment, Crime and EC Law', (2006) 18 (2) *Journal of Environmental Law* 277.

Kraemer, Ludwig, *Casebook on EC Environmental Law* (Hart, 2002).

Kramer, Ludwig, *EC Environmental Law* (Sweet and Maxwell, 2000).

Lars Emanuelsson Korsell, 'Big Stick, Little Stick: Strategies for Controlling and Combating Environmental Crime' (2001) 2 *Journal of Scandinavian Studies in Criminology and Crime Prevention* 127.

Lawson, Sam 'International Environmental Crime: Data Collection, Transparency and Auditing' in *The Growth and Control of International Environmental Crime (2007), available at* http://www.illegal-logging.info/uploads/Intenvcrime2007 backgroundpapers.pdf (accessed on 15 February 2015).

Lazarus, Richard J., 'Assimilating Environmental Protection into Legal Rules and the Problem with Environmental Crime', 27 *Loy. L.A.L.Rev.* 867, (1993).

Lazarus, Richard J., 'Meeting the Demands of Integration in the Evolution of Environmental Law: Reforming Environmental Criminal Law', 83 *Geo. L.J.* 2407, (1995).

Locke, R. Christopher, 'Environmental Crimes: The Absence of Intent and the Complexities of Compliance' 16 *Colum.J.Envtl.L.*311 (1991).

Loof, R. 'Shooting from the Hip: Proposed Minimum Rights in Criminal Proceedings throughout the EU' 12 *European Law Journal* 421 [2006].

Lefeber, R. *Transboundary Environmental Interference and the Origins of State Liability* Kluwer Law International, The Hague, 1996.

Leigh, L.H., *Strict and Vicarious Liability: a Study in Administrative Criminal Law* (Sweet & Maxwell, London 1986).

Lee, Maria *EU Environmental Law: Challenges, Change and Decision-Making,* (Hart Publishing, 2005).

Legrand, Pierre 'On the Unbearable Localness of the Law: Academic Fallacies and Unreasonable Observations' (2003) 10/1 *European Review of Private Law* 66.

Levinson, A. 'Environmental Regulation and Manufactures' Location Choices: Evidence of the Census of Manufactures,' (1996) *Journal of Public Economics* 62.

Lin, A.C. (2005) Beyond Tort: Compensating Victims of Environmental Toxic Injury, *Southern California Law.*

Lundqvist, L. 'Sweden and Ecological Governance: Straddling the Fence,' Issues in Environmental Politics (2003).

Mclaughlin, Robert, 'Improving Compliance: Making Non-State International Actors Responsible for Environmental Crimes', 11 *Colorado Journal of International Law and Policy*, 2000.

Macrory, Richard 'New Approaches to Regulatory Sanctions' (2008) 20 *Environmental Law & Management* 5, 210.

Macrory, Richard. 'Regulatory Justice: Making Sanctions Effective: Final Report' Cabinet Office, November (2006). http://www.cabinetoffice.gov.uk/regulation/documents/pdf/macrory_penalties.pdf.

Macrory, Richard and Woods, Michael. *Environmental Civil Penalties: A More Proportionate Response to Regulatory Breach* www.ucl.ac.uk/laws/environment/civil-penalty.

Macrory, Richard R. '*Regulation, Enforcement and Governance in Environmental Law*' (Hart, 2014).

M. Lynch And P. Stretsky, 'The Meaning of Green: Contrasting Criminological Perspectives' (2003) 7 *Theoretical Criminology* 217.

Mackenzie, R. (2004) The Cartagena Protocol after the First Meeting of the Parties, *Review of European Community and International Environmental Law*, 13 (3) 270.

Makuch, Zen 'The Approximation of European Union Environmental Law: Transposition and Implementation Frameworks' Carswell International (London, 2000).

Margolis, Joshua D., and James P. Walsh. 'Misery loves companies: Rethinking social initiatives by business.' *Administrative science quarterly* 48.2 (2003).

Mccaffrey, Stephen C., 'Crimes Against the Environment', in Bassiouni, Cherif M., *International Criminal Law*, 1996.

Mccaffrey, Stephen C., 'Crimes against the environment', in Bassiouri, C. *International Criminal Law:* Sources, Subjects and Contents (Vol.1) (BRILL, 2008).

Mclaughlin, Robert. 'Improving Compliance: Making Non-State International Actors Responsible for Environmental Crimes', 11 *Colo. J. Int'L Envtl. L. & Pol'Y* 377, (Summer, 2000).

Mcauley, F. and Mccutcheon, J.P. *Criminal Liability* (Dublin, 2000).

Mcgillivray, 'Valuing nature: Economic Value, Conservation values and Sustainable Development' 2002 14(1) JEL 85.

Mcgillivray and Holder, 'Locating EC Environmental Law' (2001) 20 *YEL*.

Mclaughlin, Robert 'Improving Compliance: Making Non-State International Actors Responsible for Environmental Crimes', 11 *Colorado Journal of International Law and Policy*, 2000.

Megret, Frederic, 'The Problem of an International Criminal Law of the Environment' vol.36:2 *Columbia Journal of Environmental Law* (2011).

Meron, Theodor, Is International Law Moving Towards Criminalization? *European Journal of International Law* 9 (1998).

Milieu Ltd. Environmental Law & Policy, *Final Report: Study on Criminal Penalties in a Few Candidate Countries' Environmental Law*, 6 October 2003; http://ec.europa.eu/environment/legal/crime/pdf/criminal_pen_vol1.pdf.

Milieu & Huglo Lepage 'Summary Report: Study on Measures other than Criminal Ones in Cases where Environmental Community Law has not been Respected in the EU Member States,' 20 September 2004, at 52. (B4-3040A/2003/369724/MAR/A.3).

Milieu Consortium & Legambiente, *The Illegal Trafficking in Hazardous Waste in Italy and Spain: Final Report*, GEPEC-EC, October 2003; http://ec.europa.eu/environment/legal/crime.

Mitsilegas, Valsamis. 'The Competence Question: The European Community and Criminal Law' in Guild, Elspeth and Geyer, Florian (e.d.) *Security versus Justice? Police and Judicial Cooperation in the European Union* (Ashgate, 2008).

Mitsilegas, Valsamis 'The Transformation of Criminal Law in the "Area of Freedom, Security and Jusctice"' (2007) 26 *YEEL* 1.

Mitsilegas, Valsamis, 'Trust-Building Measures in the European Judicial Area in Criminal Matters: Issues of Competence, Legitimacy and Inter-institutional Balance' in Balzacq, Thierry and Carrera, Sergio (ed.) *Security Versus Freedom? A Challenge for Europe's Future*, (Datmouth: Ashgate 2006) at 279.

Mitsilegas, Valsamis. 'Constitutional Principles of the European Community and European Community Law' (2006) 8 *European Journal of Law Reform*, no. 2/3.

Mitsilegas, Valsamis, 'The Constitutional Implications of Mutual Recognition in Criminal Matters in the EU' (2006) 43 *Common Market Law Review* 1277.

Mitsilegas, Valsamis 'Judicial Co-operation in Criminal Matters between the European Union and third states: International Agreements,' in Marisa Leaf (ed.) *Cross-Border Crime: Defence Rights in a New Era of International Judicial Co-operation* JUSTICE 2006.

Mitsilegas, Valsamis, Monar, Jorg and Rees, Wyn, *The European Union and Internal Security: Guardian of the People?* (Palgrave, 2003).

Mitsilegas, Valsamis, 'Defining Organised Crime in the EU: The Limits of European Criminal Law in an Area of Freedom, Security and Justice.' (2001) 56 *ELRev* 565.

Mitsilegas, Valsamis, *EU Criminal Law* (Hart, 2009).

Mitsilegas, Valsamis, 'The third wave of third pillar law: which direction for EU criminal justice?', [2009], *European Law Review*, 34.

Mitisilegas, V., Fitzmaurice, M. and Fasoli, E. *'Analysis of International Legal Instruments Relevant in the Fight Against Environmental Crime'*, EFFACE, July 2014. See further See http://efface.eu (accessed on 10 April 2015).

Morgan, Caroline and Faull, Jonathan, 'The Role of Criminal Law in the EU', *Journal of European Criminal Law*, vol.1 issue 1, 2006.

Mueller, Gerhard 'An Essay on Environmental Criminality.' In Sally M. Edwards, Terry D. Edwards, Charles B. Fields (eds.) *Environmental Crime and Criminality: Theoretical and Practical Issues* (Garland Pub, New York 1996).

Murphy, Sean D. *Does the World Need a New International Environmental Court?* 32 *Geo. Wash. J. Int'l L. & Econ.* 333 (1999–2000).

Nellemann, C., Interpol Environmental Crime Programme (eds). *Green carbon, black trade: Illegal Logging, Tax Fraud and Laundering in the World's Tropical Forests,* A Rapid Response Assessment. United Nations Environment Programme, GRIDA-rendal (2012); available at *http://www.unep.org/pdf/RRAlogging_english_scr.pdf* (accessed on 15 February 2015).

Nellemann, C., Henriksen, R., Raxter, P., Ash, N.,Mrema, E. (Eds). 2014. *The Environmental Crime Crisis: Threats to Sustainable Development from Illegal Exploitation and Trade in Wildlife and Forest Resources. A Rapid Response Assessment.* A UNEP Rapid Response Assessment. United Nations Environment Programme and GRID-Arendal, Nairobi and Arendal, at 4. available at http://www.unep.org/unea/docs/rracrimecrisis.pdf (accessed on 15 February 2015).

Ngarize, Sekai, Makuch, Karen E., and Pereira, Ricardo. 'The Case for Regulating Nanotechnologies: International, European and National Perspectives.' *Review of European, Comparative & International Environmental Law* 22.2 (2013): 131–145.

Nield, K. and Pereira, R., 'Fraud on the European Union Emissions Trading Scheme: Effects, Vulnerabilities and Regulatory Reform' (2011) 20 *European Energy and Environmental Law Review*, Issue 6.

Nield, K. and Pereira, R. 'Financial Crimes in the European Carbon Markets' in Stefan Weishaar and Edwin Woerdman (eds.) '*Research Handbook on Emissions Trading*' (Edward Elgar, 2015/2016, forthcoming).

Noguera Vercher, Antonio, 'Some Reflections on the Use of Criminal Law for the Protection of the Environment' (2002) 10 *Env. liability* 3 107.

Noguera Vercher, A. 'The Use of Criminal Law for the Protection of the Environment in Europe: Council of Europe Resolution (77) 28' (1990) 10 *Northwestern Journal of International Law & Business* 442.

Obokata, Tom, Key EU Principles to Combat Transnational Organised Crime, *CMLREv* Jun 2011.

Ogus, Anthony and Abbot, Carolyn 'Sanctions for Pollution: Do we have the Right Regime?' *Journal of Environmental Law* vol. 14 no. 3.

Ormerod, David. *Smith and Hogan Criminal Law* (11th ed. OUP 2005).

Omorogbe, Yinka and Oniemola, Peter. 'Property Rights in Oil and Gas under Domanial Regimes' in Aileen McHarg et al (eds), *Property and the Law in Energy and Natural Resources* (Oxford University Press, 2010).

Orlitzky, Marc, Frank L. Schmidt, and Sara L. Rynes. 'Corporate social and financial performance: A meta-analysis.' *Organization studies* 24.3 (2003).

Osofsky, Hari M. 'Environmental Human Rights under the Alien Tort Statute: Redress for Indigenous Victims of Multinational Corporations', *Suffolk Transnational Law Review*, (Summer, 1997).

Ovey, Clare and White, Robin, *Jacobs & White: The European Convention on Human Rights* (OUP, Oxford 2006).

Pagh, Peter, 'Administrative Criminal Law Systems in Europe: an Asset for the Environment?' in Comte, Françoise and Kramer, Ludwig (eds.) *Environmental Crime in Europe: Rules of Sanctions* (Europa Law Publishing, Groningen 2004).

Palmer, Karen, Oates, E. Wallace and Portney, R. Paul, 'Tightening Environmental Standards: The Benefit-Cost or the No-Cost Paradigm?' (1995) 9 *Journal of Economic Perspectives* 4, 119.

Packer, H. *The Limits of the Criminal Sanction*, Stanford, 1969.

Pradel, Jean *Droit Penal Compare* (Dalloz, 2nd ed. 2002).

Pradel, Jean and Corstens, G. *European Criminal Law* 2002.

Prechal, Sacha, *Directives in EC Law* (Second ed. OUP, Oxford 2005).

Perron, Walter, 'Perspectives of the Harmonization of Criminal Law and Criminal Procedure in the European Union' in Husabø, E.J. and Strandbakken, Asbjørn (ed.) *Harmonization of Criminal Law in Europe* (Intersentia, 2005).

Peers, S (2008) 'EU Criminal Law and the Treaty of Lisbon' *European Law Review.*

Peers, Steve, 'The European Community's Criminal Law Competence: the Plot Thickens' (2008) *European Law Review* 399.

Peers, Steve, *EU Justice and Home Affairs* (Longman, 2000).

Peers, Steve, *EU Justice and Home Affairs Law* (Second ed. OUP, Oxford 2006).

Peers, Steve, *EU Justice and Home Affairs Law* (Third ed., OUP, Oxford 2011).

Peers, Steve. Sanctions for Infringement of EU law after the Lisbon Treaty, *European Public Law* (2012) 33.

Peers, Steve. 'Mutual Recognition and Criminal Law in the European Union: Has the Council got it Wrong?' in *Common Market Law Review* 41: 5–36, 2004.

Peers, Steve 'Double Jeopardy and EU Law: Time for a Change?' *European Journal of Law Reform* Vol. VIII no. 2/3.

Peers, Steve 'Salvation Outside the Church: Judicial Protection in Third Pillar after the Pupino and Segi Judgements' (2007) *Common Market Law Review.*

Peers, S (2007) *Statewatch Analysis*, EU Reform Treaty Analysis no. 4: British and Irish Opt-Outs from EU Justice and Home Affairs Law, 26 October 2007, available online at http://www.statewatch.org.

Peers, S (2008) *Statewatch Analysis* 'Changing the institutional framework for EU Justice and Home Affairs law without the Lisbon Treaty' July 2008, available online at http://www.statewatch.org/.

Peers, S (2008) 'Can the Treaty of Lisbon be ratified or implemented? A Legal Analysis' available online at http://www.statewatch.org.

Peers, S. (2009) *Statewatch Analysis* 'The proposed Framework Decision on conflict of jurisdiction in criminal proceedings: Manipulating the right to a fair trial?' 12 March 2009, available at http://www.statewatch.org/analyses/no-76-conflict-of-jurisdiction.pdf.

Pereira, Ricardo. 'Environmental Criminal Law in the First Pillar: A Positive Development for Environmental Protection in the European Union?' (2007) 16 *European Environmental Law Review* 254.

Pereira, Ricardo. 'On the Legality of the Ship-Source Pollution 2005/35/EC Directive – the Intertanko Case and Selected Others' (2008) *European Energy & Environmental Law Review* 372.

Pereira, Ricardo. 'The Right to Reproductive Self-Determination of Indigenous Peoples under International Human Rights Law', in Berking S. and Zolkos M. (ed.) *Between Life and Death: Governing Population in an Era of Human Rights*, Peter Lang Publishing Group (February 2009).

Pereira, Ricardo. 'The Legal Basis for Harmonisation of Environmental Criminal Law in the EU: Past and Future Challenges' in Andenas, M., Baasch, C. A (eds.) *'Theory and Practice of Harmonisation'* Edward Elgar, 2011.

Pereira, Ricardo. 'The Regionalisation of Criminal Law – The Example of European Criminal Law' in L. van den Herik and C. Stahn (eds.), *The Diversification and Fragmentation of International Criminal Law*, Martinus Nijhoff Publishers/Brill, 2012.

Pereira, Ricardo, 'Environmental Regulation, Business Competitiveness and Corporate Responsibility,' in K. Makuch and R. Pereira (eds.).*Environmental and Energy Law* (Wiley-Blackwell, 2012).

Pereira, Ricardo, 'Compliance and Enforcement in International, European and National Environmental Law' in *Environmental and Energy Law* (Wiley.Blackwell, 2012).

Pereira, Ricardo, 'The Exploration and Exploitation of Energy Resources in International Law,' in K. Makuch and R. Pereira (eds.) *Environmental and Energy Law* (Wiley-Blackwell, 2012).

Pereira, Ricardo and Gough, Orla (2014) Permanent sovereignty over natural resources in the 21st century: natural resource governance and the right to self-determination of indigenous peoples under international law. *Melbourne Journal of International Law*, 14 (2). pp. 451–495.

Pereira, Ricardo, The Cartagena Protocol On Living Modified Organisms: The Regulation Of Trade In Transgenic Organisms Under International And European Environmental Law. In: Benedict, M. ed. *Transgenic Insects: Techniques And Applications*. (CABI, 2014).

Pereira, Ricardo, Pollution from Seabed Activities, in Attard, D. Fitzmaurice, M. and Gutierrez, Norman A. Martinez (eds.) *The IMLI Manual on International Maritime Law* Volume III (in press, OUP 2015).

Pinzon, Lillian M., 'The Criminalization of the Trans-boundary Movement of Hazardous Waste and the Effect on Corporations', 7 *DePaul Bus. L.J.* 173 (1994).

Posner, Richard A. 'Economic Analysis of Law' Aspen Publishers, 2003.

Posner, R. 'An Economic Approach to Legal Procedure and Judicial Administration' (1973) 2 *Journal of Legal Studies* 399.

Porter, M. and Van Der Linde, C, 'Toward a New Conception of the Environment-Competitiveness Relationship', *Journal of Economic Perspective*, 9 (4) 1995: 97–118.

Porter, M. and Van Der Linde, C. 'Toward a New Conception of the Environment-Competitiveness Relationship', in Gray, W. (ed.) *Economic Costs and Consequences of Environmental Regulation* (Ashgate, 2002).

Prinssen, J. 'Domestic Legal Effects of EU Criminal Law: A Transfer of EC Law Doctrines?' in Obradovic, D and Lavranos, N (ed.) *Interface between EU law and National Law*, Groningen, Europa Law Publishing.

Provost, Rene 'International Criminal Environmental Law,' in Good-Gill, G. and Talmon, S (eds.) *The Reality of International Law: Essays in Honour of Ian Brownlie*, (Oxford 1999).

Rachel G., Standifer R, Stone L. and Sullivan J., 'Environmental Crimes', *American Criminal Law Review*, 2003.

Ragazzi, M., *The Concept of International Obligations Erga Omnes* 1 (Oxford, 2000).

Rauxloh, R., 'The Role of International Criminal Law in Environmental Protection' in F. Botchway (ed.) *Natural Resource Investment and Africa's Development*, (Edward Elgar, 2011).

Richardson G., Ogus A. and Burrows P., *Policing Pollution: A Study of Regulation and Enforcement*, Oxford (1982).

Ringelmann, C. 'Recent Trends in Environmental Criminal Legislation' (1997) 5 *Eur. J. Crime L. & Crim. Just.* 393.

Robinson, Paul 'The Criminal-Civil Distinction and the Utility of Desert' (1996) 76 *Boston University Law Review* 201.

Robinson, Paul and John Darley, 'Does Criminal Law Deter? A Behavioural Science Investigation' *Oxford Journal of Legal Studies*, Vol. 24, No. 2 (2004).

Rothwell and Stephens, *International Law of the Sea*, (Hart Publishing, 2010).

Ross, Malcom 'Effectiveness in the European Legal Order(s): Beyond Supremacy to Constitutional Proportionality' (2005) *European Law Review* 30 (6).

Sagoff, Mark 'Economic Theory and Environmental Law', *Mich. L R*, 1980–1981.

Sands, Philip, *Principles of International Environmental Law* (Second ed. Cambridge University Press, Cambridge 2003).

Sands, P. and Peel, J. (2012) *Principles of International Environmental Law*, (Third ed., Cambridge University Press 2012).

Sally Edwards, Terry Edwards and Charles Fields, 'Environmental crime and criminality: Theoretical and practical issues', NY and London, 1996.

Schavell, S. 'Criminal Law and the Optimal Use of Non-Monetary Sanctions as a Deterrent' (1985) *Columbia Law Review*, 1232.

Schloenhardt, A. 'Transnational Organised Crime and International Criminal Law', in M. Cherif Bassiouni (ed.) *International Criminal Law* (Third Edition,) volume I.

Schroeder, Christopher H., 'Cool Analysis Versus Moral Outrage in the Development of Federal Environmental Criminal Law' 35 Wm. & Mary L. Rev. 251 (1993).

Schmidt, Charles 'Environmental Crimes: Profiting at the Earth's Expense' in Rob White (ed.) Environmental Crime: A Reader' (Willan Publishing, 2009).

Scott, Joanne, *EC Environmental Law* (Longmans, 1998).

Scott, Joanne 'Kith and Kine (and Crustaceans): Trade and Environment in the EU and WTO' in Weiler (ed.) *The EU, WTO and AAFTA: Towards a common law of International Trade* (OUP, 2000).

Scott, Lucie 'Stormy Seas Ahead? The European Court of Justice Stirs Up a Storm in Ship-Source Pollution' *JECL* [2008].

Selin, Your Money or Your Life: A Look at the Convention on the Protection of the Environment through Criminal Law *RECIEL* 10 (1) 2001.

Senat, Reunion de la delegation pour l'Union europeenne du mercredi 22 fevrier 2006, avec Judge Puissochet.

Sevenster, 'The environmental guarantee after Amsterdam: Does the emperor have new clothes?' (2000) *YEEL* 291.

Sevenster, H.G. 'Criminal Law and EC Law' (1992) *CML Review* 29.

Sharp, P. Prospects for Environmental Liability in the International Criminal Court (1999), *Virginia Law Journal* 217.

Sieber, U. 'Memorandum on a European Model Penal Code' European Journal of Law Reform 1 (1998/9) 445.

Smith, Melanie, Inter-institutional dialogue and the establishment of enforcement norms: A decade of financial penalties under Article 228 EC, *European Public Law* (2010).

Simester, A.P. and Sullivan, G.R. *Criminal Law: Theory and Doctrine* (3rd edn. Hart Publishing, Oxford 2007).

Situ, Y. and Emmons, D., *Environmental Crime: The Criminal Justice System's Role in Protecting the Environment* (Thousand Oaks: Sage, 2000).

Slapper, Gary and Tombs, Steve. *Corporate Crime* (Longman, 1999).

Somsen, H. (ed.) *Protecting the European Environment* (Blackstone, 1996).

Spencer, J. 'Why is the Harmonisation of Penal Law necessary?' in in A.Klip, H. van der Wilt (eds.) *Harmonisation and Harmonising Measures in Criminal Law,* Amsterdam (2002).

Spindler, Gerald, 'Alternatives to Criminal Responsibility of Corporations – Considerations by a Corporate Lawyer' in Albin Eser, Günter Heine and Barbara Huber (eds.) *Criminal Responsibility of Legal and Collective Entities,* International Colloquium Berlin, 1998.

Stephens, T. *'International Courts and Environmental Protection'* (CUP, 2009).

Stigler, G. 'The Optimum Enforcement of Laws' 78 *Journal of Political Economy* 78 (1978) 526.

Stone, Christopher D., *Should trees have standing? Toward legal rights for natural objects', in Should Trees Have Standing?* (Oceana Publications, 1996).

Sutherland, H. Edwin, 'White Collar Criminality' (1949) 5 *American Sociological Review* 1.

Tadić, F. 'How Harmonious can Harmonisation be? A Theoretical Approach towards Harmonisation of (Criminal) Law' in A.Klip, H. van der Wilt (eds.) *Harmonisation and Harmonising Measures in Criminal Law,* Amsterdam (2002).

Tanaka, Y., *'The International Law of the Sea'* (CUP, 2012).

Tiedemann, 'Theorie et Reforme du Droit Penal de L'Environment: Etude de Droit Penal Compare' *Revue de Science Criminelle et Droit Penal Compare* 264 (1986).

Teclaff, Ludwik A., 'Beyond Restoration: The Case of Ecocide', *Natural Resources Journal,* (1994).

Temmink, H. 'From Danish Bottles to Danish Bees: The Dynamics of the free movement of goods and environmental protection – a case law analysis' 2000 YEEL 61.

Trechsel, Stefan. *Human Rights in Criminal Proceedings* (OUP, Oxford 2006).

Tobler, C. 'Case C-176/03, Commission v. Council, judgement of the Grand Chamber of 13 September 2005' (2006) *Common Market Law Review* 845.

Tomuschat, C. 'International crimes by States: an endangered species?', International Law: Theory and Practice – Essays in Honour of Eric Suy, K. Wellens, ed. (The Hague, Martinus Nijhoff, 1998).

Treves, Tullio, 'The European Community and the European Union and the Law of the Sea: Recent Developments' (2008) 48 *IJIL.*

Tridimas, Takis, *The General Principles of EU law* (Second edition OUP, Oxford 2006).

Thieffy, P. Droit *Europeen de l'Environnement* (Dalloz, Paris 1998).

Van Dijk et al, *Theory and Practice of the European Convention on Human Rights,* Intersentia, Oxford 2006.

Ward, Angela. 'Effective Sanctions in EC Law: A Moving Boundary in the Division of Competence' (1995) 1 *European Law Journal* 205.

Vercher, Antonio. 'The Use of Criminal Law for the Protection of the Environment in Europe: Council of Europe Resolution (77) 28' in *Northwestern Journal of International Law & Business* (1990).

Wells, Celia. *Corporations and Criminal Responsibility* (OUP, Oxford 2001).

Van Den Haag, Ernest, 'The Criminal law as a Threat System' (1982) 73 *The Journal of Criminal Law & Criminology* 2.

Van Den Wyngaert, Christine. *International Crime Law: A Collection of International and European Instruments,* (Matinus Nijhoff Pub, Leiden 2005).

Van Den Herik, L and Stahn, C. (eds.), *The Diversification and Fragmentation of International Criminal Law,* Martinus Nijhoff Publishers/Brill, 2012.

Van Den Herik, Larissa, and Jernej Letnar Černič. 'Regulating Corporations under International Law From Human Rights to International Criminal Law and Back Again.' *Journal of International Criminal Justice* 8.3 (2010): 725–743.

Vervaele, J.A.E. *European Evidence Warrant: Transnational Judicial Inquiries in the EU* Intersentia, 2005.

Victor, D. Raustiala, K. and Skolnikoff, E. (ed.) *The Implementation and Effectiveness of International Environmental Commitments: Theory and Practice* (International Institute for Applied Systems Analysis, 1998).

Von Hirsch, Andrew. *Criminal Deterrence and Sentence Severity: an Analysis of Recent Research.* Oxford: Hard (2000).

Von Hirsch, A. and Joreborg N. 'Gauging Criminal Harms: a Living Standard Analysis' (1991) 11 *Oxford JLS* 1.

Vogel, David 'The Hare and the Tortoise Revisited: The New Politics of Consumer and Environmental Regulation in Europe' in Jordan, A. (ed.), *Environmental Policy in the European Union: Actors, Institutions and Processes* (2dn ed. Earthscan 2005).

Walker, Neil. 'In Search of the Area of Freedom, Security and Justice: A Constitutional Odyssey' in Walker (ed.) *Europe's Area of Freedom, Security and Justice* (OUP, Oxford 2004).

Walsh, Delmot 'Protecting the Environment through EC Criminal Law' (2005) 17 *ELM* 199.

Wang Hui 'The EU Marine Oil Pollution Prevention Regime – Recent Developments' [2004] *EELR* 292.

Wenneras, Pal, A New Dawn for Commission Enforcement under Articles 226 and 228 EC: General and Persistent Infringements, Lump Sums and Penalty Payments, *Common Market Law Review* 43, 2006.

Wenneras, Pal, *The Enforcement of EC Environmental Law* (OUP, 2007).

Weatherill, S. 'Better Competence Monitoring' 30 *European Law Review* 23 (2005).

Weatherill, S. 'Competence Creep and Competence Control' 23 *Yearbook of European Law* 1 (2004).

Webb, Philippa, *VisionBinocular: State Responsibility and Individual Criminal Responsibility for Genocide, in* The Diversification and Fragmentation of International Criminal Law (Larissa van den Herik and Carsten Stahn eds., 2012).

Weiß, Holger Tobias 'EC Competence for Environmental Criminal Law' (Bruges, College of Europe 2006).

Wettach, Christine L., 'Mens Rea and the "Heightened Criminal Liability" Imposed on Violators of the Clean Water Act,' *Colo. J. Int'l Envtl. L. & Pol'Y* 2002.

Weyembergh, A. 'Approximation of Criminal Laws, the Constitutional Treaty andthe Hague Programme' (2005) 42 *Common Market Law Review* at 1567.

Weyembergh, A. *L'Harmonisation des Legislations: Condition de l'Espace Penal Europeen et Revelateur de ses Tensions*, (Institut d'Estudes Europeennes, 2004).

Weyembergh, A. 'Le Rapprochement des Incriminations et des Sanctions Penales' *Revue Internationale de Droit Penal* (vol. 77) 187.

Weyembergh, Anne. 'The Functions of Approximation of Penal Law within the European Union' (2005) 12 *Maatricht Journal of European and Comparative Law* 2, 149.

Wils, W. 'Subsidiarity and EC environmental policy: taking people's concerns seriously' (1994) 6 JEL 85.

Wilson, John 'Re-thinking penalties for corporate environmental offenders: a view of the law reform commission of Canada's sentencing in environmental cases' (1986) 31 *McGill Law Journal* 316.

Williams, Granville 'The Definition of a Crime' (1955) *CLP* 107, at 130.

White, Rob 'Environmental Issues and Criminological Imagination' (2003) 7 *Theoretical Criminology* 483 at 485–486.

White, Simone 'Harmonisation of Criminal Law under the First Pillar' (2006) *E.L.Rev*, 31 (1) at 88.

White, Rob (ed.) 'Environmental Crime: A Reader' (Willan Publishing, 2009).

Wijman, Per Magnus, *Managing the Global Commons*, 36 Int' Org. 511.

Wijnstekers, Willem 'Protection of Endangered Species of Fauna and Flora' Comte, Françoise and Kramer, Ludwig (eds.) *Environmental Crime in Europe: Rules of Sanctions* (Europa Law Publishing, Groningen 2004).

Winter et al 'Weighing up the EC Civil Liability Directive' (2008) *Journal of Environmental Law* 20(2):163.

Yingyi Situ and David Emmons. *Environmental Crime: The Criminal Justice System's Role in Protecting the Environment*, Sage Publications (2000).

Xu, X. 'Do Stringent Environmental Regulations reduce the International Competitiveness of Environmentally Sensitive Goods? A Global Perspective' 27, *World Development* (1999).

Ziegler, *Trade and Environmental Law in the European Community* (OUP, 1996).

Zimmerman, M. The Black Market for Wildlife: Combating Transnational Organized Crime in the Illegal Wildlife Trade, 36 *Vand. J. Transnat'l L.* 1657, November, 2003.

Index

www.ingramcontent.com/pod-product-compliance
Lightning Source LLC
LaVergne TN
LVHW020650300926
849161LV00004B/885